The Tentmakers of Cairo

The Tentmakers of Cairo

Egypt's Medieval and Modern Appliqué Craft

Seif El Rashidi
Sam Bowker

The American University in Cairo Press
Cairo New York

First published in 2018 by
The American University in Cairo Press
113 Sharia Kasr el Aini, Cairo, Egypt
420 Lexington Avenue, Suite 1644, New York, NY 10170
www.aucpress.com

This publication was made possible with the generous assistance of the Barakat Trust 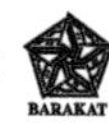

Dar el Kutub No. 11387/17
ISBN 978 977 416 802 4

Dar el Kutub Cataloging-in-Publication Data

El Rashidi, Seif
The Tentmakers of Cairo: Egypt's Medieval and Modern Appliqué Craft / Seif El Rashidi and Sam Bowker.—Cairo: The American University in Cairo Press, 2018.
p. cm.
ISBN 978 977 416 802 4
1. Textile crafts
I. Bowker, Sam (jt. auth.)
746

2 3 4 5 6 29 28 27 26 25

Designed by Jon W. Stoy

To our parents,
Bob and Jenny
Nevine and Mamdouh
with love and gratitude

Contents

Preface ix
Acknowledgments xiii
A Note on Spelling xvii

1. Early Cairene Tents: The Fatimids and Ayyubids 1
2. Tents during the Mamluk Period 19
3. Tents in Ottoman Cairo 43
4. Egyptian Tents in the Nineteenth Century 65
5. The Khedival Period 81
6. From Suradiq to Souvenir: Tentmakers and Tourists 107
7. Modern Khayamiya: Stage and Ceremony 131
8. The *Farrashin* 147
9. Khayamiya and Art 155
10. Making Khayamiya: Design and Technique 161
11. Voices from the Street of the Tentmakers 187

Conclusion 223
Notes 225
Bibliography 239
Index 247

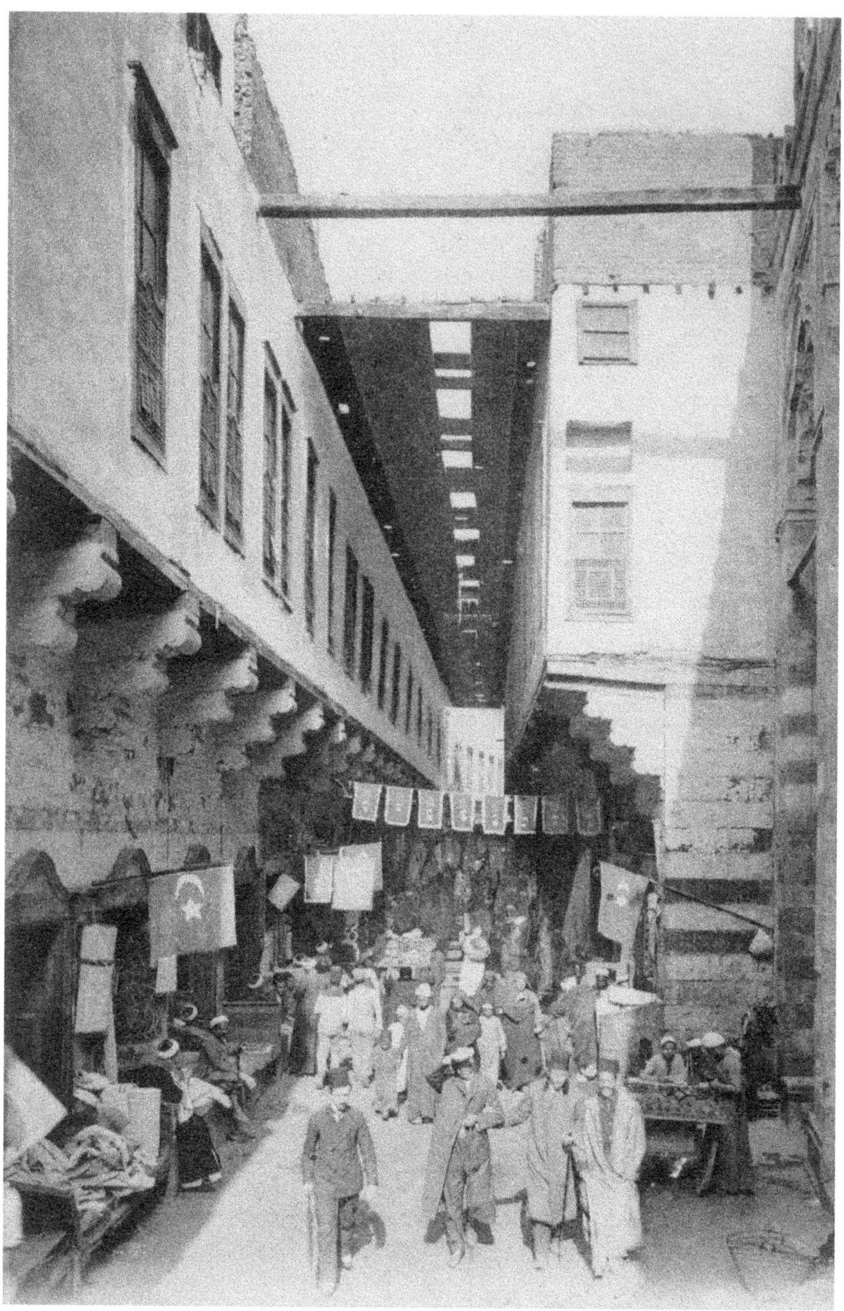

Figure 1 The Street of the Tentmakers, one of Cairo's few covered streets, in 1902. Photograph by Lehnert and Landrock.

Preface

The Egyptian tentmakers are a community of skilled artisans, primarily men. Most reside in Cairo and work from shared workshops in the vicinity of a street named after them, the Street of the Tentmakers—al-Khayamiya. This is a covered section extending from the main spine of the historic walled city of Cairo immediately south of Bab Zuwayla, a monumental city gateway. The street-spanning structure dates to the seventeenth century and is called the Qasaba of Radwan Bey.

The tentmakers sew, by hand, a distinctly Egyptian form of needle-turned cotton appliqué called *khayamiya*. This derives from the Arabic word *khayma*, which means 'tent,' so *khayamiya* is 'the art of the tent.' This follows principles of Turkish grammar widely applied in Egyptian Arabic, a linguistic legacy of shared Ottoman heritage.[1] Evidence for historic links between Egyptian, Ottoman, and Persian tentmakers can also be established through similarities in profession-specific terminology, such as the word *ustadh* or *usta*, a title bestowed upon a master craftsman in charge of a workshop.

Tents have played an important part in the social, cultural, and political life of Egypt for centuries, and as this book will demonstrate, appliqué work has existed for at least as long. There are close parallels between the technique of modern Egyptian tents and those surviving from Ottoman times, which are magnificent in design and execution, yet the relationship between the tentmakers of Ottoman Istanbul and Cairo is still unclear. The first records of visually distinctive Egyptian khayamiya in Cairo[2] coincided with a substantial decline in the working conditions and population of Turkish tentmakers in Constantinople in the mid-nineteenth century.[3]

Khayamiya are used in Egypt in two main forms. The first is as an architectural textile—literally, tents—ranging from mammoth rectangular pavilions (*suradiq* or *siwan*) used to host ceremonial events such as weddings, feasts, and funerals, to single-poled camping tents (singular *fustat*) used by travelers, particularly tourists. The second form of khayamiya is individual panels (singular *tark*), which can also take the form of screen-like bands or tent walls. This is the most significant form today because it produces quilt-like artworks for interior display rather than cumbersome ephemeral buildings. Both forms of khayamiya in the late nineteenth century regularly featured Arabic epigrams.

The color of Cairo was originally honey-colored stone—today it is that of brick and concrete. The art of khayamiya provides brilliant colors and patterns in contrast to their urban context, despite the fact that its inspiration is often architectural. These unique textiles enliven streets, bring people together, and vanish as quickly as they appear. They unite ornament, function, and ritual in a spectacular display of Egyptian visual culture.

Through their skilled work and imagination, the tentmakers of Cairo have made an exceptional contribution to Egypt. They are adaptive, creative, and proud of their identity. Their work has inspired artists as prominent as Henri Matisse, who based his paper cut-outs upon khayamiya appliqué. Khayamiya appliqués have been found across the world, from Alaska to Australia and Malaysia to Croatia, as souvenirs collected by travelers to Egypt.

This book presents an overview of khayamiya as a distinctly Egyptian textile. It surveys the changing contexts that have influenced khayamiya from the eleventh century to the present day, and the developments in technology and new international audiences which both threaten and encourage its survival. Contemporary khayamiya is displayed in art galleries rather than scaffolded along dusty streets. It is a sophisticated, competitive, and entrepreneurial art form that draws from a rich legacy of design influences.

The word *khayamiya* implies the action of making a tent. More specifically, it describes the act of embellishing canvas with hand-sewn needle-turned cotton appliqué. This skill seems to have changed very little over the last thousand years. Using large scissors, individually cut pieces of colored cotton are delicately folded to shape and deftly sewn to a canvas back.

Khayamiya were originally created for Egyptian audiences on a grand scale. They took the form of free-hanging curtain-like panels *(sitara)*, wall-like screens *(bilma)*, circular camping tents *(fustat)*, or larger, rectangular *suradiq* or *siwan*. As great walls of vibrant color and pattern, they are still used across Egypt to herald celebrations in public places. The same tent can host weddings, funerals, graduations, and festivals of all kinds—including *mawlid*s (celebrations of a saint's birthday), and Ramadan feasts (*iftaar*s). Today, during the annual Hajj pilgrimage, swathes of mass-printed 'imitation khayamiya' adorn the terminals of Cairo's airport, marking the location as an active participant in this important ritual event. From the Street of the Tentmakers to the global stage, khayamiya is one of Egypt's most vibrant forms of living heritage.

This book is the outcome of several years of constant searching for clues—in the form of old khayamiya panels, photos, records, video footage, and memories. There are still many questions that remain unanswered, and no doubt with time, more information will come to light. As a commonly used epigram on khayamiya panels reminds us, "Patience is the key to deliverance."

Acknowledgments

It is the exceptional work of the Egyptian tentmakers themselves—past and present—that justifies this book. But it is thanks to Professor James Piscatori, the former head of the School of Government and International Affairs at Durham University, that this book came into existence. James's friendship with Jenny Bowker (by the tentmakers' own accounts their *Umm al-khayamiya*, or honorary mum) and Professor Bob Bowker led to an exhibition at Durham University in 2012. This, in turn, resulted in an Arts and Humanities Research Council Grant toward a documentation project, and another exhibition in 2014. Meanwhile, in the southern hemisphere, Charles Sturt University supported a 2013 exhibition in Wagga Wagga, Australia, followed by a major exhibition at the Islamic Arts Museum Malaysia in 2015–16. Unusually for a coauthored book, our five-year correspondence was conducted almost entirely by email between the United Kingdom and Australia, fueled by our mutual obsession for all things khayamiya. None of this could have happened without James, Jenny, and Bob.

James Piscatori combined fantastic professional support with unfailing enthusiasm, sentiments echoed in Durham by Professor Anoush Ehteshami, Lorraine Holmes, Dr. Gillian Boughton, and Dr. Reem Aboul Fadl, and in the field in Cairo by Dr. Dina Shehayeb, who led an oral histories project assisted by Ayah Aboul Atta (principal field researcher and editor), Ahmed Abdelhalim (Arabic transcription), with English translation by Seif Eldin Allam and Dina Shehayeb, and additional field research by Khaled El Samman. The results of this work form the basis of Chapter 11 of this book.

Our excitement over the discovery of an old tent panel or photograph, and the new information these revealed, was frequently shared and enriched by many, most notably Ola Seif, Joan and John Fisher, Amina El Bendary, Yasmine El Dorghamy, Clive Rogers, Roba Khorshid, Christine Martens, and Randy Pace.

France Meyer, Huda Al-Tamimi, Yahya Haidar, Leila Kuwatly, and Zahra Taheri at the Centre for Arab and Islamic Studies at the Australian National University in Canberra generously translated and interpreted the epigrams on many of the khedival pieces, as did Adam Talib, Cherine al-Ansary, May al-Ibrashy, and Rasha Arous. Dr. Hassan Hilmi translated the poems about the Fatimid 'Tent of Deliverance' and that on the Harvard Tent, and Professor Robert Dankoff provided valuable assistance with the account of Evliya Çelebi.

Venetia Porter, Heba Barakat, Blaire Gagnon, Avinoam Shalem, John Feeney, Peter Alford Andrews, Lesley Forbes, Elizabeth Elwell-Cook, Roger Stewart, and Nicholas Warner gave us valuable insights into their own research; many others generously shared information that enabled us to piece things together. These include Tarek Ibrahim, Ahmad El Bindary, Tarek Swelim, Laila Said, Yasmina Abou Youssef, Iman Abdulfattah, Mamdouh Sakr, Lesley Forbes, Mohammed Amin, Ahmed El-Dabb', Kareem Ibrahim, Hany Abdel-Kader, Hossam and Ekramy Hanafy, Tarek Abdelhay, Essam Aly, Ahmed Naguib, Hany Mahmoud, Muhammad Lotfy Wahdan, Muhsin and Hussein el-Hendy, and the late Muhammad Dendon. Kim Beamish's feature-length documentary *The Tentmakers of Cairo* provided a unique visual narrative of the tentmakers' street as a microcosm of Egyptian society, developed as a concurrent project to this book. Ahmed Kamal Swedan was always keen to help us navigate the Street of the Tentmakers and their Facebook pages.

Nadia Naqib from the American University in Cairo Press provided editorial advice and critical guidance, and Katie Holland's careful editing brought the manuscript to its completed form. Ahmad Hamid and Shahira Mehrez, in recounting many personal tales of their own vast experience of Egyptian crafts, offered context, critique, and insights into the bigger picture.

Museum collections around the world enabled our research. The Islamic Arts Museum Malaysia, notably Syed Mohamad Albukhary and Sarifah Majimah Albukhary, Heba Barakat, Rekha Verma, Frederick Zink, and

Nurul Imam Rusli, has been a great patron of the history and future of khayamiya. The Doris Duke Foundation for Islamic Art at Shangri-La hosted an extraordinary scholar-in-residence opportunity, courtesy of Deborah Pope, Carol Khewhok, Sharon Littlefield Tomlinson, and Paige Donnelly. Helen Wolfe of the British Museum, and Claire and James Birch of Doddington Hall in Lincolnshire, deserve special thanks for providing access to their unique collections. Thank you also Gillian Vogelsang-Eastwood of the Textiles Research Centre in Leiden; Bonnie Browning of the American Quilter's Society; Nahla Nassar and Qaisra Khan of the Khalili Collection; Joe Green of the Semitic Museum at Harvard University; Mirjam Shatanawi of the Museum Van Wereldculturen; Mariam Rosser-Owen of the Victoria and Albert Museum; Mary Hauser of the Gregg Museum; Christa Clarke of the Newark Museum; Georges Matisse; Jennie and Hogan Smelker; and Vivian Zoë of the Slater Memorial Museum.

We are grateful for the generous financial support of the Association for the Study of the Middle East and Africa (ASMEA) for a research grant in 2015, and the Barakat Trust's grant that enabled additional fieldwork in 2016–17, and for the acquisition of many of the archival photographs used in this book, supported by the ambitious photography of Timothy Crutchett at Charles Sturt University, as well as that of Ola Seif and Ahmad El Bindary. Bernard O'Kane's endorsement of the project was very much appreciated. The Australian ambassadors to Egypt, Ralph King and Neill Hawkins, and the Egyptian ambassador to Australia, Hassan al-Laithy, provided international support for the Egyptian tentmakers.

Many friends around the world gave us support and encouragement, vital for a project like this one. We would especially like to thank Melinda Bowker, Yasmine El Rashidi, Samir Hammam, Hind Mostafa, Nasser Rabbat, Sherine Zaghow, Reham Barakat, and Guy Hughes.

Finally, our fascination with Egypt and its heritage is thanks to our parents, through whom we were able to discover it. For that, and everything else, we dedicate this book to them.

A Note on Spelling

The spelling of *khayamiya* is an approximation for English-speaking audiences, who previously referred to these textiles as 'Egyptian Quilts.' In Arabic, it is خيّامية. 'Khayamiya' has since become the most typically-seen spelling for texts written in English. It has been used by cultural and tertiary institutions, academic journals, auction catalogs, exhibition texts, craft magazines, and journalists.

It could more precisely be written as *khiyāmiyya*, but 'yy' is alien to English. As noted by Samer Akkach of the University of Adelaide, "The term *khiyāmiyya* derives from the Arabic *khiyam* or *khiyām*, the plural of *khayma*, 'tent', the verb of which, *khayyama*, means 'to camp'. Accordingly, *khiyāmiyya* (with stress on the last *y*), refers to the makers of tents, for whom the Street of the Tentmakers, *Shāri al-Khiyāmiyya*, near Bab Zuwayla in Cairo was named."

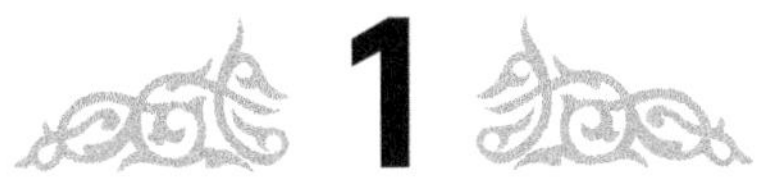

Early Cairene Tents

The Fatimids and Ayyubids

Fatimid Tents

For a sense of the importance of the ceremonial tent in medieval Cairo, the account of the fourteenth-century chronicler al-Maqrizi describing the storerooms of the great Fatimid palace cannot be bettered. The scene al-Maqrizi narrates is from an older text, capturing a time in the late eleventh century during famine, rebellions, and dire financial circumstances, when the "rogues' demands were increasing"[1] and the Fatimid state was forced to act. In order to placate the rebels and save the state, the palace storerooms were emptied and their contents sold off. We discover that the storerooms were extensive and thematically arranged: there was one for books, another for garments, one for jewels and "wonders." There were storerooms for furniture, weapons, saddlery, sugared drinks, spices, and of course, one for tents. The storerooms were kept in good order, for their contents were all highly prized items, under the care of custodians and subject to visits by the Fatimid caliph himself.

The description of the tent storeroom is attributed to a certain Abu al-Hassan al-Khayamy, meaning 'the tentmaker,' a man evidently knowledgeable about what must have been the best tents in Egypt at the time. Abu al-Hassan's heart must have skipped a beat as he undertook the exciting but probably also heart-wrenching task of emptying the storeroom of its contents and divvying the tents up.

> From the palace storeroom we brought out an immeasurable number of the walls of tents, and posts, and vases, and panels, and sections, and for-

> tresses and palaces and awnings; and tents made of *dabiqi* [linen], and velvet, and royal silk, and Armenian and Bahnasi and Cordoban fabric, and quality Aleppine of all colours and types. And also of sondos [a green silk believed by Muslims to be worn by the pious in heaven], some of which have elephants, and some with leopards, and horses, and peacocks, and birds. And others have wild beasts and people of many types, and beautiful images. Some of them are plain, and others are patterned, and lined with wondrous designs. And the posts of these tents are covered with silver pipes. There are gold-threaded textiles, and textiles without gold of all types and colours. There are ropes covered with silk and others with cotton. There are skeins of Chinese silk, and *tastari* [heavy silk], and flattened silk, and feathered silk and other types of silks of all colours large and small.[2]

The "palaces" and "fortresses" found in the tent storeroom described above are a reminder that these tents were effectively 'portable' court architecture made of wood and fabric. At its most elaborate, the royal tent structure was an encampment rather than one simple tent space as such, and in accounts elsewhere, both by al-Maqrizi and other chroniclers, descriptions of people moving from one tent space to another confirm this. What was in the storerooms was clearly a wealth of expensive, lavishly-decorated tent parts—the trappings of an entire royal tent world—used to provide the ruler with a befitting setting whenever he needed a temporary base outside one of his 'built' palaces.

The tents were part of the royal insignia of the Fatimid court, along with a wide range of items, some of them textiles or textile-related, including the caliph's parasol, his turban, and the solitaire that topped the royal turban, *al-Yatima*—the unique. The importance of the caliph's textile world in royal ceremonies is perhaps captured best in the simple fact that the royal parasol, actually a horse-mounted canopy, always matched what the caliph was wearing. It was part of who he was and part of his aura, and an object usually not even afforded to his own son. By the late twelfth century, the caliph's public appearances were accompanied by quite a range of textiles: not just tents and canopies, but banners and standards, which were as important as his symbols of physical power like his sword, lance, and shield.[3] It is in this context that the Fatimid royal tents must be seen.

There appear to have been two main types of tents in the royal storeroom. The first type was known as a *fustat*, which was essentially a round, pointed structure, in its simplest form a bit like a tepee. Many of the royal *fustat*s must have been quite elaborate, and consisted of several round tent spaces adjacent to one another. The second type was a more modular rectilinear structure, more like today's marquees, which existed in several different forms, and while it is hard to determine exactly what they looked like, it is possible to formulate some kind of idea of how they differed from the *fustat* type.

There was a flat type *(al-mustatih)*, one example of which was described as being a square 'abode' supported by six columns. Four of the columns supported the interior of the tent, while the remaining two were used to support the entrance awning. Another version seems to have been of the same design only smaller, with only two interior columns rather than four. The advantage of this type of tent, as opposed to the *fustat*, was that because it was rectilinear, it was also modular, and thus could be extended easily as required. As al-Maqrizi reminds us, the larger the tent, the greater the number of columns.

Capturing the breeze and the light was another concern, and the description of the square tents in the royal storeroom mentions their great flexibility and that an awning could be created on any side of the tent. In fact, the side chosen depended on the direction of the sun: as it moved over the course of the day, the open side of the tent would be altered, too. In some cases, a back flap existed to create a flow of air through the tent. From these basic shapes, a whole array of tent forms could be created, many of them elaborate turreted structures not unlike today's Disney castles.

As the tents in the royal storeroom were a major part of the royal paraphernalia, in many cases, their provenance, their patrons, their history, and their peculiarities were well known. Like the palaces and mosques of medieval Cairo, the tents too had their stories.

Al-Yazuri's Tent: A Story of Patience and Opulence

Abu al-Hassan the tentman recounts removing a huge tent from the storeroom, whose size and shape earned it the rather unimaginative name of 'the large round one.' It is reported to have been 500 cubits[4] in circumference with an appropriately tall central pole 65 cubits high, 6.3 cubits in diameter, and 20 in circumference. It must have been a two-tiered tent, as Abu al-Hassan records a 'wind-catcher' 30 cubits long on top. This probably would have been a perforated superstructure through which hot air would rise up through the tent, helping to ensure that it would remain cool. The architecture of Cairo masterfully evolved to deal effectively with the challenges of a hot climate, and it is perfectly logical that in this respect too, the tents reflected the engineering technology of their more solid counterparts. The typical Cairene house of families that could afford it would include a large reception room, the *qa'a*, where the central area, often with a fountain, had a raised ceiling with openings close to the top to allow for the escape of warm air.

As with all large tents, 'the large round one' was made up of sections, in this case sixty-four of them, which were tied together with cords. These sections may have had textile panels with wooden posts sewn into them, not unlike a modern partition dividing a room. Moving such a large tent would have been a monumental undertaking, and Abu al-Hassan tells us that this one required 100 camels to transport, ropes and all, from one place to another. Unsurprisingly, this tent, like most of the others in the palace storeroom, was lavishly decorated. It had a beautiful arcaded design and a border supposedly depicting every animal on earth. A giant silver basin for water, apparently dispensed via three iron spouts, was one of the tent's accoutrements. There is little doubt that the basin would have served to cool the tent, creating an atmosphere of freshness.[5]

Al-Yazuri

The patron of the large round tent was the Palestinian-born al-Yazuri, who rose in the ranks to great prominence in the Fatimid court, becoming both vizier and grand judge. Like others who saw stardom in medieval times, his ascent was interwoven with the stuff of legend. It is said that as a young man en route to Egypt, he went on pilgrimage to the holy shrines in Arabia and on visiting the shrine of the Prophet Muhammad in Medina, fell asleep in the sacred chamber. While he slept, some of the saffron which infused the walls fell upon him, and when a few of the attendants of the shrine noticed the sleeper and saw what had happened, they woke him up to tell him the news: "This is a great omen," they exclaimed, "you will be blessed with a career of great prosperity."[6] For the most part, they were right, as al-Yazuri's career really took off in Cairo. He began in the 1040s in the service of the caliph's mother, Sayyida Rasad. Rasad effectively controlled the reins of power as her son, al-Mustansir, was only a boy when he came to the throne. Predictably, al-Yazuri's rapid ascent earned him some enemies, namely the chief judge, who felt that he was rising too far above his station. Al-Yazuri pushed his luck a little too far by joining the chief judge's entourage, who would confer every Monday in one of the wings of the royal palace.

"What do you think you are doing here?" he was told angrily by the chief judge. "This isn't a meeting for just anyone!" The rebuff was humiliating, and al-Yazuri left the meeting as fast as his legs could carry him. He waited by the palace gate, following the coterie of court notables as they left the palace after the meeting. Perhaps optimistically, he then followed the chief judge home in the hope that he could appease him for the awkward incident. But al-Yazuri was ignored. Heavy-hearted, he returned home to find that thirty loads of apples from his orchards in Palestine had arrived for sale in the Egyptian market. Rather than sell them, he decided to divide the apples up, sending five camel-loads to the chief judge and each of the key members of his entourage, and two camel-loads for his guards, hoping that the gift would sway the courtiers in his favor. Day by day, he loitered by the palace gate, hoping to catch a word here or there. His patience paid off though, when a courtier, Adit al-dawla, was struck by al-Yazuri's personality and grew enamored by his conversation, always asking him to stay on longer to chat. He eventually recommended al-Yazuri to Abu Nasr, a high-ranking court official, setting him on the path of his illustrious career.[7]

Al-Yazuri's patience extended to the commissioning of his tent as well. It is supposed to have taken 150 workmen nine years to manufacture, and even if this account is slightly exaggerated, it gives an indication of the tent's opulence and scale. It cost him 30,000 dinars to make when it was produced in the mid-eleventh century. Al-Yazuri was clearly somebody who wanted to create eye-catching architecture, whether temporary or permanent. For the decoration of one of his palaces, he is reported to have hired two outstanding trompe l'oeil artists, one of whom boasted that he could paint a figure so realistic that it looked as if it were walking into the wall, while the other said he could paint a figure so realistic it looked as if it were walking out of it. Al-Yazuri put them both to the test, and ended up with a mural of a woman clad in white dancing into the wall, and another, clad in red, dancing out of it. One can only imagine what the great round tent he commissioned would have looked like.[8]

By many accounts, al-Yazuri's tenure as vizier was marked by stability, and even those who did not like him admired his ability to quell rebellion. Unfortunately though, his extravagance eventually counted against him. He was accused of filling his own coffers while the country starved and his penchant for lavish banquets, specifically, was held against him, leading to his assassination at a banquet in 1058. Could his monumental and incredibly lavish tent have contributed to his unfortunate downfall?

In a strange twist to this tale, al-Yazuri's death actually precipitated the political chaos that saw the country collapse into a dire economic state.

Among the impacts of this was the stripping of the Fatimid palace of all its contents, leading to the fascinating account of the tent storeroom. Abu al-Hassan recounts his task that day of dividing the round tent up into pieces and distributing it among the claimants. "We spent a long time to separate one section from another," he says, "and to cut it into pieces for distribution."[9]

Al-Qatul: The Great Prototype

For all its grandeur and the sense of wonder al-Yazuri's tent gave Abu al-Hassan the tentmaker when tasked with removing it from the royal storeroom, it was not without precedent. It was based on a tent commissioned by the Fatimid Caliph al-'Aziz, whose reign ended around fifty years before al-Yazuri's rise to prominence. This older tent was nicknamed al-Qatul, 'the killer,' because on the first day that it was erected one of the tentmen fell from the top of its central pole and died. Al-Qatul was reputedly even larger, more magnificent, and better than al-Yazuri's tent, and to manufacture it Caliph al-'Aziz had sent for tree trunks from Byzantium and procured two which were seventy cubits high and cost him 1,000 dinars each. One of these was later cut down slightly and reused for al-Yazuri's tent (having lost five cubits) and taken with him on an expedition to Alexandria.[10] The tent was so large that it is supposed to have covered an area of two acres (0.8 hectares) when set up.[11]

The 'House of Watermelons' and Other Wonders

The next tent Abu al-Hassan took out of the storeroom was a large paneled one of iridescent velvet, made in Tanis in the North of Egypt, also for al-'Aziz, the patron of al-Qatul. This one was known as Dar al-batikh, the 'house of watermelons.' This term seems to have often been used to refer to fruit markets, but could be used somewhat cynically to refer to other things that were a hotch-potch or overly 'busy.' For example, in the Abbasid Court in Baghdad, a tenth-century poem written by the renowned poet al-Rumi was nicknamed 'the poem of the house of watermelons,' partly because it had so many references to fruit, but also because its critics felt it to be over-wrought, 'heavy,' and excessively dense in imagery.[12] It is likely that the 'house of watermelons' tent shared these characteristics, and judging by the description of al-'Aziz's other tent, it is plausible that this one was particularly gaudy.

In terms of its structure, the 'house of watermelons' tent was pavilion-like, with a central dome supported by four columns eighteen cubits high, and two other columns at its center. In each of the four corners was a smaller dome; aisles connected the four domes together. On that eventful Cairo day in the late eleventh century, the 'house of watermelons' tent met the same fate as al-Yazuri's tent, and Abu al-Hassan recounts "doing the same to this one as we did with the other."[13]

The third tent to be divided up was a flat one made for al-Zahir li-Izaz din-Illah, the Fatimid caliph who reigned in the 1020s and 30s, immediately preceding the period of al-Yazuri. This one was also made in Tanis and was of gold brocade. At its center was a column made of six crystal cylinders, around which were six silver columns, which cost the caliph 14,000 dinars. The walls were of gold silk with large decorated Cordoban medallions.

A fourth tent in the storeroom was another round one of considerable size, but smaller than al-Yazuri's. This one was made in Aleppo, and its central post, forty-five cubits high, was said to have originally been from the mast of a Venetian ship. By royal Fatimid standards, this was a lot less ambitious in scale; it only required seventy camels and one hundred men to erect, and does not seem to have caused any deaths![14]

The 'Tent of Deliverance'

Finally, Abu al-Hassan set about removing a tent called Khaymat al-farag ('the tent of deliverance') made for al-Afdal, son of Amir al-Juyush (1066–1121), in 1121. This one was 1,400 cubits wide, 50 cubits high, and cost 10,000,000 dinars. Its beauty earned it the praise of all the poets.[15] Luckily, and quite incredibly, several of these poems still survive. Abu Ja'far Muhammad bin Hibatallah wrote:

> A luxurious tent was pitched in the place of eminence
> Lofty was it, loftier than the brinks of the mountain peaks.
> So extended was it beyond sight span that its top, methought,
> Reached beyond the highest orb for its abode
> Full were its realms of spectacular wonders
> Inspiring in thee the brilliance of the astute artisan
> Yonder seest thou gardens fertile by abundant showers watered,
> Never were they yearning for clouds' attention,
> Yonder seest thou a wild raptor soaring in the ether high,
> Yonder seest thou a snake that never venom exudeth,
> Yonder seest thou a lion that is neither common nor frail,
> And along the tent walls thou seest leaning throngs that would,
> If they only could, kneel down until their chins touched the ground.

The tent was adorned with the best, whose virtues remain boundless,
Adorned with legacy of utmost glory and supreme eminence.
Within the tent, the leader hath caused a regal sun to rise,
Thus, meditation could discern the grace of hearing and sight.
The fortunate one pledges victory shall in China pitch this tent
After having triumphantly conquered both India and Yemen.[16]

And by the pen of Abu ‘Ali Hassan Zayd al-Ansari, a court writer, writing in praise of al-Afdal and his tent:

Soft! All nations remain to thee ever inferior:
Thy resolve hath proved they are all impotent.
Is this indeed a tent that thou hast now raised, or an orb entire?
Are we really wide-awake, or is this but a vision in a dream?
How could one, before seeing thy edifice, have surmised that tents
Could be raised so high as to outdo reason’s expectation?
How could one have fancied it before thou, in temporal
Pride, hast fashioned it thus high out of lordly poise?
That it hath thee sheltered, and thou art the archetype of all folks,
Proveth that it hath been conceived to epitomize an all-inclusive orb.
One army thou commandest. Another there
On its walls depicted. Both armies swarming.
Should the breeze stir it, its convoy would be in turmoil:
Part of it advances whilst the other retreats.
Are its steeds thine own, the very steeds with which you assault thy foes?
Are they the selfsame steeds, never unsaddled, never unbridled?
Thou hast taught its heroes to advance and never retreat.
Thus unabashed, they headlong assault whenever the combat intensifies.
Thy reassurance hath made them of all peril fearless,
For swords have made peace with mountain tops.
Thy tent resembles paradise whose immortal dwellers
Suffer neither decrepitude, nor the ills of old age.
It riseth so high that it seemeth to be confiding in
A moon and a sun that both remain to its confession dumb.
No wonder that its soil should flowers grow,
For thy generous clouds cease not to sprinkle it.
O, tent, tent of deliverance whose bird is auspicious,
Thou hast become to all nations a portent of good omen.[17]

The 'tent of deliverance' has an interesting history—supposedly it, too, caused the death of two tentmen when it was first erected, and wounded numerous others. This meant that it was given the same nickname as the earlier tent of al-'Aziz: al-Qatul ('the killer'). This later tent consisted of a large central hall with four smaller halls around it, each connected by means of a passageway. The complexity of the structure meant that it required extensive scaffolding to put up, and even then it could only be erected in the presence of architects. A medieval chronicler, Ibn al-Ma'mun, notes that it was terribly cumbersome to erect, and that the users hated putting it up. (They would have much preferred to put up the two large army tents which, despite their immense size, were together smaller than this 'tent of deliverance.') Perhaps thanks to its legendary reputation, records of the tent seem to have exaggerated its size, some describing it as 1,000,000 cubits large, which is hard to believe. Be that as it may, while the 'tent of deliverance' remained in use for a long period of time, its size meant that usually only the central part of it was erected—there was hardly ever enough space for the whole tent, Ibn al-Ma'mun laments.[18]

The fact that poets wrote in praise of the royal tents is but a reminder of their role as beautiful ceremonial objects, not just spaces. With their shimmering velvet, silk, and the gold threads woven into many of them, it is hardly surprising that they could inspire the court poets to put pen to paper.

For less important occasions, the storerooms seem to have had a stock of tents of lesser complexity and rarity, but these too would have been lavish enough to portray the requisite image of royal splendor. Abu al-Hassan recounts "bringing out a large number of Cordoban type tents"; one of these, probably one of the more impressive ones, he describes as a large round tent full of decoration and finely worked. It was made up of many pieces and comprised a column 30 cubits high.[19]

Apart from the tents themselves were all of the necessary accoutrements and furnishings required for them to function: benches, seats, and glass panes of all types. There were also immense quantities of vessels for the banquets that cost men like al-Yazuri his life. These included ceramics from Ray in Iran, gilded vessels from Baghdad, and basins of poplar wood with silver handles, some of which were so heavy that even a strong camel could hardly bear the weight of two of them on its back.[20]

How Were These Fatimid Tents Used?

Perhaps what is most notable about the royal court in Fatimid Egypt is its use of ceremony, pageantry, and mystique to evoke the quasi-divine status of the ruling family. For the soldiers that paraded in front of the royal palaces on feast days and other ceremonial occasions, the one glimpse of the caliph they may have got may have been a shimmering image of a man behind a gauzy metallic curtain flickering in the breeze. He stood in a room designed for the light to fall in such a way as to create the medieval equivalent of a hologram: a picture made in light. It is easy to see how the use of sumptuous velvet and silk textiles to form the royal tents was a perfect medium for such a message to flourish.

Alongside a well-developed set of processions and parades along the main street of the walled city of Cairo, there were numerous instances when the caliph and his court decamped to the outdoors, and it was then more than ever that the royal tents came into use. One instance was the annual opening of the Cairo canal during the summer flood. The flood was an event of great importance, guaranteeing good harvests if water levels were ample, but dire consequences if they were too low. The Nilometer, a special building with a calibrated column to indicate the water level, was a key landmark of the city, as flood levels were also used to calculate taxes and thus determined Egypt's economic prospects. In 1122, for example, once the Nile had risen to 16 cubits high, orders were given for the tents to be brought out and for 'the large one'—'the tent of deliverance,' commissioned by al-Afdal, and the best one in the storeroom—to be erected.[21]

The opening of the Canal was an event the caliph attended, and in fact, the order to bring out the royal tents was in many respects a sign that an event was to have caliphal presence. Notables of the court would have had their own tents that they too brought out for such occasions. These would probably have been in a similar artistic spirit and manufacture to the royal collection, but without a doubt markedly more modest in their scale and in the lavishness of their decoration. Social hierarchy was an important feature of the Fatimid court, with a strict set of social codes designed to emphasize the caliph's preeminence and elevated status, usually by ensuring that members of his entourage publicly demonstrate their social inferiority. (The rule of having to dismount from one's horse in the presence of the caliph, for example, was one instance of such social practices.) Unsurprisingly, at public events which involved the caliph appearing in his tent, social status determined the proximity of a courtier's tent to that of the caliph.[22]

Thus, the temporary nature of the royal encampment should not be understood as a time when the court was acting informally. Quite the contrary—there was a heightened sense of drama created by the colorful royal encampment, which like a mirage would appear, impress people, and then vanish.

To that end, the social interaction that took place within the royal tents was carefully scripted. For instance, at the opening ceremony of the canal in 1122, once the caliph had arrived at his tent (decorated with humans and animals), his vizier led his horse inside it, crossing over Iranian and Andalusian carpets to the throne placed at its center. When the caliph had taken his seat on the throne, poems were recited in his honor.[23]

It should also be borne in mind that the use of tents as royal venues was not because there were no built structures in the vicinity to accommodate the court—in the case of the opening of the canal, for example, one of the royal pavilions, Manzarit al-Sukkara, was located nearby and could well have been used for this annual event, had that been desired.

The reality was that the temporary nature of these beautiful tents heightened the sense of occasion—they add color and excitement—and, like any form of temporary adornment, they were a reminder of important moments, milestones, and rites of passage.

Sutur

It is worth mentioning in passing that textile hangings often decorated the interior of built spaces as well. These were known as *sutur* (curtains or hangings, singular *sitara*) and would have been similar to tents in scale and form, except that their purpose was primarily as a decorative covering. For example, the audience hall of the Fatimid palace was hung with silk (*dibaj*, or brocade) hangings in winter and a fine linen known as *dabiqi* in summer. *Dabiqi* took its name from the small village of Dabiq in the Delta where it was made (as well as in other Northern Egyptian towns such as Tanis and Damietta).[24]

One especially lavish type of textile called Abu Qalamuni, said to have been used for the hangings in the throne room of the Fatimid palace in Cairo, was purportedly made of 'sea silk' (Byssus), which comes from a mollusc found in the Mediterranean and was used for producing very fine (and expensive) textiles up until the twentieth century. It is golden in color and iridescent, hence its appeal for such a purpose.[25] Given the scale and size that hangings in the Fatimid Palace would need to be, it is highly possible that they were made of silk imitating the color and sheen of 'sea silk,' and therefore given its name.

What Did the Fatimid Tents Actually Look Like?

The short answer is that it is hard to tell exactly. And yet thousands of fragments of Fatimid textiles survive, as do numerous brocades from cities mentioned in the account describing the contents of the royal storeroom, for example Cordoba. The descriptions of iridescent textiles ornamented with peacocks, lions, and elephants point to silks and velvets from Spain and Byzantium, which match that account very well. Many of these have survived in church collections as parts of rich vestments, or shrouding the relics of saints—a poignant reminder that the opulence of the textiles used to make the royal tents was such that they were traded and cherished around the world.

In the storerooms of another modern treasure house, the Museum of Islamic Art in Cairo, and in collections around the world, the Fatimid textiles in particular stand out for being exceptionally fine, and breathtaking in their detail, design, and color. Some of the finest of these glint with the gold thread woven into the fabric described in Abu al-Hassan the tentmaker's account; others are gilded with paint.

Wooden panels that survive from the Fatimid palaces in Cairo depict scenes of courtly life interspersed with scrolls and flowers, giving us some idea of how a royal Fatimid space would look. Although much of the color on these has gone, traces of red, the undercoat for gilding, hints at the luxury of these royal abodes. It is realistic to surmise that the Fatimid royal tents were a blend of the architecture of the Fatimid palaces and the extraordinarily rich world of the finest Fatimid textiles.

To add fuel to the reader's imagination, a depiction of tents in a thirteenth-century Arabic manuscript of the tales of Maqamat al-Hariri is possibly the closest we can get to a snapshot of what the Cairo tent storeroom would have contained, in which is described a range of color, of contrast, of patterned surfaces, and expanses of what was probably shimmering gold.

The image depicts the tents with a key feature of Islamic textiles across the ages, surprisingly omitted in the tent room description: writing. Among the trademarks of Fatimid textiles were the *tiraz* (inscribed garments), which formed an important part of court ritual. These were woven in Egypt and bestowed by the caliph upon his courtiers, in the same way that a modern monarch would give out medals. They were highly prized, and in some respects all of the other decoration was really a background for the beautifully rendered calligraphy, invoking blessings and prosperity on the user of the textile, or praising the glory of the ruler.

More broadly, it is impossible to think of a world of Islamic art without inscription bands as a focal point—they appear on every type of object and building, in every material, and in virtually every location with any link to Islamic culture. The thirteenth-century painting shows them given prominence on the interior of some of the tents, which is probably highly realistic.

Color in the Royal Tents

Scattered references in various texts suggest that the royal tents were brightly colored. For example, a description of al-Qatul when it was put up in 1122 at the opening ceremony of the canal makes mention of the central pole being wrapped in white, red, and yellow brocade from top to bottom.[26]

While brief textual descriptions may not be much to go on in order to understand color, surviving Egyptian textiles from as far back as the third and fourth centuries show an astonishing range of palette, something that continued to characterize Egyptian textiles in the middle ages and must have been true of Cairo's early tents as well.

Letters surviving from the Genizah, or storeroom, of the synagogue in old Cairo provide invaluable insights into the textile-making craft and its level of sophistication. Most of all, it is the mention of specific shades of color that shows how discerning the clientele was, and suggest how competent the textile workers, at their best, could be.

> I would like the robe to be deep red, as red as possible, and the white and yellow also to be of excellent colour. I did not like the colour of the yellow which arrived.
>
> The Sig[laton] robe is of extreme beauty, but it is not the colour which they ordered. For this is white and blue, but instead I w[ished to have] one of the blue onion colour, an open [lighter] colour, according to your taste. I wish to have the very best, as chosen by you.[27]

There were dyers specialized in the production of textiles using one specific dye, especially the more expensive ones like crimson red and saffron yellow, the two colors mentioned in the description of al-Qatul and also the subject of the first letter above. This level of specialization is reflected in the fact that some dyers became known by the specific hue of their wares, with surnames like al-Za'farani (of the saffron) and al-Qirmizi (of the crimson) being two good examples. The crimson came from the cochineal beetle found in Armenia, and there are numerous historic references to 'Armenian red.' The long list of fabrics mentioned in the storeroom account and, in fact, the tentmaker's ability to distinguish them, say a lot about the place and role of this tentmaking tradition.

Where Textiles Were Made

The description of the tents in the storeroom indicates that the textiles themselves came from different places, and not all in Egypt. Yet Egypt had a great textile-producing tradition, with different areas being renowned for different types of production.

By way of example, the Bahnasi fabric mentioned manufactured in Bahnasa—a town 160 kilometers south of Cairo—was acclaimed for its fine quality and enduring colors and for textiles with fine inscriptions, but was also renowned for the representations of animals, ranging in size and scale from the "bedbug to the elephant."[28]

Among the most important centers of production was Tanis in the Nile Delta. A surviving eleventh-century account, called the *Book of Curiosities*, describes Tanis as an island with air so healthy that despite the fact that "most of those who work there in the production of textiles eat fish and greasy food, and then return to their embroidery and weaving without washing their hands. . . . Nothing of these offensive smells sticks on them; on the contrary, their odour becomes more pleasant and their scent more agreeable!"[29]

The town had been an extremely important center in pre-Islamic times, and must have had a thriving Christian community even in the Fatimid period, as the *Book of Curiosities* mentions that it had "167 mosques and prayer niches, excluding the Friday Mosque," and "72 churches until they were destroyed by order of al-Hakim bi-Amr Allah in 403 AH (1012–13 AD), and replaced with mosques." Its importance as a center of textile production must have helped to account for the fact that it had six merchant inns, and that of its 2,500 shops, 150 were for the sale of textiles. In terms of manufacture,

> the city had 5,000 weaving looms, employing 10,000 workers, not including the men and women who embroider or adorn clothes. One thousand and five hundred sealed chests [of cloth] leave the city each year, as well as 1,000 bales. The royal treasury has right to 400 chests of textiles the like[s] of which are not to be seen elsewhere: woven gilded clothes in the form of sewn garments, selling for 1,000 dinars each; headdresses, selling 500 dinars each; mattresses/sofas, selling for 1,000 dinars each; canopies; chairs; beds; curtains; velvet cloth; eye-figured cloth; **Dabīqī** silken cloth embroidered with silver (**siqlāṭūn**), plain **Dabīqī** silk, tabby or watered cloth (taffeta), and other things which cannot be described [probably on account of their beauty].[30]

Sondos, a green silk, was believed to have been the fabric of choice for those in heaven (and in Islamic art, traditionally those believed to be going straight to heaven are depicted as wearing green turbans), while the Armenian fabric referred to in the description of the royal tent storeroom may well have been red fabric dyed with cochineal—the intense and expensive red dye from the Armenian cochineal beetle that was used for dying rugs up until the twentieth century.

Tents and Textiles in the Ayyubid World

The downfall of the Fatimids in 1169 came at the hands of one of the most renowned figures of Middle Eastern, and indeed, medieval world history: Salah al-Din (Saladin). Among Salah al-Din's key differences from the Fatimid regime he overthrew was that he was a follower of Sunni Islam, the branch followed by the majority of the Egyptian population since Islam had first spread to Egypt five hundred years earlier (the Fatimid rulers, at odds with the majority of the country, were Shi'ites).

Salah al-Din promptly set about restoring Sunni Islam as the state religion—a move welcomed by the people of Egypt. This official restoration took place on 6 March, 1172, with a large public celebration held in Cairo, the seat of his empire. One of the most visual representations of this change in state religion was through the use of ceremonial textiles. A black robe of honor—the color of the Abbasid Caliphate—was given to Salah al-Din by the Abbasid Caliph—the religious head of the Sunni Muslim community. Salah al-Din wore it the very next day, and the day after that, on March 8, traversed Cairo in a ceremonial procession. From then on, and for obvious political reasons, Cairo's imams also wore black.[31]

This black robe worn by Salah al-Din is an important reminder of two things. Firstly, that the tents, and indeed the textiles of Cairo, were part of a wider cultural picture determined not only by religious beliefs, but also by geography, tradition, and significantly during this period, by contact with the Crusaders. Secondly, textiles were of great symbolic significance. They were at the very heart of the Islamic empire, and heralded its milestones and watersheds, marked its rituals, and reflected its highs and lows.

One only has to look to the Ka'ba in Mecca, Islam's most sacred shrine. A simple cubical structure, its entire outward appearance is one created through its external textile covering of silk brocade, ceremonially changed once a year at the annual Hajj pilgrimage attended by Muslims from around the world, an event which believers see as spiritual rebirth—turning a new leaf. A famous twelfth-century Moroccan traveler, Ibn Jubayr, recounts the appearance of the sacred shrine in 1183.

> The outside of the Kaabah on all its four sides, is clothed in coverings of green silk with cotton warps, and on their upper parts is a band of red silk on which it is written the verse, 'Verily the first house founded for mankind was that at Bakkah [Mecca]'. . . . On these coverings [are] remarkable designs resembling handsome pulpits, and inscriptions entertaining the name of God Most High, and calling blessings on Nasir, the aforementioned Abbasid [Caliph]. With all of this, there is no clash of colour. The number of covers on all four sides is thirty-four, there being eighteen on the long sides and sixteen on the two short sides.[32]

These covers were actually a series of hangings, tied closely together "to appear as one single cover comprehending the four sides."[33]

In the precinct of the Ka'ba on December 19 of that year, a massive din erupted with the appearance of Salah al-Din's brother Sayf al-Din in the sacred shrine, during a brief sojourn en route to Yemen:

> The Mosque was in great commotion, being filled with spectators and pilgrims; and the voices of men in prayer for him and his brother Salah al-Din rose so high as to deafen the ears and confound the understanding. From his high post the Zamzam muezzin raised his voice in prayer and praise for him; the voices of the people rose above the muezzin's, and great was the awe of the scene to look upon and hear.[34]

The *amir* of Mecca, slightly unnerved by the presence of this legendary figure, and a bit unsure of himself, "was overcome by the crowd, . . . and hastened to his residence." But the following day, he cheerfully burst into the shrine to the sound of trumpets and drums and timbals, much to the confoundment of everyone else. He was dressed in a golden mantle like glowing coal, a cloud-colored linen turban touched with gold, and two coats of honor made of embroidered silk brocade, bestowed upon him by Sayf al-Din to affirm his standing. Round the noble house he walked, thanking God for granting him the consideration of Salah al-Din's brother "when once he had been throbbing with fear of him."[35]

Salah al-Din's family's reception was of course due to their role in fighting the crusaders, a context in which the tent played a phenomenally significant symbolic role. Less than five years after the incident in Mecca,

Salah al-Din himself was standing upon a hilltop with his seventeen-year-old son al-Afdal at a decisive moment at the Battle of Hittin near Galilee, in Palestine. Al-Afdal recounts the tale:

> When the king of the Franks was on the hill with that band, they made a formidable charge against the Muslims facing them, so that they drove them back to my father [Salah al-Din]. I looked towards him and he was overcome by grief and his complexion pale. He took hold of his beard and advanced, crying out: "Give the lie to the Devil!" The Muslims rallied, returned to the fight and climbed the hill. When I saw that the Franks withdrew, pursued by the Muslims, I shouted for joy: "We have beaten them!" But the Franks rallied and charged again like the first time and drove the Muslims back to my father. He acted as he had on the first occasion and the Muslims turned upon the Franks and drove them back to the hill. I again shouted, "We have beaten them!" but my father rounded on me and said, "Be quiet! We have not beaten them until their tent falls." As he was speaking to me the tent fell. The sultan dismounted, prostrated himself in thanks to God Almighty and wept for joy.[36]

The king of the Franks was Guy of Lusignan, the king of Jerusalem, and the incident recounted above was to lead to Salah al-Din retaking the Holy City in 1187. Lusignan's tent was known to have been red and poets saw their own symbolism in the color, which became commonly used in royal battle tents for at least the coming century.

The tents in this age of great conflict and legendary heroes like Salah al-Din and Lusignan were designed to awe. A twelfth-century account of William of Tyre, recounting the capture of the tent of Kerugha, Atabek of Mosul, near Antioch is just one reminder:

> They took and gathered the despoyles and the tents whereof they had so great riches . . . among other things, the barons assembled them for to see the tents of Corbagat [Kerugha] which was marvellous for it was made in the form of a city. It had towers and crests of diverse colours wrought in fyn silk. From the master palace were alleys into other tents, like streets in a great town. They might sit in the great hall 2000 men.[37]

Thus, even in defeat, a tent could symbolize greatness.

These accounts of the tents belonging to the ruling elite during the Fatimid and Ayyubid eras (969–1250) provide valuable insights into the importance that decorative tents held for the upper echelons of Egyptian society. While the absence of surviving examples means that the precise appearance of these historic tents can only be imagined, what is clear is that the tradition of using ceremonial tents was a well-established one. A large tent was a status symbol and an asset to be treasured. The following chapter, drawing upon accounts from later centuries, provides more detail on the place of tents and tentmakers in Cairene society.

2

Tents during the Mamluk Period

> A stately tent arrived from Syria; it was made for the Emir Kebir [the Great Emir], and required 180 camels to transport it. It was erected in the great square [beneath the Citadel]. A few days later, the Emir Kebir rode down to see it. He hosted a great banquet for his Emirs, and followed this with a banquet of desserts, followed by a banquet of fruit. It was a memorable day, and the people came out to witness the event – there was a very large gathering indeed.[1]

So writes al-Maqrizi, describing an episode in Cairo in 1357, in the middle of the Mamluk period (1250–1517)—an era when the reins of power were held by a rivalrous clique of warriors of loosely 'Turkic' and Circassian stock, whose claim to power was based on might and stealth rather than any sort of royal lineage. This context of great competition and rivalry encouraged patronage of artistic traditions inspired by the successes of a particular individual against political odds, rather than the passing on of artistic heirlooms from one generation to the next.

The scene narrated above is one that in many respects captures the spirit of Cairo across the ages: grand spectacles, private yet held in public areas, lavish, probably involving extravagant quantities of food, and a curious crowd coming to have a look at something novel. Timelessness aside, the account tells us a lot about the role that tents played in medieval times to create the places where the elite could celebrate, not entirely in the public eye, but not far removed from it, either. It is also a reminder that Egyptian society did not exist in isolation—the Mamluks governed an extensive territory ranging from what is today eastern Libya in the west, to Aleppo in the northwest and Mecca in the south, an area with similar, but not identical cultural and artistic traditions. This Syrian tent, which brought out a crowd, is a reminder that the Egyptian tenting tradition must have always been distinctive—clearly, Egyptian tents were different from their Syrian counterparts. Moreover, the 180 camels required to transport the tent are telling: they show that the Mamluk court tents, like their predecessors, must have been large and spectacular.

An account of the 'departments' of the sultan's court includes the *firashkhana* ('house of the soft furnishings'), responsible for furnishings like the royal carpets and tents. At its head was a *mihtar* (chief), aided by a team of young men renowned for their ability to set up a tent single-handedly, but also for being adept at dealing with ropes, specifically when loading mules for travel. Perhaps unsurprisingly, they were described as being among the most competent of the sultan's staff.[2]

More broadly, chronicles from the Mamluk period remind us time and time again that expensive textiles played an important part in Egyptian society. The late Mamluk account of Ibn Iyas (1448–1522 AD) is peppered with mentions clarifying the place that precious textiles held. He notes the multitude of times that sultans bestowed robes of honor upon their courtiers, and every time the sultan changed between his summer and winter wardrobes.

In times of civil strife and public unrest, it was often the shops of textile merchants that suffered at the hands of an unhappy crowd. In the summer of 1497, civil strife led to the pillaging of the area of Bab Zuwayla, leading to losses worth "100,000 dinars, without counting the tents and the uniforms."[3] A few years later in 1501, an economic crisis resulting from the sultan not being able to pay his Mamluks and the ensuing wave of excessive taxation left Cairo in crippling turmoil and friction. After a spate of stone-throwing on the part of the public, and sword-brandishing on the part of the Mamluks, numerous carpet shops inside Bab Zuwayla were pillaged. In the resulting violence which saw the loss of life, one silk merchant was robbed of 500 dinars,[4] a princely sum (which would have footed the bill of one of the sultan's ceremonial tent banquets).

Even more casual incidents emphasized textiles as economic commodities. In 1502 a band of vagabonds ransacked twenty-four shops in the market by the Mosque of Ibn Tulun, taking off with a large quantity of goods, mainly textiles. The victims, taking their plea to the sultan, were given the assurance that the perpetrators would be sought out. A thorough investigation led to the arrest of twenty or so people, who were duly sliced in two in the middle of the market, while the sultan's prefect was rewarded with a robe of honor.[5]

Of course, tents had great socioeconomic importance within this larger context. A visitor to the Cairo Citadel sometime in March 1494 would have come across a tall, 'Arab-featured' old man with a grey beard rushing to put out a raging fire that was enveloping the complex in smoke, and could be seen far across the city. The visitor could be excused for assuming that this was one of the superintendents of the royal storerooms, distraught in thinking of the explanation he was going to have to provide to his superiors. In fact, the anguished man was none other than al-Ashraf Qaytbay, one of the greatest Mamluk sultans. The royal tent collection was on fire, and despite the best efforts of Qaytbay and his men who rushed to the rescue, it was apparently too late to do much about it. The pile of tents burned for three days, and when things were finally under control Qaytbay discovered, partially dismayed, partially relieved, that just one tent survived—his most important, the sumptuously decorated round one used for the annual celebrations of the Prophet's birthday.[6] The financial loss of the unfortunate incident was estimated at two hundred thousand dinars. As the sun rose on the third day, the officials of the court went up to the Citadel to show their sympathy to the sultan, who was upfront about the fact that he was extremely depressed. In response, the courtiers felt obligated to give the sultan some of their own tents to use at his disposal. Later, aides reported to the sultan that the fire had started in the caliph al-Mutawakil II's kitchen. In consequence, the august caliph, one of the most important figures in the Mamluk empire, was forced to take his family and move out of the Citadel complex to a pavilion on the road to the mausoleum of Sayyida Nafisa—a great inconvenience (later, it transpired that the story about the source of the fire had been fabricated by the caliph's enemies, who wished to stir up trouble between him and the sultan!).[7]

Other records from the period of Sultan Qaytbay's rule remind us that court etiquette governed who entertained whom in their tent. In the spring of 1471, for example, Sultan Qaytbay spent two successive nights in the tent of his vizier, Yashbak, mulling over how to defeat a particularly troublesome adversary, Shah Suwar. The two men stayed up until dawn on the second night, deeply immersed in conversation. There was a feeling among the people of Cairo that the sultan's army would be victorious, which is what happened—but it took a long time, and was only accomplished over the course of the next year. The sultan was blamed—specifically for going into Yashbak's tent, not once but twice, which was contrary to royal protocol and custom.[8]

It is hard to overstate the importance that omens held in Egyptian society at the time—they always seemed to be present somehow. If a feast day fell on a Friday, it was seen as unlucky, because the sultan's name would be read out twice on the same day (a case of two positives making a negative, perhaps). On another occasion,

> in the spring of 1500, by chance, the feast at the end of Ramadan fell upon the same day that the Sultan switched from his woollen winter costume to his white summer one. He presided over the ceremony mounted on a white horse with a silver saddle, wearing a white silk coat, white boots with silver spurs and white leather soles. Even his cap was of white wool. It was a bizarre combination, and the fact that he was in white from head to foot was seen as a bad omen. He lost the throne soon after.[9]

Perhaps it was his ghostly appearance that was seen as ominous?

Tents and Struggles for Power

Lavish tents were not only intended for use in court ceremonies meant to remind courtiers of their ruler's glory and awe an admiring Egyptian public. They also had a prominent role to play at any occasion where the state had to represent itself, its power, and its wealth to outsiders, who were often enemies.

The vast number of military encounters and battles that took place during the Mamluk period meant that there always seemed to be a reason for the Mamluk court to represent itself publicly outside of the palace. Political conflicts at the dawn of this era included having to deal with the Seventh Crusade, which saw Louis IX of France land in Egypt in 1249, and subsequent battles that eventually led to the king's capture the following year.

An account of the arrival of King Louis and his army in Damietta, on the north coast of Egypt on June 5, 1249, tells us the following: "And on Saturday, the Franks landed on the bank of the Nile where the Muslims had their encampment. And a red tent was erected for King *Rey de France*. And they fought with the Muslims, and on that day the *Amir* Najm al-Din, son of Shaykh al-Islam, was martyred; he had been a good man. . . ." The Muslims retreated, and upon seeing this retreat the occupants of Damietta came out, "looking as if they had been pulling on their faces all night long," and seeing there was nobody left in the city at all, "they fled with the military, barefooted, unclothed, hungry, poor, with a confusion of women and children, and set off to Cairo."[10]

Although the Egyptian tents are not described in this account, there is a poignancy in the mention of King Louis's tent being erected as a key detail of a significant political event that allegedly led to the desertion of an entire city. The mention of the tent's color—red—reasserts that these tents were emblematic. Undoubtedly, this red tent, produced with expensive dyes, probably cochineal, would have spoken of the crusader king's wealth and status even from the distance of the Mamluk camp.

Impressing 'the other,' whether friend or foe, has always been a constant feature of politics and comes to the fore frequently during this period, in a time of political rivalry and a frequent shifting of allegiances. Tents were a very useful asset in this quest.

In fact, earlier in that same year, as King Louis had been in Cyprus preparing for his Egyptian offensive, he had received a delegation representing the Mongol ruler Guyuk. The emissaries came to convey a message that Guyuk was supportive of the Crusaders, wishing them defeat over the Mamluks (some accounts even maintain that King Louis was told that Guyuk had actually converted to Christianity—a fib to help foster an alliance with him). Whatever the exact details of the message to Louis IX, the sentiment was surprisingly positive, and in response to this encouraging expression of Mongol support, King Louis immediately sent his Mongol counterpart a gift of a scarlet tent decorated with scenes from the life of Christ—effectively a portable chapel.[11] The circumstances would suggest that this red tent too was probably intended to accompany the French king to Egypt as one of his royal symbols.

Muslim poets, employing artistic licence, were to see in the color red their own symbolism. When Louis was finally defeated in 1250, his scarlet-red mantle trimmed with ermine was gleefully sent by the sultan to his commander in Damascus as a token of victory, and the following verse penned: "The mantle of the Frenchman sent in homage to the Prince of the Amirs was white as paper, but our swords have stained it the color of blood."[12]

The political one-upmanship of the Crusaders versus the Muslims is demonstrated in the fact that the red royal tents seem to have been an accessory of the Mamluk sultans as well. A description of the Mamluk siege of Acre in the Holy Land tells a similar red tent story, this time from the opposite perspective:

> On 5 April 1291, the siege began when al-Ashraf pitched his red tent facing the city of Acre. . . . The Muslims poured into the city and took tower after tower. The French regiment founded by Louis IX fought bravely but nothing could withstand the onslaught. . . . Thus the city of Acre fell. . . . Within a short time Sidon, Beirut, Athlit, Jubail and Tyre capitulated as well. On 3 August 1291, when the last groups of knights left Tortosa for the tiny island of Ruad, just a mile off the Syrian shore, it marked the end of Christian rule on the mainland. Almost 200 years after the first crusaders had achieved an improbable victory at Jerusalem, their successors fled for their lives or died.[13]

This momentous pitching of the Mamluk sultan's red tent was therefore the first of a significant chain of events leading to an outcome which enabled the Egyptian writer al-Furat to say, some decades later, "No town was left in which unbelief could repair. . . . The nation of the cross has fallen; through the Turks, the nation of the Arab has triumphed."[14]

Yet the Mamluks had other military challenges to contend with. In parallel with battles for the Holy Land, there were frequent clashes with the Mongols from the east, who had invaded Baghdad in 1258 and led repeated incursions into Mamluk-controlled territory, knowing full well, of course, that the Mamluks already had their hands tied, mainly because of attacks from the Christian west.

Victory, Ceremony, and Mischief

Fortunately for the Mamluks, the beginning of the fourteenth century saw them emerge victorious, and in typical Egyptian fashion, they sought to celebrate publicly. In 1303 for example, after they had defeated the Mongols in Syria, preparations took place in Cairo for weeks in order to give the sultan and his troops a fitting welcome: the street leading to the Citadel was decorated, and Cairenes are reported to have donated both jewelry and expensive cloth for the celebration. On that occasion, all of the singers in and around Cairo were asked to provide entertainment, and to house this musical extravaganza seventy wooden 'demi-citadels' were constructed.[15] It is highly likely that these weren't just wooden structures, but tented wooden structures of some sort. (Wood has always been scarce and expensive in Cairo; moreover, the account of the Fatimid tent storeroom describes some of the tents as citadels or fortresses, very similar to this description.) The expensive cloth must have been used to create these celebratory structures.

The celebration was not all frivolous, though: 1,600 Mongol prisoners-of-war were paraded in chains throughout the city, each carrying the head of a less fortunate comrade. If that wasn't enough to convey what was being celebrated, one thousand heads mounted on lances were also paraded. Goriness and gruesomeness were as much a part of the festivities as color and music. In this instance, the sultan is recorded to have stopped at each of the pavilions to admire the way in which they had been decorated.[16]

There is a clear sense that the Mamluk sultan was a public figure who engaged in public tours in the same way royalty would today. Unlike their Fatimid forebears, the Mamluk sultans had no notion of quasi-divine status—instead for this dynasty, whose legitimacy came from military power and the ability to survive in an environment of power-grabbing and intrigue, the most they could hope for was publicly-demonstrated support on the part of the religious establishment to validate their campaigns. To that end, one of the things the Mamluks had done was to capitalize on the Mongol sacking of Baghdad in 1258 and install the fleeing Caliph al-Mustansir II as a figurehead leader of the Islamic community, effectively using him to give them religious legitimacy when they needed it. This was in return for a comfortable life in Cairo, no longer available to him in his homeland.

Unsurprisingly, displays of the caliph's support of the Mamluk dynasty took place in tents in public spaces rather than in the beautiful palaces at the Citadel, which were replete with marble and mosaics but remote and inaccessible to the public. In an age before mass media, public presence was the best way to spread news.

In 1260, just two years after the caliph had been installed in his new role, the Mamluk sultan rode on horseback to a large public garden on the outskirts of Cairo, where a tent had been erected for him. He was accompanied, of course, by the members of his court. Two of these men were responsible for transporting a set of caliphal robes that were to be bestowed upon the sultan on that occasion. Upon arrival, the sultan entered into a different tent first, received the caliphal robes, and then appeared in the main tent bedecked in his new costume. The garments bestowed by the caliph were a black turban with gold brocade, a purple stole *(dira'a)*, a gold collar, cuffs for his legs, and several swords, one of which he wore in his belt, and the others placed behind him. Two ornaments, either feathers or brooches, were placed on his head and he carried two lances and a shield. He was then presented with a mottled horse with a black bridle and head covering.[17] Black was the official color of the

Abbasid caliphate and thus there could not be a more fitting display of the caliph's approval of the Egyptian Mamluks.

After the sultan had received these gifts he called his princes one by one and bestowed robes upon them. Among the recipients was the head of the royal literary *diwan*, Ibn Luqman, who was given a robe of yellow atlas silk. Ibn Luqman then stood up, and after invoking God's name, recited a poem he had written affirming the caliph's investiture of the sultan. The poem gave thanks for the beautiful garments, rightfully earned through good deeds.[18]

The use of tents for such events was not at all unusual and continued right through the Mamluk period. In 1389, for example, the Mamluk sultan Barquq descended from his Cairo Citadel to a large tent that had been especially erected in the square below for him to receive oaths of allegiance from his princes. A number of pavilions were put around the sultan's tent to accommodate members of the court. Once the sultan had arrived and they had sworn allegiance to him, a lavish banquet was served, and following this festive meal the event drew to a close.[19]

The square beneath the Citadel, the hippodrome, was in effect the place where the sultan interacted with the public most frequently. It was not just to host celebrations (such as that of the Prophet's birthday, which was a high point of the year), but also to review his troops, judge prisoners,[20] and watch polo matches from his dais. As such, it was a space afforded great care and attention. In 1506, for example, Sultan al-Ghuri received from Syria 150 camel-loads of crates of various shrubs and saplings that were not indigenous to Egypt, including apple, pear, cherry, quince, vines, and an array of odoriferous shrubs, as well as white roses, lilies, irises, and even a coconut palm which he then had planted in the square. These were his finishing touches to what had been an ambitious program of what we would think of today as urban upgrading. He had built pavilions, belvederes, and platforms from which he fulfiled his role as a dispenser of justice and oversaw his extensive realm. His improvements necessitated bringing in a huge quantity of fertile soil for the beds where he could plant trees and plants to enable the creation of this verdant space at the heart of his empire. Apart from all of its ceremonial functions, the sultan had created a space in which he could take pleasurable leisurely strolls, amid streams of running water.[21]

It is in this context that one must imagine the celebrations that took place in the tent world of the Mamluks. On May 4, 1509 for example, the sultan held a feast on the eve of the 15th of the holy month of Muharram so magnificent that it surpassed the annual celebrations of the Prophet's birthday, seen as a benchmark of celebratory luxury.

For the occasion, he erected his large round tent around a huge pool filled up with water from the Nile and "all the flowers of Cairo." Chandeliers were hung, and magnificent carpets were placed around the flower-filled basin. Those present included all of the Qur'an reciters of Cairo (as well as four judges, representing the four schools of Islamic thought). Four hundred plates of Chinese porcelain were brought in for the meal. Marzipan confections, made in the style of Hama in Syria, each weighing half a pound, were served, while the main banquet included 500 geese, 1,000 chickens, 50 lambs, 40 sheep, and 1,500 pounds of meat. The meal probably cost the sultan 1,000 dinars, and also included fruit, desserts, and other sugary confections.

But do not let this description of mounds of food obscure the delicate image of a resplendent candlelit tent encircling a pool filled with flowers in the verdant *midan* of Sultan al-Ghuri's Cairo. The sultan, who had on that day changed from his wollen winter clothing to linen, inaugurated the polo games and reviewed the military exercises of the Mamluks. These involved archery and horsemanship, and were combined with a display of fireworks that brought out a huge crowd.[22]

The tent probably used for the occasion was one commissioned by al-Ghuri's predecessor (and nephew), Sultan Qaytbay, which had cost him 30,000 dinars. It appears to have been used on a monthly basis, as it was customary for the sultan to receive his *amir*s at the beginning of every month. Some of these audiences incorporated a series of successive events. On at least one instance in 1508, the monthly reception was followed by a procession of foodstuffs in front of the sultan organized by the prefect of the markets. The parade included meat, sheep, bread, flour, and sugar, all carried ceremonially on the backs of courtiers.[23]

Many of these occasions combined pomp with frivolity. At the celebration of 'Ashura in the year 1512 for example, the sultan, seated in his pavilion by the Nilometer, was entertained by singing and a buffoon by the name of Ali Bey, who brought the sultan to laughter with his dancing and contortions. Such events often also included the setting up of large tents to host his most important *amir*s. Events such as these ended solemnly nonetheless; after having his fill of entertainment, the sultan would get on the royal barge and depart for Bulaq, seated on a yellow satin dais.[24]

Lest we forget, the funerary traditions of Cairo also included the erection of tents. In 1399 for example, when the Mamluk Sultan Barquq died at the age of sixty, tents were erected by his grave: "And for several days, readers recited the Quran, while sumptuous public meals were spread for them; the notables of the government also resorted to the grave every night for a couple of days, and the men's grief at his loss was widespread." The chronicler Ibn Taghribirdi notes that this was the first time that a king had been buried during the day.[25]

It is evident, though, that Mamluk tents were not just used by the court for public functions—there was much more that could be done with them, not always good and not always really public. In 1387 the sultan, looking out from his citadel, caught a glimpse of what must have been a large tent erected on the banks of Nile, and sent some of his men to investigate. It transpired that two of his princes were using their tent as a place to get drunk, and the sultan subsequently had them beaten and fined: one for 100,000 dinars and 50,000 dinars for the other.[26]

And in 1516, at the twilight of the Mamluk period, to celebrate the feast at the end of Ramadan tents and canopies were set up between the two neighborhoods of al-Waruqun and al-Bunduqdariya, where singers and musicians played and lanterns and candelabra were illuminated in broad daylight.[27] It is easy to see how brightly-colored tents would have fit right into a mood of festive garishness.

Tents in the Everyday

Because many historic sources focus on the grand or politically important, many references to tents in the Mamluk period have an element of the extraordinary, but the reality is that tents were very much part of the everyday as well.

Late in the spring of 1506 for example, an island (or mud flat) appeared in the Nile opposite the port of Bulaq, immediately in front of the house of a certain Qanim Tajir ('the merchant'). Following its appearance, cucumbers and fragrant plants were planted on it; people went to celebrate without restraint, numerous tents and huts were erected, and the people of Cairo spent days and nights there, "splashing in the water until the middle of the night."[28] The following year, at around the same time, an evening celebration was held in Bulaq to commemorate Isma'il Inbabi, a local saint, and five hundred tents were set up on the new island (which eventually came to be known as Zamalek, meaning 'huts'). In addition, stalls were set up to create a fair, and for several consecutive nights people feasted without limit—the reason was simple, writes the chronicler Ibn Iyas: "We lived then in complete abundance and in complete security."

Soon after, to celebrate the *mawlid* of another saint, Suwaydan, this time on the banks of Bulaq itself, numerous tents were put up by the river. This turned out to be a less carefree occasion, however: a spark blew from the cooking pot of a woman by the water and set alight the cargo of a moored barge filled with linen, which in turn set ablaze the hay supply of a nearby sugar refinery, destroying the entire complex. It was believed that it was the saint's intercession that preserved the rest of the neighborhood from destruction, and presumably the tents as well![29]

The Appearance of Mamluk Tents

There seems to be little doubt that as far as courtly textiles were concerned, red velvet and yellow silk were the materials and colors of choice, presumably because both the materials and the dyes used (probably cochineal for red and saffron for yellow)[30] were extremely expensive. For example, on the occasions of the two main Muslim feasts (one marking the end of Ramadan, and the other the culmination of the Hajj) the Mamluk sultan would parade under a yellow silk canopy brocaded with gold, atop of which was a gilded silver bird. This contraption, the royal parasol, was a continuation of Fatimid tradition. But the world of tents seemed to have been one that focused rather more on dazzling people with an array of colors and patterns. In his account of the trappings of kingship, al-Qalqashandi, an Egyptian polymath probably writing at the end of the fourteenth century, describes the sultan's tents as being large in number and varied, including some of red, white, and blue Damascene cotton, and others made of felt or canvas of different colors that astounded viewers' minds with their beauty. He says, tellingly, that the tents were intended as stand-in palaces.[31] It would seem that in at least some instances, the most important role of the tents was to provide impressive colorful, patterned backdrops; the type of textile used to make them was less important.

Elsewhere, simply writing about the accoutrements of travel, al-Qalqashandi describes 'average' contemporary tents as either *fustat* (pointed) or domed; some, he says, were made of pieces of thick cotton. This little detail is important: the material he describes is very different from the sumptuous brocades of the Fatimid palace storerooms, and without a doubt he is describing a more commonplace kind of tent, undoubtedly cheaper and also more durable. With their wide range of uses and functions, and the fact that they were used by all segments of Egyptian society, rich and poor, the range of materials and forms used for tents was wide. Al-Qalqashandi also mentions *khirka*s, little dismantle-able tent cubicles made of thick material (cotton, canvas, or felt) stretched over a wooden frame, used inside tents to create a sleeping area.[32] In the same breath, al-Qalqashandi mentions palanquins—tented structures carried by beasts of burden, usually to transport women in privacy, or simply to provide those who could afford it with a comfortable means of transport away from the din, the dust, and the sun of what has always been regarded as a busy city. His description is of a palanquin carried by two mules, one in front and one behind. He notes that the structure is domed and at times covered with canvas, at other times with silk.[33] Just as tents were portable architecture, palanquins were portable tents, and shared many stylistic and physical characteristics. One notable difference was that palanquins were much smaller, of course. At the top of the range were extremely expensive ones that were lavishly embroidered and bejeweled. In 1475 the palanquin of the Sultan Qaytbay's wife Fatima, which was used to transport her to Mecca, was embroidered with pearls, rubies, and turquoise. Her sister-in-law, also traveling in an embroidered palanquin, was accompanied by fifty camels with litters of multicolored velvet.[34] But these were rarities, not the standard fare of the Cairene marketplace.

Al-Qalqashandi's account, mentioning the difference of materials used for the tents and palanquins, is a crucial one. Because many of the other surviving accounts of tents refer to court celebrations, they describe the most lavish items found in Egyptian society, but the reality must have been that there was a whole range of tents using different types of fabric; evidence would suggest that at least one of the Mamluk tenting traditions evolved using canvas as its base and appliqué work for decoration. It is probable that this would have been the tradition that catered to the lion's share of the market for tents in Mamluk Cairo.

Appliqué Work

Appliqué work appears to have existed in Egypt for at least one thousand years (and this remarkable time span *excludes* known pharaonic examples, such as an appliquéd leather canopy in the tomb of Isetemkheb at Thebes dating from 1040 BC). Of the textile fragments that survive from medieval Cairo, a number of the examples are appliqué work clearly from a ceremonial context, the very same context which produced tents. However, there is evidence to suggest that cotton appliqué work was not a Mamluk introduction, and was a well-developed tradition for several centuries prior. One striking example carbon-dated to the early twelfth century (the late Fatimid period) depicting a lion is thought to come from a standard (see plate 1). It is a remarkable piece—like any form of artwork incorporating a silhouette, it requires an understanding of how to simplify a complicated image without losing its character—the person who drew the lion knew exactly what they were doing. The piece exemplifies what it is that has defined appliqué work across the ages: contrast. These were pieces meant to be seen from a distance, and so to achieve this, appliqué work needs to be bold, clear, contrasting, and powerful—all qualities very obvious in the lion.

This use of appliqué work for heraldic and emblematic purposes continued—many of the surviving textiles from the Mamluk period made using the appliqué technique bear the blazons (emblems) of Mamluk courtiers: the sultan's cupbearer, his sword-bearer, his scribe. These blazons were widespread in the art of the Mamluk period, and appear frequently in ceramics and metalwork, as well as in architecture. In the early Mamluk period the blazons featured only one heraldic device, reflecting a courtier's current position in court, whereas by the late fifteenth century, the blazon combined the emblems of all the offices a courtier had held, a bit like a visual résumé made in cotton or wool. Examples of both types survive. This shows that the appliqué technique was a long-lasting one, spanning over four hundred years of Egyptian medieval history. It is easy to see why appliqué was appropriate for the representation of emblems. Legibility was important; the blazons were like logos, clear and quite simple in design, for which fabric cut-outs were ideal. Colors were bold and contrasting: reds, blues, blacks, and yellows, usually on a cream background (see plate 2).

One particularly striking example, probably the border of a standard or banner, features an inscription bearing blessings to the sultan—it is one of the few surviving textiles showing the use of an inscription (see fig. 2). However, it is unlikely that this sort of textile was in any way a rarity—Arabic inscriptions were extremely common in Mamluk art, and general blessings, or more specific praise for the sultan, were standard.

A second fragment worthy of note is one with an arabesque design forming a star pattern (see plate 3). The star pattern was a key component of Mamluk design, and was used to create a myriad of patterns, not just in textiles but in wood, stone, and marble as well. It could be found on everything from cheap copper coins to magnificent carved stone domes. Some artistic traditions survive better than others, and while the six centuries that have succeeded the Mamluk period brought with them other styles and other decorative 'components,' what is incredible is that star patterns from the fourteenth and fifteenth centuries are very similar to the standard patterns of tent textiles being produced in Cairo today.

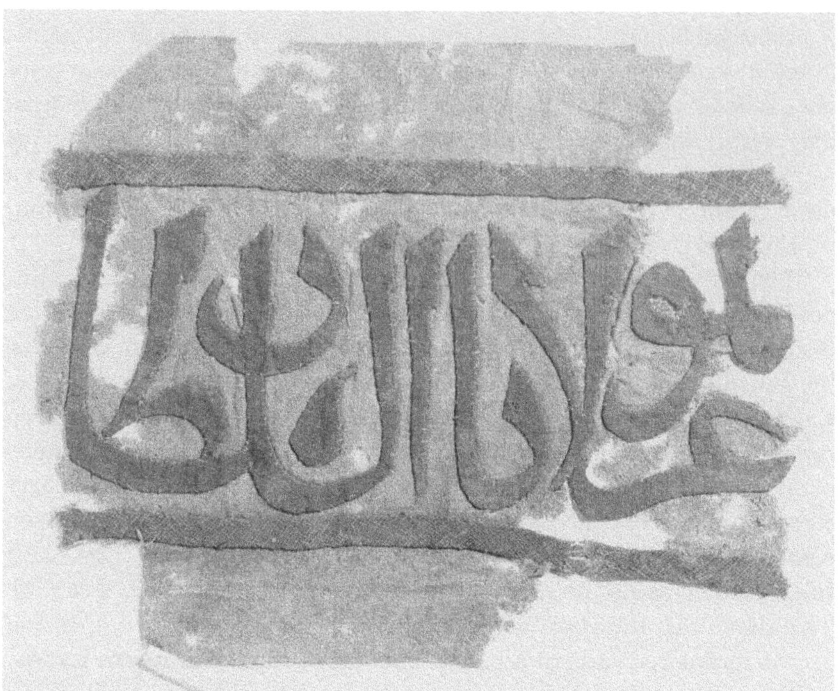

Figure 2 Appliqué work has been used by the tentmakers of Cairo for at least eight hundred years. This Mamluk piece probably comes from a banner. Photograph by Brian Boyle.

One appliqué medallion housed today at the Ashmolean Museum in Oxford, but found in Egypt, is around 60 cm long, and by virtue of its size and shape would seem to have come from a tent (see plate 4). Like other examples, it makes good use of contrasting colors—in this case blue and white—but it is also a delicate piece with fine arabesque designs. It hints at what a complete Mamluk tent would have looked like—colorful from a distance, but also captivating to those who were close enough to see its smaller details.

Appliqué of this sort appears to be very much a part of the Egyptian textile tradition used to decorate all sorts of items. There are other surviving fragments very small in scale which were almost certainly parts of garments, but their typology is the same as the pieces that seem to have come from banners and tents.

Another form of this appliqué work consists of small squares or triangles of different colors sewn together and further embellished with embroidery—usually small circular designs forming rosettes around tiny circular cut-outs in the fabric itself. The delicate embroidery added to the appliqué, the neat cut-outs, and the fact that there are several surviving examples that are very similar in terms of their bright color palettes suggest that this was a distinct type of work, as distinctly recognizable as jeans in today's world. Surviving pieces include male skull caps, bits of what were probably robes, and one intriguing little shoulder bag almost certainly made for a young girl—probably her first handbag, and probably a scaled down version of an adult's bag. It is easy to imagine the holder being bought the bag on a trip down to the textile market with her parents in the thirteenth or fourteenth centuries.

The context in which these pieces were found is unclear, but it is possible that at least some of them were found in tombs (probably of Egyptian Christians, who tended to be laid to rest in their best clothes). This sheds a bit more light on appliqué work in the context of Mamluk Cairo—it was clearly a well-developed tradition with a great variety of styles, and at its best took pride of place in the wardrobes of Cairenes of the Mamluk era.

Textiles for Mecca

Any form of Mamluk textile 'furnishing' must be seen in the context of the ceremonial covering of Islam's most sacred shrine: the Ka'ba in Mecca. The Mamluk period saw the flourishing of a tradition whereby every year specially woven textile coverings were produced in Egypt and paraded to Mecca as part of the annual pilgrimage. Because of the importance of the building and the ceremony, the textiles were of the most expensive material: silk brocade, with the most important sections embroidered in gold or silver gilt thread. The brocade itself was usually black and white decorated with inscriptions. Producing the *kiswa* (covering) was a major state-financed endeavor, carefully controlled due to the expense of the operation and raw materials involved.

The procession of the *kiswa* was a deeply ceremonial event, with the coverings carried on camelback and preceded by a palanquin, the *mahmal*, which was also usually elaborately embroidered with metal thread and a key symbol of the Hajj. The procession led the pilgrim trail from Cairo to Mecca, a long, arduous, and costly journey across the desert sands.

As the covering of the Ka'ba was changed every year as part of the Hajj ceremony, part of the ritual involved replacing the old covering with the new one that had been brought from Cairo. The previous year's covering was cut up and given as gifts to notable attendees of that year's pilgrimage, the most important of whom were given the best sections: those decorated with metal-thread embroidery, namely from the inscription band around the Ka'ba, the *hizam* or belt, and the *burqu'*, veil, or the curtain covering the door. Reflecting on this tradition in conjunction with the practice of the sultan bestowing beautiful robes on his princes as a sign of his favor is a useful reminder of the many instances in which expensive textiles took on great symbolism.

Understandably, the Ka'ba textiles were treated with even more reverence than most. In August 1498 when the *mahmal* returned from Mecca in its usual procession, accompanying the joyous pilgrims through the city, the sultan was not in his palace at the Citadel, but in the suburbs. He said he wanted to see the *mahmal*, and so after the camel carrying it had stopped and was happily resting on its knees, it was forced up again and paraded again through the city all the way to where the sultan was stationed, and then, after he had seen it, paraded all the way back. It was noted (disapprovingly) that such an extraordinary breach of tradition had never been heard of before.[35]

It is fortunate that a few significant textiles survive from the Mamluk period that are related to the sacred Ka'ba coverings, giving a hint of what Mamluk tents may well have looked like. Some of these are today in Istanbul, kept as part of the Ottoman sultan's treasures, both for their religious connotations but also for their artistic merit. Lavish and large in scale, a couple of pieces are decorated with bold embroidered calligraphic medallions. In a faith where the written word is so important, it is understandable that the decorative coverings of its most sacred shrine should be based on text.

Two very large Mamluk textile pieces survive from the end of Mamluk period. One of these is a curtain, ostensibly for the Ka'ba, of red and green silk with metal thread embroidery in elaborate patterns combining medallions and abstracted floral designs. It is a very impressive piece of embroidery, and in the center of some of its medallions are the very typical Mamluk features found in appliqué fragments: Mamluk emblems, in this case that of an abstracted pen box, symbol of the sultan's scribe, the *dawadar*. Scholarship suggests that this particular curtain was commissioned by the last Mamluk sultan of Egypt, Tumanbay II, who witnessed the Mamluk state crumble into a vassal of the Ottoman Empire following a decisive battle in 1517.

Close examination of the curtain reveals that a central panel was added slightly later, naming the Ottoman Sultan Selim as the patron of the piece, and attributing its provenance to Syria. But two details betray its origin as almost certainly Egyptian, and definitely Mamluk: the use of metal thread on a large-scale piece, given that it is known that the Dar al-kiswa ('house of the *kiswa*') was in Cairo, and the Mamluk emblem mentioned above.

Sources tell us that following the Ottoman conquest of Egypt in 1517, Sultan Selim made off with a vast range of treasures (including relics of the Prophet, which had been kept in Cairo), and that he also sent Egypt's best craftsmen to Istanbul to employ them on his projects there. It is likely that the sultan's men had come across the curtain during this period and perhaps taken it to Syria, where it was modified to name the new patron.

The second Hajj textile is the actual *mahmal* used in the ceremonial procession to Mecca—this one commissioned by the penultimate Mamluk sultan al-Ghuri, whose reign lasted from 1501 to 1516. The al-Ghuri *mahmal* is a reminder of the chromatic richness of the Mamluk textiles, and of course of their Fatimid antecedents: the intense yellow and red recalling the central pole of the famed Fatimid tent named al-Qatul described by Abu al-Hassan the tentmaker. The al-Ghuri *mahmal* is a fantastic piece of appliqué textile work, with striking red letters applied to its plain golden background. It enables us to be certain that the appliqué tradition in Mamluk Cairo was thriving until the very last days of the dynasty. Al-Ghuri was in every way an important patron of architecture: his architectural complex in Cairo was so ambitious—too ambitious—that its huge main green-tiled dome constructed to house the Prophet's sacred relics collapsed; his multiturreted minarets were unlike any seen before, and if that wasn't enough, he is reputed to have commissioned Leonardo da Vinci (who was a renowned engineer) to draw up designs for a bridge in Syria. It is telling that for the most important set of textiles he was to commission during his reign he chose appliqué work (see plate 5).

Architectural Parallels

It is hard to discuss Mamluk textiles, which are effectively portable architecture, without referring to architectural parallels since medieval buildings, by virtue of the permanence of their materials, preserve entire artistic compositions much better than most surviving textiles, which are just small pieces of a larger picture.

One very prominent decorative feature of the Mamluk architectural tradition was the embellishing of the important elements of a building with decorative panels using dynamic patterns in contrasting colors. On the façades of public buildings especially, such as mosques and water fountains, the panels were particularly common above doors and windows. Lintels in particular were often decorated with striking black-and-white strips cut to create a tessellated edge, often with delicate abstracted flowers or zigzags. These compositions formed a very strong contrast with the honey-colored stone. There was almost always a geometric structure to all of these panels, even if many of the details could include floral and vegetal elements.

A second conventional feature, as much decorative as informative, was a large inscription band, usually with verses from the Qu'ran found running across the façades of Mamluk buildings. Above that, a façade would usually be finished off with a row of crenellations, most of which resembled a three-leafed flower.

The convention for building interiors was for the lower section of the wall to be paneled, usually with slabs of stone and marble interspersed with areas of more intricate decoration. The middle section of the wall was usually plain, and below the ceiling a decorative inscription band was often placed: this could either be of plaster or painted wood. Because these inscriptions tended to be high up, contrast was important, and many of them have letters in white or gold on a blue background.

In mosques the mihrab, the niche indicating the direction of Mecca, tended to be the most elaborate feature, usually filled with a range of intricate decorative patterns. In Mamluk houses, a very common feature in large reception areas was an arcaded built-in sideboard, called a *suffa*. This too was often embellished with inlaid marble patterns.

In the interior of most grand buildings, both secular and sacred, an elaborately patterned floor was a standard feature of any building when the patron could afford it, and while the floor patterns were different from those on the walls, they too relied on contrast, pattern, and geometry. The aim of decorating the floors in this way was to create a carpet effect. In some mosques, designs of arches mimicked the design of prayer carpets. Houses often had a small fountain in the center of their main reception space and these tended to have fine geometric inlays in marble and paste.

Comparing existing appliqué Mamluk textiles with the architecture of Mamluk Cairo reveals the strongest parallels with the decorative panels that were to be found on building façades described above. In fact, some of the similarities are remarkable: by the mid-fourteenth century, it was common practice for these panels to combine different colored stones and marbles with colored paste, enabling a wider palette including blue, turquoise, pink, and red. In some examples, rather than just decorate the lintels, entire decorative panels were created in prominent areas of buildings, for example above the main doorway or in the entrance. In all cases, the object was the same: to attract the viewer's eye using pattern and color and then awe them with the sophistication of a dynamic, often kaleidoscopic, design.

Among the most striking examples is a panel above the main entrance of the mid-fourteenth-century mosque of the sultan's sword-bearer, Aslam (see plate 6). Comparing the design of this magnificent panel to a contemporary appliqué fragment, it is easy to see just how similar they are in both design and color: they both stem from a star design in their center. It may at first seem impossible to fathom how to make such a design so accurately. In fact, the designer used the same technique as schoolchildren making paper snowflakes today. By folding a piece of paper into quarters and then folding it again, this time diagonally, all one has to do is to draw a segment of the design, cut it out and unfold the paper, and the result is something a lot more ambitious. This is how all of these patterns were achieved.

A second such panel from the monumental religious complex of Sultan Hassan, built in the 1350s, is a reminder that these decorative panels could also appear on building interiors. By the late fifteenth century, inlaid panels with patterns based on a star at their center achieved incredible levels of sophistication. One of the tricks of doing this was for the stars from which the entire pattern took its structure to be placed not in the center of the panel but offset, making it hard for the viewer to understand how such an elaborate design had come about, and presumably increasing their sense of wonderment. It also helped to make a design more dynamic. Buildings erected during the reign of Sultan Qaytbay (1468–96), a noted lover of the arts, feature some of the most elaborate star compositions (see plate 7).

Unsurprisingly, this was also a period when Mamluk textiles were similarly sophisticated; surviving Mamluk carpets, although part of a craft tradition that is distinct from the tentmakers, are a good reminder of the range in color and design of large-scale Mamluk textiles.

As mentioned earlier, Sultan Qaytbay is known to have commissioned a great tent especially for the celebration of the Prophet's birthday. It is described by a contemporary chronicler as being "one of the marvels of the world" and so large that it needed five hundred servants to set it up. The tent took the form of a reception hall, with four *iwans* (chambers) recalling the layout of both mosques and palaces. The central space was covered with a pierced dome, all of fabric. It had unusual cutout designs *(taqasis)* and 'jewels' *(fusus)*,[36] recounts the chronicler.[37] It is highly likely that this marvel was a masterpiece of appliqué work.

Whether we are to judge him by the quality or the sheer number of buildings constructed during his reign, it is hard to see Sultan Qaytbay as anything other than one of the greatest patrons of architecture that Egypt had seen for centuries (see plate 7). He was prolific, and apart from constructing buildings also commissioned objects for the holy places in Mecca and Medina. His commitment to honoring the holy shrines, including the burial place of the Prophet, as well as the fact that he seemed to really love the arts, makes it likely that the description of his tent was not an exaggeration. Qaytbay's funerary complex in the northern cemetery is a masterpiece of fine, meticulous construction—its dome features a masterful superimposition of an elaborate star pattern with fine floral decoration. But it is the two caravansaries (trade buildings used to house goods and merchants) surviving in Cairo today that show how even his commercial buildings were ornamented with decorative elements of the highest quality. The stone carving above the lintels of the shops in his caravanserai behind al-Azhar show a combination of star patterns and floral designs. His patronage was one of refinement, but also of variety and playfulness.

Where Was the Tentmakers' Market?

Historic sources describe the market of the tentmakers as being to the west of al-Azhar Mosque, probably close to a site currently occupied by a mosque built by an eighteenth-century governor of Egypt, Muhammad Bey Abu al-Dahab. The adjacent sixteenth-century building, Khan al-Zarakhsha (the khan of the brocaders), still survives, and indicates that the quarter was one dedicated to the production and trade of high-quality textiles. In the vicinity were other markets related to the textile and cavalry crafts (the canvas/felt sellers, the bridlemakers, the saddlemakers and even a little clearing of dyers). Even today, the textile market of historic Cairo is but a stone's throw away.

It is not possible to tell what the tentmakers' market looked like, but the sources describe it as a 'market,' not as a building. This could mean that it occupied more than one building or that like today, the market was a street lined with tentmakers' shops. Elsewhere it is described as an open area or clearing.[38] Despite the opacity of the description, the market's proximity to al-Azhar Mosque is telling. Al-Azhar was (and still is) the city's most prestigious mosque. Being close to it indicated the social importance of the trade. Some more information can be gleaned from surviving historic accounts; for example, that with the passing of time the makers of palanquins, originally located to the north, established a presence there—where they manufactured palanquins.[39] This shows that the tentmakers' market was probably not just a point of sale, but included workshops as well. It must have been a bustling place indeed. Al-Maqrizi mentions that the palanquin makers alone benefited from a huge seasonal trade of pilgrims to both Mecca and Jerusalem.[40] Many of these may well have also purchased a static tent for the journey—which in the case of Mecca took a long forty days.

Tent buyers and sellers dealing with off-the-shelf requests in this little clearing by al-Azhar were very different from the patrons of one hundred or more camel tents described elsewhere. They needed something that looked good, but wasn't overly expensive, and presumably many of them didn't want to wait. In fact, the shaykh in the market advised that actually, the palanquin sellers didn't really have to treat their customers all that well—once a purchase had been made, they were unlikely ever to see them again.[41]

Royal Gifts

While the Egyptian tenting tradition was a well-established and distinctive one, it must not be forgotten that 'foreign' tents also came into the possession of members of the court, often as diplomatic gifts. It is conceivable that these may have inspired some of the more creative tentmakers, who could have assimilated 'exotic' patterns and techniques into their own work. In 1511 for example, 'Ali Dawlat, an envoy of the Safavid ruler Isma'il, brought the Mamluk Sultan al-Ghuri magnificent gifts from his master. As well as horses, mamluks, and two-humped camels, the offerings included a large multicolored silk tent decorated with flowering bushes, upon whose branches birds were perched. It is not difficult to imagine what this tent looked like—numerous Safavid textiles still survive today, and many of these do indeed show shrubs and bushes intertwined with birds, animals, and humans.

Along with the tent, the sultan was also given a wooden kiosk painted pink and blue, decorated with vicious animals attacking their prey. The pavilion was covered with blue hangings with tassels of red silk. Along with it was a circular carpet made to fit inside.

Ibn Iyas, the chronicler who recorded the event, notes that the kiosk and tent were the gifts of choice, and that the sultan put them on display in the royal court for visitors to admire.[42]

Tent Hangings *(Sutur)*

Let us not forget that *sutur* were an important part of the Mamluk tent world as well. In September 1507 for example, the sultan hosted a lavish reception in honor of an envoy of the Ottoman sultan. The magnificence of the Mamluk court was represented by the lavishness of the textile hangings, and the number of dishes, fruits, and desserts, as recount the chronicles. The pharaonic basin beneath the hall was filled with sugared lemonade, and at the close of a splendid evening, the guest of honor was presented with a velvet robe lined with ermine.[43] Tent hangings would have been used on numerous similar occasions throughout the year.

Two of the most poignant references to the use of tent hangings to capture the celebratory mood relate to the release of the popular hero Zayni Barakat, inspector of the markets, from prison after he had offended Sultan al-Ghuri and spent a week incarcerated. As he descended from the Citadel, he was met with a city lit with lamps burning in front of its shops and the citizens perfumed with saffron. In the neighborhood where he lived, around the Ratl pond, he found the houses bedecked with hangings of white and colored silk from their windows. Ululations, singing, and the din of drum beats filled the air.[44]

Tellingly, celebratory tent hangings were used again the following year in 1513 (this time upon the orders of Barakat himself), to celebrate Sultan al-Ghuri's recovery from eye troubles, which the more loquacious branches of the Cairo grapevine had gossiped had rendered him blind.[45] Apparently this had been an exaggeration, and after months of affliction the sultan finally removed his bandages and was able to hold court wearing his full ceremonial turban, and the whole city came out to celebrate. As Zayni Barakat and other important officials of the court paraded into the city dressed in yellow silk, led by the city's doctors dressed in their fur coats, women ululated in joy out of house windows. This time it was Barakat who ordered the residents of the houses surrounding the Ratl pond to illuminate their houses and decorate their windows. In these neighborhoods, skeins of yellow silk (the royal color) and silks of other colors were to be found hanging from the windows, drums were beaten furiously, and the sharp trills of women's joyous shrieks were heard repeatedly. Boats filled with people celebrating covered the lake and music, singing, and fireworks added to the buzz.[46]

The next day, the whole city was bedecked in street decorations. The first place to be mentioned in the long list of decorated places was the textile market, of course, preceding even great city landmarks like the Great Mosque of Ibn Tulun. "The most important Mamluk emirs decorated the doors of their houses with banners and their most beautiful tents [probably tent hangings], like on the day of the feast of Breaking the

Fast [after Ramadan]. The caliph himself decorated his doorway with the hangings of the shrine of Sayyida Nafisa while the grand judges decorated their doors with curtains of velvet and silk." In fact, the chief judge of the Hanafi rite did something unheard of in terms of luxury—he hung muslin embroidered with beads of amber (something many people thought was excessive).[47] Many of the city's religious complexes were also adorned—among the most elaborate was the religious complex of Baybars, where the chief Hanafi judge, obviously not one to do things half-heartedly, had erected a scaffold and hung from it leather hangings depicting trees and basins of water. As the chronicler Ibn Iyas reminds us, through this extravagant decoration of the city the sultan quickly silenced the rumors abounding in the east and the west that he had lost sight in both his eyes. It was his way of showing the world that he was well and on top form. The other thing the sultan did (probably by way of giving thanks) was to order the manufacture of black silk coverings embroidered with gold for the tombs of the prophets buried in his kingdom.[48]

What these events tell us is that textiles were used as markers of joyous festivity, not just by the court in shows of stately splendor, but also to express festivity among the people of Cairo. Whether they were celebrating the state, their sultan, their saints and faith, or popular heroes made little difference—they used the same decorative accessories to transform the city.

3

Tents in Ottoman Cairo

There was a rumor that on May 16, 1516, the eve of the sultan's departure from Cairo to meet the Ottoman army in the north of Syria, "lighted torches were brought, and a spark blew from them onto the Sultan's tent, and one side of it was burnt." Understandably, "the people did not regard this as a good omen for the Sultan."[1]

In fact, the dawning of Ottoman Egypt can be said to have begun with an uneasy gut feeling on the part of the Mamluk Sultan al-Ghuri a few weeks earlier, in the spring of 1516. He had received news that the Ottomans and Persians were fighting each other (after two years of hostilities that began when Isma'il, the shah of Persia, invaded the territory of the Ottoman Sultan Selim). His view was that whoever emerged victorious in this struggle would then seek to invade his own territory, and to preempt any such occurrence decided to send an expedition to the north of Syria, accompanying it himself to see what was actually going on. The announcement of his intention was met with a flurry of activity—including the convenient disappearance of artisans and craftsmen, who went into hiding for fear of being drafted to fight. The expedition date he set was only ten days away, and so a speedy exit was necessary on their part! In order to ensure that the expedition could leave on time, the sultan quickly set about paying and inspecting his troops, something he accomplished in just four days. This extraordinary speed did not sit well with the Mamluk troops, who felt that if news got to the Ottomans or Persians that administering the entire Egyptian army was a short four-day job, they wouldn't consider Egypt much of a threat, a situation that wouldn't be to the country's advantage.

Incredibly, despite all that was going on, just three days after the announcement, the sultan found the time to "come down from the citadel and go to Raydaniyya," the plain on the northern outskirts of the city, and "showed the tentmen [*farrashin*] how to set up the royal tent for the expedition." It is not clear whether the royal tent was actually there when the sultan set about giving his instructions, because around ten days later he is reported to have "sent his tents out to Raydaniyya," a move that meant that "his expedition to Syria became a certainty." The sense of haste is conveyed by the fact that Ibn Iyas, the chronicler who described the event, notes somewhat disapprovingly that the sultan had not upheld the tradition of raising the royal standard forty days in advance of departure. In fact, his instruction was that any troops that were ready should not wait for him, but should just head off straight away.[2]

The procession that left from the Citadel four days later was a striking one nonetheless, comprising 15 camels with gold embroidered finery, 300 horses, of which 100 were wearing steel armor chased with gold, some were clothed in velvet of various colors, 6 had Bedouin saddles, and 5 were decked in gold embroidered cloth. Twenty-six litters were part of the procession, 24 of which were made of yellow silk, and 2 of which were of velvet with yellow silk. Despite the excitement and the crowds that came out to watch, there were those who expressed their disapproval, commenting that there weren't enough horses and that they had seen better processions in their time. Some elements followed convention, for example the order of the procession of the standards: first the royal standard and then those of the caliph and of the sultan, but the general impression was that it could have been grander, better organized, and richer—there were only ten loads of treasure cases, for example, rather than the traditional forty.[3] When the army finally left the city on May 17, 1516, Ibn Iyas remarks that, again contrary to tradition, neither the royal tents nor the royal flute players were in their expected place in the procession—it would have been customary for them to precede the chiefs of the guard who were marching on foot, carrying axes. That said, as the sultan proceeded through the city, all trembled at his handsome presence, the townfolk greeting him with prayers for his welfare, and the women cheering him on from the windows.[4]

The next we hear of the sultan's tent is upon his arrival in Aleppo, almost two months later, on July 10. Despite ordering a sermon on the sacred traditions of peace to be delivered in the Great Mosque in Aleppo, he chose not to attend, and (to great disapproval) instead decided to pray in his tent pitched in the great *midan* (square) of Aleppo with the caliph.[5] But while the tent may have been his refuge at times when he did not wish to face the crowd, it was more than anything a symbol, not just of Qansuh Sultan al-Ghuri, but of this empire, too.

Unfortunately, things unraveled quickly, and on August 23, a day described as being one of constant ill-fortune, the Ottomans defeated the Mamluks at Marj Dabiq, near Aleppo. It is a testament to the importance of the royal textiles that "as the confusion and terror increased," one of the Mamluk Princes, Tamr al-Zardkash,

> feared for the safety of Sultan's standard, so he lowered it, folded it up and concealed it. Then he approached the Sultan and said to him: "Our King and Master, the troops of Ibn Othman are upon us, save thyself and go back to Aleppo." When the sultan understood this, a kind of paralysis fell upon him which affected one side and caused his jaw to drop. He asked for water, and they brought him some in a golden cup, from which he drank a little. Then intending flight, he turned his horse round, moved a few paces, fell off his horse, stood for a moment, and died from the shock of his defeat. It was said that his gall bladder burst and that red blood flowed from his throat.[6]

Upon learning of the sultan's death, the Ottomans set about on the men who were around him, killing some of them. Then they "trampled down al-Ghuri's tents and overthrew all of the goods and provisions stacked round them. The copy of Othman's Qu'ran was lost, they stamped upon the Fakir's flags and the Amir's banners, and plundered everything belonging to the Egyptian troops."

The sultan's personal tents must also have suffered this symbolic desecration, for later in the day the Ottoman sultan and his troops advanced

> to take possession of the Mamluk sultan's camp. He sat in the circular tent, took the wardrobe, and the costly goblets belonging to it, the armour-case, the weapons, the money chest and all the articles of value, and each of his Amirs took to himself a tent of one of al-Ghuri's Amirs. The troops occupied the tents of the Egyptian, Damascene and Aleppo troops, thus exemplifying the maxim that "the misfortunes of some are the good fortunes of others."[7]

The Impact of the Ottoman Conquest

The Ottoman conquest of Egypt in 1516–17 saw the country suddenly lose its autonomy and become part of a larger empire governed from

Istanbul. Unsurprisingly, this change had a strong political impact, which in turn led to a dynamic whereby arts and crafts were shaped on the one hand as they always had been, by a strong yet evolving Egyptian tradition, but on the other hand by a new relationship with the art of the Ottoman court, affected by changes in the nature of high-level artistic patronage.

As can be imagined, following Egypt's defeat the new Ottoman overlords had to think of how to deal with the Mamluks, who still wielded influence despite no longer being officially in control of the country. It seemed to be a perplexing issue, and tellingly, one of the things it had an impact on was style: at first the Mamluk princes were forbidden from wearing Ottoman dress. Evidently, the Ottoman regime was keen to stress that whatever roles they may have played in the old system, the Mamluks were not to feel that they were really part of the new. However, four years later, the opposite rule came into effect—the Mamluks *had* to dress in the Ottoman style. This policy was implemented by Khayrbak, the new Ottoman governor and a Mamluk himself, who had attained his position by betraying the Mamluk sultan, allowing the Ottomans to win in battle in 1516 in return for the governorship of Egypt. It is thought that one of the reasons for this change of policy was that the Mamluks and the Ottomans were constantly falling out with each other, and one way to solve the problem was to make the two groups less distinct.[8] In any case, two key questions that must have been on the minds of those comfortable enough to think of matters of identity were, Where do we fit now? and, How do we represent ourselves?

Another pivotal event as far as the arts are concerned was the fact that many of the country's best craftsmen were shipped off to Istanbul, to work for the Ottoman sultan. Although the *forced* movement of craftsmen was not all that common, the move of skilled craftsmen to places of greater prosperity and importance was a long-standing practice, and Cairo's long history as the seat of an empire meant that it had seen successive waves of craftsmen coming to find work within the Mamluk court. In this instance, the movement was in reverse. Cairo's chief administrators were now employees of a court that was based elsewhere. They were simply stationed in Cairo on purposefully short postings, not unlike today's diplomats. As such, their entire position as patrons changed; few of them had the intention of investing too much in the arts in a place like Cairo.

More worryingly, some of Cairo's buildings were stripped of their marble, which was also taken to Istanbul for reuse in the construction of imperial buildings there. Among the buildings to have suffered this fate was the Mosque of Sultan al-Nasir Muhammad at the Citadel, which is surprising, given that the Citadel remained the seat of power. Understandably, for those who had witnessed and enjoyed the splendor of Mamluk Cairo, this new turn of events was seen as unfortunate.

Ibn Iyas the chronicler, who was himself of Mamluk stock, wrote in disappointment and dismay at what had happened. Among his main grievances was that the first year after the Ottoman conquest, the celebration of the Prophet's birthday was so scaled down that it was hardly noticeable. Among the great sins that the Ottomans committed, according to him, was that they sold off the large tent traditionally used for this occasion to a group of Moroccan merchants for the paltry sum of 400 dinars—it was cut up into pieces and sold to the people as curtains. This was the tent that had been commissioned in the late fifteenth century by Sultan Qaytbay. Ibn Iyas writes, "It was one of the symbols of the Sultanic kingdom in Cairo and was sold for the lowest price. The Ottoman sultan did not understand its value, and later kings had to forgo its use."[9] In the same wave of scaling things down, the Ottomans also discontinued the traditions of distributing food to the poor and of hosting a great meeting between the heads of the four schools of religious thought.

Evidently, those in control in 1517 thought it unimportant for these large-scale celebrations to continue—to them, all of this was a frivolous and unnecessary waste of money. While the Ottoman sultan was right to celebrate religious events in grand style in Istanbul, the economic resources of Egypt were not to be squandered.

One wonders whether the sale of the tent was also a move to spite the Mamluks, and perhaps Cairenes in general. A more logical decision would have been for the new Ottoman officials to continue to use it for their own purposes, or to transport it to Istanbul along with the craftsmen and the marble that they took from Cairo.

Having witnessed what was going on, the notables of Cairo left nothing to chance. Ibn Iyas tells us that they moved their textiles to their tombs (and mosques, and the houses of the less wealthy) in order to keep them safe.[10]

Tents and Tentmakers in Ottoman Cairo—Çelebi's Account

Despite the lamentable sale of the royal Mamluk tent for a pittance, the tentmakers remained alive and well in Ottoman Cairo. The Turkish writer Evliya Çelebi says that in the mid-seventeenth century, there were 600 tentmakers in 100 shops. He adds, "Associated with them are the guilds of girth-makers (straps or trimmings), (50 shops, 150 men), tent-rope makers (300 men), ropemakers, (500 men), ironers (3 shops, 6 men), rope twisters, (200 shops, 600 men) and launderers (80 shops, 200 men). All of these march in procession behind the band of tentmakers."[11] This gives us an idea of the relative scale of things—presumably the rope twisters produced ropes for other things, while the six ironers were highly specialized, probably in working on large pieces of fabric.

Çelebi's description of tents in use is most detailed when he describes the *mawlid* of Sayyid al-Badawi in Tanta, which does not begin in Tanta at all, but in the square in front of the Ottoman governor's palace at the Cairo Citadel. He narrates that

> more than 10,000 Badawi dervishes filled up the palace square and the royal markets, playing on their drums and tambourines and displaying their pennants and banners. Some were drenched in instruments of war, with staffs or cudgels in their hands, palheng stones and skirts at their waists, and zikr on their tongues. A myriad of motley flags and banners turned the city of Cairo into a tulip garden.[12]

Seizing the opportunity of an audience with the Ottoman governor, at which the topic of conversation fortuitously turned to the *mawlid*, Çelebi sought permission to attend, and to his delight, was not only given approval but designated as an official attendant with duties to fulfill (including delivering a letter to the *kashif*, or superintendant, of the Gharbiya province "appointing him deputy of the sergeants for the *diwan* of Cairo").

To equip him for his mission, Çelebi was given one hundred gold pieces as travel expenses. He adds of the Ottoman governor Ibrahim Pasha: "He also bestowed upon me one well-furnished tent; ten quintals of biscuit and other supplies of food and drink, including 100 okkas of coffee and three quintals of sugar and 100 candles."[13]

The colorful array of flags and banners that Çelebi describes as creating a garden of tulips in the square in Cairo accompanied the entire celebration of the Sayyid al-Badawi *mawlid*. A flotilla of twelve ships sailed from the port of Bulaq toward Tanta, carrying thousands of rowdy pilgrims. This had "masts and yard arms all fitted out with pennants and banners, and on all sides . . . thousands of oil lamps and banners of the sheikhs." The event was gargantuan and apparently, twenty days before the *mawlid* actually began, all of the shop keepers and merchants of Cairo, moved to Tanta, group by group. On the either side of the main road going out of the city. . . . They start[ed] to set up thousands of shops and coffee-houses, using tents, reed-mats and reeds, carpets and embroidered kilims. Next came the Badawi sheikhs. In that arena of delight north of the city, next to these miniature markets, first the twelve vicars of Seyyid Ahmad al-Badawi [took] up quarters in the jerry-rigged pasha-pavilions, laid out tent rope to tent rope along with the tents of the dervishes.[14]

There was a convention governing the order in which they set the tents up, a social hierarchy that started with the shaykhs of the different religious orders. Following them, the *kashif* of the province of Menufiya "set . . . up his tent-pavilion with his 1000 chosen troops, armed and mustered."[15]

The encampment process was a long and happy one that took place over several days. Çelebi narrates that it wasn't only Egyptians that came to celebrate, but that the throngs of men included people from "India, Ethiopia, Persia and Aden—settling with bag[s] and baggage in tents and pavilions, joined tent rope to tent rope, so the plain becomes a tulip-garden of tents and banners."[16] It is a beautiful, quintessential Ottoman metaphor—and one thing it suggests is that there were tents of different bright colors.

Çelebi's mission to convey the news of a new appointment to the *kashif* of Gharbiya by handing him a letter from the Ottoman governor was duly carried out (once he was comfortably settled in his tent-pavilion); the letter, which included the proviso that Çelebi was to be treated with "due consideration" and conveyed back to the governor in Cairo "in happy condition," was met with the reaction that the *kashif* furnished Çelebi with a tent next to his own tent pavilion, where he spent the next few days "partying and carousing," before moving into a house as the guest of somebody else.[17]

The traveler's description is detailed enough to note that apart from a great deal of commerce, which saw a wide array of goods put on open display, "everyone decorated the front of his tent or pavilion with lamps and pennants and flags and standards." He also notes that the banners of the Gharbiya contingent of the celebration were decorated with images of dragons, and that the standards were horse tailed, "like the locks of a lovely lad."[18]

Çelebi's description of the bright lights used to illuminate the *mawlid* ground is a particularly telling one: "For the sake of a blessing, a certain benefactor planted a ship's mast, 80 cubits high, with thousands of ships' ropes stretched all around it. Every night of the celebration they string 40,000 oil-lamps on these ropes, illuminating their surroundings in a grand fashion. It is something like a vizier's tent pavilion with a central pillar. At the very top of the mast is [a] Catherine wheel that turns like a revolving sphere of heaven. . . . It is a bride to be seen, as though it were the royal pavilion of Pythagoras the monotheist."[19]

It transpires that that year's *mawlid* was ordered to be especially lavish by the Ottoman governor, who reminded his shaykhs that it was "an emblem of Islam," and that no expense should be spared. Significantly, Çelebi uses the number of tents as a measure of the fact that the *mawlid* was larger than usual, noting that there were 1,700 tents, pup-tents, and royal tent pavilions, not to mention a multitude of more modest tent structures furnished by the Bedouin, and "kilim shelters and huts, the huts of sorrows of the poorer sort."[20]

Çelebi recounts the standard worshipers present at every Egyptian *mawlid* since time immemorial, the "gatherings in tents where the faithful lovers [of God] celebrate with drum and tambourine and small kettledrum, tawhid [proclaiming the uniqueness of God] and tezkir [remembering him]." These are the sessions in which worshipers would reach an entranced state through intense, rhythmic devotion. Alongside this intense worship were "thousands of cauldrons in which delicious foods [were] cooked, and people eating and drinking."[21]

However, the presence of troublemakers at gatherings such as this was inevitable—the seventeenth-century equivalent of football hooligans perhaps, and to limit their ability to wreak havoc the multitude of tents was set up like a fortress, "tent rope to tent rope."[22]

The commercial activity that took place in the market tents shows striking contrast. While the most popular tent shops were the ones selling dried chickpeas (a specialty of the *mawlid* until today), according to Çelebi, there was a special bazaar for women—"Over 1000 tents and huts of fornication, where women's skirts are lifted and men's breeches are untied, and the women auctioned off to the highest bidder." There was another sort of bawdiness that could also be found: "Day and night a thousand boy dancers prance about with coquettish gestures, catching the hearts of lovers in the traps of their flowing locks. Other groups of entertainers—singers, instrumentalists, *ghazal* [love-poetry] reciters, itinerant musicians, mimics, eulogists, comedians, mimes and buffoons—are everywhere."[23]

Çelebi's account reminds us not just of the sheer numbers and intensity of the experience, but of how the affluent attendees of the *mawlid* kitted themselves out; the "great notables," as he describes them. They outfit their tents and pavilions with silk carpets and brocades, satins and velvets, Indian cushions with embroidered needlework and mottled velvet pillows and curtains, also various types of weapons and expensive chandeliers. The front of each tent is decorated with 100 or 150 poles topped with flags. Oil lamps and torches provide illumination. The tents are decked out with pennants and standards, like so many idol-temples of China. Night and day there are private parties and intimate conversations, where benedictions are uttered for the continuance of the Ottoman state.[24]

For all the extensive ritual and preparation that it took to create the tulip-garden-like textile mirage that is the *mawlid* of Ahmad al-Bawadi, it wound up to a climax with successive banquets in the tent pavilions of the *kashif*s (superintendents) of Gharbiya and then Minufiya, a final procession, and then quickly started to disappear. Tanta, Çelebi says,

is left as a frontier zone. The Nile submerges the countryside, the *kashifs* are left without authority; deputies and representatives seize control; and naked Bedouin brigands begin their banditeries. Now the tents and pavilions in this Badawi arena start to be dismantled. This too is a noteworthy scene, full of commotion. Myriads of horses and mules, camels and donkeys move off with their loads, and after a great deal of shouting and toing and froing, not a single pilgrim is left in this plain. For once the *kashifs* in charge have taken their leave and gone, the pilgrims and merchants are fearful of the Bedouin vermin. This too is a day of terror. The world becomes a kind of shadow puppet theatre. One moment there is pandemonium, the next moment not a fly remains in this valley. Where is that grand gathering, that hue and cry? It is scattered in a trice, and in its place only ants and snakes. Truly, the pomp of this world is no more substantial than a dream. One should take a lesson from this as well.[25]

Çelebi's is an incredibly vivid description, painting a picture not just of the physical appearance of the *mawlid* but of the euphoria, the emotion, the reverence and revelry that took place in a temporary tent-world.

His description of the lighting installation gives a good idea of the shape of these Ottoman tent pavilions—indicating that at least some of them had pointed roofs. His account of northern Sudan (Funjistan) provides even more information about the tents used during his time. He describes visiting one troop that had covered the ground with black tents and "another troop that resembled Egyptian soldiers, and even had Ottoman tents here and there." The tents were distinctive enough to enable Çelebi to say that he and his travel companions "rejoiced to see these familiar tents and baggage, and the derim tents that looked like those of the Bedouin Arabs." As he continued forward, he saw "about 2000 varicoloured tents and pup-tents and tent-pavilions, and a royal pavilion with golden balls and precious gauze. The shiny balls glittered in the sun and dazzled [their eyes]." This was the tent of the ruler Husayn Qan.[26]

Another important aspect of Çelebi's account is that it dispels the notion that *all* crafts in Egypt declined after the Ottoman conquest. In his description of carpets, in particular, he says that there were twenty workshops comprising three hundred individuals and that they wove "silk carpets and prayer-rugs in praise of which the tongue falls short. True, carpets are also woven in [the Anatolian towns of] Uşak, Kula, and Alaşehir. But nowhere will you find the quality of these Egyptian carpets, except perhaps in Isfahan."[27]

The Guild System

One thing that the Ottoman Conquest did in Egypt was formalize the guilds of craftsmen, following a model that was prevalent in the Ottoman homeland. The guild system meant that somebody would be put forward to 'head' each group of craftsmen, usually elected by the craftsmen themselves, effectively becoming their spokesman vis-à-vis the state, and representing the craft when matters arose that affected it and the community. Their role was one that required adhering to the laws and customs of the guild, *al-'Ada al-qadima* (the old custom), and ensuring that its members did the same. The position was one that was made official through its ratification by the *qadi* (judge), and until the nineteenth century, disputes that could not be resolved amicably were routinely settled in court.[28] In Cairo, the head of each guild was referred to as its shaykh.[29] It was a position that could sometimes be held for life, but this was not necessarily the case and in fact, a shaykh had to have the continued support of his guild as well as of the state to retain the position. In some cases, the position was passed on from father to son, but again this was by communal and governmental consent.[30]

While the Egyptian guild system appears to have been looser than its Istanbul model, it still imparted a structure that meant that aspiring craftsmen had to be admitted to a guild. This required guarantors who could vouch for a craftman's character and suitability. An aspiring guild member would start off as a *sabi* (apprentice), and once he had reached a satisfactory technical level, as deemed by the masters of the craft, would be confirmed as a *mu'allim* (teacher or master), often in court. In addition to being given rights the recipient also acquired responsibilities, one of which was to teach the craft to others, as the title itself suggested.[31]

By placing limitations on the people that practiced a craft, and the way they did it, its adherents could have a stronger grip on the market and presumably act collectively to put in place policies that would serve their common good. That said, unlike in Istanbul and Damascus, where 'a slot' would need to become available for a new craftsman to establish a business, the system in Cairo was less rigid, and seems to have been shaped more by market forces than by a quota.[32]

The guild system imposed a certain code of conduct upon its members: among other things, it demanded reliability, integrity, and piety, seeing the members as representatives of the craft itself and of a community that defined itself by its occupation. This code of conduct was written down in documents known as *fütivetnames*. At various times, for example, big religious festivals in which processions played an important part, the craft guilds as well as the religious sects would march in captivating displays of pageantry. The Ottoman system also ascribed holy figures that protected each of the guilds, similar to the notion of patron saints.[33] What it sought to do, in fact, was to create an organized community of craftsmen. Practical aspects of the code of honor included not stealing the customers of another member of the guild, or sending one's apprentices out to do so, or intervening between another craftsman and their client. Such principles had an impact on the physical layout of a craft market like that of the tentmakers—a number of similar shops situated cheek by jowl made a lot more sense if everyone had agreed that there was to be no dishonorable competition between them, and if there was a mechanism by which the relationships between them could be monitored and regulated by the officers of the law. Price regulation, and ensuring that profits were fair, were also aspects that were dealt with by the guilds and the authorities.[34]

The guild system had other practical implications as well: for example, the procurement of raw materials in bulk for use by a particular trade was something that could take place via the guild, but seems to have been less common in Cairo than it was in Istanbul, and took place more informally.[35] While in some instances, especially service guilds, it seemed to be common practice for the revenue coming into the guild to be collected and then divided among its members, this appears to have been less common among the craftmakers' guilds, and probably didn't apply to the tentmakers.[36]

In the seventeenth and eighteenth centuries, the number of guilds in Cairo fluctuated between approximately 200–300. Moreover, changing socioeconomic conditions affected the size of a guild, sometimes leading it to form associations with other related trades.[37]

The guild of the tentmakers must have been one that saw significant changes in demand over the course of the Ottoman period. When rivalries arose between Ottoman grandees, the market for their work would have expanded. But if these conflicts grew too serious, the demand for tents may well have shifted to much more basic 'necessity' models, leading to a slump in the higher-end work. Then as now, it was a society in which having a multitude of skills was useful—the best craftsmen would always be sought out when the demand was high. When it wasn't, many of them resorted to other jobs, and in Cairo at least, it seemed to be a fully acceptable mode of life.[38]

One interesting phenomenon that developed between the sixteenth and eighteenth centuries was the affiliation of the guilds with military corps in the Ottoman army, a relationship which meant that while each guild had to contribute to the corps with which it was associated, it also received support, protection, and privilege.[39] In the case of the tentmakers specifically, it is easy to see that such a relationship would have been more logical than most—the army and its men had always been a prime audience for the craft of the tentmakers, and official support in return is unlikely to have been seen as a bad thing.

Textiles, Trade, and Society

One characteristic of Ottoman Egypt (and a phenomenon that continued until the twentieth century), was that certain trades were dominated by particular minority groups: jewelry by Copts, Armenians, Jews, and Greeks; tailors, furriers, and weavers of gold thread were mainly Christian; and silk production was mainly Syrian, probably because the raw material itself came from the Levant (while Egypt had a booming textile industry, a large proportion of its raw materials came from elsewhere, the Levant being a prime source of these). In the late eighteenth century for example, Syria was a source of various types of silk, including white silk from Saida, Tripoli, and Latakia, and yellow silk from Beirut, but also a source of cotton. A large proportion of these raw materials were woven in Cairo, and some of the woven fabrics were then reexported to

Europe, Turkey, and in some cases back to the Levant as well.[40] There is no evidence, though, that tents were the product of a minority group (and certainly modern-day tentmakers are all Muslim Egyptians).

What was also notable in late-Ottoman Cairo was the fact that the market for some luxury goods had dwindled, a very logical development given the disappearance of the royal court. Furriers and purveyors of robes of honor, for example, so integral to the life of the Mamluk court, found that they no longer had a market for their wares, and seem to have gradually disappeared.[41] One wonders what the quality of the tents being produced in Cairo during the late Ottoman period was like, specifically whether the absence of a sultan meant that there was no longer the same market to manufacture magnificent tents. An account from 1723 maintains that the Ottoman governor Nişancı Mehmed Pasha paid more than 1,000,000 paras (a huge and probably exaggerated sum) for a tent from the inheritance of Isma'il Bey (Ibn Iwaz), a very prominent *amir* who had been assassinated that year.[42] In the same year, a rival of Isma'il Bey's, an Arab named Salim Ibn Habib—who was renowned to be a ruthless raider, having just taken off with seventy camels and seized the possessions of a wealthy Syrian merchant and an emissary from Istanbul who had dismounted to rest by the al-Hajj pond—is recorded to have set up the tent "that he had looted from the kashif of East Itfih, at the time of his flight towards Upper Egypt." Ibn Habib's opponents quickly tried to attack him but were defeated, and he went off with his looted tent, as well as all the others that belonged to his hapless opponents. Looting tents and their contents was not uncommon; in fact, it seemed to be a common occurrence, especially between the Bedouin, who thrived off looting caravans going to and from Mecca and belonging to the Mamluk *amirs*.[43]

What all of this suggests is that good tents were highly-valued luxury goods. For the chronicler al-Jabarti to know which tent originally belonged to whom says a lot. In his account of the year 1773, for example, he notes that when Muhammad Bey Abu al-Dahab, governor and de facto ruler of Egypt, was preparing to confront his former master, 'Ali Bey, he set up his tents, including the great tent pavilion *(siwan)* "that had been the tent of Salih Bey, very large and tall, of broadcloth *(gugh sayya)*, with red Atlas satin inside, and the top and columns of gilded brass."[44]

One must ask why in the top echelons of society acquiring the tents of others, rather than commissioning one's own, was so common; probably because it was easier, simpler, and cheaper. In a society so characterized by political turmoil and a rapidly-changing political landscape, expediency was probably highly desirable. Nobody knew how their fortunes would change, or how long they would stay in power. Moreover, the pages of the chronicles note betrayal after betrayal—it was an environment in which cutthroat ambition seemed to be the norm. As such, with tents as with palaces, rapidly changing ownership wasn't at all surprising. It was not something to be ashamed of; changing allegiances was a very frequent occurrence, and taking the property of one's rivals when one could was a socially-accepted practice.

It is also possible that people believed that the workmanship of the good old days was better—a common sentiment in most time periods the world over. Accounts of the textile industry in the eighteenth century present a multitude of possibilities as to the quality of textile production. There was a marked influx of imported goods, including textiles from England and France, which by the eighteenth century constituted 50 percent of Egypt's imports from Europe. With such competition, Egyptian textilemakers could only compete by reducing the quality of their work, to keep prices low. Yet on the other hand, many craft *skills* seemed to remain. One talent that the textilemakers seemed to maintain was the ability to dye thread and fabric with a multitude of hues. Apparently, one of the things they were skilled at doing was redyeing old Kashmir shawls in a refreshing hue to give them a new lease of life. Moreover, the textile industry was still so large and important that it comprised a multitude of specialisms, and factories and workshops that produced just one product. For example, businesses were specialized enough that the dyers of indigo were a community based in Giza, whereas the sheetmakers were to be found further north, in Imbaba.[45] In the grand scheme of things, even if the quality of local textiles had been reduced, there were probably enough craftsmen to create decorative tents of good quality.

Historic accounts mention numerous times that when occasion demanded, and some kind of battle or expedition was imminent, the *amir*s would bring out their tents. It seemed to be the kind of thing anybody with a political bone in their body would own, and not just because they were useful, but because they were status symbols as well. In 1786, in one of the many moments of conflict between the forces of the Ottoman sultan and the Mamluk *amir*s, the latter, realizing that they were going to have to go out and fight, went out to Bulaq especially to show off their tents before crossing the river that night and setting up camp in Imbaba.[46]

Who Were the Tentmakers?

As to the status of the tentmakers themselves, they seem to have been 'average' members of society. Some of them did not seem to make much money—for example, a shaykh or 'leader' of one group of tentmakers who died in 1735 only left an inheritance of 5,333 paras, a rather unimpressive sum compared to the estate of the head of the coppermakers, which had amounted to 144,600 paras in 1624, or that of the head of the sugarmakers, who left 801,301 paras in 1715.[47] But of course, figures can be very misleading, and it could well be that the deceased tentmaker in question was at the lowest end of the scale, being the head of a small, unsuccessful group, while the coppermaker and the sugarmaker were at the top of their entire industry.

Perhaps a more indicative piece of information is that marriages between the scholarly class and craftsmen like the tentmakers were common. For example, in the eighteenth century, the imam of the Mosque of Azbek, a reasonable-sized building, married the daughter of a certain tentmaker named 'Ali.[48] Marriage registers from the late nineteenth and early twentieth centuries show that this sort of tradition continued, and then as now, the tentmakers must have been seen as a 'respectable,' albeit ordinary, profession in terms of social standing. Of course, money made a big difference. A leading tentmaking business owner who dominated the market would be in a very different league to a modest tentmaker in a small shop in the same market. Reflecting on these financial discrepancies, a word any true Cairene of the Ottoman period might have wanted to add with a little shrug of the shoulders would be *arzaaq*—'fortunes'—meaning, of course, that one's economic prosperity was in the hands of God.

The Roving Tentmakers of Cairo

What happened over time was the growth of the area around the Citadel into the market for all things related to the military establishment, which saw the move of the tentmakers from the area around al-Azhar to the south, much closer to the markets for horses and weapons. It was the role of the tentmakers as part and parcel of the world of conquest, explorations, and travel that led to this move, along with what seems to have been the commercial flourishing of the area around the famous Citadel Square providing the commodities that sustained the parades, polo matches, state audiences, and expeditions. The accoutrements of this world were many and highly specialized. For example, also around the Citadel Square were the likes of the spurmakers, reinmakers, and horse saddlemakers, who were distinct from those who made camel saddles, based nearby.[49]

It was in 1650 that a building project that was not specifically related to tents or tentmakers inadvertently led to the establishment of the Cairo tentmakers in the street they occupy today. This was the construction of a tenement building (called a *rab'*) by an enterprising man called Radwan Bey. Radwan had dominated political life in mid-seventeenth-century Cairo, and during this time had redeveloped a huge area outside Bab Zuwayla, constructing a palace for himself set in the middle of a commercial development.[50] This included a narrow covered street lined with shops occupying the ground floor of the tenement,[51] which came to be known as *taht al-rab'* ('under the *rab'*') in reference to the fact that the building in question straddles both sides of the street, which was covered with a wooden awning, ensuring that it is permanently in shade. The *rab'* was originally intended for shoemakers—and it easy to see how the line of small shops on either side served that purpose well. Studies reveal that the Radwan Bey complex also included a dye workshop, perhaps due to the fact that the role of the tentmakers in the vicinity was already important. Significantly, Radwan Bey was in charge of the Hajj (from 1632–37 and 1640–56), and thus had a direct link to the acquisition of tents, palanquins, and banners.[52]

It took some time for the tentmakers to move into the rather cramped shoemakers' shops, but by the eighteenth century they were located nearby, just further down the street to the south.[53] By that time, there were enough of them for chroniclers to be able to refer to the 'quarter of the tentmakers,' and the area was affluent enough for horsemen of good social standing to live there.[54]

The Architectural Clues

To understand what Cairo's Ottoman tents would have looked like, we must turn, as usual, to architecture. In a nutshell, two parallel architectural traditions were to be found in Egypt in the decades and centuries following the Ottoman conquest. The first of these traditions was one which clearly bore the stamp of Ottoman-ness, a visual tool used to consciously emphasize the new regime. One of the buildings which best symbolizes this Ottoman style is the earliest Ottoman mosque built in Egypt at the Citadel in Cairo. This is the Mosque of Sulayman Pasha Sariyat al-Jabal, built in 1528, which, tellingly, is small but boasts an exceptionally tall Turkish-style minaret, towering over the city. As a building covered with a large central dome, it has everything to do with the architecture of Turkey and the Ottoman empire, and very little to do with Cairo. From the interior, it is highly decorated, also in the Turkish style, with painted decoration. Not many buildings in Cairo were as distinctly Ottoman as this one—one whose location and appearance were loaded with meaning.

The few other very distinctly Ottoman-style examples are the mosque built at the port of Bulaq in 1571 by the Ottoman governor, Sinan Pasha, and fifty years later the Malika Safiya Mosque, built by a slave of the Ottoman Sultan's wife Safiya,[55] and the Mosque of Muhammad Bey Abu al-Dahab, another Ottoman governor, in the 1770s. These examples were exceptions, but proved that an Egyptianized version of Ottoman style made sporadic appearances over the course of the next two centuries. Infrequent as these may have been, they were appearances nonetheless.

The second stream of architectural production was a continuation of Mamluk tradition, albeit often reflecting smaller purses, a constraint that was clear in the modest scale of the buildings and sometimes in the sparse use of expensive building materials such as marble. There were of course some Ottoman elements that wove their way into the repertoire of the builder and craftsman. Most significant among these was the Ottoman minaret, which almost wiped out its more complicated and costly Mamluk counterpart. Other Ottoman details that soon became part of the Cairene repertoire were Iznik tiles, striking for the beauty of their execution and design and for the freshness of the turquoise blue, red, and green. Oddly enough, there never seems to have been an attempt to produce a local version, and in view of their rarity and the encumbrance of having to import them from Turkey or Damascus, they were used sparingly. By and large, a pared-down Mamluk style continued here and there, drawing upon the Ottoman tradition often for some decorative elements and assimilating, as Cairene craftsmen have always done, bright ideas that came from other places. What it suggests is that, contrary to what one might expect, at least in the visual arts, there wasn't a gradual process of Ottomanization, but a patchy relationship with the ideas that came from Istanbul, with some people more enamored with them than others.

Unsurprisingly, the Ottoman repertoire included a wealth of floral and vegetal motifs that had nothing to do with Cairo—tulips and carnations (poorly suited to the hot climate of Egypt) and evergreen trees (usually cypresses), a symbol of immortality. These too appeared in Egyptian Ottoman art, sometimes on imported items (like the tiles) or on marblework and woodwork, which was usually locally produced.

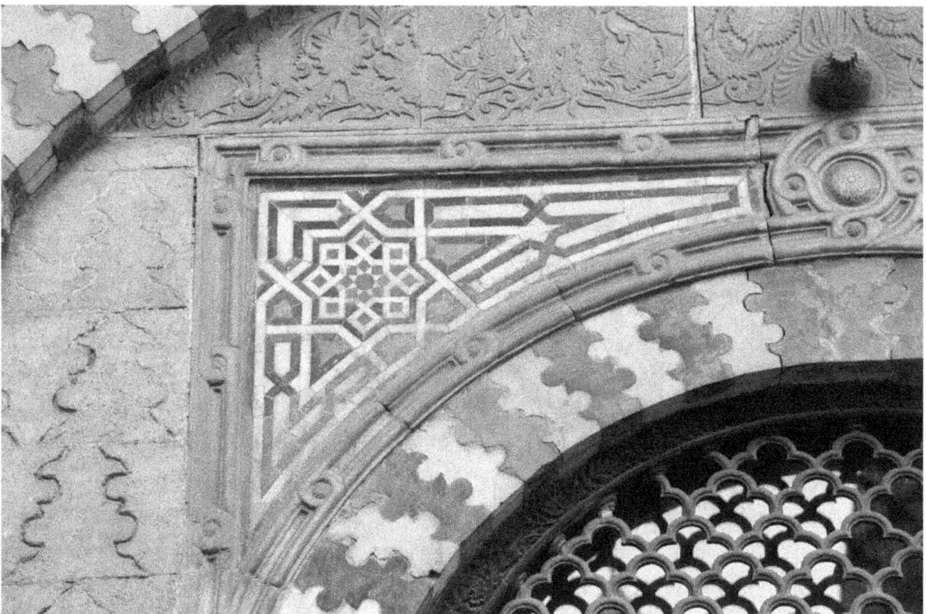

Figure 3 The eighteenth-century *sabil-kuttab* of 'Abd al-Rahman Katkhuda combines local artistic traditions like the geometric patterns with Ottoman-inspired motifs, such as the flowers. This mix was typical of Ottoman Cairo. Photograph by Ahmad El Bindary.

While it would be fair to say that, for the most part, the magnificent patrons of the arts like the Fatimid caliphs and Mamluk sultans could no longer be found in abundance in Cairo, good craftsmanship was still present. By and large, craft traditions continued; for the most part they were so well established that they retained their sense of identity.

With the scaling-down of civic buildings came the proliferation of small two-roomed *sabil-kuttab*s—public water 'fountains' or water dispensers. The *sabil-kuttab* was usually a square room with huge metal window grilles through which passersby could dip a cup into a marble water basin and quench their thirst. Above this space was often a one-room school (to teach boys the Qu'ran). Among the most architecturally famous of these *sabil-kuttab*s are two built on the main street of the city in the 1740s by a man called 'Abd al-Rahman Katkhuda, an important Mamluk *amir*. These tiny but beautifully decorated buildings combine the striking geometric patterns typical of the Mamluks with Ottoman tiles and carved white marble with floral patterns much more of the Ottoman tradition.

In some respects the buildings stand out, because a lot of the decoration isn't really Cairene and because it is more carefully executed than many of the other buildings from the period. Inside the more prominently located of these two *sabil-kuttab*s is an inscription worth remembering, as its first couplet appears on tent textiles for at least the next 150 years: "Oh opener of doors, open for us the blessings of this door. . . ."

On average, most other Cairene *sabil-kuttab*s display far less attention to detail; perhaps the best way to describe them is naively exuberant. Often their façades are decorated with carved stone panels with an array of geometric designs, some of which were probably painted. At times the carving is crude and the geometric patterns not very accurate. Other small buildings in Cairo are similar in spirit: bold, colorful, and decorative, but not always refined. Bold inscriptions with simple statements like, "There is no victor except God," or "Triumph from God and imminent victory" were common. Carving an inscription is a time-consuming and costly endeavor, and using these short, popular stock phrases was in keeping with the spirit of economy of these small-scale projects. What we really see in these small Ottoman buildings is the art and culture of the Egyptian middle class—the carefree, insouciant soul of Cairo.

The Tents Themselves

Having painted a picture of colorful Cairene Ottoman architectural exuberance, what remains to understand is what the corresponding tents looked like. Regarding style, there must have been many of them that looked similar to their Mamluk predecessors, and while a large number of these were probably made of appliquéd cotton, the most expensive ones were of silk. That used by Muhammad Bey Abu al-Dahab, the Ottoman governor in the late eighteenth century, was of red silk brocade. The question is the extent to which Egyptian tents from the Ottoman period *looked* Ottoman. One important thing to remember is that while political change was drastic in some respects, there must have been many things that stayed very much the same. It is unlikely that the tentmakers' work was markedly different in 1520 than it was in 1515, for example. That said, in terms of patterns and designs there must certainly have been Cairene-made tents on which the motifs used were Ottoman-inspired—such was the case with other applied arts, and it was easy for the tentmakers to produce new designs—something they did constantly over the centuries. One must imagine that at least some clients in sixteenth- to eighteenth-century Cairo were enamored with the Ottoman artistic style, and that there were tentmakers willing, or even keen, to produce new work with designs that may have been all the rage in Cairo, given that at least some of the ruling elite were Ottoman courtiers with a multitude of inspirations. A large collection of Ottoman-era textiles found in Egypt and now housed in the Ashmolean Museum in Oxford substantiates this claim, as many of them are embroidered with Ottoman motifs (like tulips) but look local, and in production don't differ much from earlier Egyptian textiles.

Moreover, an account from 1696 describes a great feast organized by the Ottoman governor Isma'il to celebrate the circumcision of his sons, during which luxurious furnishings, decorations, and tents were set up in the courtyard of the *diwan* at the Citadel, and "were hung with lamps and Turkish awnings." These may well have been Egyptian-produced awnings in the Turkish style, but irrespective of their place of manufacture, they are a good reminder of the Ottoman style's presence in Egypt.[56]

It is unfortunate that there are no known examples of tents produced in Egypt during the Ottoman period. However, there are several Ottoman tents surviving from Turkish conquests that shed a great deal of light on the matter.

Seventeenth- and eighteenth-century Ottoman tents are dotted around Europe and shed light on those used by the Ottoman imperial court during this period. One impressive example is an Ottoman tent captured in Vienna by the King of Poland in September 1683, and now in Wawel Castle in Kraków. The appliqué tent is magnificent in execution and design, featuring delicate tulips and carnations, as well as slender cypress trees very typical of Ottoman art.[57] What is remarkable about the tent is the delicacy with which the designs are executed, creating a sense of foreground and background, even though all of the elements are highly stylized.

Wawel Castle also includes a number of tent walls, very similar both in execution and form to the tent screens still used in Cairo today (but not the large tent panels), consisting of arcaded panels with a medallion design in each one. Wooden posts would have slotted into a 'sleeve' between the arcades to support the tent wall, and wooden pegs enabled the sides of the tent to be attached to the roof, just like today. One minor difference between these examples at Wawel and the later surviving examples in Cairo is that the former incorporate limited areas of silk appliqué.

Another example, also captured at the Siege of Vienna in 1683 and housed in Dresden in 1729, is indicative of the luxury and fine execution of these tents in an age when they still had great political meaning. Important courtiers in Cairo during the Ottoman period would have aspired to own tents as lavish as this one if they did not already.

The Dresden example is particularly Ottoman in style—especially the interior, with its large medallions reminiscent of those on the bindings of Qu'rans, as well as of the metalwork found on wooden doors. One small detail worthy of note is a geometric design that appears on the tent canopy itself—this pattern, and similar variations of it, appears quite frequently in Egyptian tents surviving from the nineteenth century, and presumably would have been found on Egyptian Ottoman tents as well (see plate 8).

One eminent scholar of Islamic textiles, Walter Denny, attributes these and other surviving examples of Ottoman tents with appliqué to Cairo, or at least to Cairene manufacture.[58] While the technique was certainly one that was widespread in Egypt, the decorative vocabulary on the known examples is very Ottoman, without a hint of the Egyptian Mamluk style, which makes it likely that even if there was an Egyptian element in the manufacture of this tent, it is far more likely to have been in the execution, rather than in the design itself. One important fragment found in Egypt (mentioned in Chapter 2 and illustrated in plate 4) shows clear similarities to both the Ottoman tents and Egyptian appliqué work (assuming the Cairo example was made in Cairo, which presumably it was).

In Walter Denny's suggestion of the Cairene provenance of the Imperial Ottoman tents he reminds us of the fact that Cairo was extremely competent at making rugs that were in the Ottoman style, and thus, if workmen in Cairo were good enough to do so, the tentmakers of Cairo could well have done the same.[59] It is certainly plausible, and worth mentioning that Cairo and Istanbul both supplied each other with new ideas and commodities in the textile industry, such as in a certain seventeenth-century line of garments known as 'the Cairo-style cut.'[60]

Prisse d'Avennes, in his richly-illustrated nineteenth-century work *L'Art arabe d'après les monuments du Caire*, depicts a red tent panel he dates to the eighteenth century that looks very similar to the walls of surviving Ottoman tents mentioned previously. His brief description provides valuable information: that these tent walls were sometimes used to line the reception rooms of grand houses in winter, and that they were of appliquéd silk on a canvas base. He notes that they were referred to as *heitha*, the Arabic word for wall. In not mentioning anything to the contrary, the assumption is that tents of this sort were of Cairene manufacture, adding weight to Denny's idea.[61]

Was Cairo the center of appliqué work tent production in the Ottoman world? It is possible, but so far hard to prove. Further documentary sources may someday shed light on the question. There was certainly a great

Ottoman tentmaking tradition, too. Tentmakers appear in processions of guilds in Istanbul, such as at the celebration of imperial circumcisions. In at least one highly abstracted and schematized illustration from the 1720s, there are hanging fabrics that look like appliqué work.[62]

Nevertheless, the colorfully decorated buildings of Ottoman Cairo, with their carved panels of geometric and sometimes floral designs, must have had tent equivalents, as had been the case under the Mamluks as well. It is extremely likely that often these tents were in appliquéd cotton, but that the most prominent members of society would have had tents lined with silk. Colors were probably bright and striking and the designs, though often largely Cairene, would have incorporated some Ottoman elements.

In closing this chapter, one of the things that should not be forgotten is that expensive textiles retained their place in Egyptian society during this period. They were considered splendid gifts in the same league as gold, ambergris, and incense. In 1726 for example, a disgruntled concubine who felt that her master had treated her unfairly gave away his secret hiding place (under a tile in the harem of his house). Inside were twenty purses of money, fine porcelain, jewelery, gold, silver, pearls, amber, aloes, saddles, embroidered cloaks, and bolts of Indian cloth.[63]

Perhaps, says al-Jabarti, the master of this house had failed to follow an important piece of wisdom from eighteenth-century Cairo: that to be well dressed, to clothe oneself in silks and pay attention to the cut of one's robes, and to have a wardrobe large enough to turn up in a different costume at every occasion, was enough to have the women of Cairo utterly devoted![64]

4

Egyptian Tents in the Nineteenth Century

It would be fair to say that for Egypt, the nineteenth century started two years early, in 1798. In the words of the chronicler al-Jabarti, "this was the first year of the fierce fights and important incidents, of the momentous mishaps. . . . Of successive sufferings and turning times; of the inversion of the innate and the elimination of the established. . . . "[1] On June 22 of that year, an English fleet of ten ships appeared in Alexandria, apparently in search of a much more powerful French fleet thought to have headed in that direction. The Alexandrian governor, Sayyid Kurayyim, hearing the reason behind the English arrival, was stunned, thinking the English claim to be some sort of trick, and by refusing to provide them with food and water, drove them off. But the English were correct, and only ten days later a French fleet did arrive and immediately took the city, raising their flag over it. It was the year Napoleon's forces invaded Egypt, on the fateful date of July 2, 1798, to be exact.[2]

Unsurprisingly, the response from Cairo was to send an army to fight. After five days of preparations, they set off after the Friday prayer, equipped not only with weapons and the utilitarian tents needed for the army, but with tent pavilions as well. But the French managed to march south with very little resistance, much to the Egyptians' grief. Before the French reached Cairo, a list of many shortcomings had been levied against them, which, quite apart from different forms of lewdness and a lack of morality, included a lack of hygiene, and sophistication too—answering the call of nature wherever they happened to be, even in full view of people, and mixing their foods and drinks. Further, say the chronicles, "they never take their shoes off and settle with them on precious carpets. They blow their noses and spit on the carpets and wipe their feet on them."[3] It seemed as if their lack of appreciation for precious textiles was one of their most unforgivable sins.

"May God hurry misfortune and punishment upon them, may he strike their tongues with dumbness . . . may he confound their intelligence. . . . " were just a few of the many commonly uttered prayers in response to these allegations.[4]

Understandably, these were times of great anxiety and confusion. The French were prolifically issuing decrees in Arabic (not always grammatically correct, according to al-Jabarti), claiming to have a respect for Islam, while trying to stir up trouble between the native 'Egyptians' and the Mamluks. Their approach added an unnecessary layer of complexity in an already unsettled time. An unlucky first skirmish for the Egyptian side, which took place in the Nile Delta in July of that year, spread the sense of worry. Not leaving anything to chance, those who had possessions of value quickly moved them from their grand, conspicuous residences to little-known houses, where they would be out of harm's way.[5]

The wider Cairene response to an impending military encounter in their city was to barricade a significant section of its northern periphery (from Bulaq to Shubra), making preparations for attacks both on land and from the river. It was a time of much fervent communal prayer, and to bring the people together the head of the Ashraf (the 'guild' of the descendants of the Prophet) rushed up to the Citadel and brought down from it

> a big banner popularly called the Prophet's Banner. He unfolded it, and carried it from the Citadel to Bulaq. In front of him and around him were thousands of people with clubs and sticks, cheering and shouting, "*Allahu Akbar*," God is Great. They clamoured loudly, using drums and pipes and other instruments. The streets of Cairo were left empty. You would have found nobody there except the women in the houses, the children, and the infirm who could not move, and who hid themselves with the women.[6]

While the religious leaders of al-Azhar sat in a small *zawiya* (mosque) in Bulaq praying for victory, the rest of the population who had fled Cairo set themselves up in local houses, mosques, or tents.

Following reassurances that the French were simply after the Mamluk ruling class, not everyone else, tensions eased somewhat, and at times there was some sort of rapport between the French officers and the ordinary people of Cairo, who interacted amicably in the markets. But it was an unsettling period for those who had traditionally held sway, and from time to time, especially when the French acted in ways that were unclear, the broader sense of general uncertainty flared up again. In autumn 1798 for example, the French "put white flags on the hills surrounding Cairo. Not knowing the reason, the people raised a din about it."[7]

Evidently, like during the Middle Ages, banners and flags were evocative in the nineteenth century and could still be used to great dramatic effect. In fact, as a symbol of their victory over 'Arish and Jaffa, the French seized the banners of the two towns and hung them on the walls and minarets of al-Azhar Mosque in Cairo.[8]

One of the things that was seen as strikingly different about the French was the way in which Napoleon comported himself when he appeared in public 'for business'—especially in comparison to the pomp and circumstance that had characterized the rulers of Egypt for centuries. When he set off to Suez in 1799, his provision for the trip "consisted of three roasted chickens wrapped in paper. Neither cook nor groom was with him, nor did he have a bed or tent."[9] It was a way of life very different from that which the people of Egypt expected from a ruler.

Yet on ceremonial occasions, Napoleon could live up to Cairene standards. Because Egypt was important to the French for strategic reasons, they made a conscious (and some would say affected) effort to show support for religious festivals like the Prophet's birthday and the *mawlid*s of saints like al-Husayn.

At the same time, the French were trying to woo Egypt with ideas of progress. In their usual custom of using the printed word to spread announcements, they broadcast the news that on November 30, 1798, they were going to show off one of their marvels—an airborne ship (a hot air balloon). To their great dismay, after the device took off the frame holding the wick fell, leading the whole balloon to come crashing down to earth, scattering a multitude of leaflets all over the ground. Even al-Jabarti, the chronicler recounting the trial, recorded the account with a hint of pity for the embarrassment suffered by the French. "In the end, their claim that this was a kind of ship that travels in the wind by artificial device and that people would sit in it traveling to distant countries . . . was not proven. Rather, it became apparent that it was like the kites which the servants construct for holidays and weddings," he said.[10]

Clearly, while the French gave the people of Egypt much to think about, they didn't always leave a particularly good impression about the way they did things. It was partially thanks to this that the Egyptians continued to do things the way *they* always had. For one thing, the processions, the lavish festivals to celebrate the feast days of saints, and the other occasions when ceremonial tents played an important role, continued to take place.[11]

In fact, it seems that it was the French themselves that started to adopt Egyptian ways. In setting off to Syria in 1799, the size of the French baggage train was noted to have "even included bedsteads, carpets, mats, tents, and litters for the women, and slave girls. . . . Whom they had taken from the houses of the *amirs*. Most of whom were dressed after the fashion of the French women."[12]

For better or worse, the French were to face a multitude of political challenges from the British, the Ottomans, and the Egyptians, and it was from a 'graceful pavilion' erected by the pond of Azbakiya in 1800 that they held negotiations with their interlocuters, seeking a truce.[13] Their Egyptian sojourn was to be short lived—they departed in 1801.

Among Napoleon's most enduring legacies is the much-celebrated *Description de l'Egypte*, a detailed account of many aspects of the life, history, and natural environment of Egypt as it was around 1800. Textual references to tents tend to focus on Bedouin rather than urban tents, although valuable information provided by the account includes that there was still a "Shaikh of the tentmakers," who would have represented his peers vis-à-vis the state, and that tents (along with string) were sold in "*el-kheyamyeh*"—the tentmakers' street, shown as being on the same street as the current market, only further south. The account mentions that a tent for four people cost 7 or 8 piasters but that there were also some for 40 or 50 piasters, indicating that they were probably better made (for comparison, a little bottle of rose essence cost 4 piasters). There is also a mention of tent fabric being used for sacks (referred to as "Kheych," pronounced *kheysh*, an Arabic word used to refer to sacking today).[14]

Thankfully, the lavishly illustrated Napoleonic volumes capture the tents of the Mamluks, showing that there was a wide range of examples, from tents that were clearly made for military use, to others that seem to have been designed especially to welcome visitors and for other hospitality-related functions. Several of the seven examples depicted are decorated, two of which with designs on their exteriors that look like the appliqué work of today. The most lavish tent depicted is an expansive, soaring, open-fronted one with a heavily decorated ceiling, displaying a design that looks quite European. The generous folds of the fabric would seem to indicate that it was probably made of some kind of silk, although it would appear that the walls and upper canopy were of a more durable material, perhaps canvas. A decorative scrolling design on the canopy is similar to patterns used one hundred years later. The construction of this tent is also interesting—it consists of what is akin to a walled lower section made up of panels held up by tapering cylindrical posts.

The chronicles indicate that in the early nineteenth century, two places seem to have been the favored locations for the erection of ceremonial tents of the type depicted: by the palace called al-Hilli by Bulaq, the riverine port of the city, and by Bab al-Nasr, outside the northern gates of the walled Fatimid city, traditionally the area where the Mamluk sultans would set up camp on ceremonial occasions, and therefore a place with a venerable history.[15] What these two places had in common was that they were the entrances and exits to the two big urban settlements of Cairo—liminal spaces where the pitching of a grand tent pavilion made a lot of sense.

In fact, when the Ottoman vizier Yusuf Pasha arrived in Cairo after the departure of the French in 1801, much to the celebration of the people, he based himself in his tent in al-Hilli (a practice that was to continue, as it was observed by his successor the following year).[16] What the tents afforded that buildings did not was portability: thus, for example, while the governor in 1802 initially pitched his tent in al-Hilli, he later moved it to Qubbat al-Nasr.

Getting rid of the French meant that there was a celebratory mood in the air, and when the celebration of the Prophet's birthday came up shortly afterwards, it was announced that the streets were to be decorated, and after much sweeping and sprinkling the streets with water, the merchants of Cairo decorated their shops "with pieces of silk and Indian cloth." The following year, tents were set up by the "pond."[17]

It was a time of rebuilding and rejuvenation under an enthusiastic governor, Muhammad Pasha Khusru, a striking contrast to the previous few years when investment in the religious and popular culture of Cairo had been curtailed by political preoccupations. For example, work was completed on expanding and embellishing the shrine of Sayyida Zaynab, one of the most important in Cairo. At the same time, Muhammad Pasha decided to demolish buildings that had been ruined by the French near his residence and construct a military barracks. He enthusiastically supervised the work himself from, of course, a tent pavilion. His personal involvement in turn led to public interest, and groups of all religious denominations and professions—the guilds—came to contribute, not only through labor, but

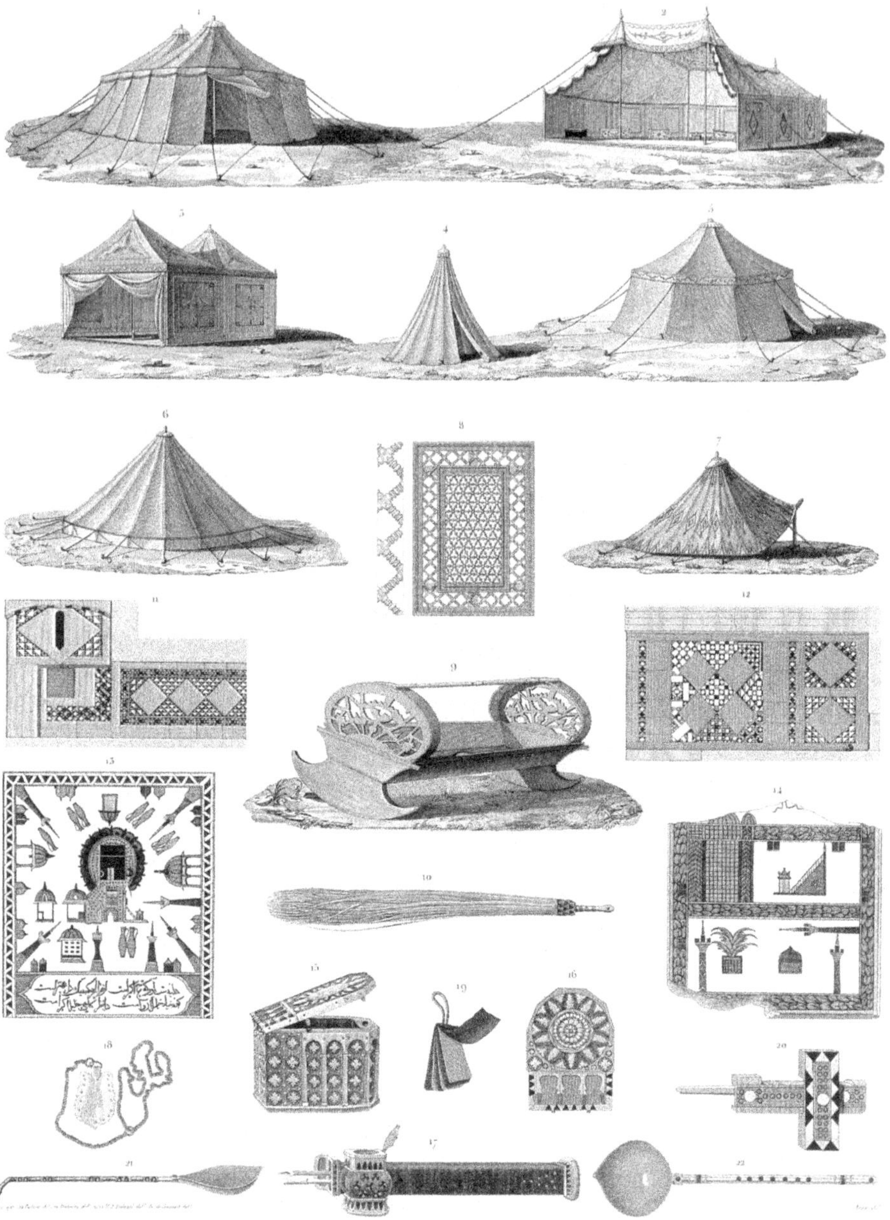

Figure 4 Late Ottoman tents as depicted within the *Description de l'Egypte*, a telling record of late eighteenth-century Egypt following Napoleon's campaign (1798–1801). Courtesy of the Rare Books and Special Collections Library, American University in Cairo.

through donations. The whole project was enlivened with musicians and dancers of all sorts, who boosted the atmosphere from their base: a musicians' tent, large enough for the older members of any of the guilds who had contributed substantially to the project to be excused from construction work and allowed to enjoy the drums, fiddles, horns, and dancing girls.[18]

The year after, in preparation for the departure of the pilgrims to Mecca, the horse-tailed banner of the Amir al-Hajj, whose duty it was to lead the caravan, was raised outside his home to the sound of Turkish music, and he was given numerous gifts by the Ottoman governor, including many tents. These undoubtedly would have been lavishly decorated, as the procession itself was recorded to be a brilliant one.[19]

It is unfortunate that out of the body of poetry that survives from late eighteenth- and early nineteenth-century Egypt only one poem describes a tent, albeit metaphorically, reminding us of the place of tents in the Egyptian imagination:

> A tent containing renown and pride
> Upon it splendour and perfect beauty
> Like a lovely garden where the doves coo
> And the joyful nightingale chants
> Over the iwan [vault] proudly rising
> Jeering at tents and tent-camp
> You would think, with its illumination
> It is the generous heaven
> Fortune says about it: in me
> The glory of the mighty vizier set up his tent.[20]

Paradisaical as this poem may be, the nineteenth century was one in which the conflicts characteristic of previous centuries, the civil strife and political rivalry, were just as common. What this meant is that elaborately-decorated Cairene tents were often used in situations of conflict, and more specifically as markers of the beginnings of conflicts, or of their successful conclusion.

Tents and Tentmakers in the Early Nineteenth Century

> Not a day passed by without disturbances and counter-disturbances, and riots in most parts of the country, whether the cause happened to be a woman, a boy, some object being snatched, . . . The necessities of life were hard to get.[21]

In the latest spate of turmoil to beset Egypt, the early 1800s saw new taxes imposed to fund military expenditure, and price increases that meant that "straw became as dear as gold" and "fruit was so expensive that only the rich, the sick, or pregnant women with a craving for it would buy it." This was nothing new in Cairo, nor the last time that it would happen, and those with a good sense of humor must have found something to smile about, for apart from the exorbitant prices, people were also complaining that, to add to their woes, unruly Albanian soldiers in Cairo were snatching their turbans from them as they walked in the streets. The resourceful people of Cairo had to tie their turbans onto their heads to prevent this from happening.[22]

In a strange twist of fate, it was not very long after this that an Albanian rose to power, but somebody a world apart from the boorish turban-snatchers—a man of remarkable ambition and personality. In a society where one's political prospects were as erratic as shooting stars, few could have predicted that this man's legacy would see his descendants ruling Egypt for the next 150 years. This was none other than Muhammad 'Ali Pasha, regarded as the founder of modern Egypt. He had been a key player on the political scene for a couple of years, and in 1805 was confirmed as the governor of Egypt, a position that was renewed many times, until he was offered hereditary rule by the Ottoman sultan in the late 1830s, and by European powers in 1840.

Muhammad 'Ali's ambitious vision for the country quickly became clear. Upon arranging the marriage of his retainer Hassan al-Shamashirji to the daughter of a prominent family, he gave clear instructions that the wedding procession be as magnificent as those of the princes of yesteryear. For the tentmakers, this sort of approach to celebration boded very well.[23] The place of textiles as valued commodities and as indicators of status during this period is demonstrated by another similar occasion—the joint betrothal of Muhammad 'Ali's son Isma'il and one of his daughters, which saw the distribution of bags containing "four pieces of Indian cloth, a cashmere shawl, a roll of brocade, a roll of Indian cotton and a roll of silk," to each of the important guests, while people of lesser standing were given a handkerchief. As textiles were an indicator of one's status in society, it is easy to see the part that magnificent tents would have had to play. For the joint wedding itself, huge light installations were erected in the Azbakiya Lake—the patterns created by the lights depicted "a boat, two lions combatant, a tree, a litter atop a camel, script spelling out "As God wills" *(mashallah)*. At least two of these decorative motifs (the lions and the *mashallah*) were also to appear in the tent textiles of the nineteenth century, the latter becoming very common. And although not explicitly mentioned, the tentmakers must have been among the ninety-one groups of craftsmen to have created floats to take part in the procession for the happy occasion."[24]

One of the most significant 'international' tensions that arose during the early years of Muhammad 'Ali's reign was the seizure of the holy cities of Mecca and Medina by the ultra-conservative Wahhabis of Arabia, whose vision of many things, including the religious acceptability of luxurious textiles, was at odds with that of the Egyptians (and their Ottoman overlords). In 1806 they prevented people from wearing silken clothes with gold or silver embroidery and threatened to destroy the cherished *mahmal* if it ever appeared in their territory again. Their view of Islam was one unwilling to accept departures from a strict code that was intolerant of anything seen as an 'innovation' from the scriptures, and one that frowned strongly upon ostentatious displays of wealth.[25]

Unsurprisingly, in 1812, when Muhammad 'Ali decided to send forces on an offensive to Arabia, and in fact to accompany them to Arabia himself, his ceremonial departure began with the erection of his own tents outside Bab al-Nasr and a five-hour long procession that took off from the Citadel to get to them, which required the dragging along of eighteen cannons and three mortars across the city.[26]

When the citadel of Medina was taken back later that year, at the very end of 1812, there was much celebration in Cairo, including the enthusiastic shooting of cannons and muskets at each of the five prayer times, a two-hour volley of rifle shots, and the procession of the police through the city "preceded by their criers calling on people to decorate the streets, shops and houses, to light the lamps and celebrate for three days." Of course, celebratory tents were set up outside the north walls of the city, at Bab al-Nasr and Bab al-Futuh.[27]

The following year, Mecca and Jeddah were also successfully taken from the Wahhabis, and when this good news reached Cairo on February 9, 1813 an order was given for the entire city to be decorated and festive tents were put up to host the celebrations. Later in the year, the *kiswa* of the Ka'ba was brought out of storage from the shrine of al-Husayn. It had been kept there for the five years of Wahhabi control of the holy sites. With Egypt back in control again, its ceremonial textiles were in high demand. The *kiswa* was unfolded and cleaned and the name of the former sultan, Mustafa, was replaced with that of the current one, Mahmud. Once again, a magnificent procession was held throughout the city.[28]

The tensions between the Wahhabis and the Egyptians and Ottomans continued for the following six years, and whenever the Egyptians succeeded, the tents were brought out and erected for the festivities; these included "the Pasha's own pavilion." Around what must have been a magnificent tent structure, 80,000 rounds of cannon shot, fireworks, and rockets burst through the air in 1818 in a celebration of victory over the Wahhabis that lasted for days.[29] Conversely, when times were politically trying, public displays of pageantry and bravado were usually suppressed or very subdued, if they took place at all.

Tents, Textiles, and the State

Muhammad 'Ali Pasha's legacy owes a great deal to his attitude toward administration, something to which he paid a great deal of attention, as he was putting in place the foundations of a modern state. For example, when he found that the money entering his treasury from the concession granted to the mint was a paltry sum, he took over its management himself and increased the treasury's revenues by around twenty-fold.[30]

His shrewd approach to fiscal policy and taxation had a bearing on the textile trade, of course. For example, the concession for the administration of customs at the port of Bulaq was driven up substantially due to heated bidding by eager competitors. What this huge price increase meant is that, in order to defray their own costs to the state, customs officials started searching shipments much more thoroughly. In earlier times, textile merchants could easily bring in expensive cloth hidden in bales of cheaper fabric, therefore paying minimal fees, and so keeping market prices low. This was no longer the case, as searches by customs officials grew thorough. What this meant is that the price of cotton, silk, and wool from Syria and Turkey increased 1,000 percent. A yard of broad cloth, a fabric commonly used for tents, went up from 100 to 1,000 paras, while silk clothing jumped from 200 to 2,000 paras, and Turkish shoes from 60 to 400 paras, according to an account from 1812/1813.[31] It is easy to see why it was often cheaper to buy or acquire somebody else's tent rather than commission a new one. Inflation in the price of raw materials could make the price of new tent work exorbitant.

With Muhammad 'Ali's keen interest in the state came the regularization of tent production for his own needs in the first decade of the nineteenth century. This was initially under the supervision of "the director of material," Muhammad Effendi al-Wadanli, known as '*topal*' ('the lame'), who lived in Abu Kalba lane, near al-Darb al-Ahmar, and used his house to make tents, saddles, and other equipment for battle. When the house grew too small for the scale of production, he moved to a larger one further west, not too far away in Darb al-Gamamiz, close to the main canal of the city. This second house and the shops around it were run down, and Muhammad Effendi set about restoring them and the adjacent buildings, establishing workshops "for the workers and craftsmen to make the supplies for the state, like cannons, cannonballs, bombs, rifles, carts, tents, saddles and the equipment for the artillery and transport units and riflemen."[32]

Among Muhammad Effendi's many other achievements was that he made "several strange looms and brought in weavers" to manufacture the colored broadcloth worn for display all around the world that was traditionally manufactured in Europe, and was "very rare in Egypt and extremely expensive." This was made of wool, and judging from the pressing process described to make it, may have also contained felt. The lame Effendi was evidently a clever handyman and a persistent 'inventor,' who was keen to get to the bottom of how things worked. He evidently had an artistic side to him as well, as among other skills he was able to make very finely decorated lacquered pen boxes like those from India, Turkey, and Europe.

Unfortunately this polymath, who can be given the credit for first establishing 'state-organized' tent manufacture, came to a violent end. He angered his son-in-law who then stirred up trouble by alleging that Muhammad Effendi planned to return to Istanbul to serve his former master (rather than to return to his village as he claimed). This rumor was spread to one of Muhammad Effendi's rivals in court, who in turn passed the information on to Muhammad 'Ali Pasha. Apparently, the result was that the hapless Muhammad Effendi was murdered in the sea off Alexandria en route home to his village.[33]

The creation of a tentmaking operation to supply the Egyptian army must have changed the dynamics of the tentmakers' market at large. The rest of the market would have focused on all of the other sorts of tents, including the decorative ones that the pasha and his entourage would have used ceremonially. This may well have been the beginning of the tentmakers' career as applied artists as we know them today.

The advances in technology in the textile industry, prevalent during Muhammad 'Ali's reign, were not without their challenges. A contemporary account mentions the complications of dyeing the color red, one of the favored hues for expensive tents.

> In a large place near Malta [in Cairo], cotton is dyed red, a difficult operation, which was first taught to the Arabs by a Frenchman, to make up for the debt of a thousand dollars which he was unable to pay the government; at present it is not nearly so well done—the colour has no brilliancy. Cotton dyed in this manner is made into square handkerchiefs, in imitation of those worn in Bearn: the stuff is coarse, and the colours less fast. There are 40 looms employed in weaving them. The workmen receive 20 paras for every handkerchief; they are sold at five or six piastres a piece, but there are few purchasers.[34]

It was a perplexing challenge, and one that was to preoccupy the tentmakers for the remainder of the century.

What Did Muhammad 'Ali's Tents Look Like?

Surviving buildings and works of art from the Muhammad 'Ali period show a very clear aesthetic, which must have been evident in the decorated tents of the period as well. Egypt's most significant cultural relationship was that with the Ottoman court—on the one hand, there was a growing sense of Muhammad 'Ali's own importance and autonomy; on the other, there was his official status as a man acting on the sultan's behalf. The fact that as late as 1820 he was still celebrating the annual renewal of his position as pasha by the Ottoman sultan is a good example of this relationship.[35] Consequently, whatever the Ottoman court was doing in terms of the arts had a strong influence on Egypt.

As it happens, the Ottoman world of the late eighteenth and early nineteenth century was one enamored with the baroque, and in the art and architecture of this period, swirling garlands and sprays of flowers intertwined with Arabic and Turkish calligraphy. At Muhammad 'Ali's seat at the Citadel, both his grand mosque and palace, as well as his residence in Shubra, capture the architectural spirit of that age particularly well. Understandably, the way in which the pasha lived and the styles he adopted trickled down the social ladder. One of the most distinctive elements of the architectural Ottoman baroque style popular at the time of Muhammad 'Ali were the sweeping curves that featured prominently, not just in the profile of arched doorways, but in large simple cornices that imparted an elegance to buildings in the way they cleverly connected sections of different heights. Carved white marble, corinthian and ionic columns, painted ceilings with swirls and ribbons, naturalistic flowers, all in a style we would call 'European,' were very common, and quite distinct from the architectural styles that had preceded this era.

Another very striking feature of this period was a new color palette that became popular—pinks and olive greens contrasted with gold was a common combination, and one only has to look at Muhammad 'Ali's mosque at the Citadel to see that this was the case.

Two *sabil*s built by Muhammad 'Ali in 1820 are exemplars of the Ottoman baroque—with very few traces of the local Cairene tradition. This was due to a conscious stylistic choice, not a sudden disappearance of the Cairene style (the local style was very much present immediately before, for example in the Mosque of Hassan Pasha Tahir, constructed just eleven years earlier, and in a multitude of later buildings for over a century afterwards). While on the interior of buildings like the two *sabil-kuttab*s discussed in Chapter 3, painted panels with trompe l'oeil work became popular, on the exterior curtains and drapes carved in marble framed the large screened window panels. It was an interesting dynamic—for centuries, textiles like tents had imitated architecture, and now architecture was copying textiles, as can be seen in figure 5. What the craftsmen were doing, really, was demonstrating their skill through the delightful tongue-in-cheek art of mimicry.

One feature of the buildings of this period, especially *sabil-kuttab*s (from the late eighteenth century onwards), were large window grilles, usually of brass, often with a repetitive, curvilinear pattern forming a lattice. Most of these were loosely in the tradition of the Ottoman baroque—often with an emphasis on the word 'loosely.'

In surviving textiles from the Muhammad 'Ali period (generally velvets with applied metal thread embroidery, like that of the *mahmal* and the *kiswa* of the Ka'ba) the same 'baroque-ish' lattice designs are to be found embroidered in silver, and sometimes silver-gilt thread. There is every reason to believe that at least some of the tents produced during this period would have looked similar, as a few surviving later examples still used these patterns. It is unfortunate but not surprising that while examples of the embroidered velvets of the early nineteenth century survive, no tents seem to. Tents were made to be used, and they were—until they disintegrated. Silver embroidered textiles were probably more expensive (meter for meter) and were guarded more carefully—unlike tents, which were constantly being erected and dismantled, many of these metal thread textiles were used in instances that did not expose them to wear and tear. One example is the final resting place of Muhammad 'Ali Pasha himself, in one corner of his mosque at the Citadel. The three-tiered cenotaph was adorned "with blue brocades, exquisitely faded and

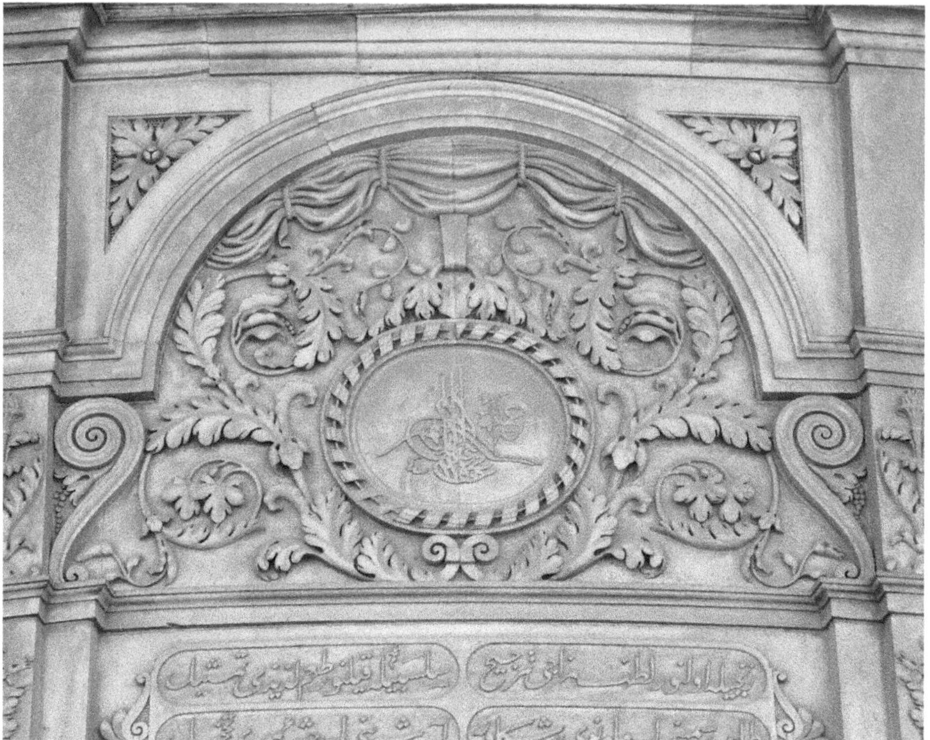

Figure 5 Variations of the neobaroque style were common in early nineteenth-century Egypt and were often combined with Ottoman motifs, such as this calligraphic *tughra* on the façade of this *sabil-kuttab* of Muhammad 'Ali Pasha. Photograph by Ahmad El Bindary.

embroidered with dull gold."[36] As these lay behind a gilded screen, their only real enemy was light.

What we can infer with reasonable certainty is that the enthusiastic adoption of the Ottoman baroque that characterized the period of Muhammad 'Ali waned, and the visual arts returned to a more or less Cairene style. However, some of the decorative elements of Muhammad 'Ali's Egypt remained and found a place in the repertoire of the Cairene tentmakers for the next century.

One of the most widespread of these was the *tughra*, the sultan's name written in a very particular form of calligraphy (see fig. 5), sometimes accompanied by a small sprig or a flower. The *tughra* was ubiquitous—it appeared on all late Ottoman coins, including those minted in Egypt, and was thus truly an emblem of the time—everyone would have known what it was. Another very simple survival was the elongated diamond shape, very popular in baroque architecture, which appeared as a discrete decorative element in the marblework of the Muhammad 'Ali period, and became a common border pattern in tent textiles.

A third distinctive feature was the way in which inscriptions were written, with the letters slightly thin and angular, unlike the more common sweeping forms of Arabic calligraphy. These two last features, in particular, were probably 'invisible features' of the time: they were so widespread that nobody would have noticed that they were very much products of the era.

5

The Khedival Period

> Amid the thundering salvoes of several shore batteries and half a dozen Egyptian and European Men of War and the music of more than a score of massed naval and military bands, a procession of 48 ships led by the empress in her own yacht, entered the canal in single file for Ismaileya, the new town on Lake Timsah. . . . Here, too, the festive preparations culminated. Besides the palaces, kiosks, and hotels, built and gorgeously furnished within the preceding few weeks—as if by the owner of Alaadin's lamp—for the more illustrious of the visitors, many hundreds of elegant tents had been prepared for those who could not be so lodged, and in these, it was given, to more than 3000 guests, the most luxurious and lavish banquet that French cooks and Egyptian money could provide—accompanied by music, fireworks, and illuminations to match.[1]

Thus is described the opening of the Suez Canal on November 17, 1869. The world would be hard pressed to find a more exciting moment in the nineteenth century, and with such a stupendously large Egyptian celebration put on, it is hardly surprising that numerous tents featured prominently.

Engravings of the event show tents of the large pointed type, and a French guest at the occasion noted that the walls of this tent city "were made of the most beautiful carpets in the world and white linens, all suffused with sunlight."[2]

Another similar description of the scene notes that the tents of the Arab desert tribes were made of colored fabrics and surmounted with standards, and that the tents to host the khedive's guests formed long rows opposite the home of Ferdinand de Lesseps, the engineer who designed the canal.[3]

The *Illustrated London News* of the following month could not fail to depict the buzzing celebration, and in a mass of large tents described as the tents 'of local people' a large number of onlookers and at least one tent of musicians are shown. This was just a sampling of what the unforgettable event had to offer.

What these accounts are describing are examples of appliqué work which since that period has been manufactured just south of Bab Zuwayla, in the covered street known simply today as 'al-Khayamiya' or the tentmakers' street, a technique which we know from surviving fragments has thrived in Egypt at least since Mamluk times.

Accounts of the tents furnished for the Empress Eugenie herself, and the main pavilions erected to host the most important dignitaries, indicate that these were not made of appliqué work, but of expensive silks instead. Those used for the days leading up to the great ceremony itself, for example when the imperial party went sightseeing in and around Cairo, were reportedly "silk ecru on the outside, and some were covered with yellow satin, others with red satin, on the inside; the colour of the furniture in each tent matched that of the interior."[4]

It would be tempting to take this contrast to mean that all that was for the empress and the upper echelons of the guest list was European in style, and what was local in style was for the locals. In fact, the artistic languages of mid-nineteenth-century Egypt, including this stellar event, were more nuanced, much more intertwined than that. Some of the furniture manufactured for the occasion still survives today, preserved in Cairo in the mausoleum of Khedive Tewfik, Isma'il's son. These sofas and chairs, though European in concept, draw their decorative inspiration from the Cairene Islamic artistic tradition. Gezira Palace, built in Cairo for the occasion itself, is similar.

It is true, however, that there was a fascination with all things European. A later account of a British man who arrived in Egypt in 1880 to tutor Khedive Tewfik's children sums it up when writing of a courtly encounter in the delta: "The tents too of the sheikhs assembled at Shibin were of great magnificence; they were adorned inside with the appliquéwork common in the country, the designs consisting of flowers, fruits, animals, conventional symbols, and verses of the Koran arranged with wonderful taste and symmetry. One tent is said to cost 2000l. The khedive's tent of French silk with silver mounted poles was no doubt costly, but much less beautiful."[5]

Fortunately, many of these tents and their panels survive—they were bought by travelers to Egypt, taken to Europe and America, and put in storage. It is easy to see why these tent panels were so appealing—they are colorful, decorative, and remarkably Egyptian. They are also portable, light, unbreakable, and therefore relatively easy to transport. In reality, many tourists took these tent panels home, only to discover that they were impractically large. Many of them were relegated to attics and storerooms, where they have been preserved, sometimes in pristine condition, for over a century. The pieces bring the numerous surviving textual descriptions of the Street of the Tentmakers to life.

Setting the Scene: Cairo's Architecture in the Late Nineteenth Century

One of the things that characterized Cairo (and indeed Egypt) from the late nineteenth century was the proliferation of European-style architecture, which spread quickly thanks to the development of new quarters of the city. There was a buzz of energy in the air—that of a dynamic society led by the modernizing ambitions of successive khedives. What this meant is that these new styles also had a strong influence on new construction in the existing quarters of the city, including neighborhoods like al-Darb al-Ahmar, the home of the tentmakers.

In these more traditional quarters especially, many of the new architectural influences were only façade deep—elements like windows and doors, shutters, and decorative plasterwork. House layouts did not change much, as the larger houses would usually still have a separation between the areas in which guests, especially male guests, were received, and the more private family apartments. Whenever there was space, a house would include a courtyard of some sort, a private space where many facets of domestic life could take place. While European influence could be found in decorative elements such as fittings and finishes, local traditions like architectural stone carving, especially on the ground storey façades of a building, remained strong, showing a centuries-old continuity that survived through craft skills being passed on from one generation to the next.

Among the new elements that were most distinctive of the late nineteenth-century architecture of the historic quarters of Cairo was the design of house doorways, which had always been an important feature of the house. A house's main façade was an indicator of status, and the doorway was the element with the greatest potential to impress. In the late nineteenth century, doorways took the form of archways constructed

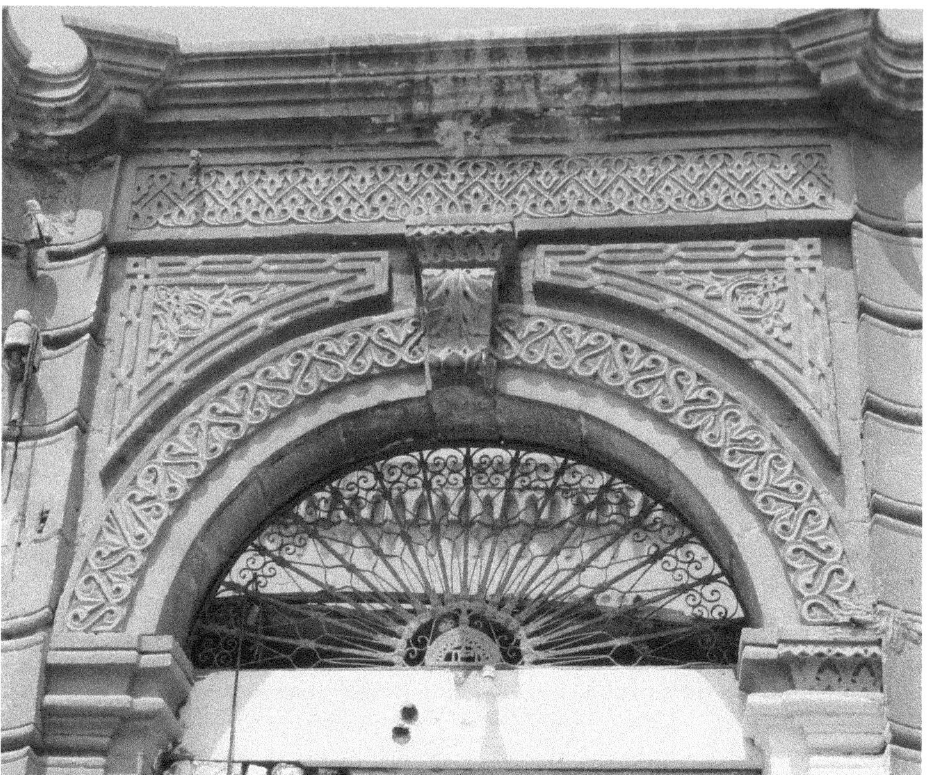

Figure 6 Doorway with embellished ironwork, Cairo. Very close parallels are found between late nineteenth-century tent panels and doorways like this one. Photograph by Seif El Rashidi.

of carved stone. A wooden double-leafed door, either with solid wooden leaves or with glass panes halfway up was typical, and its decoration often included elaborate carved panels, sometimes with geometric designs recalling the woodwork of earlier centuries, or with floral patterns. When doorways had glass panes, these were covered with decorative wrought ironwork to protect the glass. This sort of ironwork was a new European introduction to Egypt and was very fashionable.

Although the veneer of Cairene society might have been one in which European fashion was budding, traditional cultural values remained strong. The notion of privacy, for example, was an important one—essentially, that passersby would not be able to see what was going on in a courtyard, for example the women of the house involved in domestic chores wearing home clothes. The answer was often to hang a decorative curtain in the doorway to the heart of the house—the *sitara*, popular of earlier centuries, which could also double as an awning when it was sunny, or as a celebratory banner, was common. Because of its use, its decorative references were often unmistakably architectural, and because it marked the act of entering the home, it usually featured an inscription invoking prosperity upon the household. Common blessings included, "By your bounty oh house, I have attained my dreams, with happiness and joy," and "Joy has arrived and sadness has departed."

A comparison between the surviving tent panels from the late nineteenth century and the doorways of that period reveals clear links, indicating that these textiles were conceived of as architecture in cotton. Many of them show obvious references both to specific styles of architecture at the time, especially to brickwork and wrought ironwork, as well as to the older architectural traditions of Cairo: brick walls, stone arches, and columns. The one thing that was different was color: unrestrained by the limited color palette imposed by building materials, these hangings were often bright and bold (see plate 9).

Investment in Cultural Heritage: The Craftsman's Inspiration

Apart from the wave of new urban development, which had a strong stylistic impact on the historic quarters of Cairo, the late nineteenth century was an important time in terms of investment in cultural heritage as well.

There were two overlapping strands to this—one was a dramatic refurbishment of important religious buildings, most of which were the sites of significant shrines, usually related to descendants of the Prophet. In contrast to the shrine of the Prophet's grandson al-Husayn, rebuilt in the gothic style in 1874, the following few decades saw a new trend of rebuilding drawing upon the traditions of Mamluk architecture. This included the shrine of Sayyida Zaynab, the Prophet's granddaughter, rebuilt in 1884; Sayyida 'Aysha, a more distant female descendant of the Prophet, in 1895; Sayyida Nafisa, the Prophet's great-great-granddaughter, in 1897; Sayyida Sakina, another great-granddaughter, in 1904; al-Rifa'i, a Sufi saint, begun in 1896 and completed in 1912; and the construction of the Mosque of Imam Shafi'i, an important Sunni jurist, in 1891, and the addition of wings to al-Azhar in 1888 and 1894.

These were the most important mosques in the city, not necessarily from an architectural or even a historical point of view, but from the point

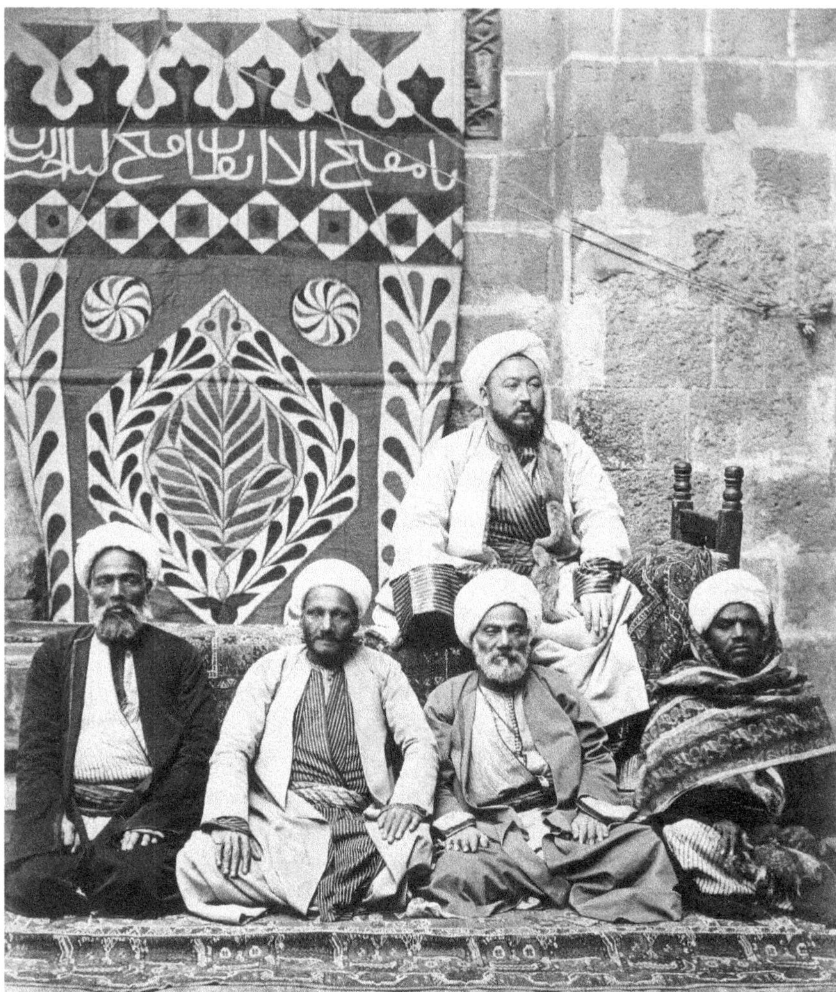

Figure 7 Emile/Henri Béchard, *Ulama* [Islamic scholars], ca. 1870s. Getty Images.

of view of community and religious value—apart from al-Azhar, which had retained its preeminent position as the seat of Sunni Islam, all of these other mosques were the sites of important religious festivals, and in the case of Sayyida Zaynab and al-Husayn in particular, among the most important mosques from a spiritual point of view. These were the places that one would go seeking blessings *(baraka)*, or for religious intercession. They were buildings that would have been frequented by large swathes of the population and their architectural patterns, their details, and their elaborately painted colorful ceilings would certainly have been familiar to craftsmen like the tentmakers, both as professionals and on a personal level as well. The tentmakers' work would have provided the tents used for ceremonial occasions like the *mawlid*s, and the banners that Sufi orders would have used to add a sense of presence and drama to their processions—an essential part of the *mawlid*. More fundamentally, these were places of great spiritual meaning, venerated by Muslim Egyptians from all walks of life.

It was not a coincidence, therefore, that these mosques witnessed great investment by the ruling family, who saw their role as rulers of the nation to encompass the preservation and support of its religious life as well.

What the average Cairene witnessed during this period was the enlargement and embellishment of all of the major mosques in Cairo, some of which, like al-Rifa'i, were of a truly monumental scale. It would have been hard for the average Egyptian not to have had these buildings imprinted in their minds, and the artist or craftsmen seeking inspiration must have thought of them as treasure houses of ideas and designs.

In parallel, 1881 saw the establishment of a national committee to conserve the monuments of Arab art, essentially what we would call today Islamic and Coptic architecture. Many of these medieval buildings were in poor condition, but fortunately the skills to repair them still survived. The Comité de Conservation des Monuments de l'Art Arabe, as it was called, undertook diligent work to restore Egypt's postpharaonic architectural heritage to its former glory. Although the Comité's work is most often noted for its legacy of preserving the masterpieces of Egyptian, and primarily Cairene, architecture, it had another parallel legacy, which was to create work opportunities for local craftsmen, and more importantly to draw their close attention to the techniques and patterns that had produced the great masterworks of Mamluk and Ottoman architecture. Restoring something accurately meant that one had to pay close attention to how it was made.

The reigning khedive of the time, Tewfik Pasha (reigned 1879–92) took a personal interest in the preservation of Egypt's cultural heritage, an interest shared by his son and successor Abbas Hilmi II (1892–1914), to which inscriptions on buildings restored during both of their reigns attest. These could commemorate the actual restoration of the building or its refurbishment, adding a wing (such as at the extremely important al-Azhar Mosque), putting in a new ceiling, donating a carved wooden screen, or installing a new pulpit. Tellingly, Tewfik Pasha's own mausoleum draws upon many of the craft traditions that would have been used to create the newly-refurbished great mosques of Cairo. In many cases, master craftsmen also signed their work, usually preceding their name with the word *mu'allim*, literally 'teacher,' but used more to mean 'master.'

What all of this meant was that the setting was an ideal one for the tentmakers—the demand for their work was strong—both within a religious context but also for domestic festivities, such as weddings.

Tents and Celebration

At the public scale, festivals like the celebration of the Prophet's birthday remained a key national event. Apart from tents used to house the festivities taking place at shrines of great religious significance, such as al-Husayn, tent 'stalls' were used to sell the sweetmeats typically consumed during this joyous occasion. The event was important enough for the khedive himself to attend, as well as the members of the diplomatic corps. Even in what was to become known as the European quarter of the city, elaborate tents were set up for wealthy pashas to hold their evening receptions. These were hung with expensive textiles, usually silks and satins (see plate 10).[6]

Tents played an important part in one-off celebrations as well, such as the inauguration of the Egyptian Museum in 1902. They provided the perfect solution to counter the sun and the heat, and to temporarily accommodate a large crowd of people. Thanks to photographic records, we can see what accounts had been describing for centuries: that whenever Egyptians wished to mount some form of public celebration on a lavish scale, they used these tents.

On a more domestic level, one account reminds us that when it came to weddings, "if a household was wealthy, and there was sufficient space, large tents were put up for the reception of male guests in front of the house. It was customary for them to be entertained for at least two nights, but often for longer."[7] The wealthier the household, the longer the celebration. The modular structure of the tents meant that they could be erected even in narrow spaces, such as the streets of historic Cairo and in its many small clearings.

Tent hangings were also a common feature of the Egyptian street, used as awnings above shops or hung above the street, and as curtains for street cafés they created a much-appreciated luxury: shade (see plate 13). By virtue of their flexibility, usefulness, and decorative value, appliquéd tents and hangings were to be found everywhere—from the small alleys of

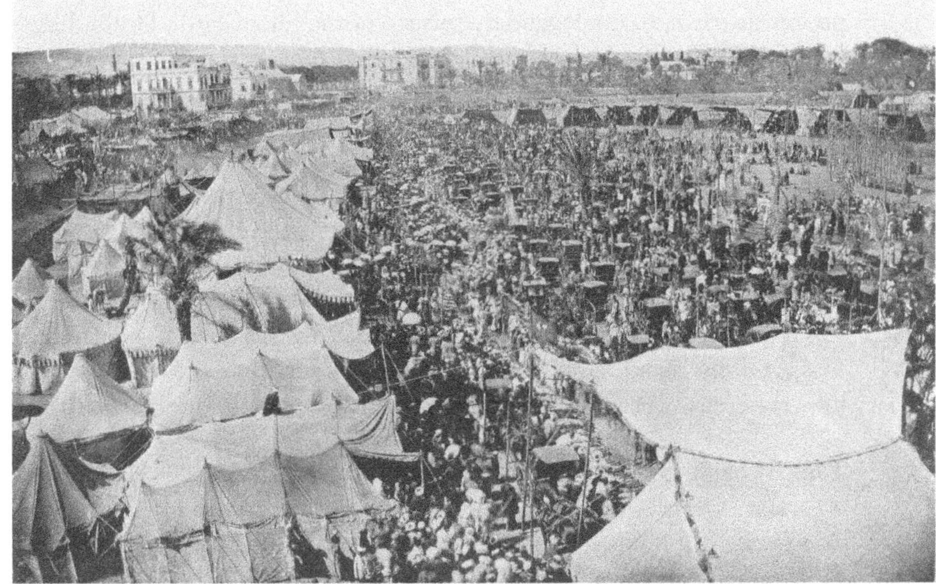

Figure 8 Emile Béchard, *Mawlid in Cairo*, ca. 1880s. Musée d'Orsay, Paris.

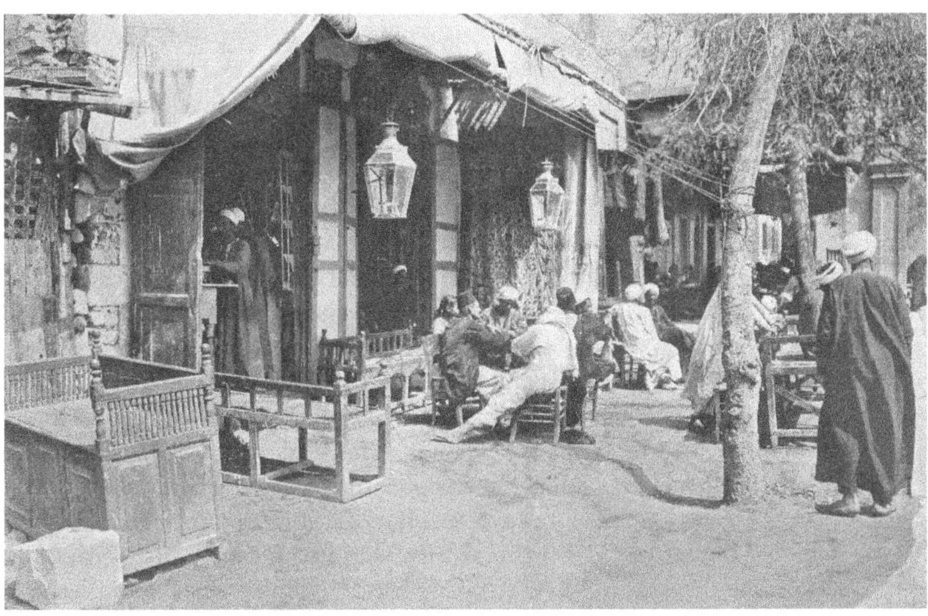

Figure 9 Anonymous photographer, *Arab Café* (Cairo). Detail from image courtesy of McLung Museum of Natural History and Culture, the University of Tennessee, Knoxville.

poorer districts, to the legendary terrace of the Shepheard's Hotel. Judging by the sheer frequency with which tents appear in historic photos of Egypt, not just Cairo, and the huge size of the tents, it is easy to see why to be a tentmaker around 1900 was to have steady employment.

Recent scholarship about the Hajj, involving careful scrutiny of historic photos, has revealed a very interesting feature—that when the pilgrims left Cairo, the *mahmal*, the magnificent palanquin that headed the procession and was elaborately embroidered with silver and gold thread, was replaced with an appliqué one for the journey through the desert. Evidently, this was to protect the more valuable and delicate one from wear and damage. It is a telling detail, emphasizing the role of appliqué as a medium that imparts a sense of richness, rather than being the height of richness itself.[8]

The Street of the Tentmakers and Its Work

There is a wealth of material that has shed light on the tentmaking tradition in the late nineteenth and early twentieth centuries, a period which, for simplicity, we have termed the 'khedival period,' corresponding to the period when the rulers of Egypt, Muhammad 'Ali Pasha's descendants, held the title of khedive.

The setting is the one that exists today; a narrow covered street lined with little shops just south of the main southern gate of the Fatimid city, Bab Zuwayla, constructed by the Ottoman grandee Radwan Bey in 1650 to house shoemakers.[9] This may seem like an odd place for the manufacture of large tents, until one remembers that these were made in panels, and that a large piece of fabric can easily be appliquéd while folded on a craftsman's knee. Furthermore, not all of the stitching was done in the shops themselves; a significant part of it was done behind the scenes, in the courtyards of nearby houses. However, rather than sit idly in the shop waiting for business, a craftsman would busy himself working on a piece (see plate 11).

According to a study of guilds in Cairo in the nineteenth century, there were seventy-two tentmakers known to be working in Cairo in 1870, as recorded by the historian 'Ali Mubarak. This may not sound like a sizeable number, but as a proportion of the population of Cairo at the time (approximately 400,000 people), it was probably not too small. By comparison, the same survey counts 53 watchmakers, 25 lead workers, 173 basketmakers, 689 stone cutters, and 1,176 shoemakers.[10] Numbers can be misleading however, and it is hard to tell whether these refer to individuals or shops. It is probably the latter, and it is thus hard to tell how many individuals were involved in the tentmakers' craft, but probably a lot more than seventy-two.

Who were the clientele? For the most part, the direct clientele were the *farrashin*, who provided the tents used in Egyptian society. In terms of the end-clients, at the top of the social scale the association between royalty and khayamiya was well established, but they were used by all echelons of society. Their clients were not only Cairenes, and a surprising piece of information that pertains to other crafts in Egypt as well (such as jewelry) is that often crafts associated with certain provincial regions were made in Cairo. For the tentmakers, a big provincial market would have been at important places of worship such as the shrine of al-Sayyid al-Badawi in Tanta and all of its adherents, such as the Sufi sects who made sure to attend as many religious events as they could and came equipped with their own tent pavilions and banners.

There are remarkable similarities between some of the tents surviving from the khedival period and the decoration of provincial homes from the same era. Both have a certain type of naivety and abstraction, especially evident in the charming representation of animals, such as lions, which were not uncommon on doors and balconies, and appear on several surviving examples of tent panels as well (see plate 12).

Egyptian Design around 1900

The early twentieth century appears to have been a turning point in the design of khayamiya. In fact, a survey of the public appearances of Khedive Abbas Hilmi II through his archival papers at Durham University reveals a chronology of changes in the appearance and form of khayamiya pavilions in Egypt.

An example depicted from 1893—a very tall and guyed tent resembling its Ottoman precursors—features a conspicuous awning bedecked with stars similar to an ancient Egyptian tomb ceiling (see fig. 10 on the next page). A 1913 tent bears a trellis structure closer to a contemporary *suradiq*, but with patterns that suggest a transition between khedival and later forms of khayamiya. A *suradiq* depicted in 1927, and three distinct pavilions associated with the khedive's funeral procession in 1944, are closely related to contemporary khayamiya for their symmetry, density of ornament, and structure.

Despite the growing interest in cultural heritage and the masterpieces of Cairene art and architecture, many of the tent pieces surviving from the end of the nineteenth century still show a primitive, vibrant exuberance, both in color and design. Moreover, the off-white-colored sailcloth material used as a base was usually striped, and more often than not, the appliquéd designs would be sewn directly onto the backing fabric itself,

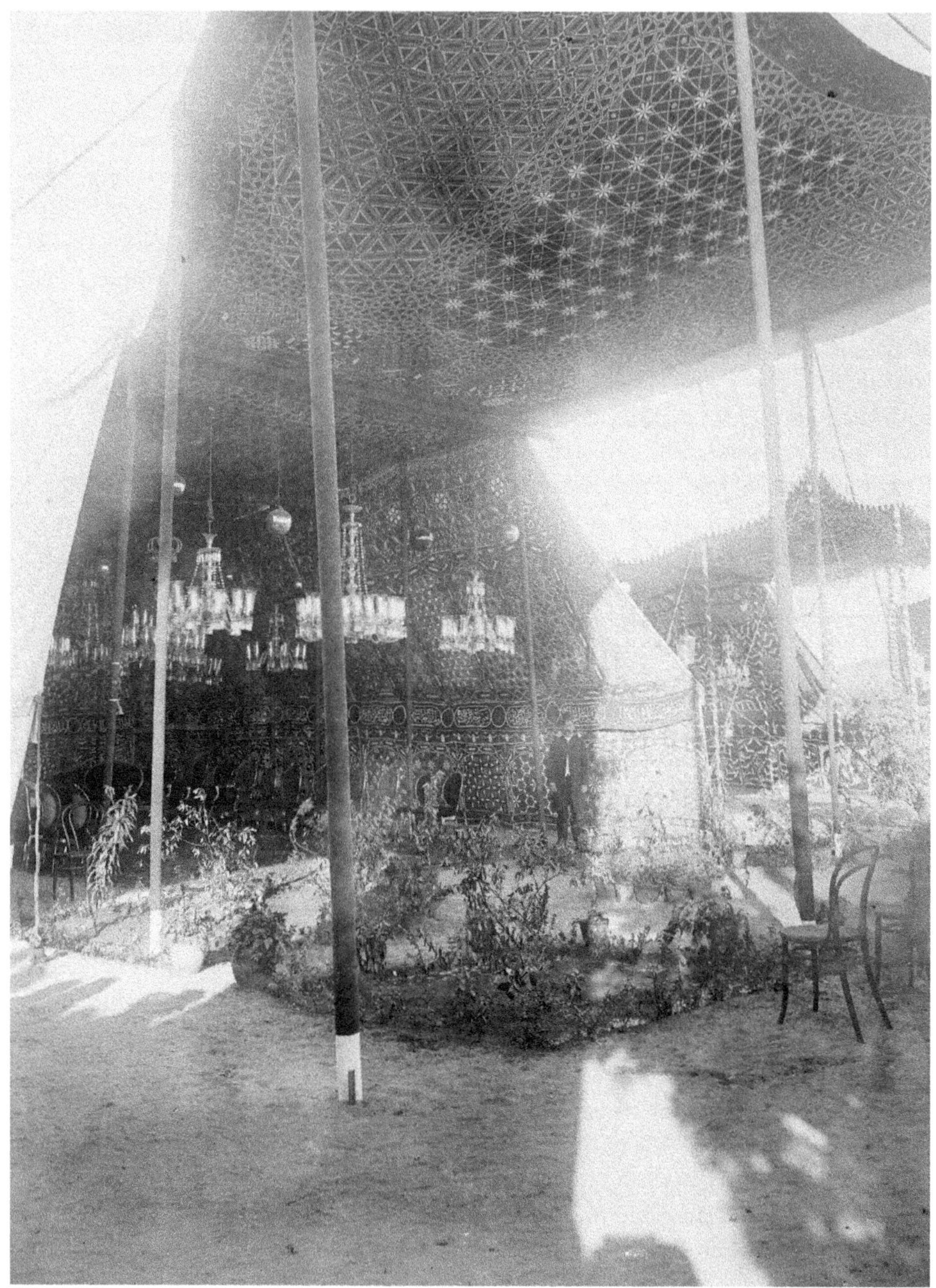

Figure 10 A photograph of a *suradiq* from 1893 in the archives of Abbas Hilmi II, Durham University. Courtesy of the Trustees of the Mohamed Ali Foundation.

leaving areas of the striped background visible. From a distance these thin stripes, spaced quite widely, would not have been noticeable, but from close up one could see them clearly. They bear witness to the fact that khayamiya was more than anything a backdrop for social life, a craft, and a form of art, but not a work of art for its own sake.

On tent panels from this period, geometric patterns are often to be found alongside sweeping fronds of an indiscernible plant. As per their medieval antecedents, many of these patterns emanate from a star design. Sometimes pharaonic motifs are thrown in for good measure—a vulture or a pair of pharaonic columns—more commonly on pieces designed as hangings, rather than tent panels (see plate 21). Most pieces have a central medallion, sometimes two, and virtually all have some kind of border framing the main design. On tent panels with two medallions, it was convention either to offset the same design within each medallion to create visual diversity between the two, or in some cases simply to use a different design in each one. The idea was to ensure that the eye would not get bored of looking at a piece, which these slight variations helped ensure. Sometimes the differences between two similar medallions are minor, and may not be consciously noticed—but they are certainly there, and play a part in animating a piece in the viewer's subconscious (see plate 15).

The most common colors used were a bright red (probably the so-called Turkey red that early nineteenth-century Egyptian dyers were trying to perfect) and a wide range of blues, ranging from pale indigo to cobalt. Green, yellow, orange, and white were also used, but usually as accents.

By the early twentieth century, there appears to have been a much more developed revival movement that in part was the result of a growing sense of Egyptian identity. The number of shops specializing in Islamic revival furniture bears witness to this trend. The owners of many of these were often entrepreneurs rather than craftsmen themselves and the names of some of these businessmen, such as Elias Hatoun (a Levantine), Joseph Parvis, and Spiro Dracopoulos, a Greek, are a reminder of Cairo's growing cosmopolitanism (see plate 14).[11]

In the world of crafts, one particular milestone was the founding in 1911 of the Ilhamiya School of Arts, *al-Madrasa al-sina'iya al-ilhamiya*, a craft school established by Amina Hanim Ilhami, the widow of Khedive Tewfik. The idea behind the school was to delve deep into Egyptian tradition and produce masterpieces that captured the lavishness and technical mastery of the Egyptian crafts of yesteryear, particularly from the Mamluk period. The main focus was carpentry, in what is popularly referred to in Egypt as 'Arabic work,' or more informally as 'arabesque,' but pieces in the neo-pharaonic Egyptian revival style were also produced. There was a strong emphasis on decoration and fine crafts such as inlay, and the general outcome was of ornate, sometimes heavy work that showed off a craftsman's skill. Some of the pieces clearly take their inspiration from architecture, and others were actually scale models of some of the city's more famous mosques. The school was evidently a success as it expanded at a fast pace; from one showroom in its original premises it had expanded to four by the time it shut down in 1930. Three of these were in downtown Cairo, of which one was in the famed Shepheard's Hotel. The fourth branch was in Port Said, to enable travelers passing through the much-celebrated Suez Canal to acquire some of their own Egyptian craft treasures.[12]

Accounts of the Ilhamiya school don't mention khayamiya, and photos of its showrooms show no indication that it was made or exhibited by the school, but the influence of the Ilhamiya approach to drawing upon traditional ornamentation was strong. Many of the khayamiya panels that survive from the period corresponding to the school's existence are much more ornate, or some might say 'busy,' than their late nineteenth-century counterparts. Moreover, they combine a multitude of patterns in a way that is very similar to the 'high art' pieces of furniture produced by the school. Other changes include the fact that new hues such as a bright purple that came from the newly developed Aniline dyes became popular, and although it may have been hard to see it at the time, the approach to traditional crafts had become a much more conscious, high-brow one, with little room for its former naive design exuberance. It was also a period when workaday, sometimes clumsy poetic inscriptions so typical of the late nineteenth century were brushed away in favor of short Arabic platitudes, much more appropriate for polite bourgeois society.

Let us not forget that this was also the age of the machine. At least one attempt was undertaken around 1900 to produce khayamiya using a sewing machine, but perhaps the experiment proved to be more trouble than it was worth, as the hand stitching continued.

Khayamiya and the Written Word

Epigrams or short messages written upon objects are everywhere in Islamic art: from the smallest coin to the largest dome, from Spain to Muslim China, from popular sayings and blessings to good wishes and poetry, to verses from the Qu'ran, itself seen as the paragon of Arabic literature.

Possibly because of the subtleties of meaning and spirit that these short texts convey, there is no single Arabic term commonly used for 'epigram'—they are usually referred to loosely by type, for example 'popular sayings' *(amsal sha'biya)*, and poetic or religious verses (*buyut shi'r* and *ayat*).

Epigrams are linked to a range of poetic and literary formats in the Arabic tradition, for example the *qit'a*, a brief poem or poetic fragment, "which lacks the structure of the full *qasida* (ode of praise)." Classical Arabic literature esteems brevity *(ijaz)*, to the extent that "every line of verse ought to be more than merely a statement of fact or a factual description; it should have a 'point' either by means of striking imagery or a form of wit." From as far back as the eighth century, the so-called 'modernizing' poets *(muhdathun)* of the Abbasid period expanded the sheer range of epigrams in Arabic literature. All major poets of this period produced them, and many minor poets went so far as to specialize in them. While the great majority of these epigrams were either satirical *(haja')*, descriptive *(wasf)*, or wisdom-imparting (*hikma* and *zuhdiya*), there were also some written on lyrical themes like love *(ghazal)* and wine *(khamriya)*. In anthologies and works of *adab* (etiquette) they abound, often grouped by subject.[13]

Most Islamic epigrams either refer to the owner or patron, such as in a blessing or attribution, or offer a reflection on the purpose and beauty of the design itself. Individual patrons are sometimes named on bespoke items, but generic statements applicable to anyone are more typical, and statements like "Blessings to its owner," "Happiness," and "Eternal prosperity" are very common.

Epigrams may also be talismanic or protective, especially when used on jewelery or clothing. Extracts from the Qu'ran and Hadith (the sayings of the Prophet Muhammad), or references to God and reminders of his power and glory are frequently used, though their sacred origin restricts these objects to specific uses—they wouldn't be used on the floor, for example, or in any other context that would be deemed inappropriate for a religious text. Epigrams of this nature include very commonly-used statements like "Glory be to God" and "God is capable of all things."

Some of these epigrams can be virtually illegible, especially when written in the highly abstract geometric script or the calligraphy used to form decorative shapes or puzzles; others may have originally been intended to fill blank spaces in a design,[14] but the object is the same: to impart some sort of blessing or wisdom, and in many cases to remember God.

Two of the most common epigrams are *Mashallah* (literally "What God has willed"), used to express wonder at God's creation, and in acknowledging God as the source of a particular wonder, to ward away the evil eye. The other is simply *Bismillah al-rahman al-rahim*, "In the name of God, the Merciful and Compassionate," a phrase used by Muslims to commence any significant undertaking—from a meal to the signing of a contract. In Christian contexts in Egypt there is also a repertoire of commonly-used religious references, such as "The pinnacle of wisdom is the reverence of God," or "Ask and it will be given to you; seek and you will find; knock and the door will be opened to you."

Within the larger context of literature and textiles in today's Islamic world, it is worth remembering that from as far back as pre-Islamic Arabia, the Arab tribes would compete with each other over who could compose the finest poetry, and the poetic work of the winners of these competitions would be written out and hung on the Ka'ba, giving rise to the term "Mu'allaqat," literally, "hangings."

Given their context, it is not at all surprising that the tents and tent hangings of Cairo, as well as boasting a rich design language of pattern and color, also developed a distinct tradition of epigrams—a tradition that holds as true today as it was in the thirteenth and fourteenth centuries, and probably before.

We are fortunate that this tradition exists, as in the absence of written records about the tents and tentmakers, the writing that survives on the older tent pieces provides many clues about their provenance and function and insights about the biographies of patrons and makers. Studying several hundred examples surviving from the late nineteenth and early twentieth centuries provides us with a wealth of information that exists nowhere else. These epigrams offer glimpses into an urban working-class profession that aimed to serve many sectors of society. It is worth noting that the later part of this period especially corresponds to two parallel and distinct developments in Egypt that had a bearing on the nature of the epigrams found on khayamiya. The first was an intensification of the Islamic art revival movement, which saw a much higher incidence of meticulously executed inscriptions of Qu'ranic verses, and the second, an increase in touristic demand for khayamiya, in many cases because they were seen by tourists as a good example of Islamic art, and something very typical of Cairo.

The panels probably intended for a tourist market tend to feature a string of short unrelated Arabic phrases, sharing wisdoms and blessings. Commonly used phrases include *Ahlan wa sahlan* ("Welcome"), *al-Adl asas al-mulk* ("Justice is the key to dominion"), *Salamit al-insan fi-hifz al-lisan* ("Man's wellbeing lies in guarding his tongue"), and *al-Sabr muftah al-farag* ("Patience is the key to deliverance"). These generic statements seem indicative of an off-the-shelf product rather than a commission tailored to the preferences of an elite patron. The numerous examples where short blessings and proverbs are strung together on the same tent panel, rather than one long epigram, make it likely that for the tourists buying these pieces the appearance of the Arabic script was more important than the sayings themselves, though a few wise Arabic proverbs may have added an additional appeal.

These sequences of short generic epigrams have very close parallels in the inlaid metalwork bowls and plates known as Cairoware, which were produced in huge quantities in the late nineteenth and early twentieth centuries, largely for a tourist market, and very rarely appear in Egyptian homes.

Thus, the audiences of these khayamiya texts varied significantly. There were many who would take great delight in the literary accomplishment of a poetic verse, or the depth of meaning of a religious passage; some who were semiliterate but would recognize important phrases like *Mashallah* and *Bismillah al-rahman al-rahim*, and others who could not read them for themselves (tourists), and would probably be told the meanings of the inscriptions when they purchased a piece—as is the case today. Even to the Arabic speaker, Arabic calligraphy can prove daunting, especially when designed to form decorative shapes, as is frequently the case in art and architecture.

Khedival-era khayamiya, especially, represent a distinctive Egyptian epigraphic tradition that lasted from the 1860s until the early twentieth century. Alongside ritual banners mounted in Sufi processions (which are still used today), the early examples were the last form of khayamiya created exclusively for Egyptian audiences. They typically feature prominent epigrams written in sweeping calligraphic strokes, variations of *thuluth* calligraphy. In many examples, we can tell that the craftsmen were not very literate by the frequency of minor spelling mistakes, usually the result of spelling a word phonetically, thereby inadvertently adding or omitting letters. In some cases, the person who wrote the calligraphy out was not the same person who actually stitched it—often the calligrapher was more literate than the stitcher who executed the work (but this does not necessarily mean that the calligrapher was always perfectly literate). Some of these mistakes would probably have gone unnoticed when acquired by clients in the provinces, some of whom may not have been very literate either.

Consistent with architectural calligraphic friezes, these 'tent texts' usually appear as a single line near the top of a vertical tent panel, just below the undulating trefoil band resembling the crenellations of mosques and known as *'arayis* ('brides'). Epigrams were usually written in white on a blue or red background, providing ample contrast to ensure legibility. The texts are often in cartouches with embellished borders, consistent with epigrams seen elsewhere in Islamic design. In many cases, smaller horizontal pieces were simply designed as calligraphic panels to be hung. These consist of a calligraphic frieze surrounded by a decorative border. Average dimensions of these are around 50 cm high by 180 cm wide.

Where panels were intended as canopies, epigrams are usually found on all four sides of a panel. In some cases, a tent panel may have a predominantly pharaonic design but still feature Arabic inscriptions—effectively hitting two birds with one stone from a tourist's perspective!

Of the 200 examples surveyed in 2015, over 170 possess legible epigrams, though only around 10 percent of these have been attributed to specific poets. These are: al-Mutanabbi (who lived in Iraq in the tenth century) and Abu Nawas (who lived in the eighth and ninth centuries), both acclaimed as being among the greatest of the Arab poets; al-Ibshihi, a fourteenth- to fifteenth-century Egyptian writer; and the late nineteenth- to early twentieth-century Egyptian poet, Salama Higazi. Most are simply what is known in Arabic as *shi'r majhul*, 'the work of an unknown poet.' Many of the epigrams are short colloquial phrases, some with an origin dating back centuries, others seemingly more recent. The late nineteenth century, when the earliest known surviving pieces were made, was the age of the printing press, and it isn't therefore surprising that the canon of Arabic literature was widespread.

When Patrons Have Influence

On rare occasions, patrons had an influence on the epigrams used on khayamiya panels; these patrons were probably very highly educated and requested specific verses from the anthologies of famous poets like al-Mutanabbi. Two examples from around 1900 that recently appeared together in Canada, with inscriptions from poems by al-Mutanabbi, have calligraphy that seems to have been crammed in to fit the available space. These were almost certainly the result of a patron requesting that the craftsman fit specific verses in—a patron-craftsman dynamic that still exists today.

Similarly, panels in the collection of Doris Duke, a noted collector of Islamic art, are unusually fine, both in terms of overall composition and complexity, as well as containing especially attentive calligraphic rendering of verses from the Qur'an. It could be that these panels were commissioned by Duke, which is consistent with much of her impressive collection in her Shangri-La mansion in Honolulu. They may have been designed using patterns from an earlier commission, due to their similarity to late nineteenth-century khayamiya *suradiqs* depicted in photographs from the archives of Abbas Hilmi II at Durham University.

On a more local scale, one panel probably dating from the early twentieth century combines verses from a popular poem by al-Ibshihi with what was almost certainly the owner's name: 'Abd al-Salam al-Gabri.

What Do These Texts Say?

Complete khayamiya tents with ceilings usually feature poems in Arabic. Tent bands or screens consisting of several panels can contain poetry, but often display collections of individual phrases. Single khayamiya panels tend toward short statements of no more than a couple of sentences, although very large panels may feature whole short poems.

It is apparent that the 'voice' of khayamiya is reverential, formal, and evocative of relationships between people, objects, and places. It can even be described as romantic. This is consistent with the characteristics of Islamic epigrams worldwide. Perhaps more interesting are the 'Egyptian' characteristics of these epigrams, evident both through their references to Egypt, in some cases, and their occasional use of Egyptian colloquial Arabic.

There are lots of references to 'the place,' which in many instances refers to the tent itself, and in the case of tent hangings to the place in which they are hung. In such instances, the tent is presented as a place of beauty or refuge. The inscriptions on tent hangings usually invoke blessings and happiness on an abode—literal or metaphorical.

The 'Look Again' quatrain

Of all khedival-era khayamiya epigrams, one unattributed Arabic quatrain appears to be both unique to the tentmakers and frequently encountered. Two panels in private collections bearing written dates ascribe it to the years 1896 and 1899:

> Look again, you will see a beautiful work.
> Behold, I have given you the proof.
> In Egypt is the most beautiful of all art.
> I see for its proof a long explanation.

There is a second verse which follows the first, but appears much more rarely; this is:

It is the country whose conditions have improved,
It has given its people great bounty
Its craftsmanship reflects its greatness.[15]

The first quatrain appears on more than twenty khedival-era khayamiya, ranging from fine works of an impressive scale through to surviving vernacular panels, in which it is also encountered in abbreviated and often slightly misspelled form.

The origin of this poem is unknown, although it could be related to the patriotic expressions associated with the age of Egyptian nationalism known as *al-Nahda* (the renaissance) with which it corresponds. It has been suggested that this poem in particular bears stylistic similarities to the lyrics of popular Egyptian songs, notably of the *mawwal* genre, which consists of colloquial narratives accompanied by musical instruments that have remained essentially unchanged since the pharaonic eras. Given the documented role of khedival khayamiya as a backdrop for traveling musical performances, the association between these textiles and musical lyrics is not unusual. The words of popular songs seem more likely to have been familiar to the tentmakers and their local patrons than classical Arabic literature, so it is possible that khedival khayamiya have preserved an oral archive of vernacular Egyptian music.

It is very likely that the poem was composed for the tentmakers themselves—perhaps by somebody local with poetic flair—its emphasis on the beautiful craft of the tentmakers being proof of Egypt's greatness and bounty suggests the work of an insider to the trade.

It is worth mentioning that upon sharing the poem with educated Egyptians today, the frequent response upon hearing it is a distinctly unimpressed one, often describing it as being unaccomplished in literary terms, corroborating the idea that it is the work of a local, probably amateur, poet. To date, we have not found any examples of its appearance in any other craft from the same period. In some respects, this is not surprising: these kinds of ornamental or votive epigrams were very common indeed. Each trade would have its own epigrams that made puns using specific vocabulary from the craft, often with double meanings. In this poem, this is seen in the words *aqamt* ('furnished'/'erected') and *sharh*, 'explanation' or 'strip.'[16]

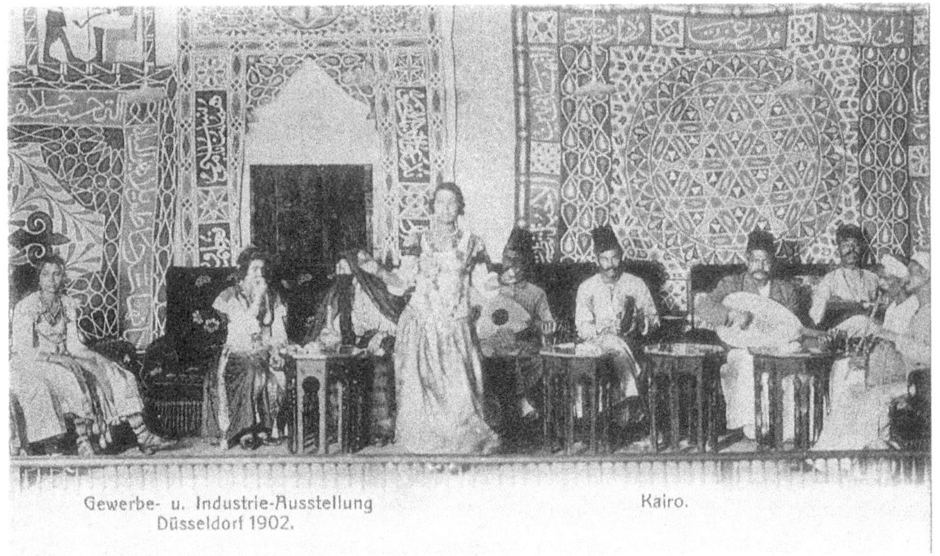

Figure 11 Egyptian musicians with khayamiya backdrop, 1902. Postcard by Friedrich Wolfrum, courtesy of Heather D. Ward.

Sharh usually means 'explanation,' but in this case it could also mean 'a strip,' as in a strip of fabric. The phrase *Aqamt lak daleela* ('I gave you the proof') features the word *iqama* (or *aqamt*), which can also be read as 'I assembled' or 'I erected,' in other words, alluding to a tent.[17] This use of puns is an Arabic rhetorical feature known as *istikhdam*, possessing widespread precedent within Islamic art.

Invocations of God and His Blessing

Epigrams to the effect of "With help from God, victory is imminent" are frequently encountered. This quote originates in the Qu'ran (61:13) and appears upon many objects, notably *mashrabiya*s (window lattices) from Cairo between the seventeenth and nineteenth centuries. "*Ya Karim*," "Oh Noble One" / "The Generous One," is noted regularly in khayamiya (and elsewhere in Islamic art) as an earnest, space-filling statement. Other extracts from the Qu'ran noted on khayamiya include "*Wa amma bina'mati rabbika fahaddith*," "Therefore proclaim the bounty of your Lord" (93:11) and "*Hada min fadl rabbi*," "This, by the grace of my Lord" (27:40).[18]

Another frequent invocation is for divine benevolence: "Oh opener of doors, open for us the blessings of this door." The first part of the saying

"*Ya Mufattih*," or the very similar "*Ya Musahhil*" ("Oh facilitator"), is a popular invocation still made by tentmakers and other craftsmen as they open their businesses each morning, and it appears on at least nine known tent pieces from the khedival era. It is also found in tilework in Cairo in the eighteenth-century *sabil-kuttab* of 'Abd al-Rahman Katkhuda (1744), as "Oh opener of doors, open for us the blessings of the door, oh king of kings, open for us the paths" (see fig. 3). This resonates with the documented use of khayamiya panels on doorways in Egyptian homes, and this particular saying spans the idea of the literal and metaphorical doorway.

Comparable epigrams include the very common inscription "*Bi-sharak ya dar qad nilt al-muna*" ("With your bounty, oh house, I have attained my hopes"), and its continuation "*Bi-l-sa'ad wa-l-afrah qad zad al-hana*," "And with happiness and joy, my bliss has been increased."[19] Other similar inscriptions include "*Bayt al-sa'ada ma a'la makanatu*" ("A home of happiness, how esteemed is its place").

The dichotomy between happiness and sadness is also common: "Happiness has come, and suffering has disappeared," and the words of the Mamluk writer al-Ibshihi, which are similar but perhaps more fervent in their aspirations: "Oh house, may sadness not enter you, and may time not turn against your owner, and may the bounty of the house make pious every guest [if the house does not get too constricted by the guest's presence]" (see plate 16).[20]

Some larger khedival period pieces combine several statements with similar sentiments. For example, the Syme Panel (see plate 17):

Welcome *(Ahlan wa sahlan)*
Patience is the key to deliverance
Whatever God has willed will be
Justice is the key to dominion
Man's safety is a charity
Be patient and good will prevail[21]

Most of these statements have also been seen on single panels *(sutur)*. This is not surprising, as their list-like structure enables independent placement.

The Egyptian tentmakers made regular use of the *qasida* on their single-poled camping tents (singular *fustat*). The most well-known *qasidas* are the "Mu'allaqat," or seven 'suspended odes,' so named for their use upon curtain-like drapes that once adorned the Ka'ba.[22] For example, the Jackson Hole tent bears an unattributed *qasida* fragment expressing warm greetings and the bestowal of love upon a friend and a nation selflessly and without envy.[23] Such an inscription is reminiscent of objects designed as gifts, and consistent with exchanges between international business partners.[24] The door panel bears calligraphy referring to "the lovers within," and might be intended as a layered reference to both function and symbolism.

Poems about the tent as a place

A *qasida* on the Egyptian Tent in the collection of the Islamic Arts Museum Malaysia (IAMM) is one that appears on other tents as well, and must have been relatively common, capturing the spirit of a tent as a place or a world (see plate 18):

> This beautiful place has no equal
> God protects it from the vicissitudes of time
> Look at the luxurious buildings and gaze
> Verily it holds the beauty of meanings
> Walk around in the *qa'a*, whose beauty impresses
> As a bride in her wedding procession of music
> Turn around it from its front and back
> You'll find in it all the desires and wishes.
> Within its boundaries runs the deer.
> Walk through the path of deer,
> Its air spreads a fragrance but
> Try it for the health of your body
> Oh how it is a *qa'a* from a beautiful place
> That was adorned with women and children.[25]

Consistent with other complete khayamiya tents, this poem personifies the tent as a witness to the beauty of an unspoiled open space. The reference to a wedding procession is likely to be a reference to the use of khayamiya at Egyptian weddings, and more specifically to the palanquin in which an Egyptian bride was once carried to the ceremony (as these were also sewn by the tentmakers).

Although the IAMM's tent was described as a 'wedding tent' by its previous owner,[26] this style of *fustat* tent is far too small for such an event, and not consistent with the *suradiq*s that were actually used to host Egyptian weddings.

Evocations of good company

Many khayamiya invoke a healthy atmosphere enlivened by delightful company. These are reminiscent of Sufi poetry, celebrating good times with friends. Other inscriptions are drawn from this genre, known particularly for its endorsement of wine. This could include the 'Blue Lions' panel in the Khalili collection, which reads:

> The person who smiles will have good fortune
> My drinking companion, let's go to the tents, and pour for me the drink of desire.
> [He] swaggers marvelously in the best of manners.

The translators of this text noted its similarity in style to the poems from the *Rubaiyat of Omar Khayyam*.[27] Khayyam was an eleventh-century Persian polymath, whose talents included poetry and whose legacy spread far beyond the Islamic world (coincidentally, his surname means 'the tentmaker').

Love and Devotional Poetry

Love in the Arabic literary tradition takes a variety of forms, sometimes romantic but at other times devotional or affectionate, the sort of love one might have for a family member, a role model, or a dear friend.

One poet whose work appears in the context of khayamiya is the celebrated Egyptian poet and singer Salama Higazi (1852–1917), who was an important figure on the Egyptian musical scene, noted not just for his love poetry, but also for musical theater. Many celebrated Egyptian performers sung his songs, which would have been very familar in late nineteenth- and early twentieth-century Cairo.

Not all poetic inscriptions were contemporary though: at least two known pieces have epigrams written by the Iraqi poet al-Mutanabbi (915–65 CE). One declares:

> When I was preparing to depart I wished to do good by you,
> And I found that most of what I had was too little compared to your greatness.
> And when souls are mighty, the bodies are wearied in their quest.[28]

The second:

Would that we were your steeds when you ride forth, and your tents
when you alight!
And our wont is comely patience, were it with anything but your absence
that we were tried."[29]

The panels were probably commissioned by an individual who appreciated specific literary references. The outcome was that the tentmaker had to compress the calligraphy on one of the panels to fit it in.

Another khedival khayamiya with an attributed epigram is the so-called Rhode Island Panel. The calligraphy is an extract from the *One Thousand and One Nights* (also known as the *Arabian Nights*), from the soliloquy of the character Anas al-Wugud, and may be translated as:

Happiness has come and swept sorrow and sadness away, then we came together and disappointed those who envied us. The perfumed breeze blew in, awakening the heart, the insides and the body, and the joy of company has prevailed, and on the horizons, bells rang our good news.

In this story Anas, a handsome soldier in the king's court, is in love with a young woman, al-Ward fi-Akmam (literally, 'rosebud'), the daughter of the king's vizier, Ibrahim. When the romance is discovered by the young woman's parents, al-Ward is banished to a distant castle. Fortunately, before she leaves, she writes a poem on the door of the palace to indicate what has happened. When Anas approaches, the door trembles in recitation of the poem. Anas himself sets off in search of al-Ward, reciting love poetry as he journeys on his quest for his beloved.[30]

The use of a quotation from the story of Anas is unusual. The *One Thousand and One Nights* is not a common source of epigrams in Egyptian crafts of the period, and is otherwise uncommon on old khayamiya panels. However, in the late nineteenth century the book was widely published in Europe and attracted a great deal of attention, coming to symbolize an exotic, sensual eastern culture, at once intriguing and reprehensible. It could be that this piece was specially made for affluent travelers to Egypt (such as those on the Grand Tour) or perhaps for a special commission (see plate 19).

Khayamiya Epigrams and the Spirit of Khedival Cairo

In their range of themes and sentiments, and in capturing both learned and less learned voices, the epigrams on khedival khayamiya are a good window onto the voice of late nineteenth- and early twentieth-century

Egypt—they are not a body of texts that existed in isolation. The most telling reminder of this is the fact that when Amina Hanim Ilhami, founder of the Ilhamiya School of Arts, which had a large part to play in encouraging the revival of Islamic art in Egypt, returned from Istanbul at the end of World War I, she was met by devoted students from her craft school, first at the railway station and then outside her palace. To celebrate the return of their generous patron, the pupils were taught a chant, which was recited as she approached the palace. Its similarity to the poetry on khayamiya from the period is remarkable:

> "The happiness of happiness has started for us, and bounty and felicity have drawn near,
> With your arrival we have attained our hopes, you goodly provider of our nations."[31]

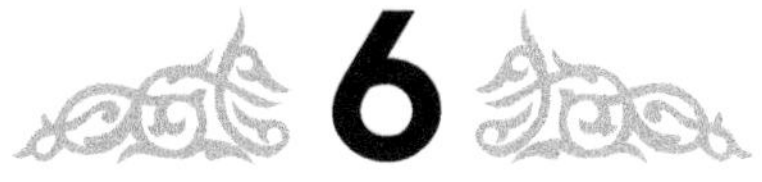

6

From Suradiq to Souvenir

Tentmakers and Tourists

Almost as far from Cairo as it is possible to be, a tiny village sits beside a highway in rural Australia. It has only one pub, and more sheep than people. It is famous locally for its hay, meat pies, and the strangely named 'Ganmain-Grong-Grong-Matong' football club. Ganmain should have no place in the story of the Street of the Tentmakers. But despite all probability, it does.

The First World War shaped Australian perceptions of the Middle East. Like so many other communities, both rural and urban, Ganmain had its own representation of soldiers and nurses sent to Egypt, Lebanon, Syria, Jordan, and Turkey. They were compelled to travel for a variety of reasons, the 'grand adventure' being part of the allure. For most, this was their first time to travel beyond Australia. Many were subsequently killed in combat or due to illness, and remembered in the ubiquitous war memorials for lives lost in foreign campaigns that are scattered across Australia.

In the local museum, two memorial plaques list the names of those who served in somber golden letters—one for each of the world wars. At the base of each plaque, beneath the epitaph "Not dead, for how can they die, while in our hearts they live?", two small pieces of khayamiya appliqué have been respectfully placed. The juxtaposition between the formality of the honor board and the informality of these humble souvenirs is striking. They make a nuanced statement about Ganmain's role in the British campaign in Egypt one century ago, and the loss of lives in war.

Both panels were collected in 1917, donated to the Ganmain museum by a Mrs. Wal Brill. Sewn into sections from the same coarse canvas, one

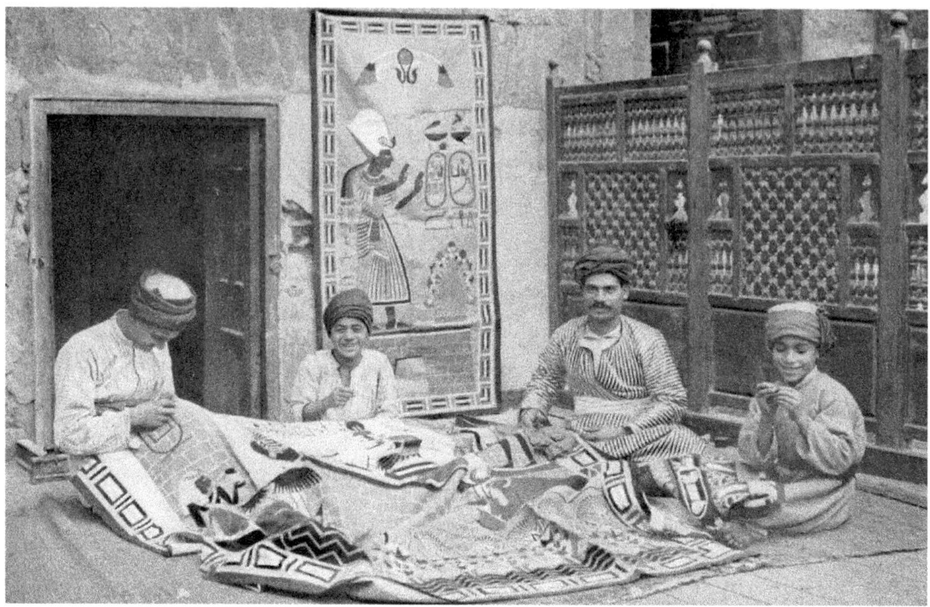

Figure 12 Donald McLeish, *Egyptian Tentmakers*, 1921. Photograph courtesy of National Geographic.

shows a crudely drawn four-legged scarab in purple, green, black, and khaki brown, framed in indigo blue. The other displays a beige procession framed in red, as two camels are gently led by a man wearing a *gallabiya* toward an obelisk, palm tree, and a pair of crooked pyramids, guarded by a bored-looking sphinx on a plinth. These were humble souvenirs from Egypt, collected as a memento for loved ones in distant Australia. They were easily folded, charming, unmistakably 'Egyptian,' and perhaps most important of all, they were not expensive.

These panels are examples of touristic khayamiya. The touristic genre is the most radical departure from the majestic, concurrent khedival khayamiya. They vividly demonstrate the impact of modernity along the Street of the Tentmakers through their revised scale, new figurative content, individual production, and international dissemination. Touristics are the most widely distributed, least appreciated, and most accessible of all the historic forms of khayamiya. They are common in antique shops, estate sales, and flea markets, but rarely mentioned in scholarship. Their references to ancient Egyptian art were reinterpreted by the tentmakers and their subsequent patrons. Their popularity with tourists ensured they were ignored by curators for anything other than the museum gift shop—these were tourist tat, not 'Egyptian' or even 'Islamic' art (see plate 20).

As Islamic art collections were developed from the late nineteenth and early twentieth centuries, their priority was the acquisition of important historical works of art and design. By contrast, khayamiya textiles were manifestations of popular culture, and none more so than touristic panels. Even the most carefully observed, beautifully made, and imaginative compositions were still made ostensibly as souvenirs, and hence rarely acquired for museum collections. No touristic panels are currently represented in any Egyptian museum. When they appear in museums overseas, they are usually a donation from a local patron who had traveled to Egypt, not purchased by curators.

Their international distribution is indebted to the recurring popularity of 'Egyptian revivals' from the late nineteenth through mid-twentieth century, as well as the popularity of Egypt as a tourist destination. Touristic khayamiya have been mistakenly attributed to the Arts and Crafts movement as products of British or American folk art—'naive quilts and embroideries'—and have been associated with the art deco admiration of ancient Egyptian design since the opening of Tutankhamun's tomb in 1922. But they are one of the tentmakers' own manifestations of modernity through khayamiya.

When seen as an expression of the tentmakers' active engagement with the visual cultures of nineteenth-century Egypt as perceived by visitors, these textiles are important. They reveal the priorities of the touristic imagination upon the work of the tentmakers. For tourists, Egypt was a picturesque land of pharaohs, donkeys, pyramids, vultures, and indecipherable hieroglyphics, wrapped in orientalist concepts of historic and mythical fantasy and the daily realities of Egyptian life. Arguably more than khedival khayamiya, touristics reveal the entrepreneurial initiatives along the Street of the Tentmakers and highlight the work of the hands of individual artisans. They appreciated the foundations of the international tourist economy, and through these they created radically new forms without challenging the materiality or working processes of khayamiya.

Following the rise of touristic forms around 1900, the first contemporary khayamiya united the colors and scale of the touristics with the elaborate geometric forms of the khedivals. These include the panels displayed at the Chicago World's Fair in 1933 and also sold by international retailers like Liberty's of London and Myer or David Jones in Australia. They are the precursors to the contemporary appliqués that now line the

Street of the Tentmakers, whose patterns are similar to the original touristic khayamiya still being sewn today.

The Transition to Touristic Khayamiya

The emergence of khayamiya appliqués as souvenirs, carrying designs that were quite unlike the abstract patterns and geometric, calligraphic, or vernacular motifs that defined the khedival panels, was a dramatic departure from the previous roles of khayamiya in Egyptian society. Unlike the architectural scale of khedival khayamiya, the most popular format for touristic pieces are small squares (45 cm wide), modest rectangular panels (typically 45 cm x 100 cm), and panels or archways no larger than a household door. These are small decorations, not pieces of architecture.

With very few exceptions, touristic khayamiya do not feature Arabic calligraphy. Improvised hieroglyphics are common, usually without meaning and symetrically repeated. Some ancient texts are accurately rendered from their source materials, particularly if the stitching is especially fine, though the tentmakers did not read ancient languages. Some hieroglyphics were apparently invented by tentmakers, or may have been selected because their shape was appealing to the tentmaker or their patron, independent of meaning, or possibly in an attempt to spell a name. None made before 1986 appear to have featured written English or other languages.

Although the khedivals and touristics may appear unmistakably different, hybrid forms are also known. For example, the archway in the collection of the Museum of Man in San Diego, acquired by Emily Michler in the 1890s, is khedival in form, except for the inset panel featuring the pharaonic motif of Nekhbet, a vulture seen as an architectural motif over ancient temple and tomb entrances. Dr. Warner's Egyptian tent in the Adirondack Museum, acquired in 1921, displays a relatively crude figurative touristic wall band with a dynamic abstract khedival ceiling. Other examples of tent bands are known which alternate between khedival and pharaonic designs (see plate 21).

Further challenging the khedival-touristic binary opposition, some khedival panels also possess elements that are touristic on closer inspection. Simple calligraphic statements like "Welcome" are generic messages that may have been intended for non-Egyptian clients. References to literature more familiar to non-Egyptians, such as the Rhode Island Panel's quotation of a passage from the *One Thousand and One Nights*, also suggest a convergence (see plate 19). These are strange textiles that look khedival but sound touristic.

The composition of large touristic panels is closely related to the composition of the khedivals. From the top down, both usually feature two wide bands, the top one bearing a repeating *'arusa* pattern inspired by alternating crenellations or fleur-de-lys, often reinterpreted as Egyptian lotuses on touristic examples. The lower band normally features calligraphy on khedivals, while depictions of Nekhbet (stylized vultures with wide wings) are common on touristics. Beneath these bands, a central medallion fills the upper center of the composition, framed by two column-like borders. At the bottom, a solid form provides a base to the panel. Though the content of each of these sections reflects the imagination of the tentmakers and the diversity of sources at their disposal, the overall layout is consistently similar for large panels, be they khedival or touristic.

Although visitors' accounts of the Street of the Tentmakers in 1908–11 are known, it is unfortunate that no evidence survives of the tentmakers' own perception of the emergence of touristic khayamiya in the early twentieth century. Innovation is prized and frequently challenged within the Street of the Tentmakers, so it is reasonable to assume that the first touristic panels were quickly copied by other workshops. The discovery of khayamiya caches featuring khedival tents in conjunction with touristic appliqués suggests that the tentmakers sold both forms simultaneously. Individual tentmakers may have specialized in particular genres, but they remain anonymous.

Through the production of touristic khayamiya the tentmakers could generate a more regular and autonomous income, as opposed to irregular payments for long-term team projects. Touristic khayamiya were quick to make, easy to sell, and promoted individualism along the Street of the Tentmakers.

By comparing their diversity in style, skill, scale, imagination, and appropriation, we gain a sense of the tentmakers' street as a working community, as shown in Donald McLeish's 1921 portrait of master and apprentice tentmakers working together on touristic panels, hinting at the interactions between them. Touristic panels were sold along the Street of the Tentmakers as well as in the diverse shops of Khan el-Khalili (about two kilometers north of the Street) by street hawkers, and from souvenir stalls near attractions like the Giza Pyramids, Luxor, and Karnak. They were also sold from the gift shop of the Egyptian Museum and thrown by vendors from small boats to the waiting cruise vessels at the Aswan Dam.

Touristics in Context

The earliest known touristic khayamiya are associated with travelers who visited Egypt between 1880 and 1890, although the majority in circulation today appear to have been made after the 1922 excavation of Tutankhamun's tomb. Unlike scarabs and other tourist-oriented products like beads, scarves, carpets, and counterfeit antiquities, touristic khayamiya are rarely mentioned in travelers' accounts of the markets of Egypt. Usually, it is the behavior of the vendors which is more closely described, their insistent refrains or comical quips in various languages, rather than the items being sold. The earliest known panels possess simple forms, rudimentary single-color borders, and are sewn into coarse woven canvas without the blue stripes widely associated with khedival khayamiya. The distraction of the fine blue woven stripes within the backing canvas was not a concern when sewing large tents, but it was consciously avoided in all known touristic panels.

The first clear familial provenances for touristic khayamiya were recorded by participants during the First World War in Egypt. For example, Jane McLennan served as a nurse in Cairo for three weeks in 1916, where she acquired the panel now in the collection of the State Library of Queensland (acquired as a donation alongside her diaries). The Borree Creek Panel, which shows a scene based on *Nebamun Hunting in the Marshes*,[1] was collected by Ernest Cameron Moffat of the First Light Horse regiment in early 1915. It was sent to his sister with a letter, noting: "I am sending you a bit of a table centre, I hope you will like it. I would have liked to have sent something better but two shillings a day won't stand for it."[2]

Beyond making exotic souvenirs, touristics were also used as decoration on barracks. A photograph of an open-air Allied Soldier's Club near Cairo on New Year's Day, 1916, depicts soldiers from New Zealand in a 'comfortable setting' enhanced by four appliqués bearing an array of deities, Isis with wings outspread, and a departing solar boat (atet). The ABC television series *ANZAC Girls* (2014) acknowledged this use of touristic khayamiya by using a basic but genuine World War I-era specimen as a production prop, acquired by the perceptive set designer via eBay.

Perhaps the most important photographic evidence connecting the tentmakers with the rise of touristic khayamiya is Donald McLeish's 1921 depiction of four smiling tentmakers—two adults and two boys—wearing *gallabiyas* and turbans as they sew a large touristic panel together with a second, smaller panel suspended upon the wall behind them (a version of the suspended panel was noted in a private collection in 2012, along with a cache of other touristics of similar date). This image, like its 1880s predecessor by the Zangaki brothers, showcases the intergenerational skills of the tentmaker workshops (see fig. 23). In this case, it also highlights the warm relations between the group depicted, the patience and focus required to hone this craft, and their easy familiarity with a visiting photographer. Even before the opening of Tutankhamun's tomb in 1922, these artisans were quite used to visitors.

The international popularity of Egyptian appliqués was well established after World War I. They were frequently mentioned under various names by interior decorators as an easy way to add charm to a plain room. Exhibitions were displayed as far away as the Otago Women's Club in New Zealand's South Island.[3] One Australian newspaper columnist praised them as home décor in 1923, adding the odd warning that "Australian women will have too many painful a recollection of our troops in Egypt before and after Gallipoli to be attracted by camel scenes. The men would say they gave them 'the hump.'"[4]

That said, the tentmakers benefited from the continuation of the demand for touristic khayamiya during the Second World War. The Australian War Memorial features a 1944 photograph by Laurence Craddock Le Guay in which Australian soldiers are holding a large touristic khayamiya among other souvenirs collected in Cairo. Other photographs of the same era depict the interior of the Sisters' Mess Tent of the Twenty-first Casualty Clearing Station in Amiriya (by Dorothy Vines) and the Dutch Nurses' tent (by Willem van de Poll), both of which are furnished with touristic khayamiya. The Ashcroft panel, acquired by 'Jack' (John) Ashcroft in Port Said around 1944, while serving with the Pacific Steam Navigation Company on the SS *Orbita*, also offers an extant example with a clear World War II provenance (see plate 20).[5] As further examples come to light, we may yet establish a stylistic or material differentiation between 'typically' World War I and World War II touristic khayamiya, though making this distinction is currently challenging.

Beyond the direct influence of the world wars, touristic khayamiya also appeared as foreign 'curios' in international quilt shows and were known ambiguously as 'Egyptian Tent-Work' by retailers across Europe, the United Kingdom, Australia, and the United States.[6] It is not clear how these retailers sourced their khayamiya, but they were widely exported through department stores and interior designers, as demonstrated by catalog advertisements, newspaper columnists, and business labels either stamped, sewn, or tied upon khayamiya. These designers ranged from specialists in rugs and carpets to interior decorators such as Goodyer's of 174 Regent Street, London, and Liberty's of London, as well as American dealers based in New York and other cities. As most of the advertisements were ambiguous, these listings included both touristic and late-khedival khayamiya.

Interior designers usually praised these 'gay' appliqués as inexpensive, colorful, and charming ornaments for the home and nursery, suggesting that their readers were familiar with them by the early 1930s. The most common use was as cushion covers, but appliquéd panels with touristic figuration were also inserted into room dividing screens, laid out as upholstery for sofas and chairs, and over beds. Some appear to have been specifically designed for such varied purposes, though most were adapted to suit these unconventional formats. One example in the British Museum (acquired in Sudan in the 1920s) features several panels sewn together, creating a cover that would fit over a child's bed like an ancient Egyptian sarcophagus. Another example in the Doris Duke collection has been displayed upon a wall, but given its shape (a central circle surrounded by petal-like rectangles), was probably designed as a cover for an ottoman stool.

Clothing featuring touristic khayamiya also indicates that fashion designers were aware of the Egyptian tentmakers in the 1920s and 1930s. Some appliqués were sewn upon jackets and dresses, though a mid-1920s white silk shantung coat in the collection of the Fashion History Museum in Ontario, Canada, appears to have been designed in considered collaboration with the tentmakers (see plate 22). This simple art deco garment features a well-balanced composition of figurative pharaonic motifs, including carefully positioned portrait medallions on the back, a decorated nape, elaborate processions on the cuffs and lower hem, and fine stitching throughout in mahogany, black, yellow, cream, pink, navy blue, and pale blue. Similar garments are illustrated in French, Italian, American, and British fashion catalogs, though they are rarely encountered as extant textiles. They also suggest a future direction for the work of the Egyptian tentmakers—khedival khayamiya patterns, for example, are yet to be seen upon clothing, though a handful of contemporary designs have been adapted as bespoke jackets.

Critical Reception—Douglas Sladen

Douglas Sladen wrote about the tentmakers regularly following his visits to Egypt between 1908 and 1911. He noted their work and the Street of the Tentmakers as a destination for tourists in his books *Queer Things about Egypt* and *Oriental Cairo: The City of the "Arabian Nights"*. He described the Street of the Tentmakers as "a blaze of colour [and] also a blaze of vulgarity and impudence."[7] In his chapter "On the Most Interesting Things to Buy in Egypt If You Have Not Much to Spend," he guides his reader to the Khayamiya:

> Where the Sharia Kasabet-Radowan draws in to the Suk of the Tentmakers there is an avenue of stately buildings, native mansions with rich portals and balconies, and mosques with pattern'd stonework and massive bronze grills clustered together. . . . Two sides of the street almost meeting overhead warn you that you have reached the Tentmakers' Bazar, through lovely lines of mosques and minarets and old palaces with *meshrebiya*'d oriels. It is always cool and dark and picturesque in the Tentmakers' Bazar, just the right environment for the gay awnings and saddle-cloths and leather work that are made in its tiny shops. . . .
>
> One of [the Dragoman's] happy hunting-grounds is the Tentmakers' Bazar, which might have been designed for tourists. Its shops, in a sort of arcade which has a College behind it, are larger and opener and there is enough colour here for the whole of Cairo. Most of its shops have their owners hard at work embroidering till a victim passes; the floors are covered with embroidery in the making, the walls with canvases appliquéd with texts from the Koran [sic] and caricatures of the tomb-paintings of the Pharaohs.[8]

Sladen's advice for visitors has since been echoed by many other guides to shopping in Cairo:

> The moment when you have said that you are not going to buy anything is rather a good time to buy. They put the prices down very low to tempt you. They don't mind if you do break your word in this way. Price the same sort of thing at different stalls which are a long way from each other. It helps to give the real price and to show which stall is cheapest.[9]

But in regard to the use of khayamiya, Sladen provides slightly more context:

> The Arabs use [khayamiya] in enormous quantities for decorating the insides of the canvas pavilions which they erect on any provocation, some-

> times in the street of a wedding, or the return of a pilgrim from Mecca; sometimes in a regular encampment for an occasion like the birthday of the prophet; and which they use a great deal in mosques. The tentmakers affect texts from the Koran [sic] and arabesques in brilliant colours, the red-white-and-blue [-like] battle flags being the favorite combination. These, even when new, do not look more than pleasantly garish. But when they are faded by fifty years of use—being dyed with good vegetable colours—their effect is adorable.[10]

> Red, white, and blue blended are the quietest tints used; they may have yellow added, and a violent violet and a gaseous green are also very popular. The colours of some of the new texts intended for purchase by tourists are crude enough for a factory-girl's summer hat. But the faded texts which have done duty for mosque or marriage for many years are exquisite. Their colouring was probably flowerlike in its beauty when they were fresh; they have faded into tints like nature's own. The parodies of the pictures of the Pharaohs are soberer in their colouring; the black of hair and the Venetian red of naked bodies play such a large part in these compositions.[11]

Sladen's enthusiasm for the Street of the Tentmakers was quite distinct from his attitude to the tentmakers themselves, particularly the development of touristic khayamiya. Of these he wrote: "Their imitations of the wall pictures in ancient Egyptian tombs are generally beneath contempt, except in price." For Sladen, touristic khayamiya were "odiously vulgar . . . in shocking taste and bearing hardly any resemblance to their originals."[12] His passionate denouncement of the 'caricatures' made by the tentmakers renders his criticism uniquely intense:

> The tentmakers are the most hopelessly vulgarised of all the denizens of the bazar; elsewhere I have inveighed against them for prostituting their art by substituting coarse caricatures of the ancient Egyptian tomb paintings for the beautiful texts and arabesques which are on the awnings and tent linings they make for Arabs. They talk incessantly to every foreigner who passes: "Look here, sir, you want to buy very nice. Come in— no sharge [sic] for examine"— and so on.[13]

> I should like to shoot the whole lot of tentmakers for the vulgarity with which they caricature the scenes painted in the Tombs of Memphis and Thebes, playing down to the ignorant tourist's sense of humour. It would

be far better if they took their designs from Mr. Thackeray's inimitable "Light Side of Egypt"—it would be more Egyptian and more amusing.[14]

Sladen's vitriolic and eurocentric opinion cannot be left to stand without comment. His advocacy for the designs of an English cartoonist overlooks the entrepreneurial purpose and social context of touristic khayamiya. It also ignores the difference between the tentmakers' agency as Egyptian artisans and Thackeray's privilege as an English satirist to comment on their patrons (who were basically the same people).

The tentmakers were deliberate in their selection and reinterpretation of ancient Egyptian motifs, responding to reproductions in their own manner, choosing topics that they either related to or which they imagined would appeal to visitors. They were 'safe' choices, in the sense that they did not seek to satirize the tourist's experience of travel in Egypt—tourists don't appear on touristic khayamiya. Thackeray, by contrast, was working as a British cartoonist, acerbically commenting on the behavior of his fellow expatriates. It would have been contrary to the business interests of the tentmakers to disparage their patrons.

Though not of the sarcastic style of Thackeray, a sense of humor is evident in the touristic work of the tentmakers. It may be a consequence of the camp or kitsch treatment of ancient artworks, such as a procession of somber deities, interrupted by what appears to be a flatulent Anubis, or the improbability of scenarios like the juggled juxtaposition of camels, donkeys, and tiny tilted pyramids. The humor implied in these objects may have been the collectors' rather than the tentmakers', providing a reason for their acquisition and preservation to this day; ironic souvenirs selected for jovial awkwardness as much as deliberate precision.

Ancient Motifs

The pharaonic content of touristic khayamiya is indebted to postcards, souvenir papyrus sheets, and illustrated books of ancient Egyptian art. One book known to have been used by the tentmakers was *A History of Art in Ancient Egypt* (1883) by Georges Perrot and Charles Chipiez, in which the sequence of illustrated plates has been adapted (often inverted) as compositions in touristic specimens. The most memorable of these features almost consecutive illustrations from this book, creating a scene in which a sword-wielding left-handed pharaoh drives his chariot through a swamp, while his fleeing enemies are flung into the river and hide in the reeds, and nesting waterbirds are stalked by a mongoose. In the original illustrations, the pharaoh was right-handed, driving on solid ground on his mown-down enemies. The waterbirds, once isolated to their own page, only had the mongoose to worry about.

Other arrangements suggest multiple sources were drawn upon by the tentmakers. For example, on the Beylerian Warrior Panel, an ancient ceramic plate bearing three overlapped fish appears as a space-filling motif beneath an unrelated scene of a lethal fight between two warriors.[15] Today's tentmakers have explained that their regard for such appropriation is based not upon similarity to the original source, but the ability to interpret or combine sources into a 'new' design.

A curiosity of referencing illustrations occurs when khayamiya depict pharaohs or deities at an unusual 45-degree angle facing the viewer. This appears to be the result of copying an illustration of a sculpture rather than a two-dimensional painting, which was set at this angle. Naturalistic perspective is rarely seen in the work of the tentmakers, and tends to be imprecise when it is followed, notably on the designs based on the prints of the nineteenth-century Scottish orientalist David Roberts or Egyptian cinema posters in appliqué.

Of the innumerable symbols offered by ancient Egyptian visual culture, the Egyptian tentmakers clearly had favorites. These resonated with tourists as easy to identify and distinctly Egyptian, and were subsequently reproduced on postcards, guidebooks, posters, and papyrus. They include processions in honor of a pharaoh, colorful groups of ancient deities, and humans interacting with animals—notably the procession of the donkeys of Ty.

This very popular motif originates in a sculptural frieze in the Mastaba of Ty at Saqqara, dating to the Fifth dynasty of the Old Kingdom (circa 2474–44 BCE), in which donkeys have been gathered to thresh grain with their hooves—a detail not usually visible when translated into touristic khayamiya, where they simply look like a row of donkeys. However, at the front of this orderly queue, one donkey leans down to eat the grain, to the chagrin of the gesturing overseer. The finest renderings of this procession evoke the elegance and subtle intelligence of the original donkeys, but the more common versions cut the donkeys into rectangles with simplified triangular ears. The original frieze also depicts eleven cattle, which are less frequently represented in touristic khayamiya. In each case the repeating motif of animals' heads is distinctive, but the expressions and exasperated gestures of the accompanying herdsmen are also memorable. In the original sequence, these men bear hieroglyphics indicating words like "Drive them," "Go," "Watch out!" and "Block them," though these are rarely copied with accuracy by the tentmakers (who were, and still are, unlikely to read hieroglyphics—like most Egyptians). Most examples feature a self-contained composition framed in the same manner as the original frieze—a rectangular panel with dot-dash borders typical of touristic khayamiya.

Another popular motif in touristic khayamiya is Nekhbet, a vulture with a pair of shen rings in its claws, sometimes replaced with a maat feather (a long feather with a stem to one side and curling over at the tip). This usually appears set into a rectangular composition reminiscent of the conventional appearance of Nekhbet over ancient temple doorways, facing toward the ground. It can be presented alone or as part of a larger panel.

The ancient Nekhbet or the Bennu (heron) may also provide the source for the recurring touristic motif of a small flying bird carrying what could be a leaf or feather in its beak. This simple bird is not obviously drawn from ancient Egyptian art, though it often appears on touristic khayamiya. Charming but mysterious, the bird appears on ancient and *sha'bi* (folkloric) panels, usually tucked into an empty corner or flying over human figures. Though stylized birds sometimes appear on khedival khayamiya and earlier Ottoman tents, they do not resemble this odd little thing. It is a relatively recent invention, possibly a signature for a particular tentmaker or workshop, or perhaps a space-filling device.

The representation of birds in ancient Egyptian art has been thoroughly studied.[16] From the early 2000s, contemporary khayamiya panels consisting entirely of birds started to appear along the Street of the Tentmakers. These were initially inspired by ancient sources like the *Birds of the Acacia Tree* in the tomb of Khnumhotep II at Beni Hassan (reproduced in paintings by Nina de Garis Davies (1932) and others) or *Nebamun Hunting in the Marshes* (in the British Museum since 1821), such as the Booree Creek Panel of 1914, featuring the distinctive black cat eating a bird.

Since the year 2000 the 'Birds' have become a well-established genre of contemporary khayamiya, drawn increasingly from the imagination as fanciful herons, colorful ducks and parrots, long-necked flamingos, and crowded flocks of songbirds linked by sweeping foliage. The tentmakers' depiction of fish has followed a similar course, starting with references from ancient Egyptian art and now drawing more from color-saturated advertisements for coral reef resorts like Sharm al-Sheikh and Hurghada, rather than the native fish of the Nile.

Sha'bi (Folkloric) Motifs

Just as modern Egyptian artists looked to the fields of the fellahin for an expression of Egypt's national identity, so did the tentmakers of Cairo. Ancient sources dominate the touristic khayamiya, but modern life in Egypt was also a popular subject matter. These can be called *sha'bi* khayamiya, shaped by local references. These were selective—we don't see urban scenes of rising city skylines in *sha'bi* appliqué, nor planes, trains, and automobiles. We do find cruising feluccas with sails expanded, boisterous camel riders, exuberant wedding and Hajj processions, and stick-bearing donkey boys. The tentmakers also depicted the 'timeless' labor of water carriers and operators of the *shaduf*—an ancient irrigation device lifting water into fields from the Nile river. Veiled women, sometimes peering from palanquins (also sewn by the tentmakers), were carefully appliquéd with elaborate jewelery. Musicians and dancers drawn from ancient and modern sources also appear on a variety of khayamiya panels.

Though some of these motifs may have been seen by the tentmakers along their own street, the majority of *sha'bi* khayamiya were drawn from the orientalist photographs of the Zangaki Brothers, Lehnert and Landrock, Bonfils, J. Pascal Sebah, and many others. These images were rearranged as the tentmakers saw fit, having already proved their commercial appeal as postcards for tourists. The photographic aesthetic that upheld a nostalgic and picturesque version of Egypt, rather than the progressive and changing realities of the early twentieth century, appealed to tourists' expectations. Images based on the prints of the nineteenth-century Scottish artist David Roberts are now being revisited in lurid colors and complex patterned fabrics, as the tentmakers continue to adopt Orientalist references for the production of new khayamiya designs.

The Tents of Tourists

Perhaps the most ambitious application of touristic khayamiya was also the most infrequently seen: the complete tent. Yet their international distribution is also extensive and surprising, as some were collected as very large souvenirs by wealthy travelers. The most typically collected of these were circular and single-masted enclosed tents known as *fustat*, which bear close similarities to the Ottoman tents used and depicted by Napoleon's savants during the compilation of the *Description de l'Egypte*.

The popularity of khayamiya tents as mesmerizing dining spaces and hotels is well documented through numerous photographs from the early twentieth century, including a noteworthy collection of glass slides in

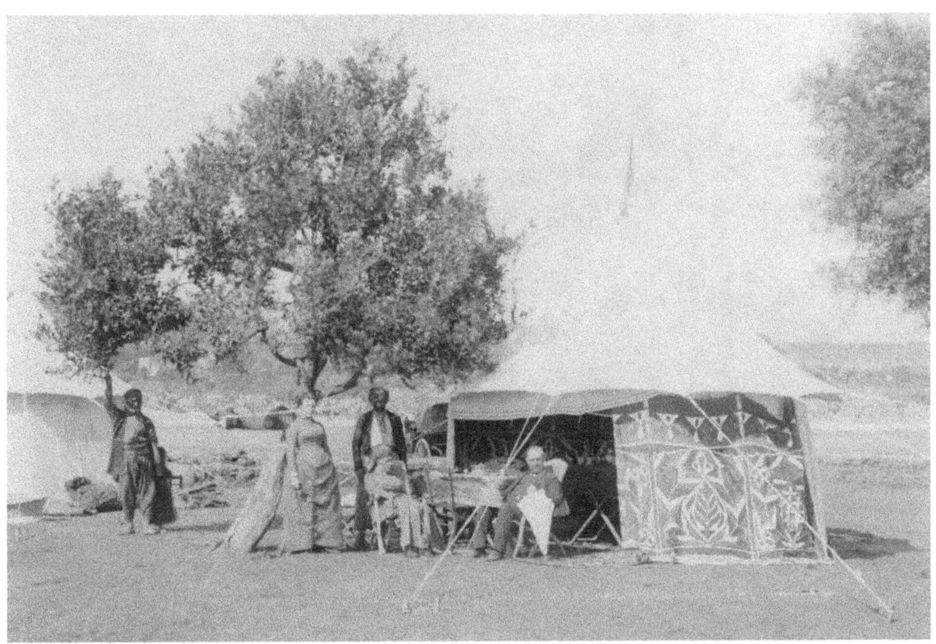

Figure 13 Travelers with an Egyptian tent, likely 1880s–1900s. National Library of Congress.

the Library of Congress. These include records of the American Colony missionaries in Jerusalem, who traveled with a series of impressive khayamiya screens and enclosed tents in the early 1940s. The Thomas Cook agency used khayamiya tents as dining areas in Egypt and Jordan (specifically near Petra), some of which were described as a 'Jewish Tabernacle Tent' in photographic archives. In 1914 the American-British writer Alice Muriel Williamson described an oasis lunch within a big "open-fronted, awninged luncheon-tent . . . lined with Egyptian appliqué work in many colors, the porch-like roof extension supported by poles." This description evokes the khedival tents depicted by Reginald Barrett in 1907, as well as the structure and scale of the *suradiq* now in Doddington Hall in Lincolnshire, England. Although Williamson did not describe the ornament within her tent, she noted that it was a picturesque feature within the Egyptian landscape, complemented by a frame of green palms, against a "silver-white desert, hotter than gold" casting "turquoise blue shadows."[17]

Records exist of khayamiya tents specifically made for European travelers and archaeologists, such as Max von Oppenheim's 1893 tent used at the Tell Halaf expedition in 1929, or the anonymous travelers depicted in

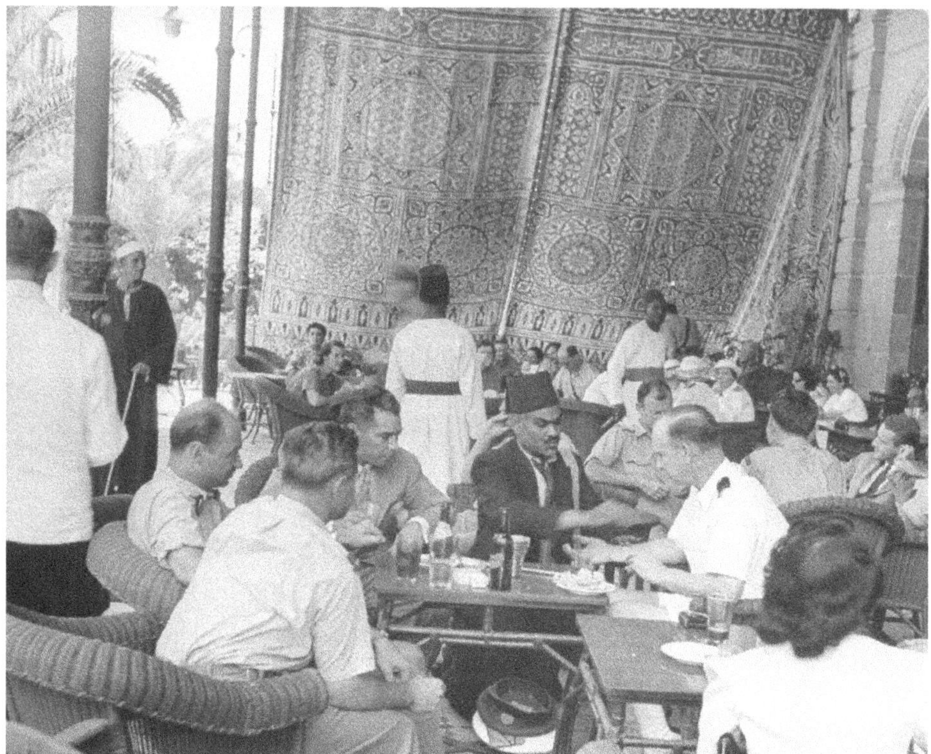

Figure 14 Robert Landry, *Terrace of Shepheard's Hotel*, Cairo, 1956. Getty Images.

Palestine from the collection of the Library of Congress (fig. 13).[18] Some of these were fixed in place as venues for photographs and meals, such as the record of Rosicrucians visiting the Giza Pyramids (also in 1929), or the souvenir from the Khomais restaurant (once located at 8 26th July Street), which depicts two tired tourists seated before an appliquéd *mahmal* procession to Mecca led by riders on camels and a donkey.[19]

Mary Roberts Rinehart in *Nomad's Land* (1926)—which was also cited in Blaire Gagnon's study of tentmaker appliqués in 2003—describes her experiences of well-catered tents while on safari in the Egyptian desert:

> Three large circular tents were our shelters, erected umbrella-fashion on great central poles, each pole carried in two sections; the tops were extended by ropes fastened to stakes driven into the sand, and the side walls were then hung from the tops.[20]

Though their sleeping tents were unadorned, their large dining tent was the centerpiece of this trio:

> No ordinary tent this, but one of the finest specimens of the tent-maker's art. It had been made in the Street of the Tent-Makers in Cairo, where all day long men sit cross-legged on the earthen floors of their workrooms, their hands calloused from the heavy canvas, cutting out designs in vivid colours and sewing them to the thick cream-coloured base. Here was Cleopatra, in red and blue, reclining on a yellow barge upon a bright green Nile; here was Seti I as a youth, in a rose skirt and not much more, except the double crown of Upper and Lower Egypt, here were slaves in golden yellow collars, and Sphinxes and camels, pyramids and donkeys, and gods with heads of beasts and sacred bulls—all in strong and primitive colours. All sewed with millions of stitches to make our tent a gorgeous thing, and to bring into the desert the colour it so badly lacks.[21]

Douglas Sladen's visit to the Karun hotel also accounts for a 'delightful' scene, once his vociferous opposition to touristic khayamiya is overlooked:

> Everyone who sees this hotel, called the Karun, is delighted with it. . . . The hotel is built of canvas—the gay awnings of the Arab tentmaker. It stands on a stretch of gravel, with patches of gay flowers at its edges, and a thick fringe of reeds twelve feet high all round; and sometimes in winter it must be all upstairs, for the basement, built of more substantial materials, is probably under water in flood-time. The upstairs, divided into the drawing and dining rooms, is simply a tent of rich Arab stuffs and awnings covered with parodies of ancient Egyptian life . . .
>
> The sleeping arrangements of this hotel are very pleasant for those in need of a thorough change after the artificialities of Cairo; the bedrooms are two huts and as many reed-thatched sleeping-tents as happened to be required. As the dining-rooms and drawing-rooms are also canvas, one combines the pleasures of camping out with the comforts of a fair hotel.[22]

One of the most dramatic recorded uses of khayamiya for tourists were the terrace awnings of the Shepheard's Hotel in Cairo, which also erected a small *fustat* tent on a high balcony.[23] Though replaced several times, and likely burned in the catastrophic fire of January 26, 1952, these huge hand-sewn panels transformed the terrace of the hotel into a semi-permanent *suradiq*, including a long calligraphic fringe (see fig. 14).

Comparable awnings are still featured in the Old Cataract hotel at Aswan, though these now consist of imitation khayamiya fabrics. The Grand Hotel Helwan also suspended khedival khayamiya awnings under a veranda, providing a fine view for those reclined below.[24] The staircase and 'Egyptian Salon' of the Hotel Continental, as photographed by Gabriel Lekegian around 1870–90, was wrapped in khayamiya ceilings, awnings, and cornices, reflected in large mirrors and echoing the woven carpets underfoot.

Camp Tents

The Scout movement is indelibly associated with tents, and khayamiya tents were used by delegations of Egyptian scouts for many years as a distinctive expression of national identity. An example was raised at the 1933 World Scout Jamboree in Hungary, described by a young American witness with enthusiasm:

> The Egyptians were well worth photographing. They looked very exciting with their red *tarbouches* [red fez] posing in front of their temple-like gateway, or their picturesque tents. We wondered for a moment whether these boys hadn't the right idea about tents. The outsides were plain light colors, but the insides were gayly [sic] decorated with designs, such as you see on oriental wall tapestries. When you sat down in them, you immediately felt in a festive mood. But the really dangerous part of them was the trying to get out. In front of each tent was a mob of people, craning their necks to get a peek of the strange looking interiors. You couldn't blame them. That's what they had come for—to see how the other parts of the world live.[25]

This exoticism is also seen in the tent commissioned by Dr. Lucien Calvin Warner, a lingerie manufacturer, for the Adirondack League Club around 1906–08. Although it was used for camping expeditions in New York state, the appliqué and original colors of this tent remain very well preserved. The wall panels present a frieze of ancient deities loosely inspired by the Book of the Dead. By contrast, the ceiling is adorned with vibrant khedival abstractions in orange, yellow, light and dark blue—the same palette as the walls, which suggests these separate parts were designed by the same workshop. Strangely, the Warner tent does not possess an *'arusa* border, nor any alternative pattern to replace this motif. It now lends a dramatic accent to the Adirondack Camping Museum, which also sells a souvenir umbrella based on the ceiling of this remarkable 'camp' tent.[26]

Comparable tents, alternating between panels in touristic and late-khedival styles, have been found in several other collections—notably the vibrant example in the Gregg Museum in North Carolina[27]—but not all touristic tents were as gaudy as these. The finely-sewn tent band owned by Randy Pace (in Houston, Texas) depicts a sequence of eleven deities. It has been very carefully prepared, including details as subtle as fingernails, patterned hair, and clothing with delicate embellishments, unlike the ad-libbed hieroglyphics and wide columns seen on other touristic tents.

This band was allegedly linked to the excavation of Tutankhamun's Tomb in 1922—the story being that it sheltered objects displayed for dignitaries making site visits. This story is feasible, but not conclusively documented. A single-poled Egyptian tent was installed near the excavation for this purpose by Carter and his team, but the style of the interior is unknown. Comparable tents are also owned by Elmer and Lillian Elsea, acquired in 1931,[28] and one was allegedly given by King Abdullah of Jordan (grandfather of King Hussein) to Sir Henry Cox, the British Representative in Transjordan until 1939.

A Note on Provenance

Unverifiable but alluring provenances of khayamiya are quite common. Given that many of these were acquired as follies (ornamental structures for occasional enjoyment, rather than regular rigorous use) or sold on by second-hand dealers, their origin stories are likely to be embellished. One of the most colorful accounts belongs to the Egyptian tent in the Saunders Museum in Berryville, Arkansas, which is primarily a collection of guns and hunting trophies. However, Colonel Charles 'Buck' Saunders and his wife Gertrude also acquired a khedival khayamiya tent during an expedition to Egypt, which was allegedly won as a prize following a shooting contest with an Arab shaykh.[29] It is prominently displayed upside-down in a souvenir postcard from the 1960s alongside several touristic panels and what appears to be the gold-embroidered calligraphic band from a *mahmal*. The caption reads:

> The late Col. Saunders traveled extensively in Arabia where he obtained many objects for his famous collection. A sheik's harem of 200 wives made this colorful tent, hand woven and embroidered. The panels, of Egyptian origin, are decorated with threads of gold. Also on exhibit is the harness for a camel.[30]

The late-khedival tent now in the collection of the Islamic Arts Museum Malaysia was also delivered with a fanciful provenance story (see plate 18). It was acquired in 2001 from the collection of James D. Burns, a Seattle-based lawyer and textile collector, who noted that it had been erected annually on his lawn to celebrate his mother's birthday. The unlikely part was the attribution to "a wedding for one of the daughters of Abbas Hilmi II, the last Khedive of Egypt, in 1903." This is unlikely, as Hilmi had four daughters, only one of whom married, and that was in Istanbul on May 5, 1923.[31] Heba Barakat, the Head Curator of the IAMM, also noted that the design is inconsistent with an Egyptian "bridal" tent.[32] It is now thought to have more in common with tents like that held in the collection of Killruddery House in Ireland, or the tent of the Jackson Hole Historical Society (the Smelker Tent) in Wyoming,[33] as a vibrant folly from the late 1920s or 1930s.

The 'Morton Tent' of the Oriental Institute in Chicago has a very well-documented provenance, with appliqué comparable to, if stylistically later or more modern than, the tent in Kuala Lumpur. The shape is quite distinct, bearing four sides in a square format; it was commissioned for the Morton family who used it to host receptions from the 1930s onwards. The curator John Carswell described it as "a splendid example of its genre, in almost perfect condition."[34]

Individual khayamiya panels are even less likely to retain a well-documented provenance. One example in the British Museum was donated by a Mrs. Henry Perrin in 1939, claiming it had been brought to the United Kingdom by Captain Tristam C. Speedy on his return from Ethiopia (then Abyssinia) in 1868. Speedy was a well-known figure in British history whose travels were extensive, but the design of this panel is more consistent with panels in the Newark Museum in New Jersey, collected and commissioned by John Cotton Dana in 1929, than the designs of the 1870s. The lesson to be taken from this is that a good narrative helps these textiles to sell, regardless of its veracity.

Khedival Tents

It is incorrect to assume that all tourists' tents were touristic in style. Several touristic tents in khedival styles are known around the world, most held in private collections. Three of the most spectacular and accessible are the nineteenth-century tents of the Semitic Museum at Harvard University and the Tent Room of Doddington Hall in Lincolnshire (United Kingdom), as well as the early twentieth-century tent of the Islamic Arts Museum in Malaysia.

Rebecca and Francis B. Greene collected their *fustat* tent during their Egyptian honeymoon in 1879–80, following a camping expedition to Giza.

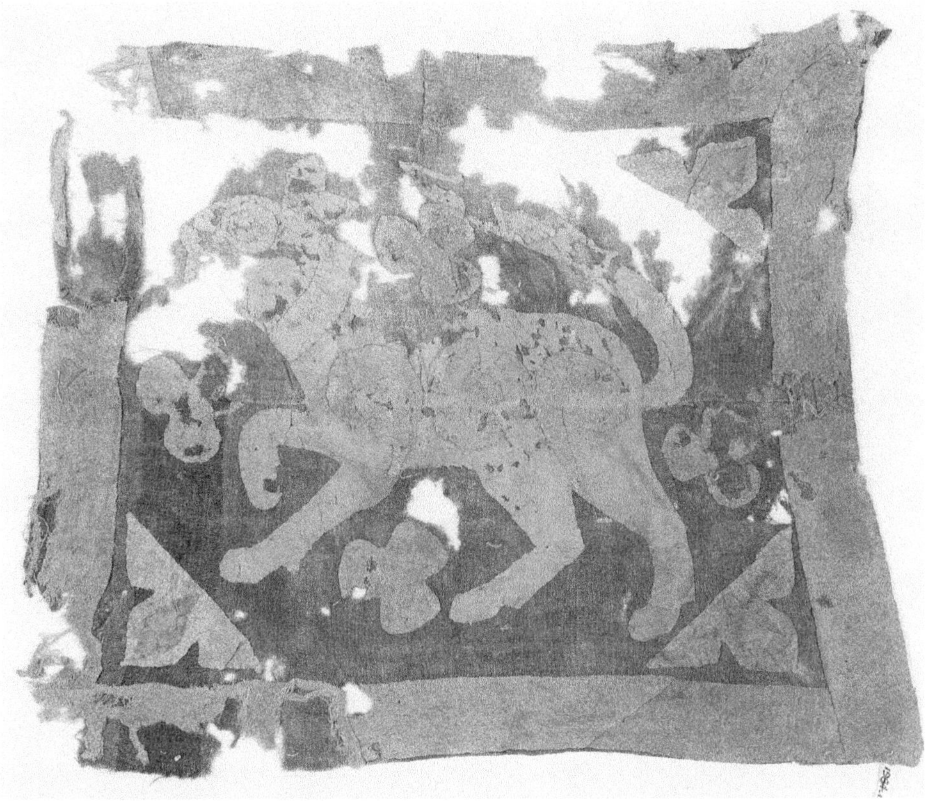

1 A Fatimid appliquéd panel from Cairo. This piece probably came from a banner or standard. Photograph courtesy of the Ashmolean Museum, Oxford.

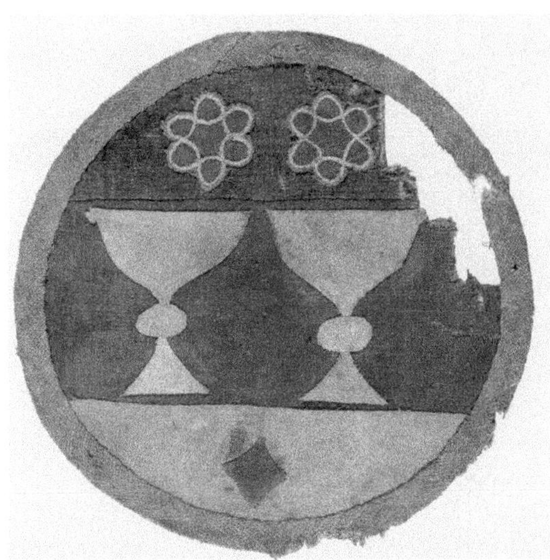

2 Appliqué is particularly effective for executing bold designs relying heavily on contrast, ideal for Mamluk heraldic emblems such as this one. Photograph courtesy of the Textile Museum, Washington DC.

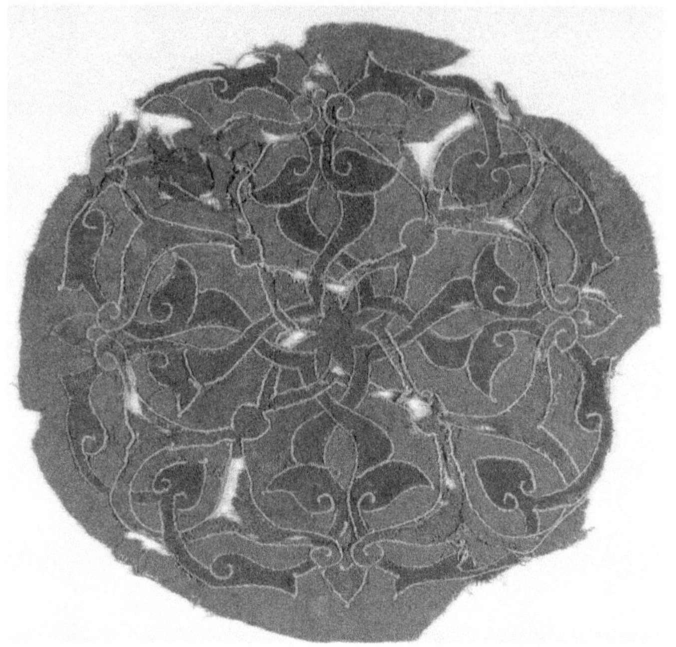

3 Elaborate arabesque designs were a common feature of Mamluk art, as seen in this appliquéd textile from the fourteenth or fifteenth century. Similar designs are still produced today. Photograph courtesy of the Ashmolean Museum, Oxford.

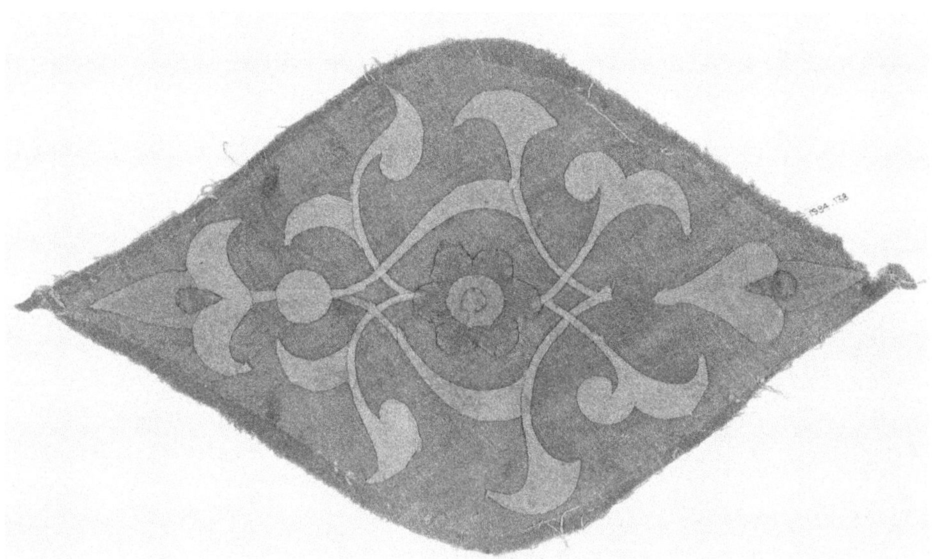

4 Large appliquéd fragments such as this one, measuring 55 cm x 39 cm, indicate that the same technique was used in 'architectural textiles' for centuries. Photograph courtesy of the Ashmolean Museum, Oxford.

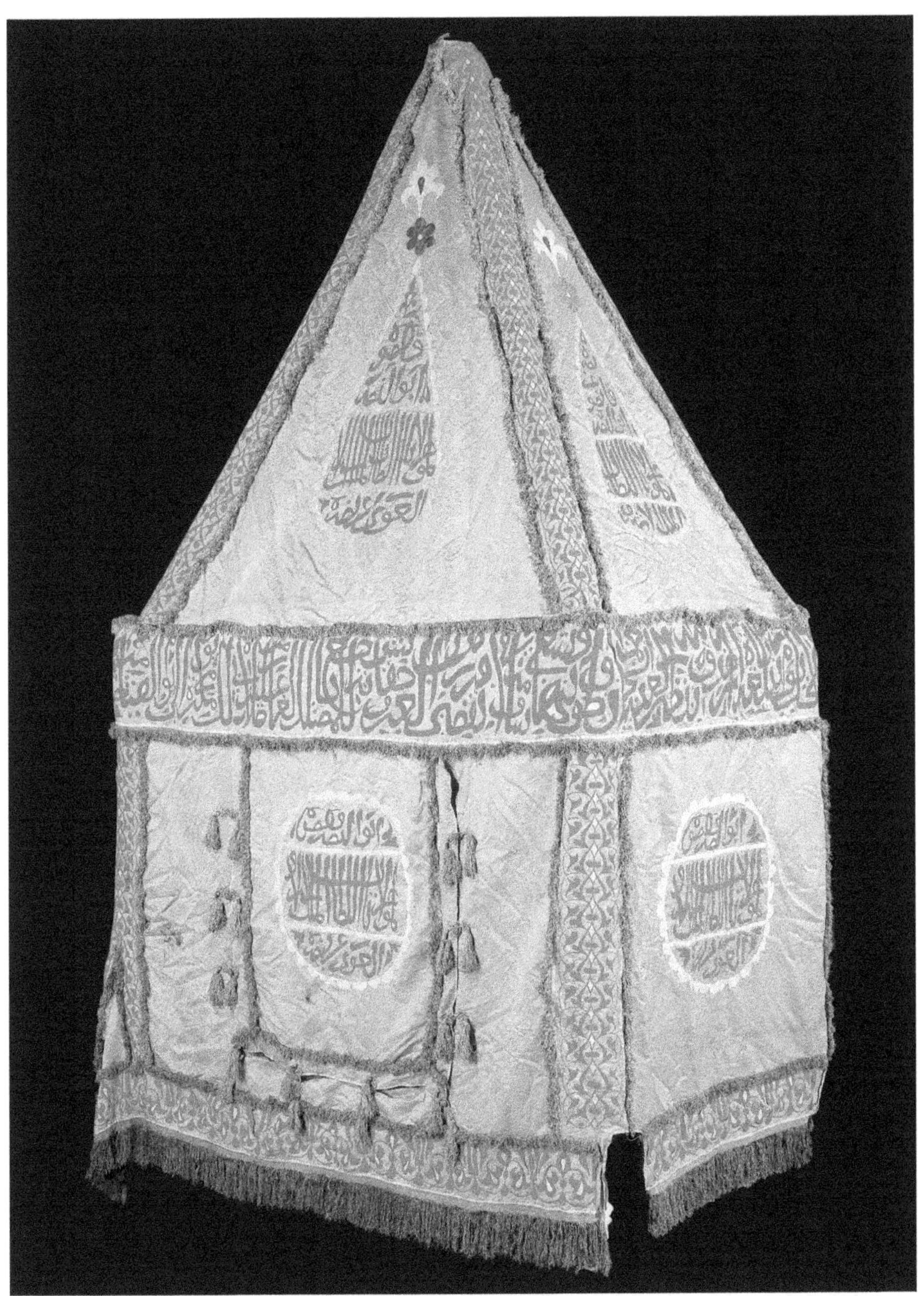

5 Mamluk chronicles often mention red and yellow textiles used by the court. This appliquéd *mahmal* of Sultan al-Ghuri, dating from the early 1500s, is one of the most impressive surviving examples. Photograph courtesy of the Topkapi Palace Museum Collection, Istanbul.

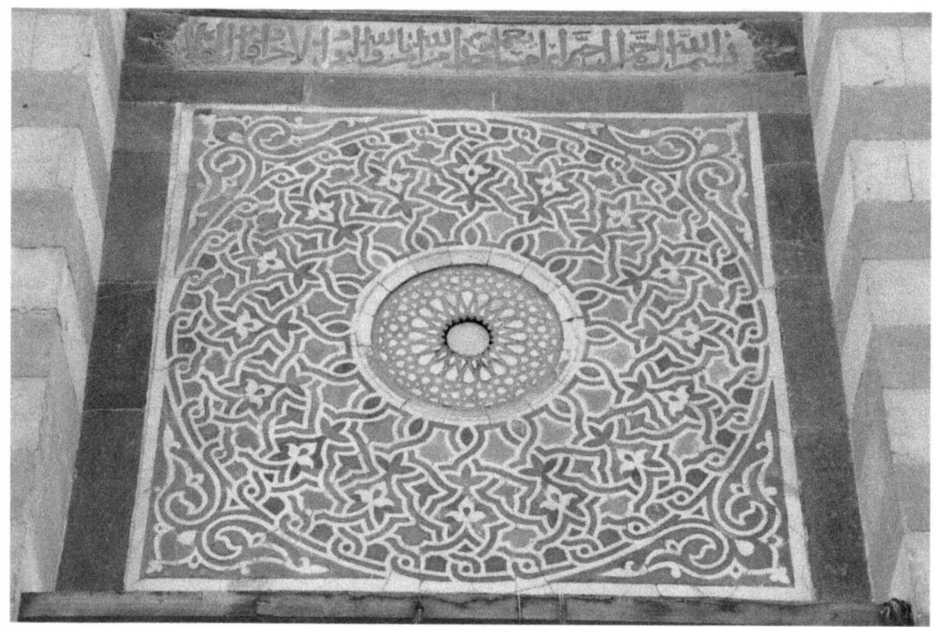

6 Inlaid marble panel from the Mosque of Aslam al-Silahdar (1300s). Note the similarity with the appliquéd textile shown in plate 3. Photograph by Ahmad El Bindary.

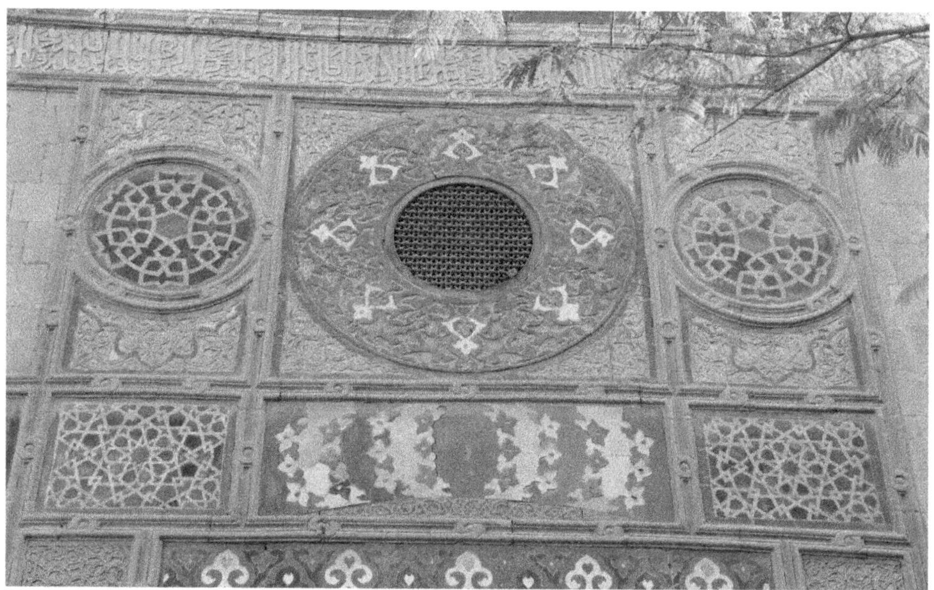

7 The *sabil-kuttab* of Qaytbay on Saliba Street. The parallels between Egyptian appliqué work and Mamluk architecture are striking—the tents of Cairo were essentially temporary architecture. Photograph by Ahmad El Bindary.

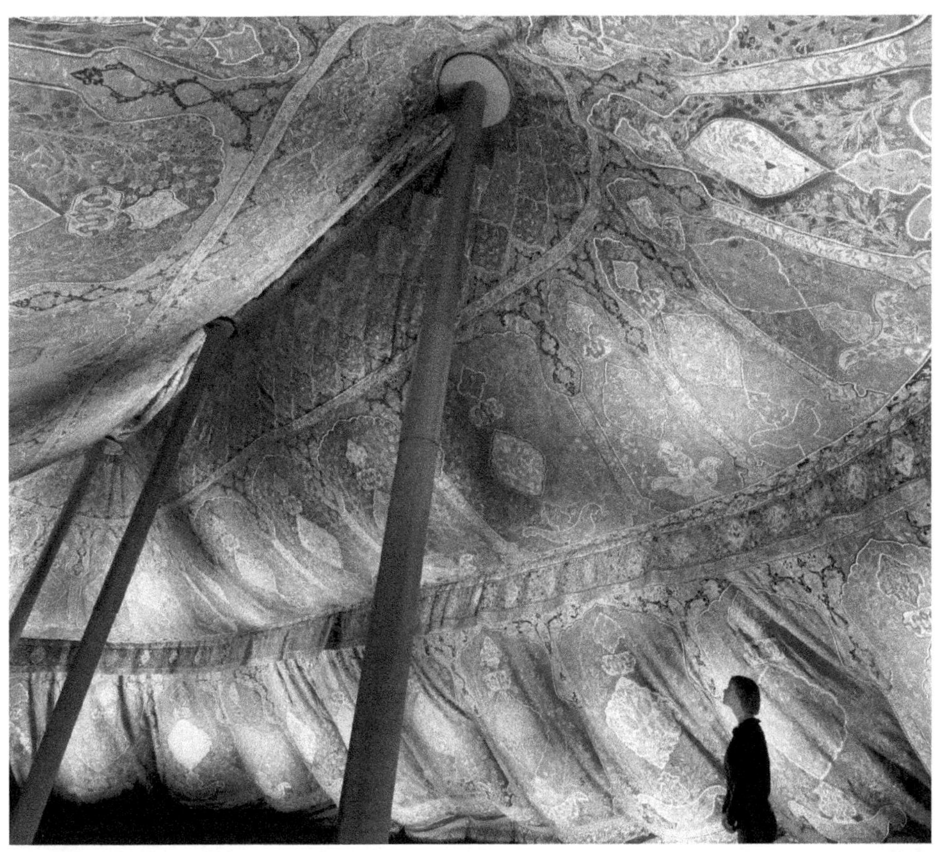

8 An Ottoman tent captured in 1683 at the siege of Vienna. Dresden State Art Collections. Photograph by Ralf Hirschberger, 2010. Alamy Stock Photo.

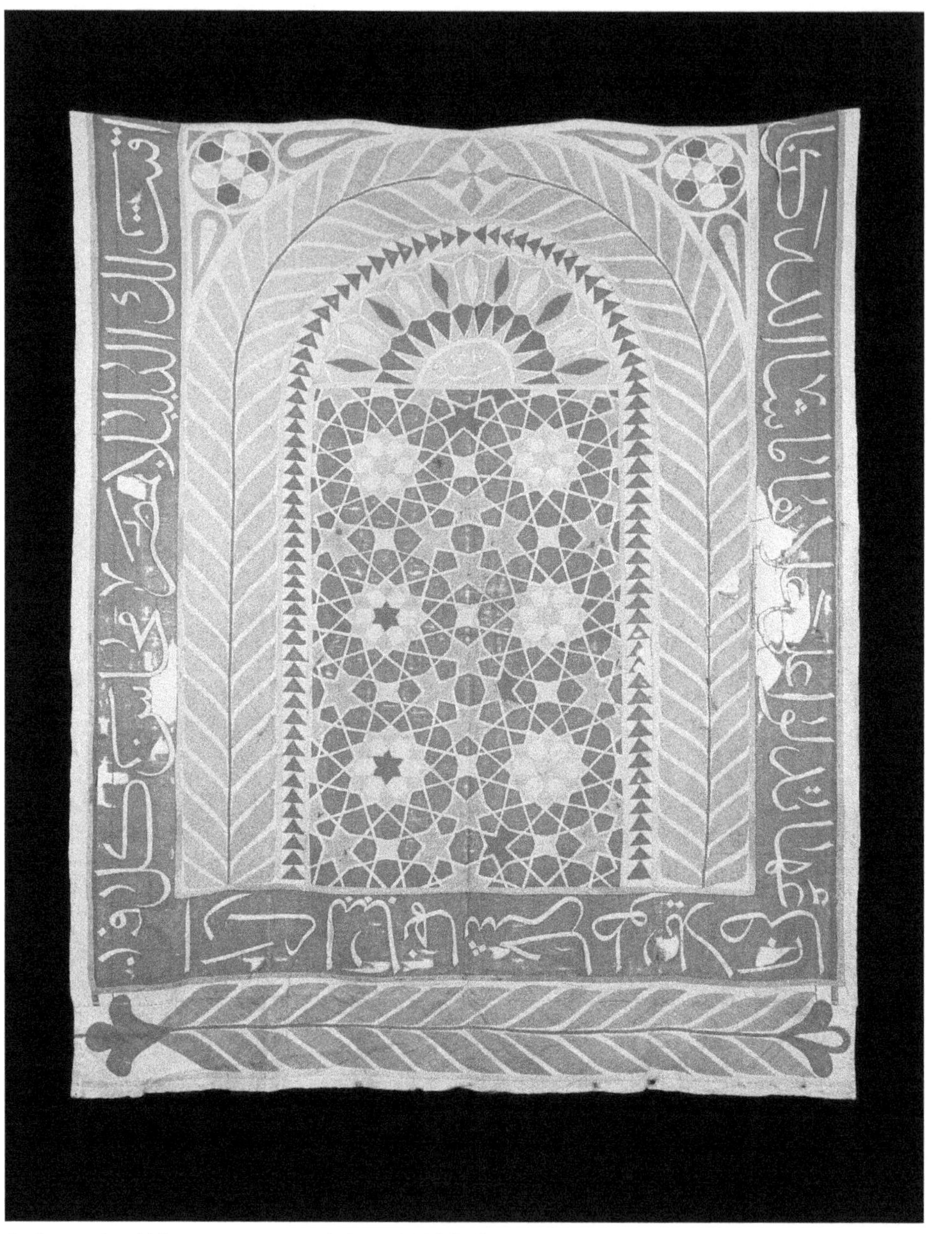

9 An arched khayamiya panel dated 1899. Compare this to the doorway dated 1883/1884 in figure 6 (p. 84). Private collection. Photograph by Oliver White.

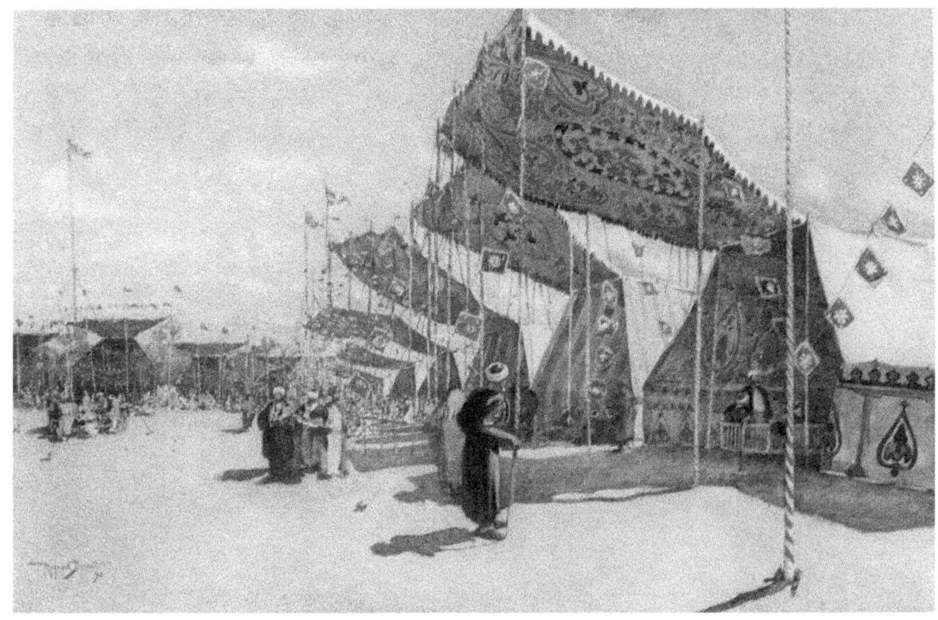

10 Reginald Barratt, *The Mawlid*, 1907.

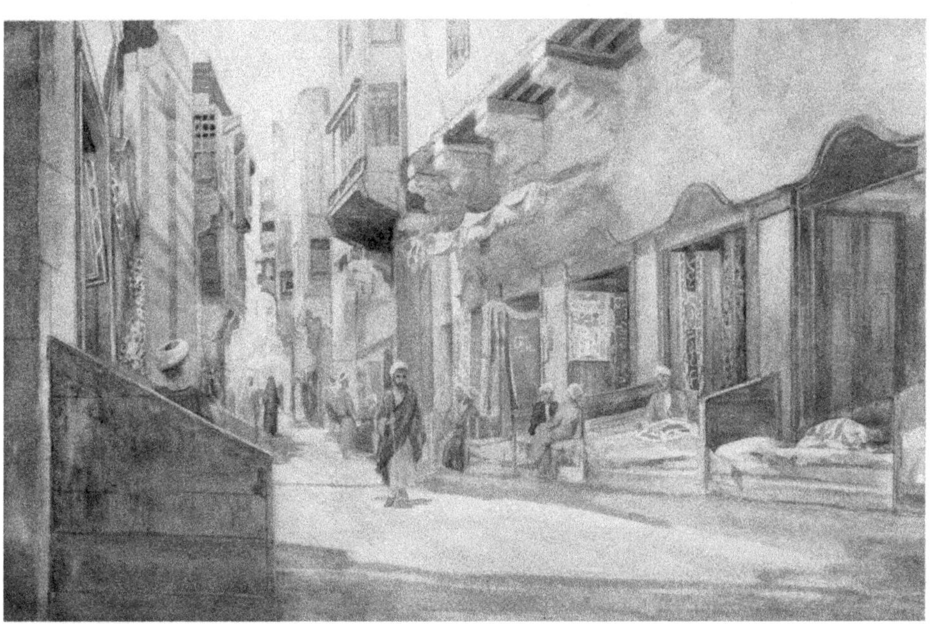

11 Reginald Barratt, *The Street of the Tentmakers*, 1907.

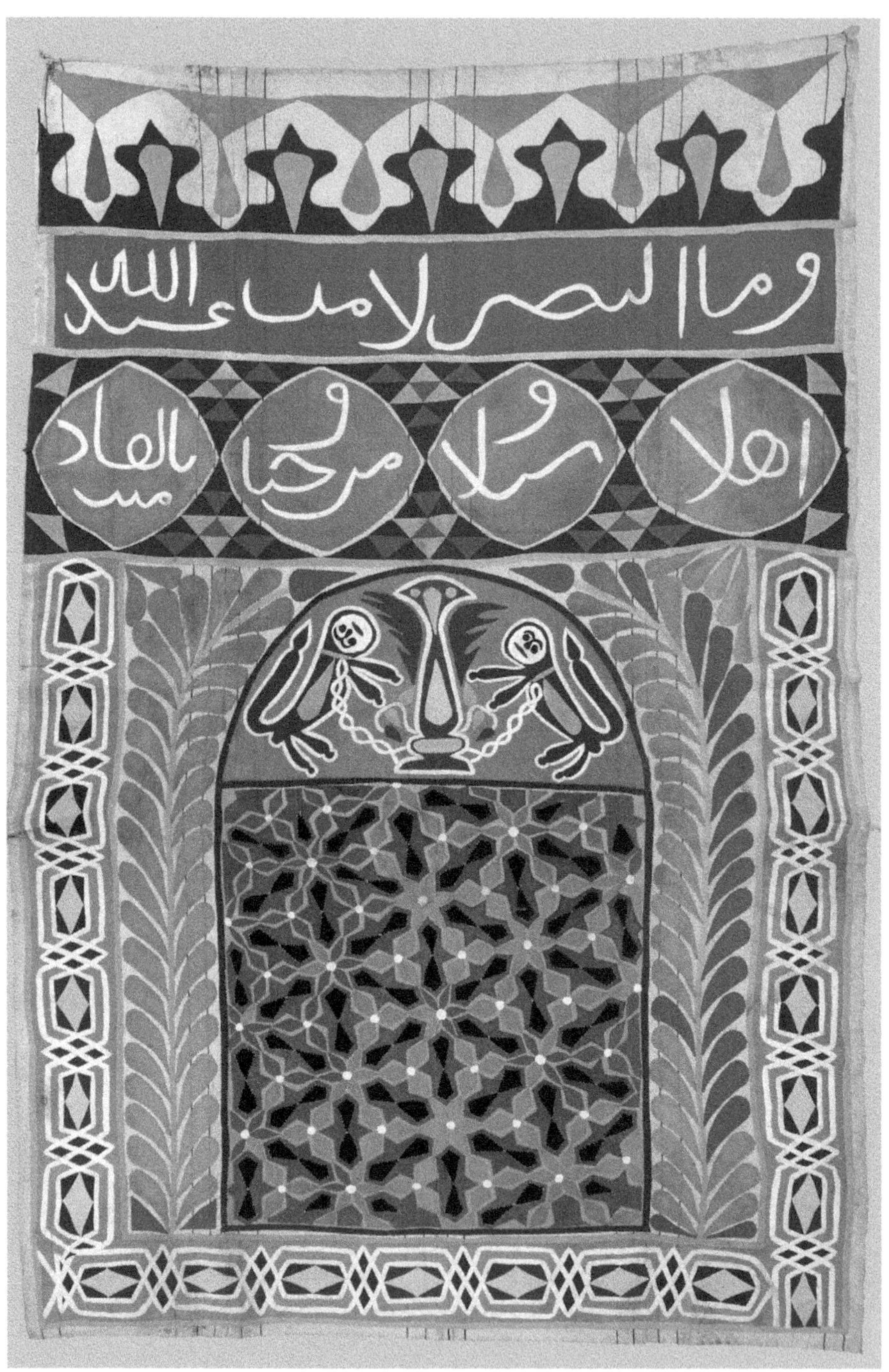

12 The khedival-era 'Two Lions' Panel of the British Museum, pre-1928. Photograph courtesy of the Trustees of the British Museum.

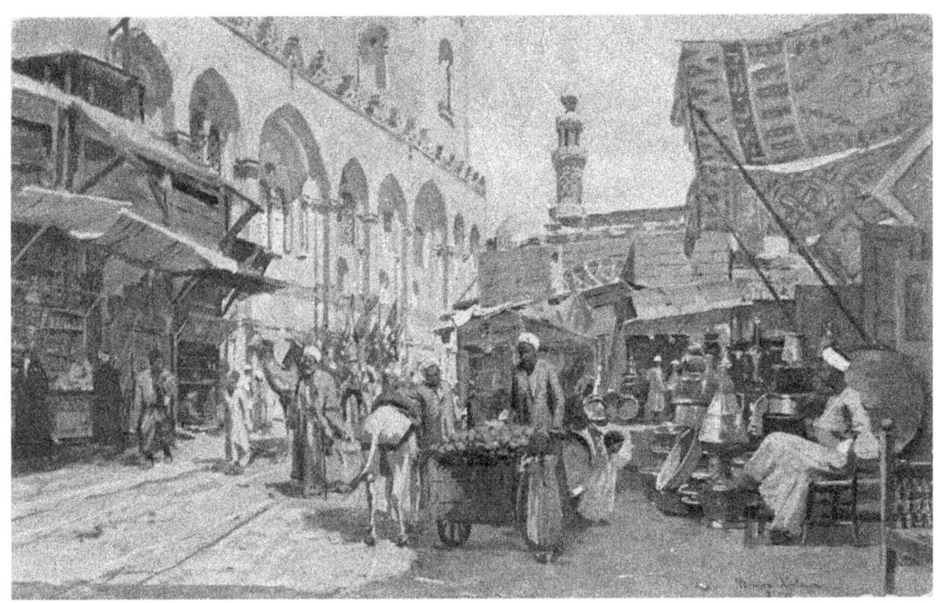

13 Khayamiya awnings on shops along the main street of historic Cairo, today known as al-Mu'izz Street. Print after painting by Alberto Rossi.

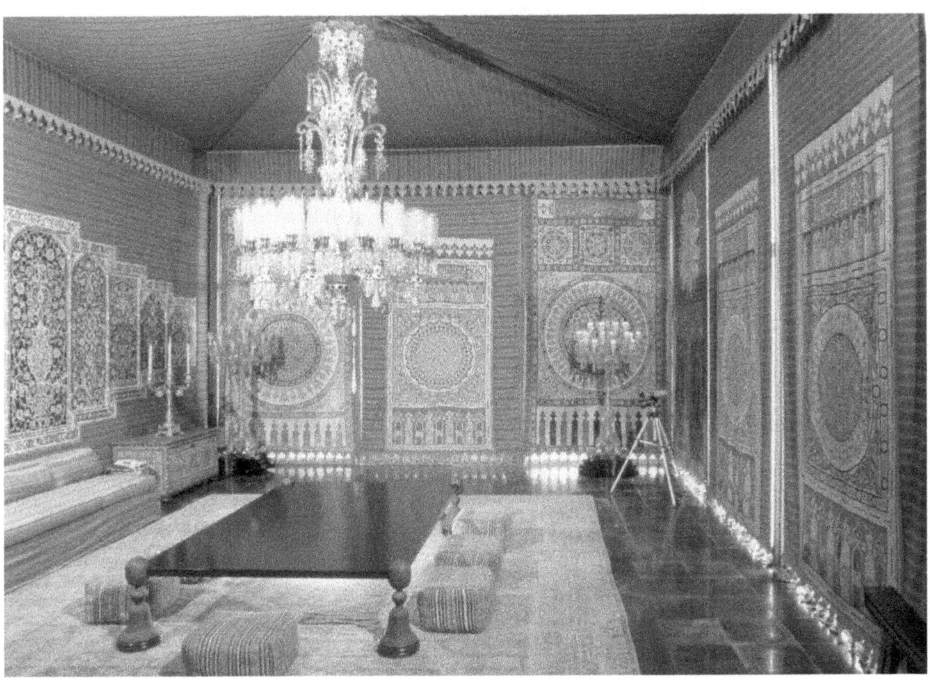

14 The dining room of Doris Duke at her Shangri-La mansion, Honolulu, features elaborate appliqué work from the early twentieth century. Photograph by David Franzen.

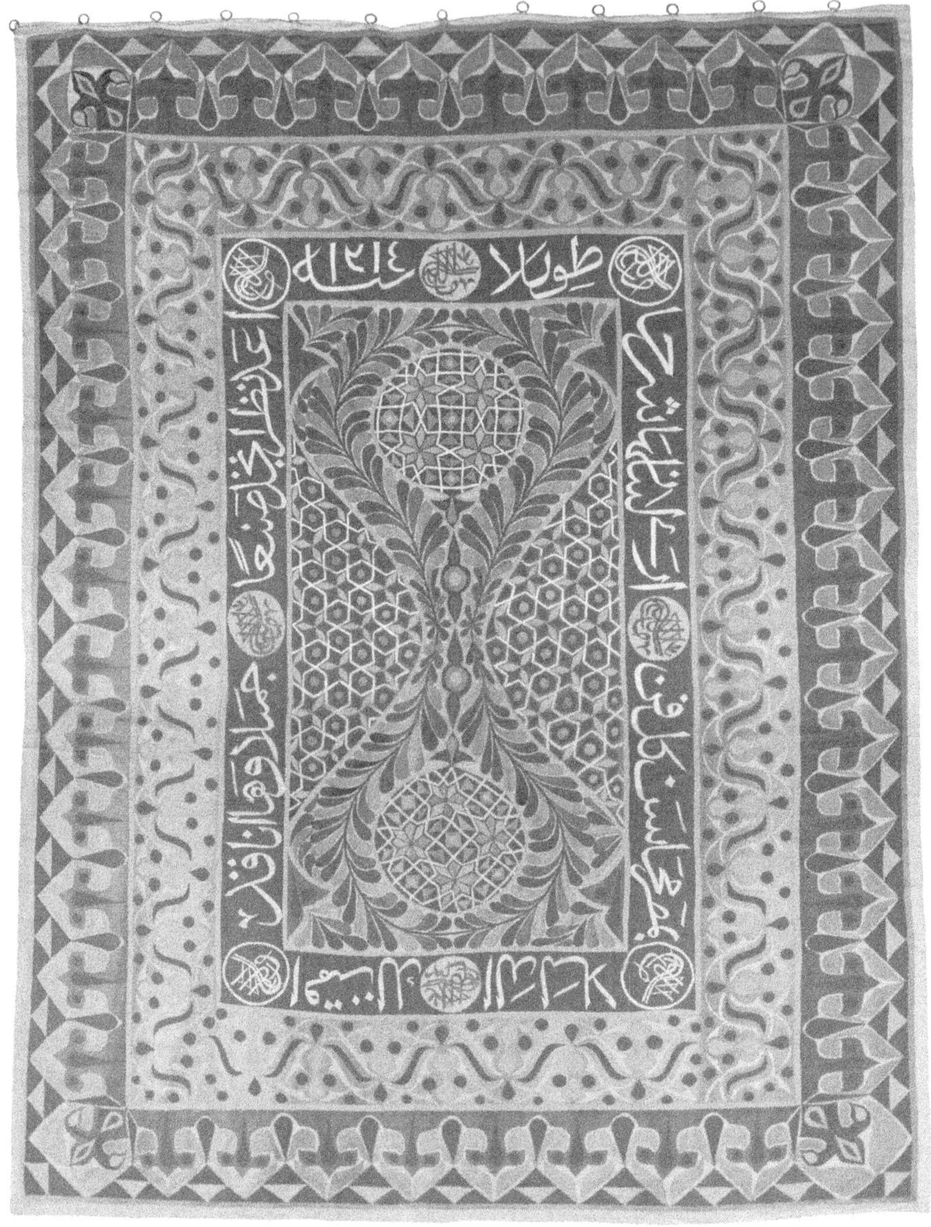

15 The Milan Panel, 1899. Private collection. Photograph by Timothy Crutchett.

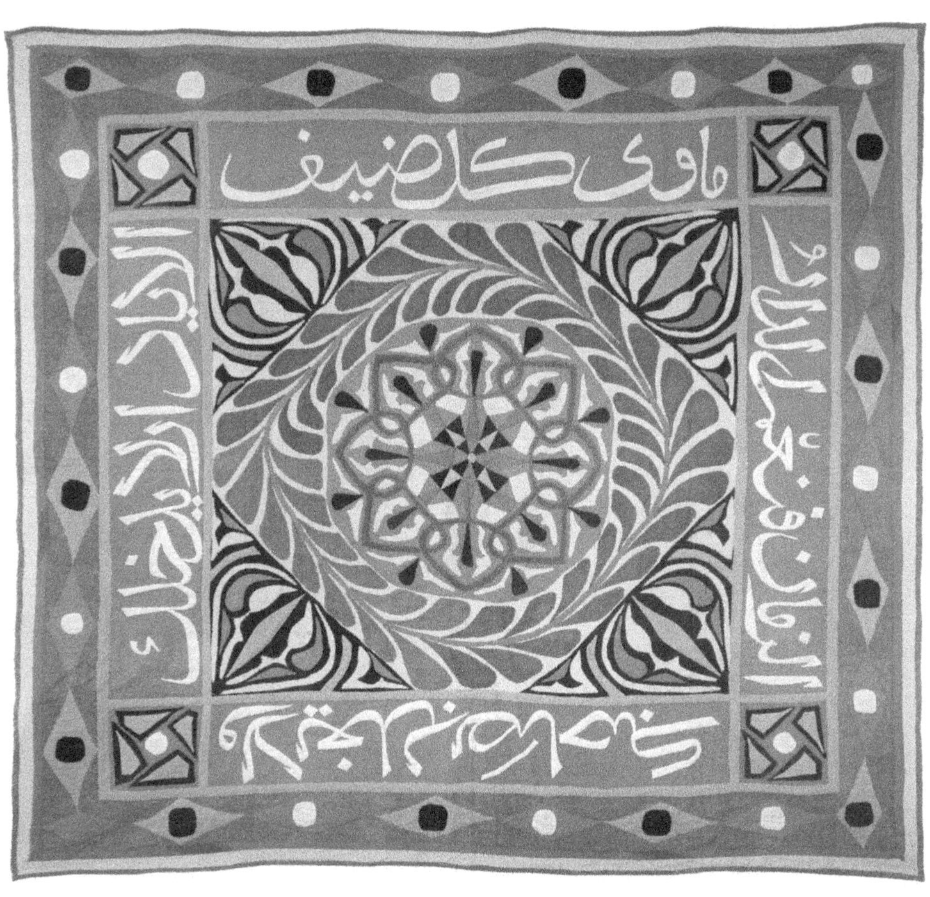

16 The Bath Panel, ca. 1900. Private collection. Photograph by Seif El Rashidi, edited by Timothy Crutchett.

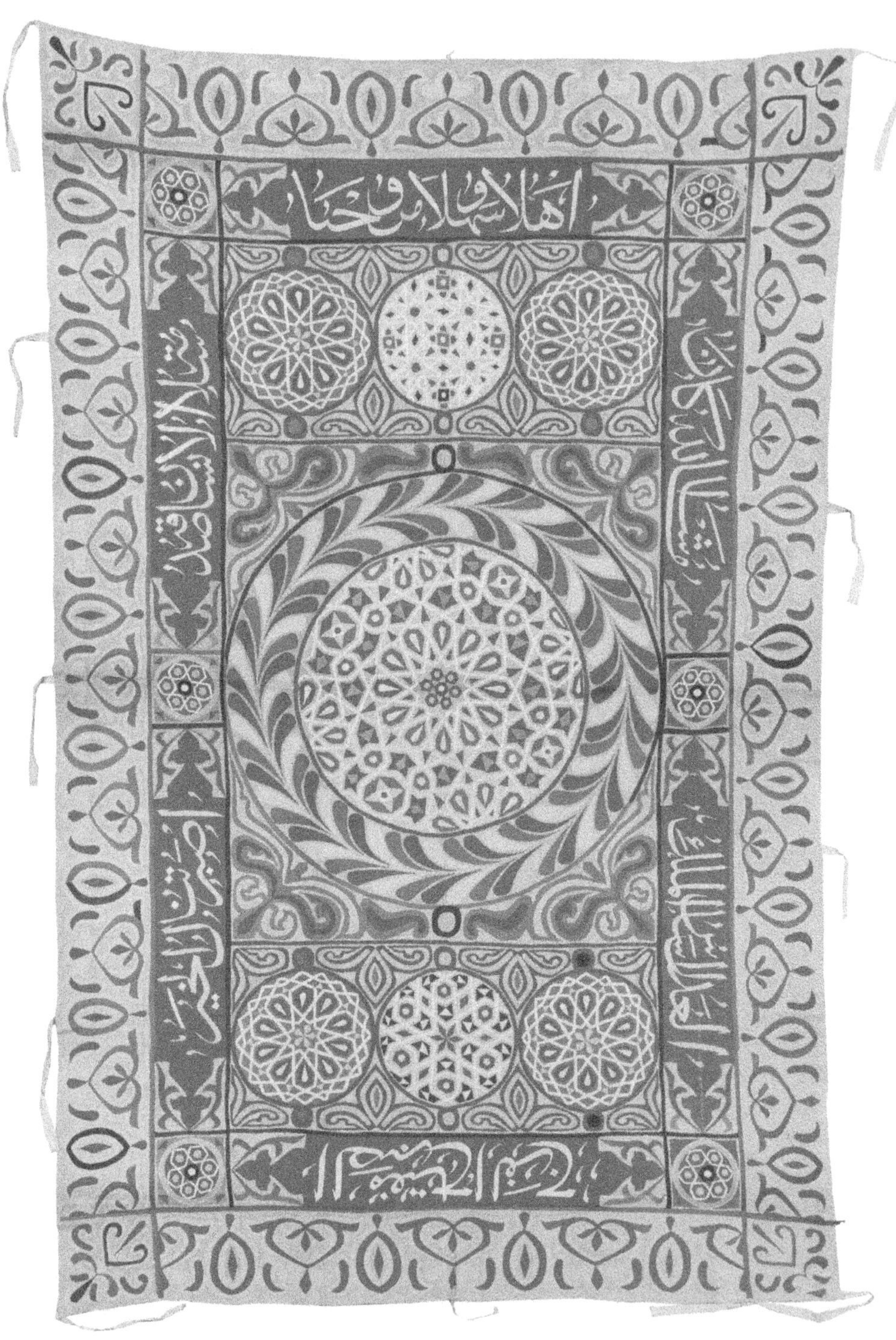

17 The Syme Panel, ca. 1900. Private collection. Photograph by Timothy Crutchett.

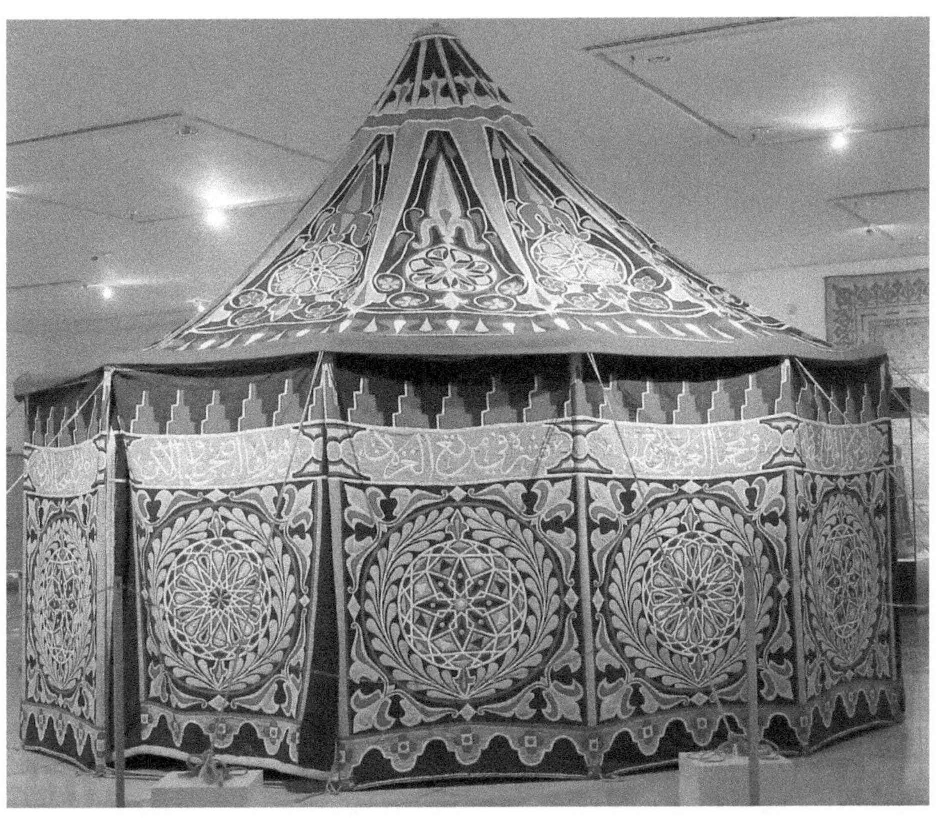

18 The Egyptian Tent of the Islamic Arts Museum Malaysia, Kuala Lumpur. Photograph courtesy of the Islamic Arts Museum Malaysia.

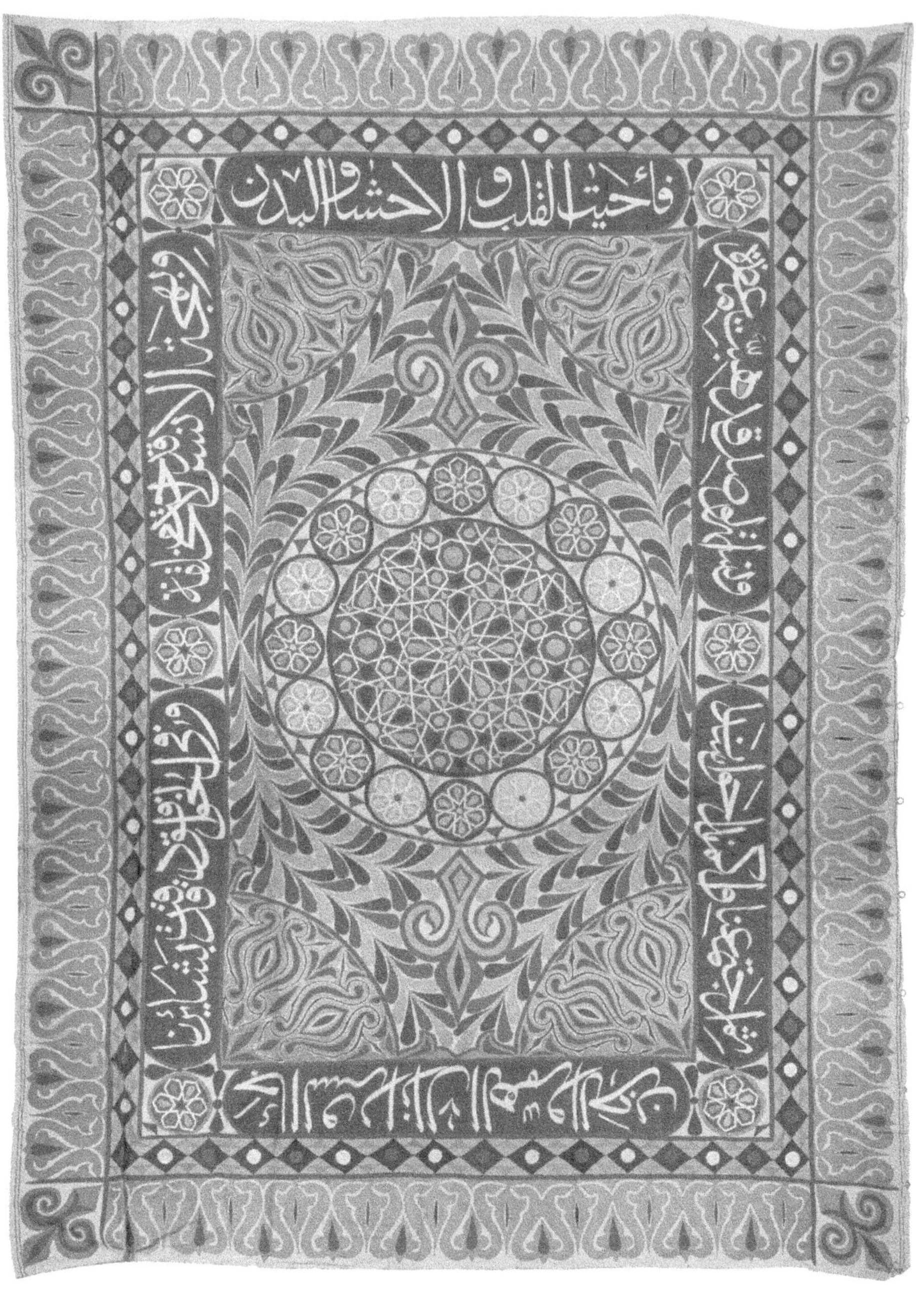

19 The Rhode Island Panel, ca. 1900–30s. Private collection. Photograph by Timothy Crutchett.

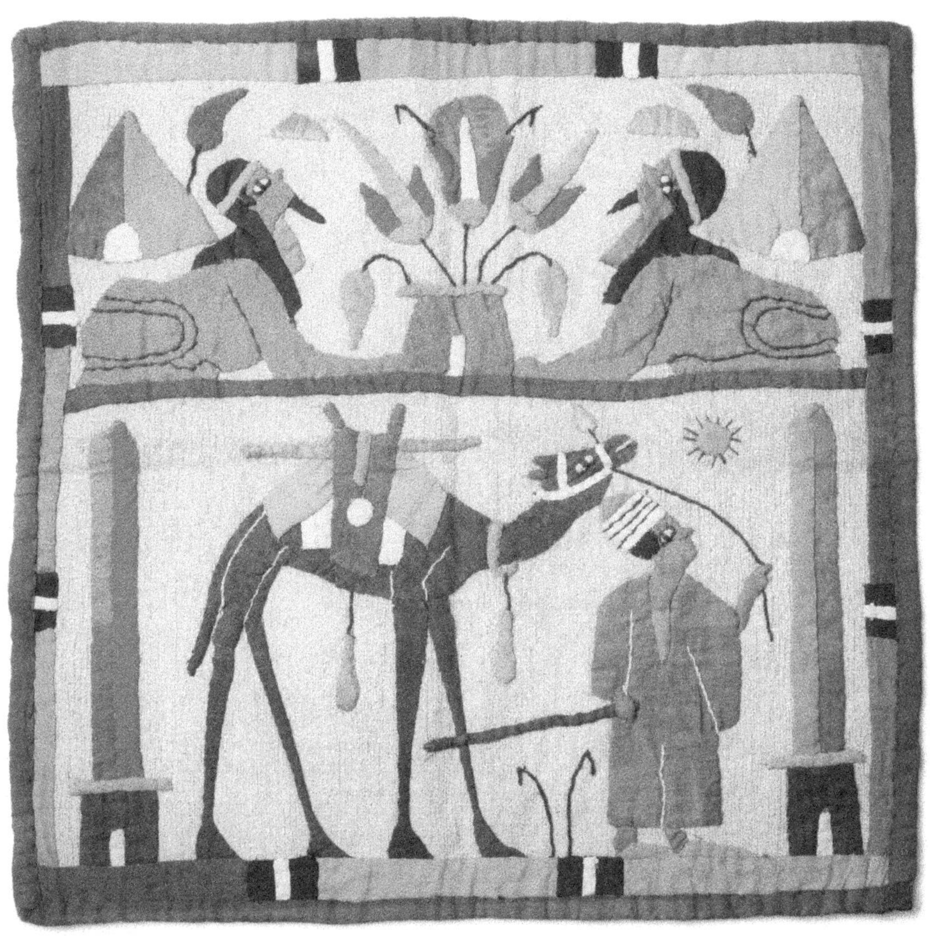

20 The Ashcroft Panel, early 1940s. Private collection. Photograph by Timothy Crutchett.

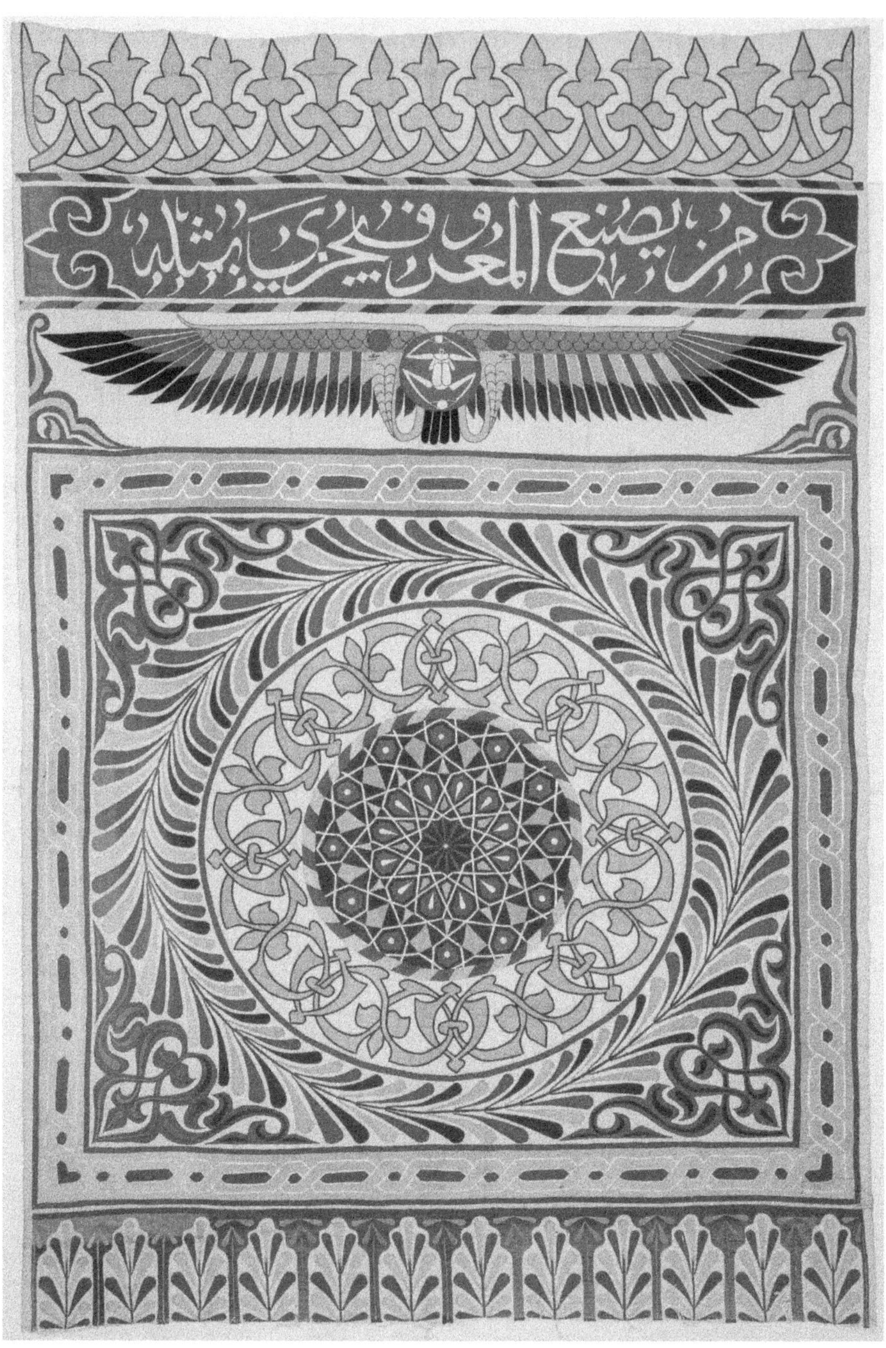

21 A late khedival khayamiya in the Islamic Arts Museum Malaysia, featuring hybrid aspects of the touristic genre. Likely late 1920s. Photograph courtesy of the Islamic Arts Museum Malaysia.

It returned with the newlyweds to North Dartmouth, Massachusetts. In 1896, the Greenes donated it to their neighbors (the family of Oliver Prescott), where it was used as a children's cubbyhouse. In 1986, after nine decades of service in the Prescotts' backyard, the tent was gifted to the Semitic Museum of Harvard University.[35] There it is pitched by a team of four people for the annual Commencement on Divinity Avenue, in order to host guests. This echoes the ceremonial use of khayamiya in Egypt and creates an opportunity to inspect the condition of the tent.[36]

The structure of the Harvard Tent is typical of most surviving khedival-style tents. A circular perimeter band connects with wooden toggles to a bell-like top, 4 m high and ca. 4.8 m in diameter. This is held in place by a central pole secured by about twenty ropes, reinforced in turn with wooden slats concealed within the walls at regular intervals.

The white canvas is hand-appliquéd with khedival-style designs in red, green, yellow, blue, and black. These ornaments bear similarities to earlier Ottoman tents, particularly in the alternate-repeat band of circular motifs capped with tri-lobed fleur-de-lys or *'arusa* motifs, surrounded by a floriated wreath pattern. Compared to earlier Ottoman tents, here we see a more 'vernacular' composition, distinguished by broader pieces of appliqué drawn from a brighter and more limited color range. This results in a dynamic and lively interior showcasing the gusto of the Egyptian tentmakers against their more elegant Ottoman predecessors, in which finer figurative realism of vegetative forms might be anticipated. Joseph A. Greene (director of the Semitic Museum, and no relation to Francis B. Greene) has associated the khedival ornament of the Harvard Tent to the 'Mamluk Revival' design movement. Typical of most khedivals, an Arabic inscription in white *thuluth* calligraphy runs in a frieze around the top of the interior walls, just below the crenellated border.

The Harvard Tent is one example of a tent whose inscriptions can be attributed, in this case a love poem, "The Blush of the Crimson Cheeks," composed in the late nineteenth century by Salama Hegazi (1852–1917), a celebrated Egyptian poet, singer, and performer. The poem on the tent differs slightly from Hegazi's original—it does not include the whole poem and an alternative ending has been used, probably so that the inscription can fit. A mistake has been made in the execution of the poem: a missing letter renders "the crimson cheeks" into "the free cheeks." One of the most important aspects of this poem is that it shows the link between contemporary literary culture and the poetry used on tents.

The blush of thy crimson cheeks

Inquire the blush on thy crimson cheeks
About my smitten, infatuated heart
And the pearls yonder between thy lips
About mine lovesick, ever weeping eyes.
Overlook thou not the gleaming glance
In the eyes. For surely a fatal saber it is,
To my stabbed bosom, and a charming
Allure to my pensive distracted wits.
(You left me in love.)[37]

A comparable tent once belonged to the Ellwood family, the ceiling of which is now part of the Ellwood House Museum in Dekalb, Illinois. It is thought to have been collected by Harriet Ellwood and her daughter in 1894, and is documented in photographs from 1906.[38] Unusually, the calligraphy was attached to the interior of the ceiling rather than sewn to the top of the wall. It features the traditional khayamiya ode dated to at least 1896 ("Look again, you will find a beautiful craft . . . "). Others are known from private collections, including the Kintore-Gunston Tent in the United Kingdom.

Unlike these khedival *fustat*, only one khedival *suradiq* is known to exist today. This is the 'Tent Room' of Doddington Hall in Lincolnshire, United Kingdom. This was also manufactured in the late 1870s, like the Harvard Tent. It features no calligraphy but was collected in association with a red Sufi processional banner. This remarkable *suradiq* was used by Viscount Harry Crookshank to entertain guests on the lawns of garden parties, likely in much the same manner as his parents when they originally acquired it in Cairo.[39] One documented example was the 1903 gathering of the Primrose League at Saint Hill, in which over one hundred guests were received in their Egyptian tent before other activities and entertainment began. The event did not run entirely as planned:

A deluge of rain and hail, accompanied by a 'West Indian' hurricane, descended for a full five minutes. In a large tent, 90 feet long, thirty women were preparing for the tea hour. The wind seized hold of the tent and shook it in the manner a dog shakes a rat. The centre poles snapped with a loud crack and the three feet iron stanchions one inch in diametre, supporting the ropes, were bent and twisted in all shapes and torn from the ground, bringing

> with them bucketfuls of turf. The canvas collapsed, and when the women had been extricated from the smashed crockery it was found that all had miraculously escaped injury. A second, but smaller, tent was carried bodily away a few yards. After the elements had subsided efforts were soon made to clear away the wreckage. Tea had necessarily to be taken upon the lawns.[40]

It is not clear if the collapsed tent was the same as the Egyptian tent. That said, Crookshank gifted his khayamiya tent to Colonel Charles Jarvis. James and Claire Birch subsequently commissioned a restoration by Indian tentmakers in Gujarat in the 2000s. At that time they were residing in India, and believed their tent was of Indian origin. Comparably appliquéd tents are a recurring feature at festivals in India, and the Gujarati tentmakers made no comments about the tent of Doddington Hall being unlike the tents they normally made.

The use of hand-appliquéd khayamiya tents as traveling accommodation for tourists is now very rare. Desert safari expeditions across Egypt frequently use imitation khayamiya to provide a decorative dining area for camping expeditions. According to Will and Deni McIntyre, at least one antique khedival specimen was employed by Fergany El-Komaty in this manner during the 1990s, accompanied by two 'neo-Khedival' replica tents.

Lost Tents

There are many khayamiya tents waiting to be rediscovered beyond Egypt. Newspaper references to the use of 'Egyptian tents' at public and private events indicate that these were widespread but unusual attractions. For example, a wedding in the regional Australian town of Bendigo was held in a 'pretty Egyptian tent' in 1899.[41] Others were noted between 1890 and 1940 in Sydney and Melbourne as stalls for fetes (such as clairvoyants with crystal balls or cards) or as backdrops for musical theater, popular dances, and university lectures.

Egyptian tents are more likely to exist in British and American estates, as references are widely recorded in the social pages and classified advertisements of British and US newspapers. For example, a "grand Egyptian tent" was displayed in the Public Library Hall on Ocean Road, South Shields (near Newcastle-upon-Tyne in Great Britain) in 1880 by a Mr. W.M. Guthrie, who used it as the backdrop for an orchestra.[42] Another "splendid Egyptian tent" was displayed on the grounds of Cobthorne in Oundle, Northamptonshire, as part of an 1894 bazaar to raise funds for the Union Workhouse Chapel. This tent had allegedly been captured by Captain Arthur W. Moore of the Royal Navy at the Battle of Tell al-Kebir in 1882.[43] Other British examples of khayamiya tents included those belonging to a Lieutenant-Colonel Fitz Stubbs in 1889,[44] and Francis Greville (the Fifth Earl of Warwick) in 1912.[45] Similarly, an Egyptian tent was acquired 'during travels in the East' by Major and Mrs. W. Cornwallis West, which was used as a market stall on the grounds of Ruthin Castle from 1879.[46] More of these travelers' tents are likely to be discovered, as they provide remarkable spaces for hosting events at home.

From Architectural Textile to Souvenir

Touristic khayamiya were developed by the tentmakers in the late nineteenth century to engage with the Orientalist perceptions and expectations of Egypt held by foreign visitors.

One could argue that tourism was a contrary pressure upon the status of the *suradiq* as the most typical manifestation of khayamiya in Cairo. From the 1890s, but particularly from the 1920s, tourists frequently acquired souvenirs of khayamiya in the form of wall hangings, not 'hanging walls.' Designed with visual references to ancient pharaonic cultures, these touristic khayamiya were more carefully crafted so they could be closely considered as intimate artworks, rather than as walls from a distance. Most significantly, such souvenirs were smaller, faster to make, and provided a better profit per item for the individual tentmaker.

On the basis of tourist demand alone, the entrepreneurial direction of the tentmakers slowly moved away from the original concept of khayamiya as an architectural textile. Tentmakers continued to work within the authentic principles, materials, and techniques of their highly skilled profession, but toward the production of radically revised objects. The labor distribution that favored souvenirs over large structures held substantial implications for the tentmaking economy when 'imitation khayamiya' was invented.

7

Modern Khayamiya

Stage and Ceremony

If there is a line to be drawn to herald the rise of modern khayamiya, it is probably the beginning of the reign of King Fuad in 1922. It was a time when Egypt had become its own nation, and one of the greatest symbols of this nationhood was the figure of the Egyptian nationalist leader, Sa'd Zaghlul, who came to represent Egypt's fight for independence against colonial rule. Upon Zaghlul's return from exile in 1924 to become prime minister, crowds greeted him and his equally respected wife, Safiya Hanim, with much euphoria. "Egypt welcomes the arrival of the great leader," one magazine headline announced.[1] In a grainy print of a photograph of the occasion, published in October 1924, a huge crowd of well-dressed ladies, some bearing parasols and one with a banner depicting the crescent united with the cross, await the arrival of Zaghlul's wife, known affectionately as 'the mother of the Egyptians.' The crowd, of course, is waiting in a huge tent pavilion, its walls decorated with geometric patterns in colorful appliqué.

In the Egypt of the 1920s, representations of nationhood were everywhere. Most ubiquitous was the newly-created Egyptian coat of arms, a common feature around the nation to the extent that it was carved in stone above the doorways of hundreds of houses in the traditional quarters of Cairo. On another level, the interest in Egyptian heritage that had been flourishing since the nineteenth century continued. This took many forms—including royal visits to national museums, such as King Fuad's visit to the Museum of Coptic Art in 1920, and again with the King of Italy in 1923;[2] the building of the monumental neopharaonic mausoleum

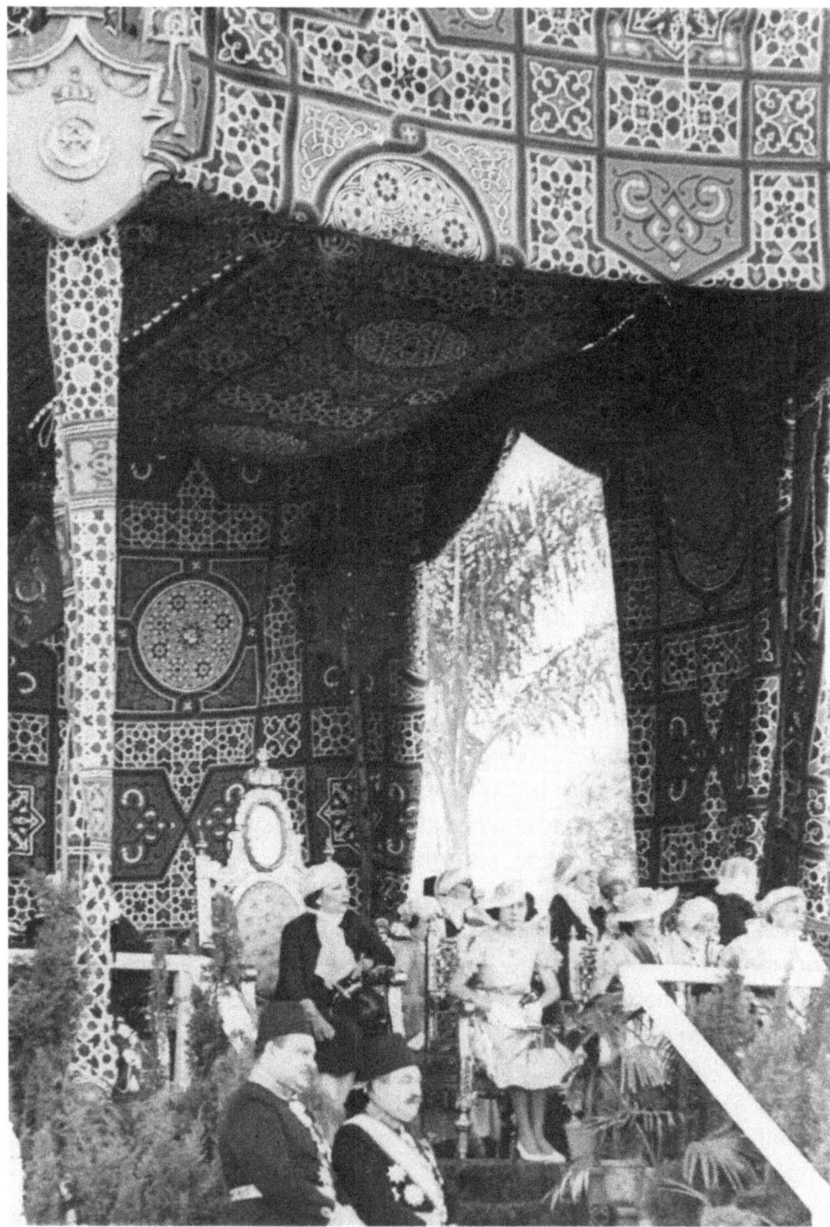

Figure 15 Queen Nazli Sabri, then the Queen Mother, reviews soldiers on parade from her *suradiq* following the coronation of her son, King Farouk, in 1937. Associated Press.

in 1927 for the great leader Zaghlul himself; and the construction of buildings in the neo-Islamic style by members of the royal family, such as the palace of Prince Muhammad 'Ali (Amina Ilhami's son) in Manial in the 1920s, whose foundation inscription attests that it was built 'to revive and honor Islamic arts.'

The idea of Egyptianness was one that was on everyone's minds, and gave rise to an artistic vocabulary of its own. The unveiling of the great Egyptian sculptor Mahmoud Mokhtar's *Egypt Awakening* in Cairo in 1928 was one such occasion. This monumental work, depicting a sphinx rising and an Egyptian peasant woman standing with confidence and resolve, symbolic of the national mood of an Egyptian renaissance, was given pride of place in front of what was effectively Cairo's most important gateway: its railway station. Footage of the momentous occasion shows a tent pavilion of exceptional quality and size with the royal coat of arms hanging on a shield at its entrance. King Fuad sits on his throne on a dais in the center, surrounded by his courtiers and a range of dignitaries, all dwarfed by the magnificent open-fronted pavilion, with elaborate appliquéd panels hanging at intervals, hiding the wooden posts holding the structure up. In the background, passing traffic tootles by, momentarily obscuring the crowd gathered to witness the scene.

This period saw the development of elaborately-manufactured appliqué panels much more finely decorated than their nineteenth-century counterparts, and often more finely stitched. It is hardly surprising that in 1931, at the eighteenth conference of Orientalists held in Leiden, King Fuad's representative, Murad Kamel Bey, attended with a variety of top-quality handicrafts from Egypt as gifts from the king. These included a few wooden Qu'ran stands in the style of the Ilhamiya school and an impressive collection of khayamiya hangings, now in the collection of the National Museum of the Netherlands. These were probably not commissioned specially for the occasion, but bought from a high-end gallery, like that of Elias Hatoun.

While hangings such as those gifted by King Fuad feature exquisitely designed Arabic inscriptions, the convention for tent panels seems to have been to omit them. This gave tents multiplicity of use, lending themselves to a wider range of occasions.

In the particular case of King Fuad, he appeared frequently in a grand tent pavilion, effectively a portable throne room. This traveled with him as he traversed his kingdom, inaugurating hospitals, reviewing military parades, and visiting his subjects far and near. Figure 16, by the court

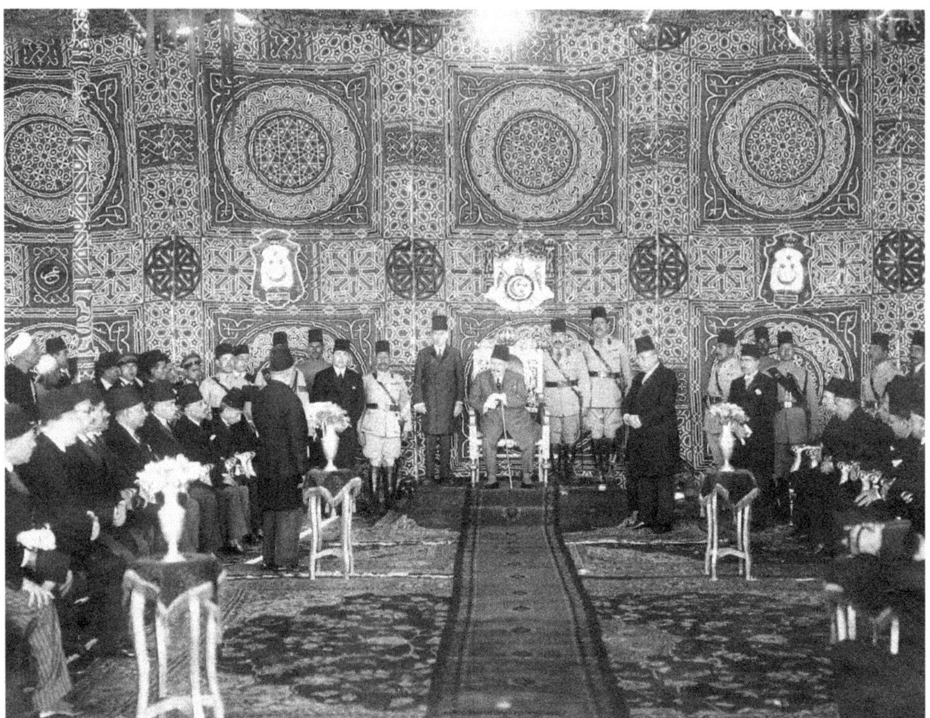

Figure 16 King Fuad I at the opening of the Egyptian Spinning and Weaving Company in al-Mahalla al-Kubra, 1927. Photograph by Riyad Shehata.

photographer Riyad Shehata, shows him with the great industrialist Talaat Harb, founder of the National Bank, attending the opening of the Egyptian Spinning and Weaving Company in al-Mahalla al-Kubra in 1927. This provides a clear demonstration of the visual intensity of the khayamiya pavilion as a mobile platform for visiting dignitaries. The juxtaposition of palatial khayamiya against dusty streets appears incongruous, but it is consistent with their purpose as a decorative backdrop—a textile to define spaces claimed within public places.

The tent pavilions used by King Fuad are pretty much of the form that has survived until today—a box-like structure, every surface entirely decorated. This is known either as a *suradiq*, a classical Arabic word mentioned in the Qu'ran, or a *siwan*—two interchangeable terms referring to a walled tent. Their modularity is perfect for the urban settings in which they were most commonly used: they could be erected to fit in a narrow Cairo street or a huge open space.

The *suradiq*s of early twentieth-century Egypt followed their rulers across the course of their lives. Unsurprisingly, a huge one was erected to host the funerary events marking King Fuad's death in 1936, which was no different from the tents that had accompanied him, and other members of his family, at the high points of their reigns.

This type of *suradiq* continued to be used under King Fuad's son Farouk at a wide range of celebrations, including the young king's coronation travels in February 1937:

> In Minia Al-Qamh, the Abaza family had solicited palace authorities to permit the royal train to stop briefly in their village so that the king could partake in refreshments offered in a large, magnificently ornamented tent they had erected in the train station. The municipality, railway authority and other government agencies in Zaqaziq festooned their city with a variety of decorative displays. Of particular note are those that were created by the eminent Abdel-Rahman Radwan Bek on his cotton ginnery, his school and his other properties facing the train station.[3]

Suradiq tents followed this king around, too. They appear in football matches that he attended, visits to mosques and shrines, and in 1949, on the 100th anniversary of Muhammad 'Ali Pasha's death, when a pageant was held at the Cairo Citadel, the longstanding seat of power.

With the *suradiq* so prominent a feature of court life, it is hardly surprising that it was widely used by all members of society, rich and poor. At a household celebration of King Farouk's birthday in 1951, a large balcony is covered with a *siwan* to accommodate well-dressed guests and protect them from a chilly December evening. In the poorer quarters of the city, the *suradiq* transformed a space, creating a temporary illusion of wealth. In a society which placed weight both on impressing one's community as well as hospitality, even those with modest homes could entertain in style.

Khayamiya in the Second Half of the Twentieth Century

The overthrow of King Farouk in 1952 by the so-called Free Officers witnessed a populist movement come to power that transformed Egypt into a republic, and under its second president, Gamal Abd al-Nasser (1956–70) especially, energetically rallied the public across the country. Although most accounts of this period portray it as the antithesis of the era it succeeded, in terms of his frequent and widespread movement around Egypt, the president followed in the footsteps of previous Egyptian rulers. It was also a time

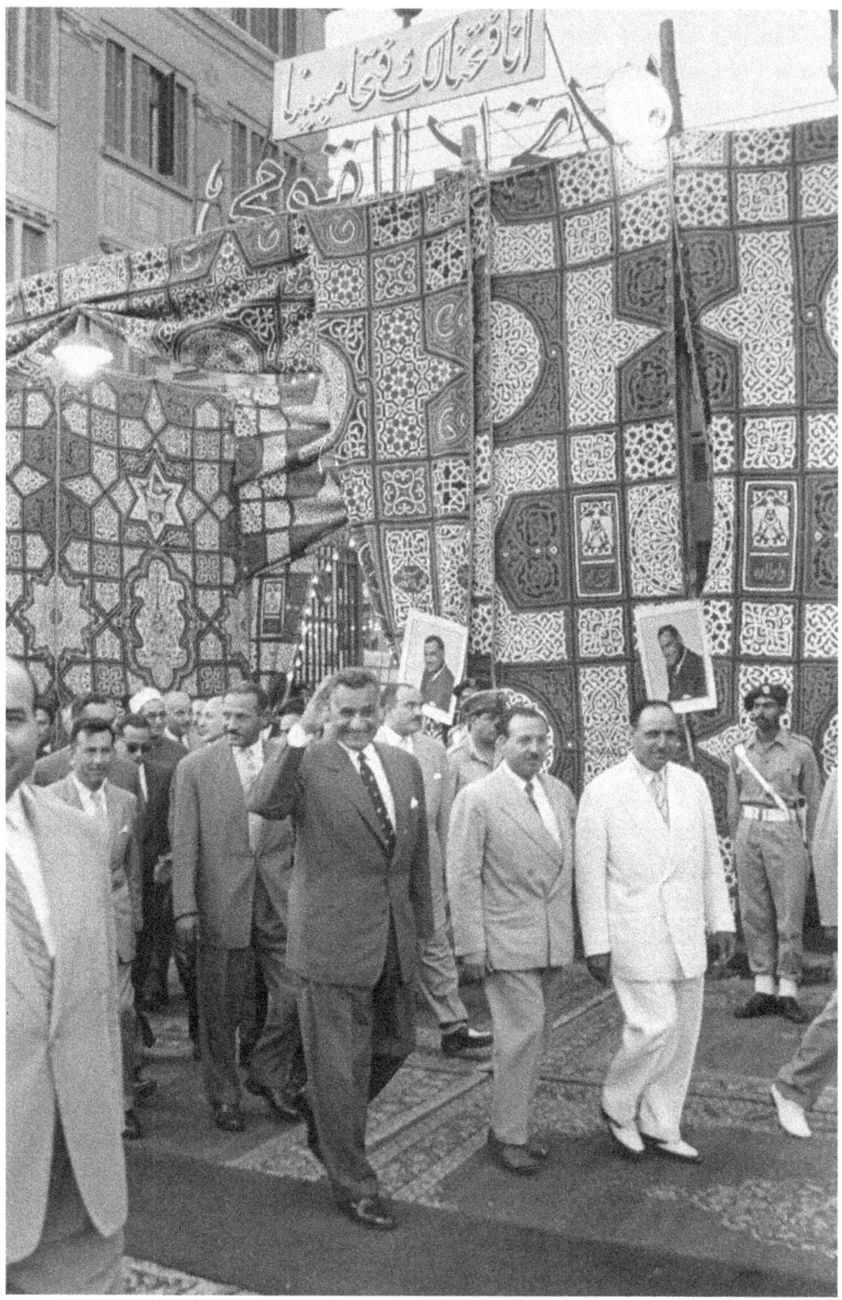

Figure 17 President Nasser at the sixth anniversary of the July 23 Revolution, 1958. Photograph by James Whitmore. Getty Images.

in which Egypt aspired to excel in the production of everything from the 'needle to the rocket'—which meant that there were numerous occasions on which the president appeared in public at inaugurations, for which, of course, a *suradiq* was in order. One of the key differences was the spirit of these events, which meant they no longer featured the ruler on a throne, holding court, and felt a bit more like the venue for an election campaign. The setting was therefore the same, but the atmosphere different.

One seminal event was the nationalization of the Suez Canal in July 1956—an event which saw the president triumphantly raise the Egyptian flag over the canal to a cheering crowd under a huge open-fronted *suradiq*. It was one of the most significant events of the era in that it showed western powers exactly what Nasser thought of their involvement in Egyptian affairs. It came with a heavy price, of course—military aggression against Egypt followed soon after.

What Nasser's era hammered hard was another wave of pride in being Egyptian, one aided by the fact that it corresponded to a gung-ho postwar industrialization and mass production movement taking place the world over. Images of factory workers, modern buildings, and transport systems abound—it was one of the calling cards of the era. While the arts of the Islamic eras of Egyptian history were still alive and well, it was the art of ancient Egypt that witnessed an intensification of interest in the fifties and sixties. Ancient Egyptian gods, kings, and queens like Isis and Horus, Ramesses, Nefertiti, and Cleopatra, and emblems like the key of life, the scarab beetle, the sun, and most of all the lotus, were used ad infinitum as logos for hotels, public sector industries, banks, and pretty much everything else. Perhaps the best example of the use of the lotus as inspiration is in the design of Cairo Tower (constructed between 1954 and 1961), for decades the tallest structure in Africa.

One particularly iconic event that captured this interest in ancient Egypt was the move of the statue of the great pharaoh Ramesses II in 1955 from the outskirts of Cairo, where it was found, to the square outside the main railway station, where Mokhtar's *Egyptian Awakening* statue had been placed twenty-five years earlier. It was an event described as restoring the glory not only of Ramesses but of Cairo itself, and led to the renaming of the square after the pharaoh.

The interest in ancient Egypt and the use of its symbols to reflect a new dawn found its way into khayamiya as well—mainly through the use of the lotus, which became widespread. While some tent panels from the Nasser period are dominated by lotus motifs, on others it appears incorporated

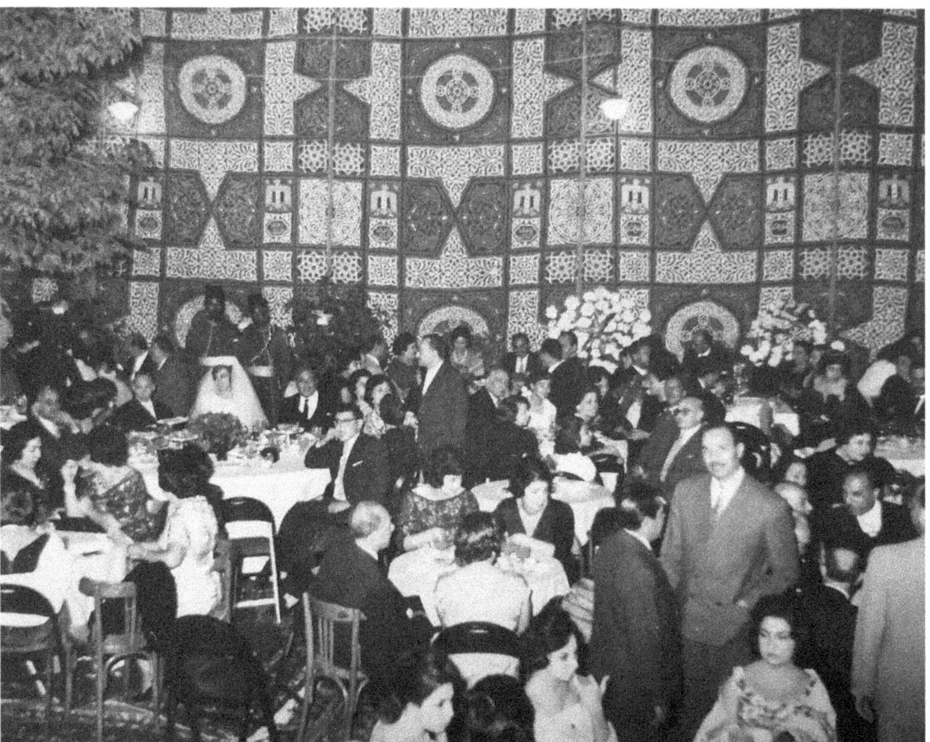

Figure 18 A magnificent tent used for the wedding of 'Aziz al-Bindary and Naila Ibrahim in 1960. Note the 'toothed' *(sanan)* khayamiya design and appliquéd Egyptian national eagle. Photograph courtesy of Naila Ibrahim.

into panels of Islamic inspiration, both as an open flower and as a bud. It was a perfect symbol in many ways, and remains a standard element in Egyptian tents until today.

Another interesting feature of the tents from the 1950s to the late 1970s is the frequent appearance of the Egyptian coat of arms in appliqué work. The coat of arms was modified several times, and the appearance of all of its different versions indicates that the tentmakers were paying close attention to the different iterations of the symbols of nationhood as they changed over time—something that is perhaps unsurprising, given how closely linked to the reins of power these tents were. Between 1953 and 1958 the coat of arms was an eagle with a crescent and three stars on its breast; between 1958 and 1970 the shield was changed to two stars (with no crescent), representative of the union between Egypt and Syria;

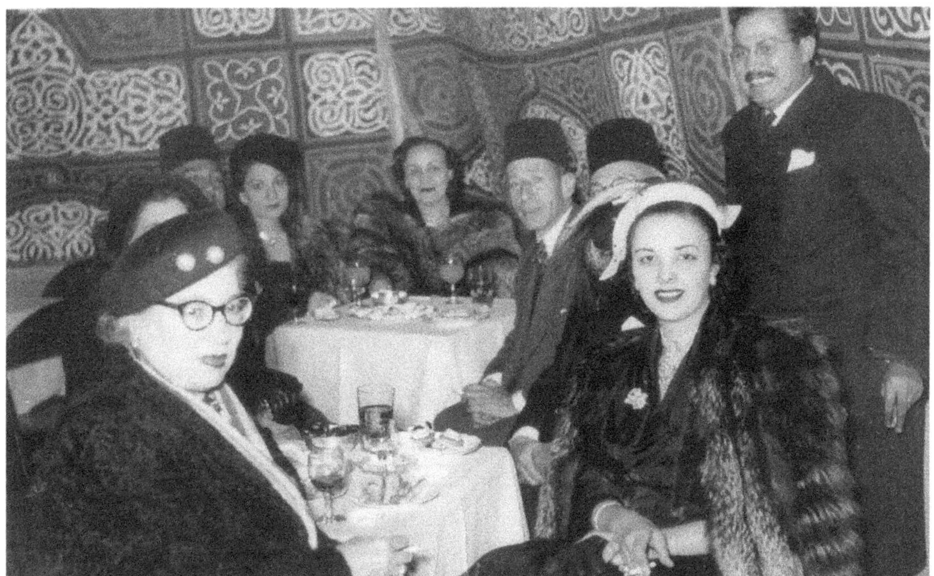

Figure 19 A party celebrating King Farouk's birthday on February 11, 1951. A tent encloses a terrace in Zamalek, Cairo, to create a temporary space and keep the guests warm. Photograph courtesy of Nevine Hussein.

from 1970 to 1984 the eagle was replaced by a falcon (looking right, while the eagle had looked to the left); and from 1984 the eagle was reinstated, but the shield on its breast replaced the stars with three vertical stripes corresponding to the stripes on the Egyptian flag itself. The emblems constitute easy dating devices (although there is no evidence to suggest that tents stopped being used when the coat of arms was changed).

The link between the work of the tentmakers and the activities of the state is well documented in press photos of both presidents Nasser and his successor Sadat (1970–81), capturing various parts of Egypt bedecked for their arrival, often in open-topped vehicles, which were very popular in the era before major security worries. Often the roads leading into towns and cities would be decorated with khayamiya in the form of 'triumphal archways,' as a way of showing welcome and celebration. These provided a perfect structure upon which to hang banners proclaiming public support, and in other contexts, to advertise parliamentary candidates—a practice that still continues today.

Sadat's assassination while reviewing a military parade in 1981, although not from a tent, probably precipitated the decline in the use

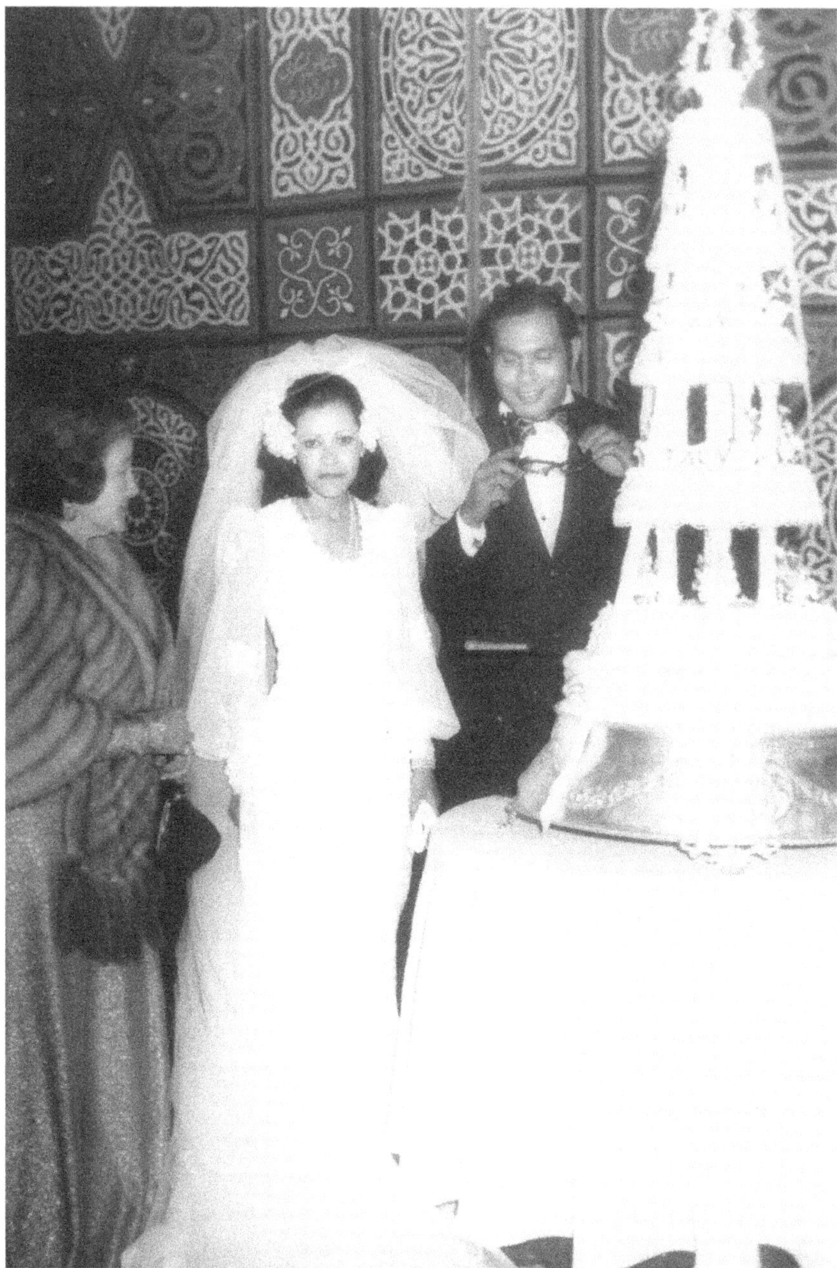

Figure 20 An Egyptian wedding *suradiq*, Zamalek, Cairo, 1974. Note the *farrash*'s name and phone number on the tent—Abbas al-Bakry and sons. Photograph courtesy of Nevine Hussein.

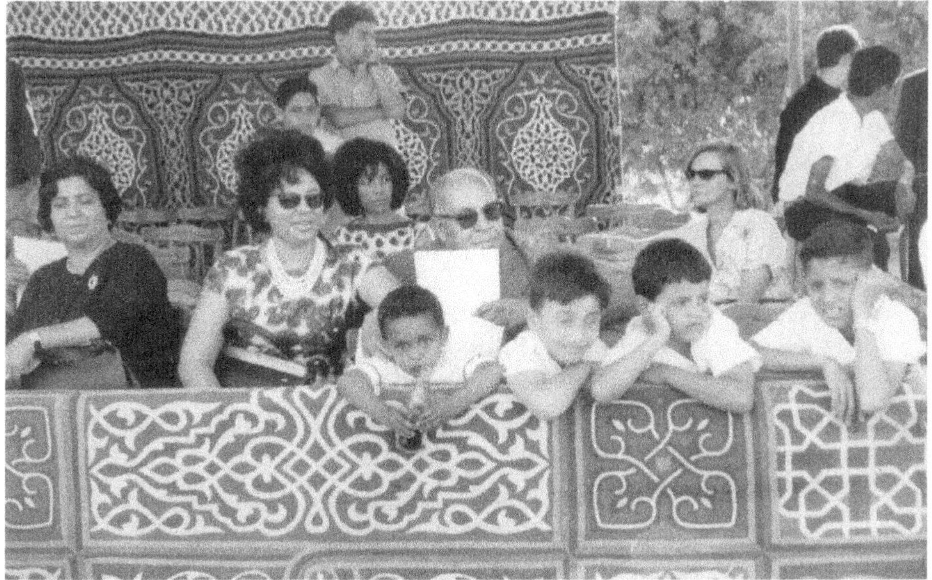

Figure 21 A *suradiq* raised for spectators at an athletics event, ca. 1965. In the background is a typical khayamiya *bilma* (screen). Photograph courtesy of Mamdouh El Rashidi.

of the *suradiq* to host top level political events, reflecting an Egypt more concerned about the safety of its top players. The use of the *suradiq* in other spheres of social life continued—in every family album khayamiya will appear in the background of every sort of event. As the use of the camera proliferated in the 1960s and 70s, and as informal photographs have grown more common, so have visual records of khayamiya, its uses, and its designs.

The khayamiya used by dignitaries and for weddings are uniform repetitions of panels with consistent compositions. By contrast, in less formal, less affluent contexts, several panels of unrelated size and chaotic compositions can sometimes be used together. Some of these have been repeatedly repaired—and are subsequently cheaper than new panels. Traditionally these sorts of pieces formed exuberant flowing backdrops for musicians and dancers, and were likely owned by the theatrical/music troupe and used until it disintegrated.[4] At the lowest end of the scale are faded and worn panels used to screen off building sites, especially when shops are being repaired or buildings demolished. The height of the tent panels effectively ensures that passersby are shielded from dust, rubble, and noise.

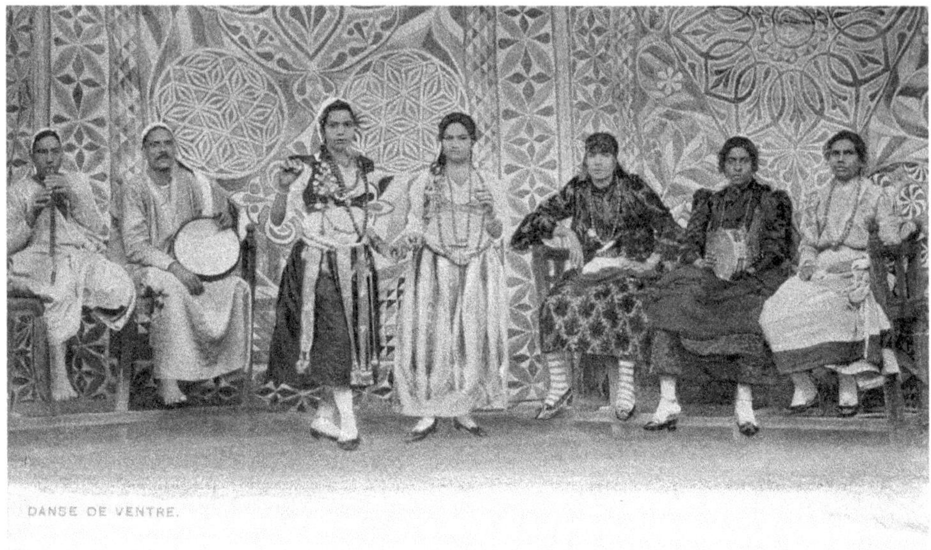

Figure 22 *Suradiq*s were often used as temporary performance spaces. This image probably dates from around 1900. Postcard attributed to Fritz Schneller.

Although many examples we have cited present tents from an Islamic context, the use of khayamiya is not a specifically Islamic custom, and the same tents were used by Muslim, Christian, and Jewish communities alike. For example, a large *suradiq* was in use at the Fourth African Churches Congress in St. Mark's Cathedral in Cairo on February 18, 1976. Many ministers, state officials, and diplomats attended the opening session, which included representatives from 118 churches in thirty-one African states, as well as delegations from Europe, the Americas, and the Middle East, and was hosted by Pope Chenouda III, Pope of Alexandria and the patriarch of St. Mark's Cathedral.

Khayamiya in Cinema and Performance

Unsurprisingly, *suradiq*s are seen frequently in Egyptian cinema from the Nasser period (1956–70), particularly as backgrounds for wedding scenes, such as Nagwa Fouad's dancing scenes in the comedy *Shahr assal basal (The Ruined Honeymoon)* (1960) or *Kulub el azara (The Hearts of Virgins)* (1959). Khayamiya tents have also been used behind the scenes as convenient bases for other cinematic productions in Egypt. In November 1955 Ralph Crane photographed the director Cecil B. De Mille pacing in the shade of the awning from a *suradiq* which provided on-site quarters for his crew during the filming of *The Ten Commandments*, a role echoed by another on-site *suradiq* during the production of Mel Gibson's *The Passion of the Christ* in 2003.

Perhaps the most active use of khayamiya in cinema was the 1966 film *Khartoum*, directed by Basil Dearden and Eliot Elisofon, with art direction by John Howell. In this film, Charlton Heston's performance of General Charles Gordon is contrasted with Laurence Olivier's portrayal of Muhammad Ahmad (the 'Mahdi'). This character is invariably depicted in front of a bright khayamiya screen typical of the twentieth century's vibrant street tents, rather than the relatively subdued khedival forms that were in use around 1885. This orientalist touch evokes the Mahdi's exoticism through dramatic color and complex patterns behind his otherwise plain robes, which further exaggerates the contrast between the leading characters. It could be argued that this jarringly modern (1960s) tent acts as an extension of Laurence Olivier's costume in this film, more authentically sourced than the actors themselves!

The use of khayamiya as a stage-like backdrop for performances by theatrical groups and musicians is as old as the tradition itself.[5] The versatility of such backdrops is illustrated by their appearances at Egyptian performances for international expositions as far back as the 1902 Gewerbe Industrie-Ausstellung in Dusseldorf, or the 'Assuan Village' pavilion at Earl's Court, London, in 1903, but textual references indicate that this was a common practice as far back as Mamluk times.

Today's Tents

The *suradiq* or *siwan* is a prominent feature of celebrations across Egypt throughout the year, but Ramadan is an especially good time to assess the state of affairs of tents in Cairo, given that it is a month-long cause for public celebration. Banquets are hosted by those who can afford to feed the hungry fasters at sunset, and these are held in tents. Some of these are the traditional soaring *suradiq*, especially around prominent mosques, which are always actively engaged in charitable activity on a large scale and have the funds donated though almsgiving and other sources to host the most lavish banquets. In other instances, for example, meals are organized by generous residents for the poor of their neighborhoods, and for passersby who may be caught with nowhere to eat at sunset. These tents are lower in height and serve rather as screens to shield the people eating, and more symbolically to define the space reserved for these 'Banquets of the

Merciful,' as they are called. These lower enclosures are not often roofed, as they are only used at sunset, when there is no need to create shade. They are constructed either by turning the traditional tent panels on their sides (in landscape rather than portrait format), or by using purposely-designed screens about 2 m in height known as *bilam*, the plural of *bilma*, from the Turkish word for screen.

In parallel, printed khayamiya fabric has truly taken off as a popular symbol of Ramadan. From place mats to table cloths, fabric lanterns to bunting, it has become an Egyptian equivalent of Christmas decorations. Most of these items are made or sold by the tentmakers themselves, showing an adaptation to markets unwilling to pay large sums of money for handmade work, but interested in imparting a local touch. The ubiquity of these printed fabrics is astonishing—they feature prominently in places as unexpected as hospitals and airports. Some of the patterns are traditional designs, but others depict Ramadan symbols like the lantern and the crescent, or feature the traditional Ramadan blessing, *Ramadan karim* ('Blessed Ramadan').

The tent has come to symbolize shisha café culture as well. Usually of printed material, the traditional *suradiq*, or at least one red fabric wall is conventional, almost to the point of becoming an emblem of the trendy shisha café. This is probably an evolution of the nineties fad of the Ramadan tent, an evening meeting place where friends would spend several hours and perhaps partake in a predawn, prefast meal. Today it is a standard way to spend a summer evening.

Open-fronted tents and tent archways are a good way to mark the lead-up to a celebration as well. Before Ramadan, for example, lanterns, a traditional Ramadan symbol displayed in homes, shops, and in the street, are sold in their thousands out of open-fronted tent pavilions; for the Prophet's birthday, the traditional sweets consumed for the occasion are presented in the same setting.

In the lead-up to feast days in general, cake shops and butchers are likely to have tents and awnings of this sort to indicate the relevance of their wares to the upcoming celebration, and to create an additional display space. Tent structures of this sort aren't only the preserve of religious ceremonies—the opening of new shops is a common occasion when the tentmakers' product is used to create a visual announcement of something exciting.

The funerary tent is still commonly used, not for funerals themselves, but to receive people coming to pay condolences *(azza)*. In more traditional neighborhoods, it is erected in the street beside the residence of the deceased, and the entrance is typically from one of the narrow sides.

Sometimes the tent is subdivided to create a separate section for women, but traditionally it has been the preserve of only men. A *bilma* is usually placed at the entrance of the tent, like a fabric wall forming a backdrop to the short line of male family members standing at the entrance of the tent to receive those coming to pay condolences, and to thank them on their way out. Inside the tent, chairs are arranged in rows parallel to the sides of the tent. A shaykh is usually hired to recite verses of the Qu'ran during the *azza*, which starts after the sunset prayer and lasts beyond the evening prayer.

The *azza* tent is often found in front of mosques as well, sometimes in the street but other times on land owned by the mosque. The format is very similar, except that these tents tend to be much larger than their neighborhood counterparts. Apart from the type of preacher, the format of tents used for Christian *azza*s is the same.

The *mawlid*, the celebration of a saint's birthday, is another strongly upheld tradition in which tents are still used, both to house travelers coming from far afield to pray and receive some of the blessings *(baraka)* of the religious figure they have come to venerate, as well as to create the space where this veneration can take place (see plate 23). Huge tents are erected by religious orders who use them to host *dhikr* (remembrance) events, which involve communal chanting and prayer. As described by Evliya Çelebi in the chapter on Ottoman tents, the *mawlid* creates a temporary world that seems to appear out of nowhere. This usually starts several days before the celebration day itself, and reaches a climax with the 'Big Night,' *al-Layla al-kebira*, the actual commemoration of the saint in question. The *mawlid* of al-Husayn and Sayyida Zaynab are two of the largest celebrations in Cairo, receiving hundreds of thousands of people, while that of al-Sayyid al-Badawi in Tanta is also huge. There are sites all over the country where such events take place, though not all are conveniently located in cities and towns. One particularly hard-to-reach *mawlid* is the one of Shaykh Shazly in the south of Egypt, located in the desert halfway between the Nile and the Red Sea. It marks the place where al-Shazly, an important Sufi leader, died on his way to Mecca for pilgrimage in 1258. Usually, the shrines of important saints will also have a weekly sufi *hadra* (gathering), which often takes place in tents. One thing is for certain: the one thousand-year-old tradition of using tents for any sort of celebration is very much alive.

8

The *Farrashin*

It is impossible to think of the tentmakers without recalling the *farrashin*, the people that put the tents up. They are distinct from the tentmakers themselves. The root of the word *farsh* means furniture or bedding, in its broadest possible sense, and explains the role of the *farrashin* (singular *farrash*): it is to them one goes if one wants to have a tent put up for any occasion, but more than that their responsibility is to create the tent space, with whatever furniture and other accessories are required. Unlike the tentmakers, who have historically existed as a community of craftsmen that produced tents in close proximity to one another (in the tentmakers' market), the nature of the *firasha* business is very different; the *farrashin* operate on the neighborhood level, serving its tent requirements as well as those of the surrounding areas, whenever possible. Thus all of the older historic neighborhoods of Cairo have several *firasha* businesses dotted around them. In physical terms, *firasha* businesses tend to occupy a small front office, which looks like a small shop but is known as a *maktab*, an 'office,' rather than a shop, because in fact, the transaction between the client and the *firasha* business is a sitting-down-at-a-desk affair to discuss the client's requirements, agree payment, find out the location where the tent is going to be, and when exactly it is needed. Goods are not sold, it is more a service being procured.

The typical *firasha* shop makes it clear from the window what its business is, with the size of the window determining which elements of their wares they can put on display. The office of the el-Hendy family in the Abdin neighborhood, for example, boasts a shop window with a gilt chair set against a backdrop of a piece of printed tentmaker's fabric and several examples of old serving dishes, which would have traditionally been rented out for events such as weddings and parties. Also in Abdin, though more tucked away, is the office of the Wahdan family, who furnished many of the tents required by the royal court during the reign of King Farouk (1936–52) and the presidential *diwan* until the 1970s. It has just a few examples of this gilt tableware in the narrow window, simply as a symbol of what their business is. In reality, finding a *farrash* is usually through word of mouth—somebody asks somebody else, who tells them where to go. The shop window is often just an indication of the fact that you have arrived, rather than being the actual source of the business.

One way that *firasha* businesses advertise their service is by embroidering their name on the tent panels themselves, and sometimes a phone number as well. Some of the more enterprising ones also provide a brief note of their location so that if one is looking for a *farrash*, it is easy enough to head off to the neighborhood where their business is and ask for so-and-so, the *farrash*. Somebody is bound to know. Ibrahim Mohsin in Ras al-Tin, or simply a name like Sayyid Hanafy, are enough to give the tent-seeker somebody to look for.

Apart from his office, the *farrash* will usually have a nearby storage area where his wares are actually kept, usually very carefully arranged for ease of access and efficiency. Unlike the tentmaking process, which takes a long time, the business of the *farrash* is dependent on speed and efficiency as his clients often want a tent erected quickly, usually within a couple of days, sometimes on the same day, if the tent is needed for a funerary event. As such, having everything ready is essential.

The main components of the *farrash*'s storeroom are the tent panels (singular *tark*), usually kept folded up in matching sets of thirty to fifty pieces, the six-meter-long wooden poles used to create the structure of the tent, and ropes. Most *firasha* businesses will also have numerous tent screens used for the entrances of tent pavilions, to close off shops, or to create tents where height is not required. Each screen, known as a *bilma*, is usually around two m high, and five or six m wide, usually with a design of arcades. They will also have rugs for the floor, which were traditionally hand woven and usually crude and garish, but today often replaced with machine-produced work. Light fixtures are also essential, as many of these events will take place at night.

Chairs, now stackable, and sometimes small side tables, used for resting one's coffee cup at funerary wakes, are the standard furniture used by a *farrash*'s business.

The *farrash* business owns its kit, but subcontracts out the actual putting up of the tent to skilled men who know how to do it. They don't work for the *farrash*, but are employed on an ad hoc basis. Typically, these tent-erectors sit at a local coffee shop and are called upon (by telephone) by a *farrash* when their skills are needed. These workers are accompanied by less-skilled men called *shayyalin* (carriers or lifters), whose job it is simply to carry and move all of the tent components and help the tent erector to put them up. The *shayyalin* that show an aptitude for putting up the tent—a job that requires skill, agility, and no fear of heights—eventually become tent erectors themselves. Their profession sees them master the use of the ladder, moving around on it with the deftness of circus performers on stilts. The third type of hired hand to be found at these cafés are the servers or butlers, who are hired to serve the coffee at funerary wakes. It is usually the more historic neighborhoods that have these *farrashin* coffee shops where one can find the required workers, often as many as twenty people. Neighborhoods with important mosques popular for their spiritual links to members of the Prophet's family, and therefore used frequently for family events and funerals, are a big hub of tent-related activity and will therefore have a *farrashin* café nearby. The neighborhood of Sayyida Zaynab, which takes its name after an extremely important shrine dedicated to the Prophet's granddaughter, and is surrounded by some of the city's most important mosques, has a café (Zahrat al-Midan) used as a base by the tent-erectors, for obvious reasons. The central midan in Giza has a similar café.

When a client calls in asking for a tent to be erected, the *farrash* will find out what is required, agree the cost, and immediately call upon his contacts at the coffee shop to get the men ready for the process of putting the tent up. He will often send somebody to the location itself to see whether there are any special requirements that need to be taken into account. Some locations may well be familiar, and therefore not require a site visit. In such cases, a truck is simply loaded up with all the necessary items and sent off.

If the tent requires blocking off a section of the street, something that was very common for funerary tents but also for smaller local weddings, usually in the alleyways and smaller streets of less affluent areas of the city, permission must be obtained from the local police station in order to do this. It is sometimes the *farrash* business that obtains this permission, and given that many of these businesses have existed for decades, they know how to go about doing it. The standard practice is for a tent to be dismantled immediately after the conclusion of the event, and therefore it may be up for as little as six or seven hours. The smallest *suradiq* measures 5.5 m (two tent panels) wide and 16.5 m (six tent panels) long. In 2018 prices, a complete tent of this size with all of the requisite furnishings will cost around LE2,000 to rent for one night.

The *farrash*'s business, like the rest of the Cairo tentmakers' world, has seen many changes over the past few decades. In general there is far less demand for their work on a daily basis. Most mosques now have function halls where funeral wakes are held, taking away much of the traditional day-to-day business of the *farrashin*. Similarly, weddings are rarely held at home or in the street—even in the poorer areas of historic Cairo, where street weddings were common, now local social clubs tend to be used for festive occasions, reducing the need for tents. At the other end of the scale, affluent Cairene families tend to resort far less to the *farrashin* to transform their homes into spaces to host huge gatherings such as weddings and engagements, which were common until the seventies and eighties. Until the 1950s and 1960s there were enough wealthy Cairene families living in houses large enough to host such events. The wedding of the son of al-Bindari Pasha, former minister of health and an eminent diplomat, in 1960 was held in the bride's family home in the Manial district, and is a good example of how the traditional *farrashin* were still serving the uppermost echelons of society. Similarly, the typical upper-middle-class family album of the 1960s and 1970s will show a range of events held at home and in other places, where tents have been used to create an indoor gathering space. New Year's Eve parties, replete with scantily-clad belly dancers and amused besuited onlookers, were common. Tents were especially important for social events held in winter, when it would have otherwise been too cold to sit outdoors.

Over the following three or four decades, the move from villas to apartment buildings and the parallel proliferation of high-end hotels (starting with the Nile Hilton in 1958) saw the move of lavish weddings into hotels. In Egypt, weddings are the ultimate show of social status, with the venue, scale, food, decoration, and guest list all being important. In more recent years, the wealthy have once again come to occupy villas, this time usually in new developments on the outskirts of Cairo. Weddings are once again being hosted in the most expansive of these properties, but the traditional tents are seen as old fashioned and unsophisticated, and billowing white marquees in European style are much more popular, if a tent is required at all. At an elegant Cairo wedding in the garden of an old villa in the wealthy neighborhood of Zamalek in the early 2000s, one of the guests remarked on the refinement of the tenting used to screen the garden off from the street. "Look how nice, all of this white—not like those terrible traditional colors," she said, crinkling her nose at the mental image of khayamiya garishness. It was a sentiment reflecting a social class that has come to see the traditional tents as unsophisticated.

The el-Hendy brothers, Muhsin and Hussein, seated in their shop in Abdin one Saturday, quietly reflected on the changes they have seen over the past forty years or so. Muhsin, the elder of the two, runs the business set up in 1948 by their father, who was then a young man of around twenty. His own father, Muhammad, had been a tentmaker, and they had other relatives still in the tentmaking business. Hussein, the younger brother, chose not to enter the business and worked for al-Azhar University instead. Now retired, he often keeps his brother company at the office. Despite never having really worked in the family business he knows all about it, and goes to great length to explain the essentials of the trade, while his brother is busy in the storeroom preparing for a job that has come up.

The tent panels are produced and stored in sets of around forty pieces. They still have a set of handmade panels, although the ones they use most frequently are the printed ones, which started to appear on the market around thirty-five years ago, copying the traditional appliqué, partially because the demand for tent panels then exceeded the supply. "It takes about twenty days to make each panel," Hussein says. In the trade today, there are three distinctions: the handmade work, which is very rarely produced and is known as *naqsh* (decorated), the printed work, *matbu'* (simply 'printed'), and 'computer' work, the result of a modern production process that enables the manufacture of satin panels that look appliquéd, but are actually simply made by machine.

In 1990 one of the el-Hendy brothers' tentmaker cousins, Fouad, proposed the manufacture of a new set of handmade panels for their business. It was a period of a slump in the tourist market for smaller appliquéd goods due to the Gulf War, which had considerably reduced Middle Eastern tourism, and it seemed like a good time to replenish their stock. The idea was to manufacture a set of twenty new panels, and a prototype was made, but it was found to be too expensive and the project was shelved. The el-Hendy brothers still have the prototype, with a typical lotus design, but the trimmings and ropes that would have made it into a finished panel were never added.

"It's not the same as it once was," Hussein says. "How many people do you know that still have events in a tent? Very few. . . . It's only in the provinces really—they still have the space for tents like the ones we erect, and are still more traditional."

In early January 2017, trying to call upon Muhammad Lotfy Wahdan, whose father provided the tents to the king's palace, proves to be a difficult endeavor. While everyone seven or eight blocks away knows where he is, and the small office is open, there is nobody to be found and enquirers are directed to his neighbor, who has known him for decades. "You'll find his number above the door of the office," the neighbor says. "Call him and tell him what you want."

We do, and he quickly affirms that they "did all of King Farouk's work." That week it turns out that he isn't available for comment because he's in the Red Sea resort of Hurghada, "Bringing back all of the work from New Year," he says, matter of factly. It turns out that these are modern German tents: "We can't use the traditional ones in places like Hurghada, because they are afraid of fire," he says.

In reality, more and more of the *farrashin*'s trade is for local and foreign tourism, not just New Year's events, but the plethora of Ramadan tents that play host to thousands of Egyptians who stay up drinking tea, smoking shisha, and at times getting something to eat in the evening hours during Ramadan, when the normal day is turned on its head and Cairo becomes strongly nocturnal.

Muhammad Wahdan is a forty-two-year-old who started spending time in his father's shop at the age of five. His family business was started by his grandfather, Madbouly Wahdan, who managed to become the *farrash* of the royal *diwan*, furnishing King Farouk's court with the tents that they needed for events all over Egypt. When the monarchy was replaced by a republic in 1952 Wahdan continued as the tent-furnisher to the presidential *diwan* until his death in 1955, at which point his son Muhammad took over, retaining the privilege until the 1970s, when ill health prevented him from catering to the needs of the presidency. One of Muhammad's two brothers also works in the *firasha* business but is based in Sixth of October, an affluent new neighborhood developed on the outskirts of Cairo, while his other brother is a doctor.

Muhammad's recollection of his father's business in the late 1970s and early 1980s was that they had two tentmakers, two chair repairers, and two gilders as part of their staff to produce and fix the tents and associated furniture the trade required. Further back in time, Wahdan recounts, "my grandfather was one of thirteen main *farrashin* in Cairo. One of the privileges he had was a permit for his horse-drawn carts to travel anywhere in the city, which was uncommon. Sometimes, smaller *firasha* businesses that needed to transport tents across the city would rely on my grandfather to arrange things for them, so that they wouldn't need to get permission themselves."

Wahdan notes the reduction in demand for their business, which he says has become all the more noticeable after the political events in Egypt in 2011. There has also been an increase in the number of *farrashin*. According to him, with the proliferation of printed tentwork the capital investment required to start up a *firasha* business has been reduced, meaning that it is easier for newcomers to enter the business, and his own family has much less of an advantage than they once did. He sees keeping up with the times as being essential—hence his work by the Red Sea, which is different in nature to his business in Cairo.

Although closely related to the tentmakers, the *farrashin* have their own jargon; for example, the decorative panel used at the entrance of a tent pavilion is referred to by Wahdan as a *sibinsa* (coming from the word for caboose, the last carriage in a train). It reflects the fact that this is the last panel to be erected, after the entire tent has been set up. It is a word that means nothing to the tentmakers themselves. "We simply call it an entrance," two of them say.

"Today, trusty workmen are much harder to come by," Wahdan says. "Unlike in my father's day, I find that I have to supervise most of the work myself. In days gone by transactions were often dealt with on-site by my father's workers. He never actually had to go to the site himself."

That said, he adds, "Even though in the past five years we've had less work, of course I expect my sons, once they are old enough, to take the business over—just as we did."

9

Khayamiya and Art

Matisse and Khayamiya

Interior with Egyptian Curtain (1948) was one of Henri Matisse's last oil paintings (see plate 24). It can be divided into three sections that are, on their own, typically Matisse. The view through a glass window frames the flourishing fronds of a palm tree, above a still life of yellow fruit in a white bowl, which casts a dense black shadow upon a pink table. The most striking feature is the 'Egyptian Curtain,' a khedival-era khayamiya acquired around 1920, reinterpreted as a dynamic composition of black, red, white, and green. Although Henri Matisse never met an Egyptian tentmaker, the khayamiya appliqué process is remarkably similar to his *papiers découpés* or paper cutouts. These are now regarded as one of his most significant contributions to twentieth-century art, so their association with the tentmakers should be more widely recognized.

Matisse was an avid and lifelong collector of textiles, recently demonstrated on an exceptional scale through the exhibitions *Matisse: The Fabric of Dreams* (2005) and *Matisse in the Studio* (2017). However, examples of khayamiya were not included in exhibitions of Islamic Art known to be visited by Matisse (such as the exhibitions in Paris in 1903 and Munich in 1910).[1] His biographer Hilary Spurling notes that Matisse never visited Egypt, so his khayamiya was likely acquired in France before 1920. This is demonstrated by the appearance of this textile in *Interior in Nice* (1921), where it can be seen hanging to the left of the seated woman, echoing the colors and pattern of her garments in a similar manner as the blue shutters echo the bedspread to the right.[2]

In short, Matisse's appreciation of his khayamiya was based on its aesthetic appeal. He used it in his studios at Nice and the Villa Le Rêve in Vence as a curtain, consistent with their use in doorways. On a bright day, this illuminated the appliqué like stained glass, darkening the folded-cotton borders of each sewn shape and enlivening the bright colors. The shape of this rectangular textile panel against a larger arched window can also be seen in Matisse's design for the 'Tree of Life' stained glass windows at the Chapelle du Rosaire de Vence.

Matisse's khayamiya is echoed in other works made prior to 1948. The drawing *Pomegranates on a Table, Vence* (1947) anticipates the development of *Interior with Egyptian Curtain* the following year. The three-part composition is readily apparent (pomegranates, palm tree through window, and elaborate textile), but note Matisse's attention to the composition of his khayamiya. His typically fine pen quickly renders a summarization of the foliate wreath with a series of crosses, which changes to a sequence of short curving lines in response to the columns at the base of his khayamiya.

A black-and-white sketch for a painting very similar to *Interior with Egyptian Curtain* appears on the wall to the rear of *Large Red Interior* (1948). Given that these were both made in the same year, it seems reasonable that a sketch for a subsequent painting would have been in his studio at that time. The changes between the final painting and this prototype emphasize the khayamiya as a major component of the painting, rather than concealed behind a floral arrangement and grid-like pattern.

Another clear indication of the development of *Interior with Egyptian Curtain* is the *Still Life with Pomegranates* (1947). The inclusion of his khayamiya provided a means to resolve the spatial ambiguities of *Still Life with Pomegranates*, which lacks the dynamic arabesques and visual intensity of its successor. The placement of a female face in profile (resembling *Interior with Black Fern* of 1948) and a relatively dull zigzag border, as well as a curiously formless orange and white pattern, gives reason to believe that Matisse felt this composition deserved revisiting. Even the palm tree through the window becomes an "explosive motif" in this revision.[3]

Matisse's decision to exchange the beige canvas of the original khayamiya with an imaginary black background evokes his fauvist work from 1905. The use of a black background is unusual but not unprecedented for Matisse, as demonstrated by *Laurette in a Green Robe (Black Background)* (1916). Black backgrounds do not appear in any khedival khayamiya due to the use of tent canvas as the base for appliqué.

Many commentators agree that these Egyptian appliqués were a contributing element in Matisse's development of his celebrated paper cut-outs.[4] As the art writer Brian Oard wrote, "It is impossible at this point not to see the Egyptian Curtain as a prefiguration of Matisse's next artistic direction: the late cut-outs which consist entirely of symbols arranged on flat surfaces."[5]

The process of making the paper cut-outs mirrors the process for sewing khayamiya. Colored pieces are cut to shape, retaining their organic flowing lines, then applied to a background surface. For Matisse, the pieces were painted paper, cut precisely before being carefully arranged and adhered with glue. For the tentmakers, colored cotton is cut approximately before being adhered with an initial stitch. The edge of each piece is then tucked and sewn into shape. Both processes may be described as 'drawing with scissors.'

Matisse's cut-outs also drew on existing collage practices in cubism and surrealism and on his lifelong association with the material properties of textiles. That said, the main textile previously cited as an influence on Matisse's cut-outs are the *tifaifai* quilts of Polynesia. These have a strong claim as Matisse traveled to Tahiti in 1930, where he collected both *tifaifai* and tapa cloth. These sources can be seen in his subsequent prints, paper cut-outs, and drawings. Additionally, the influence of *tifaifai* benefits from the wider awareness of those Polynesian quilts. They have been featured in international exhibitions, scholarly and popular books, and diverse interdisciplinary articles. [6] By contrast, khayamiya remained obscure beyond Egypt until quite recently.

Affinities such as these aside, Matisse was probably more interested in both *tifaifai*'s and khayamiya's mutual regard for shapes of designated color, flat simplified forms, and their elegant use of spatial relationships. As Ann Dumas summarized Matisse's use of textiles in his painting:

> Used traditionally at first, as mere background elements in his compositions, textiles soon became the springboard for his radical experiments with perspective and an art based on decorative patterning and pure harmonies of color and line.[7]

His *Egyptian Curtain* now has a name and its own context. It can be seen referenced beyond the 1948 painting, and deserves recognition as a contributing factor in the development of the paper cut-outs. Matisse was not alone in his use of khayamiya as a subject in painting; however, the implications of his applications of khayamiya are profound. Matisse's act of homage to the tentmakers of Cairo spurred some of the most significant innovations in twentieth-century art.

Khayamiya and Orientalism

It is surprising that neither the Napoleonic savants (active in Egypt between 1798–1801) nor Emile Prisse d'Avennes (1858–79) recorded Egyptian designs attributed to khayamiya appliqué. They described decorative tents in Egypt featuring intricate floriated patterns more typical of Ottoman tents, but these are distinct from the bold forms of khedival-era khayamiya after 1870.

The earliest depiction of khedival-era khayamiya is a photograph featuring a tableau of Islamic scholars *(ulama)* by Emile/Henri Béchard, dated to the 1870s. Several alternative sittings for this photograph are known, suggesting that these scholars were models rather than an authentic record of a faculty meeting. Regardless of which image one considers, as in *Interior with Egyptian Curtain*, the khayamiya is the most striking feature. However, it is not merely an ornamental prop. The calligraphic epigram in Arabic reads "Oh opener of doors, open for us a blessed door," a request that is consistent with the aspirations of a religious scholar. Similar uses of khayamiya as backdrops for street businesses like cafés, fruit vendors, healers, and entertainers have been documented elsewhere.

Such fantasies were appealing to Matisse, especially in his earlier years, where he would frequently evoke odalisques reclining in harems through the strategic placement of exotic textiles collected from the Maghrib. Fabio Fabbi (1861–1946) was a prolific Italian orientalist painter known for colorful female dancers swirling or luxuriating in harems, or stripped naked for sale in slave markets, drawing upon Egyptian sources to create ambiguous fantasy settings. By contrast, Matisse never referenced Egypt as a setting for his odalisques. His work after 1905 ceases to resemble Fabbi's approach, focusing less on titillating narratives and more on pattern, rhythm, harmony, and color. In Matisse's harems, the nude woman provides a justification for the layering of textiles and brilliant colors. For Fabbi, the harem justifies the nude woman.

Fabbi's khayamiya appears variously as a wall hanging inside a harem and as an awning over a street, both verified by photographic and documentary evidence as authentic applications of khayamiya in the early twentieth century. On close inspection, one notes that these khayamiya feature the same composition. It was typical for orientalists, including

Matisse, to recycle objects from their studio across several artworks. However, this panel is identical to the one photographed by Béchard in the 1870s. Fabbi more than likely adapted this photographic reference for his own needs, just as he adapted the poses of the young dancers.

Fabbi was not the only painter to draw from Béchard's photograph. The English painter Walter Charles Horsley (1855–1934) exhibited his painting *Unwilling Evidence* at the Royal Academy in 1882 (see plate 25). Horsley's orientalism situates sentimental Victorian narratives as scenes set in Cairo, conspicuously lacking flirtatious dancers or nudes. *Unwilling Evidence* presents viewers with a trial or interrogation; an adult in yellow and red robes is beginning to lose his patience with the reluctant testimony of a young Nubian boy, and discretely reaches for his cane. The boy is cowering as he notices a young woman, hiding in the doorway behind Béchard's khayamiya, who gestures to ensure the boy remains silent, perhaps keeping a secret for her. Onlookers watch the courtyard drama unfold, including two women behind a *mashrabiya* screen. Narratives drawn from the perspectives of children served a popular Victorian-era demand for relatable scenes or conversation pieces, in contrast to Fabbi's ambiguous erotica and predating Matisse's fauvist modernism. The questions prompted by Horsley drive a narrative—what has happened, and what will happen next?

Horsley's use of khayamiya draws on a second photographic source. Gabriel Lekegian photographed the courtyard of an Arab home in Cairo around 1880, which was also published as a postcard. The khayamiya in this scene is different to the one in Béchard's image, but the configuration of the courtyard in *Unwilling Evidence* is consistent with Lekegian's photograph. Horsley has retained the open doorway and square *mashrabiya* windows above the bench, as well as three tiers of the stepped archway over the suspended khayamiya and the band of calligraphic tiles, which he has painted in blue and red.

Unlike Fabbi and Horsley, Matisse did not rely upon photographic references when depicting khayamiya. Other painters also had first-hand access to these textiles, such as Walter Tyndale and Reginald Barratt, who depicted khayamiya in ethnographic contexts akin to Lekegian's image. Axel Herman Haig included khayamiya as incidental details within his Egyptian streetscapes, suspended against walls, doorways, or overhead as awnings.

George Joy's history painting *General Gordon's Last Stand* (1893) features a khedival-era khayamiya fixed to a pole and carried as a banner by Mahdist soldiers preparing to execute Gordon. The tentmakers made appliquéd banners for ritual processions, as depicted in paintings by Jean-Leon

Gerome in 1824 and a century later in photographs by Gervais Courtellemont, but Joy's depiction of a khayamiya waved as a marshaling banner is unique. Like the *jibbehs* (patchworked garments) worn by the Mahdists, Joy's khayamiya was based on a looted souvenir of the Sudan campaign.[8]

Another khayamiya souvenir appears in a portrait by Henry Brokman-Knudsen (1868–1933) of his family. The artist's mother, wife, son Erik, and his nurse recline at a picnic in a shaded garden, where a striking khedival khayamiya serves as a splendid background. Brokman-Knudsen's original textile emerged at an auction in France in 2015, stained and bearing calligraphy that was removed from the painting.

The French painter Emile Bernard (not to be confused with Emile Béchard, an alias of Henri or Hippolyte Béchard) also suspended a khedival khayamiya sideways in his studio, as documented in a photograph from 1895.[9] Following his visit to Cairo in 1908, Douglas Sladen also described the use of large appliqué panels like this as interior ceilings in the residence of a Swiss diplomat in Cairo.

Reminiscent of Matisse's studio odalisques, the use of khayamiya as a decorative textile screen is consistent with their Egyptian use as mobile theater sets for dancers and musicians. Similar aesthetic intentions can be seen in the kitchen of the Bristol household on Massachusetts Avenue in 1937 or the dining room of philanthropist Doris Duke at Shangri-La in Honolulu, or the wall-filling panel at Oak Alley in Florida, collected by Josephine Stewart between 1906 and 1923. Khayamiya continue to make appearances in depictions of private spaces like musician Marianne Faithfull's four-poster bed canopy in 1969, or the bedroom of American actress Ellen Pompeo in 2010, where khedival khayamiya were suspended as decorative backdrops. Each of these surprising appearances embraces the startling aesthetics of khayamiya, very much in keeping with the tentmakers' intentions today.

10

Making Khayamiya
Design and Technique

The making of khayamiya has remained unchanged for at least five hundred years. Though the composition and forms have adapted to new demands for these textiles, their design process remains intact. Like many Egyptian crafts, the tentmaker's skills are taught from generation to generation, and every stage involves learning by hand. The years required to develop these skills and the intimacy of their acquisition through apprenticeships form a considerable investment for a tentmakers' workshop. For this reason, the tentmaker families form a close-knit economic and social community. A tentmaker's skill and loyalty was once rewarded by lifelong employment within a workshop hierarchy that would have been familiar to artisans within the guilds of the Ottoman Empire. Today relationships are slightly different—the average tentmaker's long-term goal is to set up their own business, rather than to work for somebody else.

Designing within a Framework

One important feature of the tentmakers' trade that held true until the 1970s was the fact that their primary occupation was to make tents and that these tents followed certain conventions of size, dimension, and decorative repertoire. Although there was ample scope to innovate within the tradition, the framework was a clearly defined one.

In the nineteenth century, for example, a typical khayamiya awning was 2 m wide by 3 or 3.5 m high. In the twentieth century, the tent panels became a standard size of 2.75 m wide, and 5.5 m high, and the predominant color was usually red. The other colors included dark blue, orange,

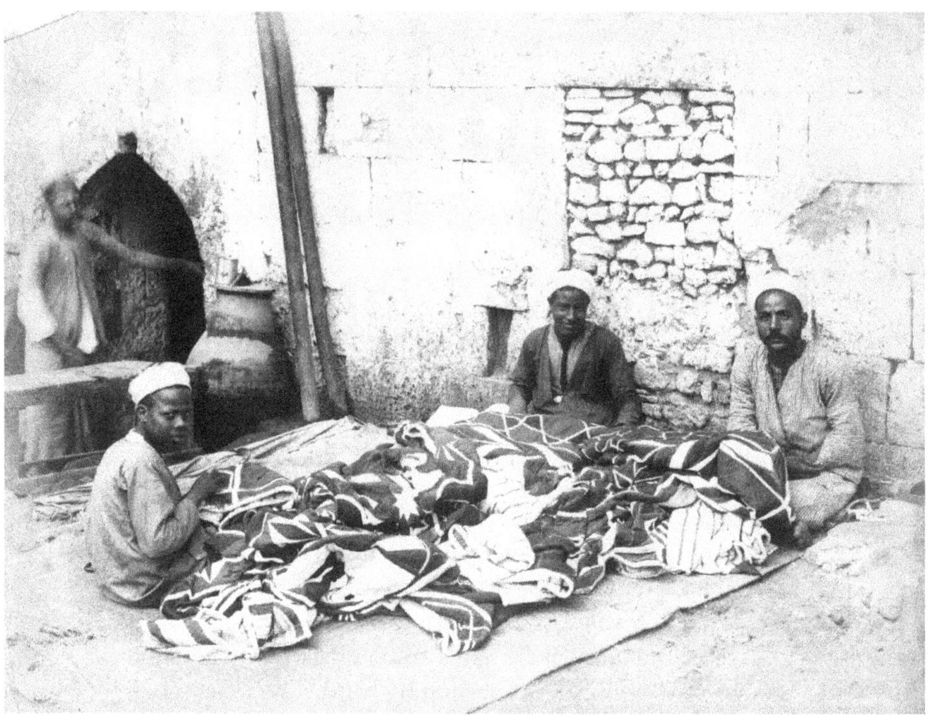

Figure 23 Tentmakers photographed by the Zangaki Brothers, ca. 1880s. Photograph by the Zangaki Studio.

a strong green, and white. The standard patterns were either a geometric lattice, known as *al-sanan* (toothed), panels with large medallions resembling the cover of a Qu'ran, called *dahr al-mus-haf* (the back of the Qu'ran), and something that was a hybrid, given the name of *turunga*, a colloquialism with no apparent formal meaning, but referring to a medallion.

The tentmakers would be working within these parameters, with a defined palette of colors. Because the tents were designed to be modular, they could be erected at any size that was a multiple of the unit of measure at the time (in other words, in the twentieth century, a tent could be any multiple of 2.5 meters wide). This meant that the individual tent panels needed to be similar enough not to look mismatched, and for this reason they were usually produced in sets of between thirty and forty panels.

In reality, so long as the design of each panel was more or less the same, and the lattice structure coherent, differences in small details would go unnoticed to the average member of the public. What this meant was that the smaller details, for example the flowers used to decorate the main medallion, could differ slightly without it being too much of a problem. There was certainly room for innovation, but because these were functional tents, the artistic element of the craft was in many respects determined by its use. A glance at photos of *suradiq*s (tent pavilions) over the course of the twentieth century shows that some were indeed much more accomplished from a design point of view than others, but to an untrained eye the panels appear very much the same.

The compositions of vast *suradiq* panels (each known as a *tark*) are as modular as the panels themselves. Individual units within these panels possess names known to the tentmakers, but meaningless to almost everyone else. Some of these, like *ranq* (a circular blazon), pay homage to Mamluk design conventions; others, like *makhadda* (cushion), refer to the size and shape of the unit (a small square). Some terms are obvious, like *rub'* (quarter), referring to a quarter of a *tark* panel, the standard unit which was repeated four times, or *tu'* (collar). Some terms refer to the intricacy of the design, for example, *turunga was'a* (a wide medallion), refers to plainer panels with a central medallion, four quarter medallions in the corners, and a relatively plain field, except for some lotus scrolls.

Apart from the three standard *suradiq* types referred to above (*dahr al-mus-haf*, *al-sanan*, and *turunga*), more specific patterns sometimes refer to the individual who developed that design, but this oral history varies from workshop to workshop. Other names are descriptive of the motif's appearance, such as the *dhakar* (male), *kaff* (palm of the hand), and *ras te'ban* (snake head), the way in which one piece of fabric curls over another. Given the enormous scale of these panels, templates are developed for separate units rather than entire compositions. Unlike smaller forms of khayamiya appliqué, *tark* are sewn collaboratively.

Smaller panels, made for other uses, appear to have been popular from the late nineteenth century at least. One can see the reason for such a solution: people liking the tentmaker's work for its artistic craft-related merit, not because they need a tent for a grand occasion. The outcome was that the designs of the components of larger tent panels were used to create small individual pieces. With this sort of essentially decorative work anything was possible—but, figural panels aside, most of the other work made clear reference to the artistic tradition of the tent pavilion itself.

It was with the demise of the handmade *suradiq* in the late 1970s that the artistic backbone of the tentmakers' craft was fractured. There was no longer a framework setting boundaries within which one could innovate, and in recent decades there has been much more experimentation. For good or ill, this is probably the most significant factor that has had a bearing on design over the past two centuries, but it is by no means the only one.

From Apprentice to Master

Traditionally, an aspiring tentmaker would begin as a 'server,' or *khaddam*, as a boy of maybe eleven or twelve. His tasks would involve bringing the raw materials and fetching food and drink, and in the process he would carefully observe the craftsmen *(sanay'iya)* as they sewed. Eventually he would be invited to become an apprentice *(sabi)* through the gift of a cushion, which is used to support a tentmaker's back as he works. The gift of this cushion demonstrated that an apprentice had earned their right to a 'place' in the workshop. By sewing next to an experienced tentmaker, threading his needles and sharing his scissors, an apprentice would learn the intricacies of the craft. The irregular quality of an apprentice's work usually involves a great deal of unpicking and resewing to the satisfaction of their supervisor *(usta)*. The tentmaker's sewing tools are simple: just a large pair of tailor's scissors, a thimble, and a needle.

When an apprentice's skills had developed, he earned his own pair of scissors. This was a practical and symbolic statement of independence. For experienced tentmakers within a workshop setting, borrowing scissors would be regarded as embarrassing and inconvenient. However, interchangeable, inexpensive items with a short lifespan like tentmaker's needles and thimbles were not accompanied by any overt symbolism.

Today, the rites of passage marked by the receipt of a cushion and then a pair of scissors are far less frequently upheld. In fact, one of the tentmakers, when asked about the symbolism of the scissors, responded, "Yes, it's true, but when I first traveled abroad to an international exhibition, I couldn't help but purchase a new pair of scissors for the trip."[1] In this case the scissors marked a rite of passage, but in a different way.

Overall, the structure of the contemporary tentmaker's workshop is a lot more fluid. Nowadays, several tentmakers 'outsource' their work to stitchers who may not be based in Cairo at all; this is especially true of more inexpensive work, referred to as 'the work of the market' *(shughl al-suq)* or 'commercial' *(tuggari)*.

Earning the title of *usta* is described by one of today's tentmakers, Yasser el-Leithy, as being "like a coronation." The most skilled and respected tentmakers usually receive this title when they come to manage or employ a team of *sanay'iya*—their acknowledged skill as a master tentmaker being a requisite. They designate work, select or invent designs, and informally own the 'copyright' to specific compositions and motifs. The *ustawat* (masters) of the tentmakers are now regarded as the last pinnacles of an endangered legacy. Nonetheless, the process of the craft remains the same.

The Tentmaking Technique

Tentmakers sew by hand, sitting cross-legged with their backs supported by a cushion against a wall. This posture was once shared by many other Egyptian artisans and goes as far back as ancient Egypt. Older tentmakers noted that their 'retirement' usually coincided with the point at which their knees could not sustain this position. Sewing machines are only used to sew large panels together, often when making imitation khayamiya.

Khayamiya designs begin as a hand-drawn composition transferred onto a stencil. These are created with basic equipment—a large sheet of paper, white chalk or crayon, sometimes carbon powder, and a pencil. Asymmetrical designs (such as the narrow bands characteristic of touristic khayamiya from the early twentieth century) are drawn straight across the paper. Symmetrical designs are drawn across half a sheet of folded paper, then pricked with a needle ('ponced') to transfer the second half of the composition. Radially symmetrical designs are folded repeatedly to form a triangular segment reaching from center to border. The top of this segment is drawn upon, then poncing transfers that drawing through the entire composition. The completed stencil is then laid across the backing fabric to be dusted with chalk, iron oxide powder, carbon powder, or charcoal diluted in kerosene.[2]

This provides fine patterns for reference, which are redrawn over the fabric with chalk or pencil. Some of these paper templates are archived and used many times, and several templates can be combined into a single panel. One design may be interpreted through a multitude of variations in color, giving very different effects.

The needle-turned appliqué begins with the cutting of each cotton piece to approximately the right size. Their edges are then folded under to create a precise shape, sewn into place with a deftly-handled hemstitch. These are primarily overcast stitches, though straight stitches are also performed on thin borders. The invisibility of all stitches is prized by the modern tentmakers (but did not seem to have been as important in the nineteenth century). Embroidered details are frequently seen on touristic forms of khayamiya, typically couched and performed with conspicuous skill.

Multiple working sites are dedicated to the construction of a single *suradiq*. These include the drafting workroom, where patterns are drawn to scale and transferred to canvas; a machine room, where large sheets of canvas or finished modular panels are sewn together; and an open area, where the colorful appliqué is skillfully sewn. This was once the primary function of the open-air roof of the Qasaba of Radwan Bey, now known as the Street of the Tentmakers, in addition to several private workshops in the vicinity.[3]

Designing Khayamiya

The design process of the khayamiya of the nineteenth century can be inferred from the panels themselves. The tentmakers of the khedival period relied primarily upon freehand approximation, with templates used to a much lesser extent. This change can be seen in the comparison of complex geometric sections and calligraphic insets. Geometric design is a sophisticated and nuanced field that requires extensive preplanning, so casual approximations are especially evident in the most vernacular examples from this period. These idiosyncrasies result in highly animated compositions, livelier for their accidental distortion; refined precision is a characteristic of only the highest quality tentmaker work. Calligraphic panels reveal underdrawing from templates that may have been derived from an original freehand composition, but in many cases the writing of Arabic calligraphy was performed freehand, with variable skill. Spelling mistakes, running out of space, inadvertent omissions of words, or mistakes in the dots integral to the Arabic script, are extremely common, indicating a greater spontaneity in the design process than is found today.

As mentioned in Chapter 7, the 1920s saw a conscious revival in Islamic art, which is very clear in the design of khayamiya as well. The contrast between the somewhat sketch-like tent panels from the late nineteenth century, and the meticulously executed and inscribed 1920s and 1930s panels shows a clear change in the design process. In looking at the work produced today, most of it falls into the latter category, although for simpler designs the experienced tentmaker, having produced them so many times, will sometimes draw a quick outline with a pencil and work from there.

Color and Composition

The selection of color is imperative within khayamiya design. Any pattern may be reinterpreted through multiple color combinations, traditionally the decision of the workshop, but sometimes at the request of the client. The tentmakers value striking combinations of color, focusing upon the intensity and contrast of vibrant tones. The colors of contemporary khayamiya reflect individual tentmaker's tastes, but some aspects of color are consistent with specific genres and periods in khayamiya design. For example, the modular panels designed for a *suradiq* showcase primary colors as well as orange, green, black, and white. Small medallions in green provide space for the addition of the tent owner's (*farrash*'s) name and phone number, usually written in yellow appliqué. The framework underpinning *suradiq* patterns is typically white, forming a lattice through the entire panel, evoking the gaps of unadorned canvas once visible between the patches of appliqué. As the objective of these architectural-scale textiles is to create compelling backdrops, so the tentmakers create vast fields of bright color and mesmerizing patterns to juxtapose the everyday with the extraordinary. In direct contrast, contemporary 'Islamic' or calligraphic designs are relatively monochromatic, typically in somber white, browns, dark blues, and black, recalling the ink on paper calligraphy and the inlaid marble panels on the walls of Mamluk mosques, both of which inspired this work.

One of the factors often overlooked when thinking about color palette is which colors are available. For example, the dyes available to the Egyptian tentmakers in the late nineteenth century resulted in the preference for white, indigo blue (light and dark), and red (both organic and inorganic). These popular colors were described by the traveler Douglas Sladen in 1911 as resembling battle flags, "pleasantly garish" when new, but "adorable" once faded through fifty years of use.[4] Less common lemon-yellows and "gaseous" greens became associated with touristic forms of khayamiya in the early twentieth century, described by other writers as "strong and primitive colours."[5] By the 1920s purples, orange, and pinks were introduced to the tentmaker's range, sometimes including patterned fabrics recycled from clothing. Through these fabrics the tentmakers "were trying to accommodate the aesthetic tastes of a foreign clientele, but were constrained by the color range used within Egyptian society."[6]

Today, Egyptian cottons in almost every color are available to the tentmakers, and perhaps one of the most striking developments is a greater tendency to use a wide range of colors on each piece. Some pharaonic-style panels from the nineteenth century showed a wider range of colors, but nothing in comparison to today's higher end pieces, in which incorporating a wide range of colors seems to be an aim in itself. Greater exposure to international quilting circles may be behind this shift.

Fabrics and Thread

The history of khayamiya reveals changes in fabric technology, from hand-dyed organic hues sewn into hand-spun backing canvas used until the khedival era to the adoption of synthetic dyes and commercially produced fabrics in a vast range of colors today. Early twentieth-century experimentation with silks and recycled fabrics led to colorful and imaginative embellishments such as donkey riders with dapper striped silk garments, embroidered eyes, metallic sheens, or fish and birds inlaid with vibrant patterns.

Khayamiya feature two or three layers of fabric. In all panels, the back is a plain canvas described as *tark*.[7] This was once the exterior wall of the tent, and is retained as a durable base for all khayamiya appliqués. Some appliqué stitches may penetrate this canvas to become visible, but this is avoided as it is seen as a sign of haste or inexperience. During the late nineteenth century this canvas was made of many woven variations in linen and hemp blends in narrow repeating strips, usually 40 cm wide and sewn together by hand. Such backing canvas was often distinguished by vertical blue selvedge stripes, also seen on undecorated awnings suspended over Egyptian streets and reminiscent of sail cloth, as well as pilgrims' tents documented in photographs of Mecca. The use of indigo-dyed fibers to create thin blue lines in linen and other textiles is widespread around the Mediterranean and Europe, and has been noted in ancient Egyptian linens as well.[8] Although not designed for the tentmakers, the thin stripes help create a grid which stitchers used to create panels of regular size and design.

Early twentieth-century panels are backed with a variety of plain canvases, sometimes in a dull green. Contemporary *suradiq*s are sewn to soft but very thick canvas usually marked with black selvedge stripes. Since at least the 1970s contemporary khayamiya cover their backing canvas entirely with an intermediate layer of cotton, upon which appliqué is sewn. This means they also meet the definition of a 'quilt,' as three layers of fabric held together by thread. Meeting that definition was not important for the tentmakers—the middle layer probably began as a means of hiding the selvedge stripes so the pattern could stand out. Today the canvas fabric itself is made in the Nile Delta and brought by truck to Cairo twice a week. Tentmakers buy it in rolls directly from the truck.

The appliqué fabrics, made of a smooth and supple Egyptian cotton, are acquired from sources located near the Street of the Tentmakers. Some of the fabrics used for early twentieth-century appliqué were adapted from discarded clothing through the *zabbalin*, the community that provides Cairo's recycling network.[9] Older tentmakers also recall dyeing their own fabrics when they were children, which they carried to their family workshops. Traditional dyer's workshops continue to work near the Street of the Tentmakers today. The modern fabric is thicker than it was one hundred or so years ago, when a lighter, slightly gauzy *batista* (batiste) was used. Incidentally, the traditional Egyptian fabric seller's cry, "In every color, oh batista," today used to refer to any mishmash of bright colors, is a good indication of why the fabric was relied on by the tentmakers of yesteryear. Cottons of a single color are normally used, but there are touristic examples that playfully borrow printed or woven patterns (notably in reclaimed silk, often as garments for pharaohs), and some very recent designs of butterflies or garish tropical fish consist entirely of small pieces of highly patterned fabrics.

In the nineteenth century, the threads used by the tentmakers were a uniform white, and stitched at a uniform but slightly wider distance with less discretion. Modern and contemporary khayamiya feature threads color-matched to the appliquéd cotton, sewn to appear almost invisible. The difference is the perception of the textile as an 'artwork' rather than 'architecture'—a shift that emerged as the tentmakers embraced the genre of touristic khayamiya.

In a similar vein, it is common in the older pieces for the backing canvas, broadcloth with distinctive thin blue or black vertical stripes, to be visible, and indeed the stripes themselves can often be seen in the places where the canvas is visible. The reality is that people would not have noticed this when the tent was erected—it was a backdrop, and a space for social activity, not an object of scrutiny.

The tentmaker Muhammad Hashem recalled a 'suggestion' from the Egyptian government in 1953 (following the coup of 1952) that the tentmakers cease using Egyptian cotton, as it was a "scarce fabric" that was more valuable when exported. Due to protests from local clients—the *farrashin* or tent renters—this 'suggestion' was ignored.[10]

The Grammar of Ornament

Although khayamiya was not noted in Owen Jones's 1858 book *The Grammar of Ornament*, each genre of khayamiya possesses a 'grammar of ornament' developed by the tentmakers. The composition of every khayamiya panel possesses continuity from the base or border to the center. Orientations are implied as either clearly vertical, horizontal, or universally symmetrical. Bases and tops are emphasized by frequently repeated motifs and borders are defined by an 'outer chain' that surrounds the entire panel.[11]

These principles were as true of khayamiya during the 1980s as they were during the khedival era between 1867 and 1915. However, the uniformity of khedival-period khayamiya after 1860 is notable, and is usually at least loosely inspired by architecture. From the top down, one will find an alternating border (known as *'arusa*, meaning a doll or bride; the term used to refer to mosque crenellations and battlements) above a calligraphic band, usually in white text on a red or dark blue field. Beneath that band one might find a series of niches that may also hold additional calligraphy. Below that, a dominant square holds a circular motif, consecutively layered, containing a geometric design. The lowest portion of the panel consists of a series of thin columns with ornamented capitals, recalling the marble paneling on prayer niches and around the walls of Cairo's wealthier seventeenth- and eighteenth-century houses. The entire panel is encompassed with a fine border.

For touristic khayamiya, this border is usually an alternating 'dash and dot' sequence of yellow or grey divided by short black-white-black intervals. This bold pattern is adapted from the borders of ancient tomb paintings and is not normally associated with khedival compositions. Contemporary khayamiya possess a straight border of a single color, either evoking the background of the appliqué field or selected to serve as a frame.

The tentmakers of the khedival period developed many combinations within this methodical structure, but their adherence to this tall, rectangular format was challenged only when the scale of the panel was increased, usually to make an awning or a canopy. In such cases, the canons of vertical architectural order are superseded by the traditions of carpets and decorative ceilings.

The twentieth century saw even greater standardization and the use of the same tents for many different occasions. One impact this had was the disappearance of calligraphy from the standard tent panel, thereby increasing flexibility of use. With one of the common uses of appliquéd tents being funerary occasions, inscriptions wishing happiness and prosperity would have been inappropriate. Similarly, verses of the Qu'ran would have been inappropriate for some occasions, for example Christian weddings or funerals, and the solution appears to have been for the standard tent panel not to have calligraphy at all.

Makers Versus Designers

Individual tentmakers play diverse roles as designers. Many do not design their own work, specializing in sewing from templates instead. The masters or *usta*s periodically invent new compositions, but there were also specialist designers among the tentmakers. Such individuals were commissioned to create new designs or would sell the rights to new designs to workshop owners. The career of Yasser el-Leithy, narrated in detail in the final chapter, demonstrates the progression of his work from tentmaker to khayamiya designer.

> Raouf Ayoub would come to me with a piece of paper and say, "Our work is becoming outdated, come on Yasser, give me a treat," and I would ask him, "What should I draw?" He would reply, "Whatever your hand yields." My hand would produce heavy work; elaborate, difficult to implement, what we would call *danah* (heavy cannonball) work. To give you an example, appliquéing a bedspread at that time would take twenty-five days to a month to finish, while a 1 m by 1 m piece in *danah* could take two months. . . .
>
> In the year 2000 I decided to leave Raouf. I felt I could not work as an employee to anyone any more. . . . Raouf was accepting but he had one condition; that I would not replicate any work that I did for him during those ten years. I told him not to worry, as that was like a code of honor between us. He was right . . . Raouf paid me three times; once for the design, once when I stitched and finished the piece, and a third time if I sold it myself. I would set my price for each piece. As for my percentage of sales, he would buy my designs on paper, irrespective of when and if we would implement them. That is why I only sell designs to different merchants and workshops, and I stopped sewing altogether.[12]

The Dynamics of the Street of the Tentmakers

The popular Egyptian saying "My brother and I against my cousin, but my cousin and I against the outsider," is very true of the tentmakers, who form a community vis-à-vis the outside world, but are competitive among themselves. As demand has waned, competition has increased further and the nature of the Street of the Tentmakers, a row of small cubicle-like shops offering no privacy whatsoever, means that the only way to keep one's best ideas a secret is to guard them elsewhere. The tentmaker Mahmoud Farag even moved his business to the suburb of Maadi partly to avoid the copying of his elegant figurative designs of folkloric dancers and musicians, and also to reach the affluent expatriates living there.

The storerooms (*makhazin*, singular *makhzan*) of the tentmakers are distinct from the small and uniform shops lining the Street of the Tentmakers, which display relatively similar work to pedestrian traffic. It is in these private spaces that visitors are invited to consider designs unique to that tentmaker's workshop. These innovative or unique pieces are jealously guarded, for intellectual property is not easily protected. Similarly, even when revealing designs to visitors in shops along the street, customers are usually seated at the back of the shop facing the street, and their prospective purchases are held up to face them; in other words, with their backs to the street, therefore not divulging the design.

Complications arise when a designer, using their anonymity to their advantage, sells the same design to multiple workshops. This leads to accusations of theft and copying, and accumulated grudges can last a long time along the street. The ownership of designs can also be inherited and sold, such as the calligraphic template for a panel of the ninety-nine names of God used by Muhammad Dendon, which was sold by his widow to another tentmaker workshop (see plate 29).

Women Tentmakers

Few of the Egyptian tentmakers are women. This stems from the traditional role of men as the breadwinners, and the perception of the tentmakers' spaces as typically 'male,' including the public shops along the Street of the Tentmakers and their private workshops. There is a separation between family and public life—for example, it is customary for tentmakers to not mention their wives by name unless the person is well known to them. Women learn sewing skills from their partners and one another, not as formal apprentices employed in workshops, resulting in work that is more likely to be used for cushion covers than large or complex commissions. This is partially because these can be accomplished quickly as a side activity while a woman runs the household.

As khayamiya appliqués were usually sewn anonymously, it was not until the American Quilter's Society's insistence on signed appliqués for the US market in 2012 that the names of women working as tentmakers became attributed to their work—and this was a side-effect of a policy intended to promote the tentmakers as artists, not to discern their genders. Some of the oral histories recorded by Durham University acknowledged that women had also served as tentmakers in previous generations, but much like today, their roles along the Street of the Tentmakers remain invisible.

Khayamiya within a Larger World

It is worth mentioning that cotton-on-canvas appliqué is not a peculiarly Egyptian tradition, but perhaps what is surprising is its architectural scale and the fact that it has survived so long in Egypt. Other similar traditions include those in Ottoman Turkey (possibly of Egyptian origin) which lasted until the 1860s, Syria, Iran, India, and Morocco (the latter using a velvet base). Some examples of these would have found their way to Egypt as gifts. The tent heritage of central Asia also features decorative appliqués and other methods of construction—notably felt and woven tent bands—as well as leather work that are distinct from the Egyptian tentmakers.[13] Similarly, the woven black or goat-hair tents of the Bedouin are not related to Egyptian khayamiya, the first being a seminomadic residence, the latter being an ephemeral pavilion for primarily urban events or short expeditions.

In some respects, the sewing of khayamiya is technically similar to Kenyan appliqué, South American Mola textiles, or Polynesian *tifaifai* quilting, though the speed of sewing, intricacy of composition, and architectural scale of khayamiya set it apart from these comparable textiles. The appliqué of Turkish, Iranian, Pakistani, and Indian tentmakers appears more closely related to Egyptian khayamiya, and they may share a common point of origin. These textiles serve ritual and social roles as forms of conspicuous display made by skilled individuals who exercise creative agency by adapting accepted conventions of design.

Mapping the shared lineages of diverse decorated tents globally raises other questions of knowledge dissemination, differences in patronage, locality and materiality, and review of extinct traditions. The relationships between these pathways are challenges for future scholarship.

Quilting and Khayamiya

Of all comparable contemporary craft networks, the tentmakers of Cairo have found a thematic link to quilters around the world. They have also proven to be supportive and admiring patrons, namely because quilters recognize excellence in craft as well as long-held tradition and experimental innovation (see plate 26). Blaire Gagnon's 2003 thesis, one of the first scholarly investigations into Egyptian appliqué, was inspired by her work as a quilter. Quilters were also responsible for the crowdfunding of the 2015 documentary film *The Tentmakers of Cairo* by Kim Beamish.

Quilters have generated independent platforms for the display, peer review, and publication of their work as craft and contemporary art. Theirs is both a craft and a thriving industry, simultaneously demanding the recognition of its past and encouraging the sustainable continuation of the work to new generations. By contrast, the tentmakers are a small and competitive group of skilled workers driven by professional demand but culturally and geographically isolated, with no independent means of publication. The 'amateur' or 'hobbyist' so valuable to the quilt industry does not exist within the Street of the Tentmakers. Broadly speaking, quilting has been perceived as women's work, but the tentmakers are usually male.

The affinity between khayamiya and quilts consists of similarities and juxtapositions. While quilts have faced the challenge of being perceived as horizontally displayed utilitarian objects, khayamiya has always been accorded the tapestry-like 'dignity' of vertical display, even in a strictly functional context—though perhaps this has been offset by their exposure to harsh outdoor conditions (dust, heat, and direct sun) versus the indoor security afforded to quilts. Quilts serve private needs within domestic contexts, while khayamiya are temporary displays for a wide range of outdoor ceremonies. Quilts are privately owned objects that can aspire to retire as family heirlooms, but khayamiya screens are hired as objects for public display, sometimes repaired but usually discarded as rags when faded.

Both crafts have struggled to be seen as 'art.' Neither has yet found their due representation in museums and art galleries, though this is changing. Both quilts and khayamiya are a form of folk art, ancient in origin and still made with similar techniques, materials, and technology. They are equally concerned with display, ornament, and transcending the functional into the spectacular. For much of their history, both quilts and khayamiya were made anonymously. They both embrace a complex heritage, and recognizing their shared context as contemporary crafts is mutually beneficial. As producers of a tangible cultural heritage, the tentmakers demonstrate the continuity of historic and increasingly rare skills that cannot yet be outsourced to sewing machines.

Interaction with quilters beyond Egypt has had several influences on the work of the tentmakers, not least of which has been the introduction of motifs, patterns, and colors that had not been part of their repertoire, including everything from kingfishers to tropical fish and roses. However, it has promoted the esteem of the tentmakers within Egypt, especially among themselves. The tentmakers have been described as 'rockstars' following extensive participation in major international exhibitions, such as those coordinated for the American Quilter's Society in the United States, the Santa Fe Folk Craft Festival, the Art in Action festival in

Oxford, United Kingdom, the Siyadala Quilt Festival in South Africa, and at cultural institutions such as the Islamic Arts Museum Malaysia and the Art Gallery of South Australia. Jenny Bowker, the curator of the first exhibition of tentmaker appliqué in Australia, said the tentmakers were swarmed by crowds of fascinated quilters. They were "so utterly humbled by the interest in what they had believed was an unimportant and menial skill."[14]

The more talented of the tentmakers now see themselves as artists rather than craftsmen. Although this has not stopped them from producing their traditional work, it has led them to focus on a separate line of detailed, complex multicolored pieces, many of which will be sold abroad, where appreciation of the skill is greater and wallets are larger. There is now a tendency for pieces to be signed by the craftsman, and arguably for greater individualism in design.

This is an interesting shift. International demand for the tentmakers' work is at least 150 years old, and even pieces from the turn of the nineteenth century sometimes show an awareness of tourist demands (combining pharaonic with Islamic motifs, for example). The difference is that the tentmakers had never been part of the international craft network. Their horizons today are far wider than ever before. Perhaps their biggest challenge is how to retain the artistic traditions of the craft, to develop it in a way that is true to itself, and to retain the strong foundation upon which khayamiya has been built.

This is made all the more difficult by the fact that there is very little awareness of khayamiya history within or beyond Egypt. International audiences are perhaps more impressed by the skill of the craft than by its aesthetic traditions. For example, decorative panels depicting flower arrangements and clusters of birds on trees are growing more common because they appeal to western audiences. Some of these motifs originated in the ancient tomb paintings reproduced as touristic panels, or floral bursts from eighteenth-century Ottoman tents, but through the Egyptian tentmakers these subjects developed their own conventions. Today, these are often at the expense of the guiding principles that once defined well-balanced khayamiya.

"It isn't really part of our tradition to hang textiles on the wall, but it is part of our tradition to hang pictures," says John Fisher, a UK-based textile expert who organizes khayamiya exhibitions around the world. "What the tentmakers have done in response is make textile panels that look like pictures, and there is clearly a demand for these."[15]

The impact of quilting can also be seen in recent khayamiya that evokes the structures of western quilts, such as compositions that feature one bold color in each corner, nine-patch grids, embroidered highlights, and border-on-border repetitions. The tentmaker Ahmed Naguib courted controversy by copying the 2009 quilt *Renaissance Revival* by Mariya Waters (inspired by an Ottoman ceiling panel in the Islamic Arts Museum Malaysia) without seeking permission. This misunderstanding was privately resolved, but as he encountered this design through a quilting magazine, it sets a precedent for future interactions.

The patronage of quilters has also led to the tentmakers' creation of sewing workshops to teach khayamiya appliqué skills. These *Stitch like an Egyptian* classes offer the tentmakers a sustainable income that respectfully situates the heritage of khayamiya as a process and product. There is ongoing appeal in learning these endangered sewing and design skills—especially from a master craftsperson whose work is mesmerizing to watch. However, this also prioritizes different skills, for these teachers need to possess patience, charisma, languages beyond Arabic, and a passport or visa for other countries. Some of these skills are already present along the shops of the Street of the Tentmakers, but they are now seen as especially desirable for ambitious tentmakers.

The relationship between quilters and tentmakers takes other commercial forms too. The American Quilter's Society (AQS) developed an unprecedented three-year contract to exclusively promote and sell the work of the tentmakers in the United States from 2012 to 2015. The work was purchased directly from the tentmakers in Cairo then sold to American audiences at exhibitions and online. The profits were used to provide transport and accommodation for tentmaker representatives at AQS events across the United States.

In the lead-up to the tentmaker exhibition at the Australasian Quilt Convention in Melbourne in 2007, curated by Jenny Bowker, the representation of the tentmakers was carefully considered. The most important of these was to feature a high standard of work across the diverse repertoire of the tentmakers and ensure that all tentmaker businesses were represented in every exhibition. This approach initially led to mistakes, as multiple shopfronts could belong to one business, and retailers were mistaken for managers, causing tensions during negotiations. Whenever possible, these exhibitions feature tentmakers' products while other tentmakers work alongside, so they can explain the craft in their own words.

> It is important that the men are there to demonstrate in the exhibitions I have organized. It is partly to let people see how fast they stitch, how simple their tools are, and how skilled they are—but also to establish their clear ownership of the work.
>
> One thing that I have truly sought to change is that all work to be sold in exhibitions is signed. At first we asked for the tentmaker to sign it, and found that some shops were simply making up names rather than giving credit to a worker. Then we asked for shop names, followed by the stitcher's name, and it started to work. This gives ownership and additional provenance for the work, but many tentmakers still cannot see a lot of point in adding their signatures.[16]

Imitation Khayamiya

Since the late 1970s the appliqué work of the tentmakers has been replaced by factory-printed fabrics bearing patterns derived from khayamiya. This 'imitation khayamiya,' known by the tentmakers as *tab'* (literally, 'print-work') was developed by one of the tentmaker families. The handmade panels were getting too expensive to produce and this seemed like an ideal substitute. From early forms consisting of silk screen fabrics printed by hand, it is now produced commercially with sophisticated machines. Imitation khayamiya is appealing to consumers—including the *farrashin*, the assemblers of tents—because it is cheaper, lighter, versatile, and easier to display than handcrafted khayamiya. By making such vibrant decorative fabrics more accessible, imitation khayamiya has undermined the ability of the tentmakers to sustain their skilled profession. Imitation khayamiya has also introduced novelties like the repeating patterns of Ramadan lanterns *(fawanis)*, hearts, cartoon characters, and religious motifs such as the Ka'ba, mosque skylines, and Arabic script. Recent forms of imitation khayamiya have included digital portraits of imams, political figures, and Egyptian celebrities. Although its primary function is to line the interiors of tents and awnings (commonly used for Cairo's thriving café culture, for example), imitation khayamiya has also been resewn into clothing, handbags, tablecloths, upholstery, and other items for export. Significantly, the most common color palette mimics that of the traditional hand-sewn *suradiq*s: predominantly red, with accents of blue, yellow, purple, white, and black (there is also a turquoise variant, but this is less common).

In more recent years, a plusher form of imitation khayamiya has been introduced into the market. This is known as 'computer' work because it involves the machine printing of appliqué work in satin fabric. A design repertoire clearly inspired by the traditional patterns like *dahr al-mus-haf* (the medallions found on the back of the Qur'an) with a range of variations can be found, as well as a wide range of other designs, including 'one-off' decorative panels used as entry panels to the traditional pavilion. These capture important elements of popular culture. One common design is a calligraphic panel with the ninety-nine beautiful attributes of God, *Asma' Allah al-husna*, which have seen a rise in importance in recent decades, probably since they were popularized by leading pop star Hisham Abbas, who started singing them at weddings in 2000, and became the standard first wedding song played by DJs in all social circles of Egyptian society.[17] There is also a panel specifically for a Christian context, featuring a very Catholic-looking Virgin Mary. Printed catalogs show the range of designs from which the *farrashin* businesses can choose.

While purists may shudder at these computer-printed panels, they are not bereft of creativity. A particularly striking example depicts a famous Egyptian shaykh, and one of the country's most popular preachers, Muhammad Mitwalli al-Sha'rawi (1911–98), seated on a prayer rug reading the Qu'ran. An inscription above his head quotes the Qu'ran, stating that there is no fear for God's representatives. Two green hearts frame the unusual composition (see plate 27).

The tentmakers' role in the production of these panels is sewing the printed satin onto the canvas backing and finishing the piece—in other words, adding the trim and the ropes to enable the panels to be tied to the wooden structure forming the pavilion itself. One striking difference in this computer work is that the color palette is not traditional. Many of the designs consist of cream, ochre, and pale blue, while some others comprise a dark blue background with yellow and red decoration. There are also modern-day *surqadiq*s which are made up of gauzy fabrics in different colors, often creating attractive geometric patterns. A final form of tent-work consists of simple pleated fabric in one or two colors—often exported to Sudan. Two typical color combinations are red and white (for weddings) and blue and yellow (apparently often for funerals).

Though imitation khayamiya resemble the designs once sewn by hand, they lack the soul and textured surfaces of the authentic Egyptian tentmaker appliqués. Imitation khayamiya is a logical conclusion of technological modernity along the Street of the Tentmakers. However, it is not the conclusion of this Egyptian art form. The machine-produced khayamiya is only a superficial replacement of the work of the tentmakers, designed as a solution to problems associated with hand-sewn appliqué in an architectural context. The development of imitation khayamiya is driving the need for the tentmakers to exploit new alternatives for their craft. These include collaborations with designers, artists, and the teaching of sewing skills as new commercial alternatives to the sale of khayamiya itself.

Contemporary Khayamiya

Khayamiya has long featured in the background at public and private events but has equally been ignored as an art form in Egypt. For example, despite its spectacular scale and rich design heritage, khayamiya designs were never adapted for use on Egyptian currency or postage stamps. Nor did they make significant appearances in the work of Egyptian modernist artists, writers, musicians, or poets, although they have served as settings for Egyptian theater performances. Khayamiya was not associated with the perception and promotion of Egypt overseas until quite recently, and very few historic examples of khayamiya are held in Egyptian museums and galleries. This disregard has meant the tentmakers have been regarded more like manual laborers than cosmopolitan artists. This stigma is problematic for the recruitment and retention of young tentmakers, especially given the long apprenticeships required to become a master.

Although few young Egyptians beyond the tentmaker families are being trained in this craft, tentative signs of a revival can be seen in the tentmaking profession. Some trained tentmakers have returned from alternative careers to support family businesses, others because their previous professions provided poor conditions and lower social status.[18] Some have tertiary qualifications, and have chosen this profession over other careers because they enjoy the nature of this craft.[19] Encouraged by international opportunities, some tentmakers have ruptured employer-apprentice relationships to open their own shops (such as Hany Abdel-Kader and Tarek el-Safty). As stated to filmmaker Kim Beamish, "This is our future, we cannot keep working as we used to. I am sure that our children will not make the work we know today, they will be making new designs."[20] These tentmakers see the importance of their own work as innovative in both design and enterprise, and as part of a professional legacy.

Two challenges now face the tentmakers. The first is to find and develop Egyptian demand for their handmade textiles. The second is the need to promote their own work while acknowledging the aspects of their heritage and craft practice which appeal to regional and international audiences. Although the tentmakers have demonstrated the capacity to change their craft to suit new audiences, they need to organize their own participation in international exhibitions and online markets (like Etsy, Instagram, and Facebook). When this happens, the balance of complex commercial interests in the Street of the Tentmakers will be tipped toward the entrepreneur. Like any other occupation, if the tentmakers are to survive as a self-sustaining community of artisans, they cannot rely on Egyptian governmental assistance.[21]

Artists, Designers, and Khayamiya

The tentmakers are open to collaboration, including ambitious and innovative projects by contemporary Egyptian and international artists, architects, designers, and sometimes even book illustrators.

There are many local initiatives that involve Egyptian designers working with craftsmen to produce modern Egyptian craft pieces for a wide range of audiences, often trendy, affluent Egyptians—Egyptian chic, it is sometimes called. Markaz is one such place, working with a range of communities to produce crafts using traditional techniques, but incorporating designs, colors, and materials that provide some sort of artistic twist. Khayamiya is one of these. The Markaz collection consists of cushions of different sizes. The fabrics used are not necessarily those used by the traditional tentmakers—the range is wider, some including patterned printed fabrics, others thick cottons. The palette is subdued and restrained, the motifs derived from the traditional arabesques or inspired by traditional geometric patterns and lotus flowers.

Despite the quality of the output, Mohammed Amin, founder of Markaz, says:

> In the traditional marketplace, the best, most expensive products are displayed on the top of the crate, beneath them is the lower quality stuff—our fabrics are the top of the crate—but that means that it isn't always easy to sell our work, because the prices are significantly higher than the average 'market' work. A large part of that difference in cost is due to the quality of materials and finish. It took us a long time to find craftsmen who were interested in working on something different from the standard cushions being sold on the market. Our challenge is that Egyptians haven't really been taught to appreciate their heritage; we never study it as part of our history, nor really see it as part of our identity. People know little about it. It isn't well documented, or taught at school, either. If you wander around the tentmakers' street today, many of the shops are selling other things—that's because the demand has dipped. What we try to do is

produce high-quality, useful, but decorative things. That's really what can sustain crafts in the long run.[22]

Taking a very different perspective, inspired by touristic khayamiya, in 2004 the American patron Sarah Gauch coordinated a collaboration between Hag Hamdy Muhammad Fattouh and Hany Abdel-Kader to design and sew khayamiya, respectively, that would illustrate the stories of Goha, the 'wise fool' of Egyptian folklore. Translations of these well-known Egyptian stories had been collected by Denys Johnson-Davies and photographs of these appliqués were published as a book for children and adults. The fable of "Goha and the Donkey" remains very popular along the Street of the Tentmakers to this day, as many of the tentmaker shops now sell a version of it. Read from left to right, it tells the story of Goha, his nephew, and their donkey as they walk down the street, attracting criticism from bystanders no matter what they do—the moral being that 'You can't please everybody.' Though this is a charming representation, the naive depiction of sequential figurative narratives for Goha influenced Hany Abdel-Kader's design of the *Revolution Khayamiya* in 2011.

Moving from the literal to the metaphysical, *The Invisible Masters* (2010/2011) consisted of a series of large banners suspended as a vast installation, combining Rachid Koraichi's drawings and enigmatic calligraphy with black-on-white tentmaker appliqué. This artwork evoked the forms of khayamiya across the ages in scale, function, and mysticism, drawing on the skills and heritage of the tentmakers as a physical and symbolic legacy. For these reasons, it was awarded the prestigious Jameel Prize through the Victoria and Albert Museum in 2011. This is a global competition designed to "explore the relationship between Islamic traditions of art, craft and design and contemporary work as part of a wider debate about Islamic culture and its role today."[23] Since this project was completed, innovative variations inspired by its austere use of black and white have appeared along the Street of the Tentmakers, such as Hossam Hashem's monumental canvas bearing a single black *hamza* or 'Hand of Fatima.'

Ahmad Hamid's collections in the 1980s and Chant Avedissian's collaborations in the late 1980s with the tentmakers evoke their historic artistic architectural heritage as well as a flowering from the seed of indigenous modernism planted by their late mentor, the architect Hassan Fathy. In the case of Avedissian's work, this results in streamlined compositions guided by subtle Nubian patterns and a preponderance of right angles not usually

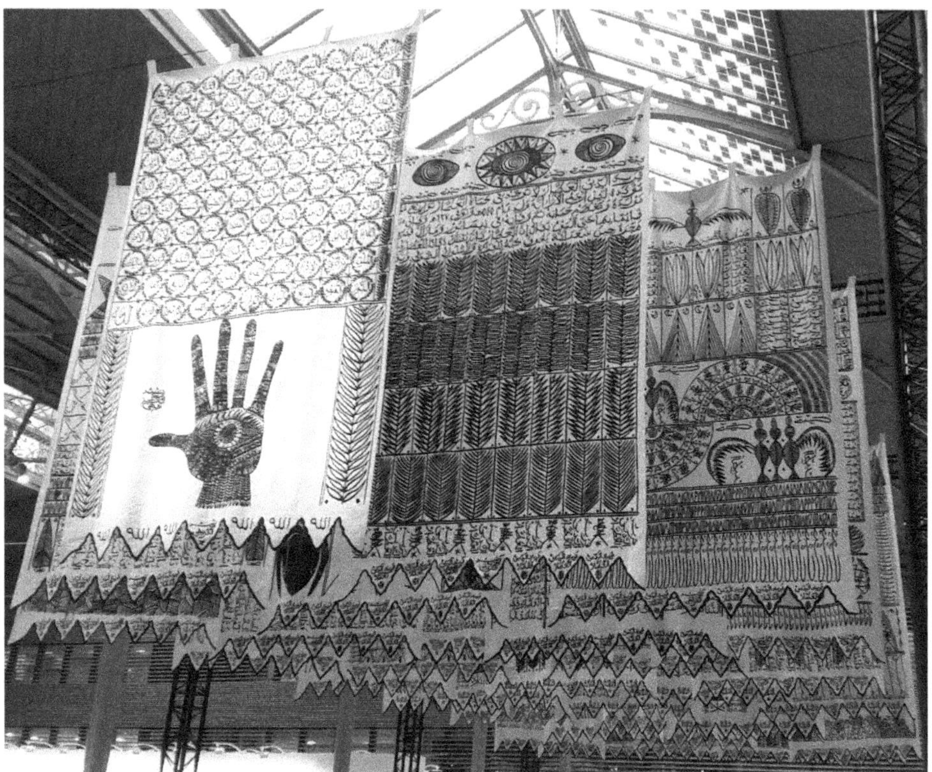

Figure 24 Installation view of Rachid Koraïchi's *The Invisible Masters*. Photograph courtesy of the October Gallery, London.

seen in khayamiya.[24] Some of his simpler pieces are beautiful evocations of the subtle tones of Mamluk marble paneling, delicately capturing the subtleties of patinated stone and marble. Hamid's collections modernize tradition in a different way: they are bold in palette and playful in color, inspired by the audacity of the masters of Islamic miniature painting and in fact of the very spirit of khayamiya, which was never timid or faded.

Hassan Fathy did not make noteworthy references to khayamiya in his work or publications, though he displayed khayamiya panels in his home. Though *suradiq*s are significant Egyptian structures, they are not as durable as residential architecture, nor were they affordable before 'imitation' khayamiya was invented. Capitalizing on this impermanence, another architect, Abdelhalim Ibrahim, relied on the *farrashin* to erect a scale model of the new children's park he was designing in the Sayyida

Zaynab neighborhood in the 1990s, enabling local residents to visualize his design and critique it before it was built.

Can the incorporation of aesthetic, functional, and cultural elements of the *suradiqs* sustain new directions in architectural forms beyond Egypt? Some of these have been considered in the work of Philip Drew, a specialist in contemporary tensile architecture, as well as Simon Schleicher's research into robotic and digital enhancements to shade-casting 'toldo' awnings.[25] These proposals could develop new directions for khayamiya in the twenty-first century, though they depart from the actual work currently produced by the tentmakers.

Though it has yet to be realized, a hand-appliquéd *suradiq* could be a spectacular contribution for a contemporary arts biennale, challenging the concept of an 'Egyptian Pavilion.' Though these are the most spectacular manifestation of khayamiya, they are awkward objects for museums. Like Syrian *ajami* rooms, traditional Egyptian *suradiq* pavilions are complex installations to store, preserve, and display. A new kind of *suradiq*, designed in collaboration between tentmakers and artists, could provide a purpose-sewn space for performances, soundscapes, digital interfaces or multimedia projections, social commentary, or anything desired by those brave enough to take up this challenge.

In the art sphere, Egyptian artists like Susan Hefuna and Moataz Nasr situate their collaborations with the tentmakers in terms defined by international and civil conflict. Hefuna's installation *I Love Egypt* (2011) invited audiences to explore tents reminiscent of the structures seen in Tahrir Square during the 2011 Revolution. Nasr's collections of propaganda flyers dropped by the United States in Iraq following the invasion of 2003 were resewn as appliqués by the tentmakers, in addition to his own original calligraphic compositions in black and white. After 2011, Nasr also adapted the ornate patterns of twentieth-century khayamiya appliqué to form fields using thousands of matches—a delicate and incendiary sculpture in subtle shades of red, yellow, blue, and green, referencing Egyptian heritage against political unrest.

Revolution Khayamiya

Throughout the twentieth century, large khayamiya screens adorned streets behind parades of tanks, artillery, and personnel, shading dignitaries and other guests at gatherings of international leaders in Egypt. They were backdrops to spectacular displays of authority. Hany Abdel-Kader's *Revolution Khayamiya* reject this passive role; they record the events of the Revolution of January 25, 2011, which culminated in the removal of President Hosni Mubarak. They are provocative manifestations of the first politically-motivated art by the tentmakers of Cairo.

Abdel-Kader's *Revolution Khayamiya* were sewn by hand in secret. They depict the events in Tahrir Square as the artist witnessed them, as his friends informed him, and as they were shown in Egyptian media, for radios and small televisions appear in all the shops along the Street of the Tentmakers. They capture the banners and slogans of protestors, the police barricades and tear gas, and the innumerable crowds gathered under the Mugamma' (a government administration building). This was a distressing and anxious period so, at his wife's suggestion, he recorded it in appliqué.

The lack of tourists after the 2011 Revolution meant that for five and a half months, he secretly drew and stitched the *Revolution Khayamiya* in his home. This personal project was not declared to his employer, for the *Revolution Khayamiya* were to be entirely his own work. Competitive secrecy is normal when developing new designs, but this was not just a new design. It was an unprecedented response to a controversial event. From Abdel-Kader's perspective, it was a personal tribute to the 2011 Revolution at a time when the results of this event were being widely questioned.

At the request of the Oriental Museum at Durham University, Hany Abdel-Kader described the content of the *Revolution Khayamiya* in a handwritten statement in Arabic:

> The work depicts the Revolution of a nice and kind people who have endured and fought thirty years of poverty and the deprivation of their legitimate rights. I have represented Tahrir Square in the middle, because it is very famous among Egyptians. I included the slogans that the Egyptians were shouting, for example, "Go!", "Get out!", "Down with the Regime!", because the Egyptian people are free and cannot be enslaved by anyone but God. I also represented the tanks, the armored vehicles that carried the police forces. I added something essential to me, my name on the border, as well as on its back. I hope I will continue to work on such new and timeless ideas all my life.[26]

Although some of the optimism following Mubarak's departure had faded by the time the *Revolution Khayamiya* were complete, these panels were intended as a personal narrative and legacy for future generations of Egyptians. They demonstrated that khayamiya could serve as a uniquely

Egyptian form of contemporary art directed by the tentmakers themselves, both departing from and drawing upon their own heritage. The prospect that other tentmakers might follow this precedent to create conceptually challenging, politically active, or socially responsive khayamiya now seems unlikely. Most tentmakers never saw the *Revolution Khayamiya*—they were made in secret and then acquired by British collections (the first was purchased by the Oriental Museum at Durham University in 2011, the second *Revolution Khayamiya* was acquired by the Victoria and Albert Museum in 2016). Perhaps more importantly, the demands of the 2011 Revolution failed to be met. As recorded by Kim Beamish's documentary *The Tentmakers of Cairo*, it is remembered with disappointment and nostalgia (see plate 28).

The income from the sale of these artworks contributed to Abdel-Kader's decision to open his own business near his original employer, just beyond the Street of the Tentmakers. This ruptured long-established relationships along the tentmaker's street, where lifelong commitments to employers (as master and apprentice legacies) were the norm. Although invisible to most observers, this sort of departure created tensions that deepened as others followed this example, forging their own pathways. These schisms reveal the expectation that once a tentmaker is trained, he is expected to work for a particular workshop for his entire career—perhaps a legacy of the Ottoman Empire's guild systems, but one that is somewhat unnatural, and therefore has been breached many times across the centuries.

Future Directions

The formation of museum collections highlighting both contemporary and historic khayamiya should prompt greater critical esteem of this art form within and beyond Egypt. In particular, the omission of khayamiya from the collections of the Museum of Islamic Art and the Textile Museum in Cairo ought to be addressed. These important museums are located just a short walk from the Street of the Tentmakers. For these institutions, khayamiya provides one of many ways to link and interpret their historic collections with the living heritage of the city of Cairo. This collaboration between past and present is an essential step in recognizing the contributions of the tentmakers to Egyptian society.

Through all of these collaborations, khayamiya provides a means of juxtaposing the old and the new, shaping Egyptian contributions to international contemporary art. However, misjudging the relationship between khayamiya and other crafts could jeopardize the authenticity of this art form. For this reason, increasing the recognition of khayamiya as a dynamic yet authentic art form is a vital consideration when establishing future collaborations. To sustain its cultural integrity, khayamiya must never be anything other than 'Egyptian.' As Yasser el-Leithy said when interviewed in 2014:

> We are the last generation of khayamiya who know these rules, who can transmit this heritage. But the survival of this art is not in our hands, it is in yours. It needs clients that recognize this craft and its associations with our identity, with who we are and what we stand for. At any time now we could stop working, and it will be gone forever. Ours is an art that others consume—if they cannot savor it, if they do not see its origins and its passion, it will diminish.[27]

That said, there is still hope along the street. Master craftsmen like fifty-year-old Tarek el-Safty are optimistic. The quality of his work is such that he has little to fear, he knows that he will always have a market somewhere. He has acquired a second shop along the street, and has plans to teach the craft through workshops to the public in the 'khayamiya mall' behind the Street of the Tentmakers. Most encouragingly, his eleven-year-old son Muhammad is involved in the shop, during school holidays of course. In his spare time, he is stitching a small piece at home. Time will tell whether he has inherited his father's skill. Tarek is keen that Muhammad learns the skills of the trade, even if he doesn't become a master stitcher himself. He will have other skills, Tarek says. "For example, I don't speak English well, but Muhammad will. It will help internationally—an important market for us."

Together they bring out some of their recent masterpieces. One of them is inspired by Ottoman tiles, another is a copy of a famous Klimt painting, *The Kiss*. He has also been collecting some of the older pieces, to learn from their skill.

"You know, I don't really have to worry about other people seeing the best pieces—I know that nobody can really copy them. It's the new ideas one has to guard." He brings some of these out from behind one of the hangings in his shop. "What do you think?"

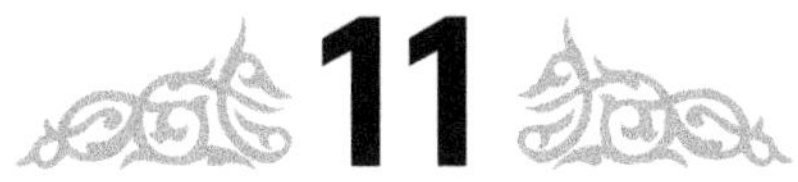

11

Voices from the Street of the Tentmakers

Some of the material in this section comes from interviews conducted in 2014 and 2015 by Dr. Dina Shehayeb, Ayah Aboul Atta, Ahmed Abdelhalim, Seif Eldin Allam, and Khaled El Samman as part of a project sponsored by Durham University and funded by the Arts and Humanities Research Council.

Yasser and Moustafa el-Leithy: Choosing a Path in the Tentmaking Business

Yasser is a distinguished tentmaker of the younger generation. Unlike the older generation of masters, *ustas*, he became specialized in one aspect of the craft: design. He does not stitch any more himself, but focuses on designing classic and innovative patterns that he sells to different workshops as well as implementing them in his own workshop, which he set up in partnership with his elder brother, Moustafa.

Yasser: "My beginnings here started simply as a member of a khayamiya family. I am the youngest of three brothers and we all started as servers to our six uncles, two of whom were masters, and the rest were craftsmen working with them. Our grandfather's house (the family house) and the workshop were both in al-Khalifa, but in the time of President Abd al-Nasser (1956–1970), new apartments were given out for free in Sayyida 'Aysha nearby, so we moved there."

Moustafa: "My uncle set up a workshop in an old house just next to our home,

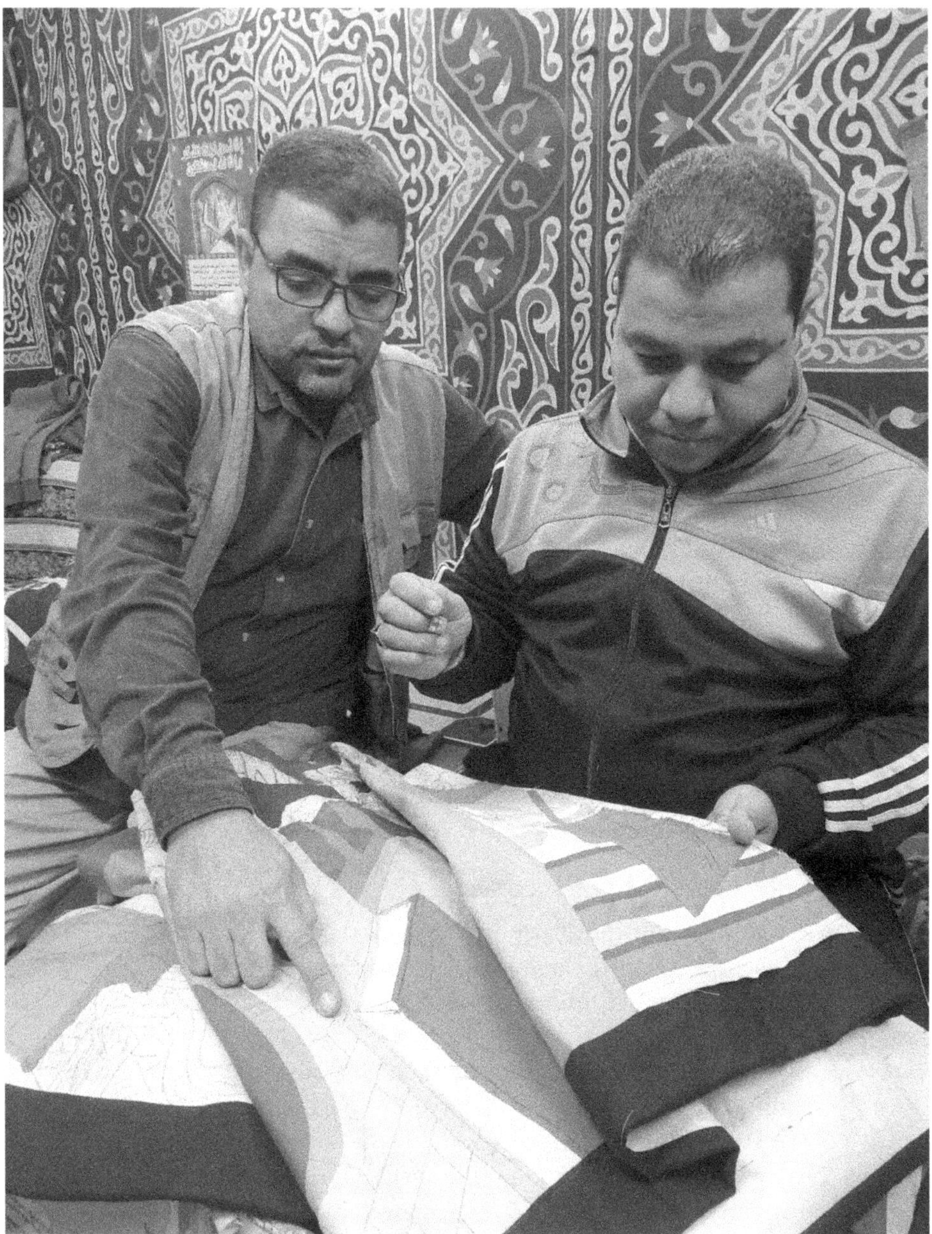

Figure 25 Moustafa and Yasser el-Leithy, tentmakers. Photograph by Ola Seif.

so as a child, I used to escape from home and go to the workshop to sit among my uncles and the men and learn the craft, learn about our world . . . so one day people would call me *usta* . . ."

Yasser: "Back then we had not yet earned the title *sabi*, or beginner. I was just ten years old, we all started at the age of ten; our job as a server was to fetch raw materials, fetch food and drink for the workers, and just sit and watch them work. Imagine how it feels when your uncle is the business owner and you have to serve all the employees! We found it demeaning, but later on we understood the wisdom behind it. You would think of those craftsmen whom you served, those *sanay'iya*, and you couldn't help having the highest respect for them and considering them the *usta*s of today.

"We stayed like that for almost one year, it was around 1980. Then my uncle, the big *usta*, started observing each one of us; what we were doing, who would succeed and continue in the trade, and who would be fired. . . . He saw that Moustafa, my brother, started to like the Islamic Arabic style, the Qu'ranic verses and so on. As soon as his mind was made up, he ordered a pillow to be added in the workshop for Moustafa. This meant that he was promoted to *sabi* status. Having a dedicated pillow to sit and work on is the indication of being a *sabi*. The *sabi* only accomplishes one step in the production process: he either frames a piece or assembles the basic canvas, but he never completes a piece."

Moustafa: "I started by sitting beside one of the workers to thread the needle, to hand him the scissors, to bring over anything he needed. When I had the courage to hold the needle and imitate him, he would allow me to go on working beside him and watch what I was doing. If I did something wrong, he would fix it. If not, he would let me continue. I was very young then and the needle would often prick my finger, so I started practicing wearing a thimble. It is hard at the beginning because they tie your middle finger to your palm until, slowly, you learn how to use it. I hated it . . . and soon I untied the bandage and could use the thimble well. It was time to have my own pair of scissors, because it is shameful to ask for another worker's pair; he uses it constantly. I took one of the older pairs of scissors that were lying unused, and went to have it sharpened. Later on, I would buy my own."

Yasser: "As for me, my uncle saw that I liked to draw, so he assigned me the 'pencil tracing' of his work. This meant that once he finished outlining and scaling the design in chalk, I would trace this outline in pencil; this is still all on paper. This in itself was a learning process. . . . The challenge in our Islamic style is to know the beginning and the end of each line . . . of each color. You should be able to slide your finger along each line uninterrupted; this way you learn when a drawing is correct or incorrect. And then there are the names . . . while tracing, I would ask my uncle about the name of each motif: *dakar* (male), *kaff* (palm), *ras te'ban* (snake head). . . . I only dared to ask once—if you asked twice he would say: "Asking is for dim-witted [people] . . . learn with your eyes . . . " I was tired of sitting there tracing, not doing real work. Moustafa was already a worker and was getting paid. Reda [a third brother] never really got the hang of it, he would only 'prepare' the work.

"Eventually, I got a pillow to sit on and worked with a needle. My uncle would assign me the 'special' work; designs that required time and a certain mood . . . 'showcase pieces' that he would unfold first to engage a new client. I stayed three years in this ordeal; one day you work on a certain design, a week later you do not touch it again and you are working on a new design . . . Moustafa, on the other hand, produced good work fast; he was the type who would sit and work for hours at length—those were times of standardized work. My uncle was one of the few innovators in the vocation. Typically, if a client liked a bed cover 2.5 x 2.5 m, the next thing you knew, the same design was implemented as a 1 x 1 m design. It was all repetition: once you rotate the flower to the left, another time to the right. . . . All designs were produced the same way; by folding the paper three times, drawing and piercing one eighth, and then unfolding it to reach the final size. At the end of those three years, I started to be known . . . known as the nephew of Abdallah el-Leithy. . . . I come from one of the two greatest families in al-Khayamiya: el-Leithy and Abdel-Aal. That was it . . . that was the life that awaited us . . . like my uncles who spent their entire life coming to their workshop together every day and leaving together, each going to his home. . . . This was not what we wanted, Moustafa and I . . . so we started to pull out . . .

"First my uncle was annoyed . . . but when he saw that we were persistent, he would go around telling the merchants that we were his nephews; that we were taught by him as a recommendation. [The compromise we reached was that] my uncle allowed us to work for our own account but insisted that we stay in his workshop; this way he would extend to us the good reputation of his workshop . . . respectable craftsmen . . . craftsmen of excellence. . . .

"We stayed like that from 1985 until 1989; both of us, Moustafa and I, would work a separate piece and go down to the market to sell it. In 1989, Moustafa accepted to work for *usta* Muhammad Hashem, one of the last generation of *ustawat*. I continued receiving orders from different merchants; orders to implement a typical design but with some modification. I still resented the typical designs, but they were all that merchants ordered.

"My dream was to work with a 'genius,' and finally one day I went to the market to deliver a piece, but the merchant was not in his shop, so I walked accidentally past an exhibition at the beginning of al-Khayamiya [the Street of the Tentmakers], right in front of al-Salih Tala'i Mosque on the first floor. I needed the money, so I decided to climb up and check out this new merchant—maybe I could get more from him for my piece. There I met Raouf Ayoub. . . .

"Raouf Ayoub was known to have a workshop in al-Zaytoun, but he was new to the market. He was a lawyer who learnt our craft and worked from home, supplying bazaars in Coptic Cairo. Eventually his business expanded; he hired young women to do the stitching, and here he was opening a shop in al-Khayamiya. He eyed my work as a connoisseur, not a merchant, and told me, "Your work is very nice, your hands are beautiful . . ." Then he added, "But my work is not like what you see in the market . . . come have a look around." His work was different and that was what I liked about it. Seeing my enthusiasm, he offered me to sit beside him and gave me a needle and a thimble and a beautiful piece with an Arabesque design that he kept beside him. I did not know then that this was a test, or more like a trap. The original piece is actually very beautiful and hard to replicate; only the most professional craftsman's scissors could reproduce it. He realized I was starting the piece from the inside out and not the easier way, from the outside in; that was a technique he himself had never tried, so he kept on watching me work until

I finished. We stepped outside into the daylight and, narrowing his eyes, he scrutinized each stitch and line, but could not find a trace of pencil showing, or a millimeter of asymmetry, so he slowly turned his head to me and said, "Tomorrow morning you show up at my shop, I want you to work for me . . ." And that was a turning point in my life.

"He helped organize so many exhibitions, here and abroad . . . there was no exhibition we did not participate in . . . I was always with him setting the display, taking part in the interviews. . . . For almost ten years I worked with him; I never left him . . . we complemented each other. He had a gap in Islamic design and I filled it; he had no clue about it, but then he was a genius in Egyptian scenes; landscapes . . . portraits . . . and I learnt that from him. . . . It was God's doing . . . I was blessed. He would come to me with a piece of paper and say, "Our work is becoming outdated, come on Yasser, give me a treat," and I would ask him, "What should I draw?" and he would reply, "Whatever your hand yields," and my hand would yield heavy work. Elaborate, difficult to implement, what we would call *danah* work . . . meaning as heavy as a *danah*, that is, a cannonball. To give you an example, a bedspread at that time would take twenty-five days to a month to finish, while a 1 m x 1 m *danah* work could take two months.

"A regular merchant would complain, saying that he would never be able to sell such workmanship, but not Raouf. He was selling it in exhibitions abroad. Each Egypt Air office abroad had a piece from Raouf . . . every exhibition organized by the Egypt Tourism Authority had to include his work. . . . Marketing was never a problem for Raouf; the owner of a bazaar in a Las Vegas Hotel once visited the shop and was so impressed, she ordered a lot to be sent to her, yearly. He was an expert salesman. This is an important skill that is lacking in the rest of the market. He would make the customer feel they are buying something unique; something special. He always said that handmade work should be appreciated by the tourists. When I was left in the shop to sell instead of him, he would caution me, "Do not cheapen my work, if I tell you to sell a piece for LE1,000, it is because this is its worth, no matter how much it cost me. If it sells, it sells; if not, then this is God's will.

"Because of this policy, the clients that came up to our shop were always upper end; clients who appreciate your work . . .

who make you realize its value . . . Raouf had his philosophy, his school of thought; he would order tea for the client, sit and explain how the piece was made, and would never attribute to himself what he did not make himself. . . . He would tell the client, "See that boy inside . . . he is the one who does this Islamic design, sit with him and he will explain to you." Japanese clients are the most difficult to convince that this work is all handmade; I would have to show them all the steps from the very beginning . . . from the penciled paper. After that when Raouf states his price, the client does not bargain; they pay the price you say. He would never get a shop assistant to do the selling, like other bazaars did. He would let the craftsman do it; he would say, "No one knows the piece better than the one who did it."

"It is the design that sets my work apart. For seven years, the secretary of the American ambassador would buy each new piece I designed at Raouf's; she would call me and say, "Yasser, did you make anything new?" She mounted them in her home, like a private collection. You don't learn design . . . what I gained at Raouf's was the chance to design; to be creative. I excelled . . . but my measure of excellence was not the foreigner, but my fellow craftsmen and the merchants of khayamiya . . . when you see the look in their eyes as they come up to the shop and look at my work . . . when I impress the craftsmen I know for certain the foreigner will be impressed.

"The years went by and I finished my bachelor's in commerce while I was still working with Raouf. I would often spend the night in the Old Cairo shop, go to university early in the morning, then come back around 1:00 p.m.; that is when the market picks up really, not before. In 2000 I decided to leave Raouf . . . I was all grown up and I felt I could not work as an employee to anyone any more. [In the meantime] Moustafa, my brother, had bought a workshop here in al-Khayamiya in 1995. Raouf was accepting and had no problem with that, but he had one condition; that I would not replicate any work that I did for him during those ten years. He said that he had bought all those designs from me so I should not implement them again. I told him not to worry, and it was like a code of honor between us, not to hurt one another. He was right . . . Raouf paid me three times; once for the design, once when I stitched and finished the piece, and a third time if I sold it myself. I would set my price for each piece.

"He would buy my designs on paper, irrespective of if and when we would implement them. That is how it came about that today I only sell designs to different merchants and workshops and have stopped the needlework altogether for the past two or three years now. But back then, selling a design only was unknown to the market here in al-Khayamiya . . . everyone was imitating one another . . . it was a jungle. I also found out that Moustafa was completely monopolized. He worked for one merchant family only. They appreciated him immensely, and he likes stability, so he was happy. . . . He didn't mind, but I did. I told him, "I did not leave one employer to be an employee again . . . this is not my style. It is not what I want and I will work with anyone and everyone who likes my work." And so that was the first year."

Moustafa: "My father turned sixty and with his pension he bought us this workshop. It reunited us three brothers. I worked in our workshop for wonderful people. For example, the Fattouh brothers, we owe them a lot . . . we ask for money, they ask for more work . . . we are like engineers, we produce . . . like a factory, we produce this multicolored fabric. We do as we please . . . choosing designs, choosing colors . . .

"When they asked me to work in the shop itself, I did, but that does not mean I am a 'follower.' We still had our workshop open . . . it keeps our family's name. Nowadays, things are different . . . they only know how to hold a needle. . . . In the past you would earn the title *usta* after years of experience . . . like a coronation . . . an *usta* is like a project manager; not only does he design a new pattern every now and then, but most importantly, he orchestrates who will do what and when; he prepares the work for others to do it. . . .

"To be able to modify a design needs experience. See, khayamiya designs have three sources; either an idea brought by the client, or the Islamic mosques around us, or books like *Description de l'Egypte* for the Ancient Egyptian style . . . you cannot innovate there.

"Yasser's design capacity surpassed the skills of most of the craftsmen."

Yasser: (smiling) "I would sell a design to a merchant; he pays for it and all, but then he would ask around and fail to find a craftsman who can implement it. He comes back to me complaining, so I tell him about Moustafa. Whether they agree and Moustafa does the work or not isn't my business, but with our longstanding experience in the craft, I know the capacity of most craftsmen . . . I can design a part that I know would make the merchant come back to us to implement. . . . We are independent, but we complement each other . . . it comes naturally, really.

"If it were for the money, we would have made much bigger profits. No, it is for our love for this craft that we go on working. My home is open and my family is provided for, but that is because I am an accountant in a private petroleum company, it's been eleven years and I am now a department director. In this vocation, you do what you see beauty in, but it is still not appreciated enough by the merchants. . . .

(sighing) "Design . . . design . . . it exhausts me now. I sit and scribble for three or four hours; I scribble and I erase, I draw something and then I realize I drew something similar before and I discard it. I've been drawing for so long. . . . Then if I am working on real scenes, like a street view of a monument, I can make a mistake in the shade and shadow; a small mistake that the client won't notice, but it bothers me and I could discard three days' work and start anew. More important than pleasing the client is that I am pleased with the work.

"It was only with the advent of the 1980s that khayamiya entered the world of decor; by 1981 the handmade *tark* for *siwan* tents disappeared and we started making smaller pieces. The tourist would see the large 5.5 m x 2.75 m *tark* at the merchant's place and ask for smaller, more portable pieces. From there came the idea of taking one motif from the *tark*, framing it and selling it as a pillowcase or a tablecloth. Only then did we start to understand the meaning of tourism. . . ."

Moustafa: "In the old times, we would work with the four basic colors known to the *tark*; black, red, yellow, and navy blue. The *tark* is formed of several units, different geometric motifs. Some were named after the craftsmen who invented them. We would take a motif in a square module, a *tarbi'a*, and repeat it; two square modules would make a frieze or *herz*, four would make a 90 cm x 90 cm piece . . .

and so on. We would make curtains; we would make bedspreads and large tablecloths. But then we thought of more elaborate designs to raise the level of difficulty . . . to raise the price. Pharaonic design friezes had existed since the beginning, but you could not innovate in that domain, so in the late 1980s what we call the *rumi* work appeared . . . more curves, more overlaying.

"In the 1990s there was a focus on religion and we worked on large pieces as big as the traditional *tark* with Islamic and Christian iconography. Yasser was good at depicting the Virgin Mary and Jesus; these *tarks* were to be hung in churches. I would do the Islamic *tark* with the ninety-nine names of God, or verses from the Holy Qu'ran. Arabic calligraphy is the most difficult work; craftsmen like me and Amm [uncle] Mahmoud who work on Islamic designs can do pretty much anything . . . the moves you master with your pair of scissors to cut the curves qualify you to do anything. But the point is not to produce more, it is about authenticity; that is what makes it art. That is why Naguib Mahfouz got the Nobel Prize. It is from going deeper into the local that you reach the global. That is why my work is expensive; my experience in design, in choosing color combinations, in the degree of difficulty comes from the rules of the craft we inherited.

"We are the last generation of khayamiya who know these rules, who can transmit this heritage, but the survival of this art is not in our hands, it is in yours . . . it is in clients that recognize this craft with its associations with our identity, with who we are and what we stand for. Any time now we could stop working, Yasser and I, and it will be gone forever. Ours is an art that others consume and if they cannot savor it, if they do not see its origins and its passion, it will diminish to a playful product driven solely by innovation like so many other leisure items in modern times . . . the beauty of my work and my knowledge is that it is contained within a meter by meter . . . no noise there . . . only a pair of scissors, a needle, and a thimble."

Atef Fattouh—From Stitchers to Merchants

Atef Fattouh comes from one of the prominent tentmaking families—one of the largest in Cairo, whose work involves exporting tents to Sudan. They also have a stake in a factory that manufactures stackable chairs for weddings and other events, complementing their tentmaking business.

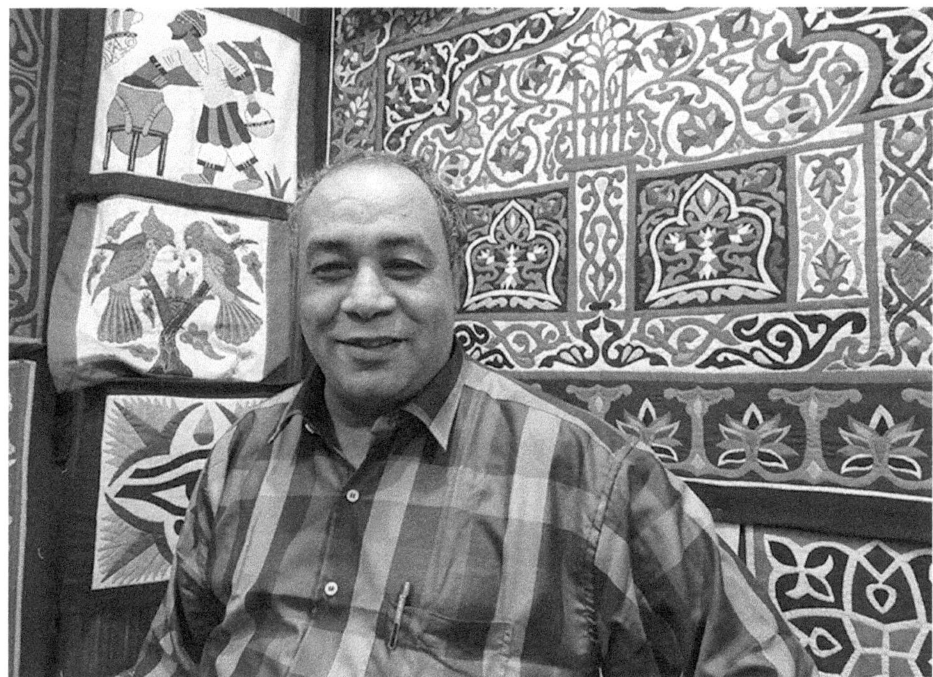

Figure 26 Atef Fattouh, tentmaker. Photograph by Ola Seif.

From time to time they exhibit their work in shows abroad, but complain that business isn't as good as it once was. As many of the shops along the street are small, Fattouh has two units, and also like the typical tentmaker business, most of his work is hidden from his competitors' eyes in a back showroom, which he calls his 'storeroom,' many times the size of the cramped street units. "This is where I hang the special pieces, pieces I would not put in the shop outside; I show them only to those clients who would appreciate the work," he says. The storeroom has a mezzanine level where piles of folded finished pieces are kept, arranged by size. When a client shows interest in buying a piece they are taken from the front shop to the workshop, offered a glass of tea, and then piles are brought down from the mezzanine and spread out on the floor. This process is usually handled by the shop assistant, but it is Atef to whom the client must turn once they have chosen their pieces to agree a price. Asking the price while still looking always elicits the same response: "Just see what it is you want first," meaning: if you buy more than one piece, you'll get a better deal. Atef no longer puts needle to thread himself, but knows how to stitch.

A family tradition

"I was born into a family of tentmakers; my father, my grandfather . . . both my grandfathers were tentmakers. My grandfather from my mother's side was an *usta* in the craft; one of the best craftsmen. He was famous, going by the name of el-Mikkawy [referring to Mecca] because he worked in the annual covering of the Ka'ba. Making the *kiswa* of the Ka'ba had its rules; they would not hire any craftsman to work on it, it had to be an *usta* and he had to be someone who prays, a family man with a good reputation.

"Although my paternal grandfather was also a tentmaker, my father worked with el-Mikkawy, his father-in-law. The workshop was a large 6 m x 7 m room along the courtyard of el-Mikkawy's old family house, just around the corner in Zuqaq al-Misk. It was so large it could house as many as thirty workers when large orders were placed. My father took over the workshop after the death of his father-in-law in 1968 because el-Mikkawy's only son was still too young to manage the work alone, but only for a few years. Soon after, my father opened his own workshop in al-Maridani Street. All the khayamiya workshops were dispersed one here and there . . . this market you see today is just, a '*moda*,' a fashion. In the past, the merchant who needed a job done would go directly to the workshops . . . the merchant would negotiate the terms with the *usta*, and if they agreed, he would place the order."

Learning to manage

"Then came the war of '73, work was hard to come by, and sold for almost cost price. A few years later, my father died. I was only thirteen then, and my eldest brother was twenty. He had just finished his military service and was not experienced enough to take over our father's business. That was when el-Shaykh Taha came into my life. I owe this man everything . . . my brothers and I would not have continued our education; we would not have achieved what we are today if it weren't for him. El-Shaykh Taha was a colleague of my father but he had learnt the khayamiya work at an advanced age. When father died . . . we were young and inexperienced, my three brothers and I. God blessed us with this man . . . it was him who overtook the workshop business and taught my older brother the craft and its management; how to deal with the workers/stitchers, how to deal with customers; what type of work to focus on depending on the market demand. . . . He was my brother's mentor, he practically adopted my brother, guiding and advising him step by step, helping him sustain our father's business. He worked alongside my brother until he died at over eighty years old. He was a man who honored work relations. In the past you would find such people like el-Shaykh Taha, *usta*s or workers who would lend the business owner the money needed to get a job done, trusting that they would be repaid later; trusting them because he is a good and honest man . . . those were the work codes of the past."

Opening our own shop

"My elder brother went to work in Saudi Arabia from 1980 to 1986. Those were times when rich Arabs from the Gulf would come to Cairo and buy large quantities of *siwans*—rectangular tents made of multicolored stitched patchwork. One order could amount to two hundred or three hundred pieces, so the merchant would pass by different workshops and commission a few here and a few there. He would buy a piece for LE100 from the workshop then sell it to the Gulf Arabs for LE200. The Arabs only knew the Street of the Tentmakers' market; they did not know the stitching workshops, so we were at the mercy of the merchants in the market.

"It was around that time that el-Shaykh Taha started convincing my elder brother to open a shop for us in the market. My mother had to intervene to help convince my brother that this was a step that would improve our situation. Until he agreed to open a shop in 1990 we were barely sustaining daily living . . . we were nothing then. It was important to get my elder brother to agree—family customs were that elders should be respected and their word obeyed, regardless of how unsound their decision. But tradition gave all members of the family the chance to discuss matters in their daily gathering over the evening meal, and moreover on weekend mornings. In 1990 we bought the shop in the market, the one I sit in now, but then it was el-Shaykh Taha who sat in it until 1996, when he passed away. Those years were the best; orders flowed in non-stop, as if he were a man with a mission to set up a place for us in life, and when he did, he told us, "Now you go on from here. . . ." This was a new step, this unprecedented mix between being a stitcher and being a merchant. The two complement each other; I look at colors, my brother looks at designs. We used our education to complement our experience in the craft. Since 1990, God has been generous to us. We opened two shops in the khayamiya market, a workshop in the back, and a factory in Giza for handmade and machine-made tents.

"Even my mother worked in the Khayamiya. It is a craft that both women and men can do equally, but she did not do the design, she would only stitch from home. Women in those times never worked in the workshops, but they still did all they could to assist their husbands to provide for the family; food for this one, education for that one. They sacrificed a lot to sustain the family.

"Today there are some skillful women stitchers, but they tend to work from home."

Learning the trade

"When I was a boy, all my school holidays were spent in the workshop in al-Maridani stitching *siwans*. It was very close to home. There was this friend of mine, a neighbor my age, who also worked with me at the workshop. As boys, we would often stay till dawn in the workshop working side by side, listening to songs. . . . That was how much we passionately loved this craft. All my brothers worked in the Khayamiya, we all did, including the one who was a bank employee; for years he worked both jobs. My love for khayamiya doubled when it became associated with foreign tourism. When you are young you feel a sense of pride that foreigners from abroad appreciate your work and buy it. The advent of the foreign client changed the product of khayamiya; new designs, new colors . . . and the pieces themselves became smaller and of all shapes and sizes. I lived through this transformation and took an active part in it; I would look at different designs in catalogs brought by foreigners and try them out, but more importantly I learned to read the client: to understand their mindset, their psyche. These days for instance, if Egyptian clients walk in, I show them something cheerful and optimistic because I know the general state of mind in the country; I first show them bright colors, an uplifting verse of poetry to open the door to do business with them, and then I introduce the other themes. Foreigners, on the other hand, are a cocktail. Each country has its general preferences; for example, Americans like bright colors and pay more attention to color than design. People from Spain are pretty much the same, but the Germans prefer earth tones and the Swedes go for low contrast; they would buy work with shades of the same color. The French, however, are unique; they are the pickiest clients, and the ones with the most taste; they would not buy just anything . . . this is the business side of our craft . . . and this is what I do now."

The rules of the trade

"The evolution in the craft can only succeed if you sustain certain principles inherited from the trade; following those principles in the production process is key to the success of new designs. First the designer pencils one-eighth of the design on paper and pierces it; he then imprints it on the entire fabric by 'powdering' it, but this may take up to two days just to adjust the proportions of the assemblage . . . If after that the designer is satisfied with the design, he will add the colors; usually each tentmaker will have his own signature colors and combinations. Then comes the role of the stitchers; a most critical rule is to depend on *usta* stitchers and not go for the inexpensive labor from the countryside, or amateur girls. The last and simplest step is the finishing; adding a background and a frame. In our business, sustainability is essential. Most important is to sustain the skilled labor that makes your team. If you have twenty workers, you keep them producing at the same rate, even when the market is slow. You devise new products . . . you explore new markets . . . this is your role as a merchant. . . . No matter what, you never let your workers go, because in times of hardship they were the ones who stuck with you and didn't leave you. . . ."

Being a businessman

"I am no longer a craftsman, I am the businessman in this vocation and proud of it. It is this vocation that made me and sustained my family, my home. I will teach my son this vocation and will present him with better outlets than here, maybe a bazaar somewhere else. . . . I will make him understand that it is an art as well as a business, and that with a college education and the knowledge of languages he can elevate this art, he can be an ambassador for it as well as a businessman. Muhammad Daghash did it right, the vocation was passed down to him through generations, but he added scientific knowledge to it; he studied tentmaking in the United States. Now he has his tent factory along the ring road close to where he lives. . . . The decline we are suffering now is because of intruders who perceive it as any other income-generating business and fail to see the art in the craft."

Ahmed Gomaa—Starting in the Street of the Tentmakers

"My connection with khayamiya began back in 2003, and I was the first member of my family, which includes two younger siblings, to enter this business. My brother Muhammad entered the business about four to five years ago, while Moustafa joined a little later. Muhammad now owns two shops in front of the mosque on the extension of the Khayamiya Street.

"I entered the business out of passion toward the craft; even though I cannot sketch or stitch with my own hands, I love the craft all the same.

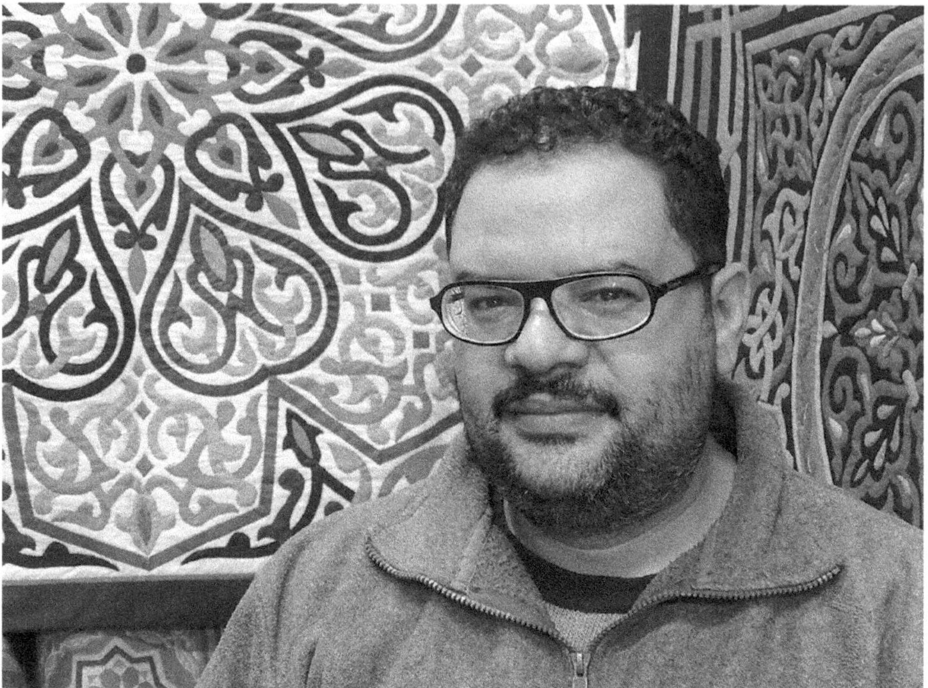

Figure 27 Ahmed Gomaa, tentmaker. Photograph by Ola Seif.

I have been here in al-Khayamiya Street for twenty-six years now, I basically grew up in this shop, you see, and it was originally my mother's.

"I am honored that my mother, back in those days, used to sell live chickens here on this sidewalk. It is an honest job, and along the way God was kind to her and she was able to buy this very shop. In later years, when the income from the shop was not really covering that much, especially since my mother had fallen sick at the time and had to stay home more often, my brothers took over the shop and I decided that my sixteen years of education were quite enough and that she need not provide for me any more. She had already paid for my education, I was at university and was embarrassed to ask for any more than that; she had done enough for me and it was about time I bore my own responsibility. I worked alongside my mother in the chicken shop until the Qasaba was renovated. That was when the government set a law banning water and sewage from entering the shops and stalls in our street. It was then that we had to consider shutting down our business. We stalled for a while, but we had to shut down sooner or later. My mother offered me to make use of the shop as I saw fit in return for paying her rent, and I agreed."

Being introduced to the craft and having a 'mentor' along the Street

"I was lucky back then to have someone like Hagg Sayyid Aziz stand by my side during those hard times, and it was him who introduced me to the craft; I merely had a shop at the time, but nothing to sell.

"God stood by me and whenever I sold a piece, I would give Hagg Sayyid his share of the profit, and I would not pocket my profits. Instead, I would add some money to it and use it to buy two pieces, sell them and then buy three, and so on; he was my lucky charm. Of course, my mother and my brothers still owned their shares in the shop, but with time and God's blessings, I managed to buy them out and the shop became my own. I struggled for ten years until the shop was finally mine, in spite of the circumstances and the instability our country faced. Maybe a month or two would go by without selling anything, and this was my only source of income. This forced me to start selling colored fabric alongside dealing in khayamiya, just to be able to cover my expenses and be able to pay my workmen—otherwise, what is to keep them from seeking new employment elsewhere?"

The craftsmen's role

"To be honest, I am lucky to have the craftsmen I have; people willing to help me this much in my work, all of whom are very decent, who admire and respect me, and even though many were presented with several tempting work opportunities elsewhere, they decided to stay by my side. They say that I treat them well; I never treated any of them as people who work for me . . . you see, I gain wealth from the fruits of their labor, and because of that, their burdens are my burdens, and I must treat each and every one of them with the same respect I would expect to receive myself. I never tell any of them, "This is what you will earn" from this or that piece, because I do not practice the craft myself and therefore I cannot put a price on the amount of work he did—it is his work, his effort. The craftsman puts the price he sees fit for his time and effort, that is my policy, and if I feel he's getting a little greedy he would make me the piece, I would sell it, but from then on we go our separate ways. Even though I do not know how to practice the craft myself, I do however know enough by now to know when I'm being swindled. When I first opened this shop, many of the tentmakers did not expect I would last long, since neither me nor my family were craftsmen, and this was the challenge that gave me motivation to persevere. Thank God, over the years I have achieved success that no one, including myself, would have imagined."

The range of products and quality

"At first I dealt in the more commercial, popular products, since I was mainly looking to earn good money. This commercial level of work is usually of lesser quality; the levels of stitching are not necessarily intricate or so nice. We have different names for different types of stitching. There is the 'snake's head' for example, where one piece has another piece overlapping it and both have to have the same precision and the same craftsmanship; both should be identical, otherwise the shape would be deformed. However, the typical client just looks at the color, and when business was good it didn't really matter to me whether the customer was here for the colors or the design and the craftsmanship itself. Business was business and I was selling well. Usually we used to get people just looking for something to buy that would remind them of Egypt, a souvenir. But now the people who come to buy are the ones who know and understand khayamiya and are looking for quality craftsmanship."

The source of his workforce

"As the demand for quality craftsmanship has increased, I have started employing people from the countryside. They have their own style of work; the work itself is not that fantastic, of course, but is better needlework than the local popular work, and less expensive.

"First I used to deal with girls from Mansura [a city in the Delta] and other places. I married one of them actually—that is how I met my wife, through work, and until now she works with her own hands when she has the time.

"Now it's mostly young men from Upper Egypt. Any of those young boys sitting or standing at the shop entrance is sure to be from Qena [a governorate in the South of Egypt], no exceptions. They all come from one place there, it's like we are a second Libya; one person comes, finds a job then brings his brothers and relatives, and it goes on. Some have a bit of education and they learn the craft. When they do, they bring others from their hometown and teach them; they don't always stay as errand boys, you see, they evolve into craftsmen who can produce their own work and sell it to the shop owners."

His aspirations

"I constantly try to improve myself, not as a craftsman of course, but as a shop owner—I want to have quality merchandise. Sketching the designs was never for me; someone else mostly did the designs. There is this very respectable man, I must say, who goes by the name of Yasser el-Leithy; he is possibly the best designer among the Khayamiya. I rely on him. Bit by bit my business flourished, more foreigners would come to my shop and each would buy three, maybe four, pieces instead of buying one or two."

His clients

"One of my most prominent clients is Margaret Scobey, the [former] American ambassador; I even took a picture with her once. When she used to come here, the entire place would be crammed, the mere fact that she entered our street is already a success to us as merchants. She would come and buy from us; she even bought a few pieces from me personally! And it wasn't just once or twice, she would visit our street regularly. Our business is completely dependent on tourism; barely any Egyptians ever come here to buy. For example, when I decided to collaborate with the Aga Khan project they helped me participate in many exhibitions, and through them I got to know the Craft Improvement Center, with which I traveled to Paris in 2010. The Paris exhibition was like a dream to us. I did some really good business there, and we were based in a place they called 'The Market.' When I think of it, some of the best exhibitions I've been to were through that Center. When it comes to the type of clientele we get in exhibitions, I think the Egyptian clients, no matter how few they are, are better than your average tourist. You see, the few Egyptians who buy from us are a more refined class of customer, and they appreciate our craft and the time and effort spent on each piece."

Recognition of the craftsmen

"They are the ones who do the work, it is through their experienced hands and craftsmanship that the pieces are made. They are the ones who work night and day; as for me, I am just a means for their work to get to the market. It is their right to seek to improve their income, they too have families and homes to provide for. It is their right to have ambitions, to have their own personality and integrity independent of me, the shop owner. They are my only source of income, and if it wasn't for them, we shop owners would be nothing."

Hany Abdel-Kader

As per the tradition of the craft, Hany started out working for other people along the street and then set up his own shop, in his case, three years ago, at the age of forty. Atypically, his shop is not in the Street of the Tentmakers, but about one thousand meters away, in an alley off the street that leads to the tentmakers. It is in the textile market of al-Ghuriya, which sells a wide range of products, from blankets to *gallabiyas* to underwear. An older stitcher, Amm Hassan, and a young assistant are employed in the small square shop, and Hassan is usually seated at the doorway, working his way through a new piece.

Like others along the street, Hany is related to many of the other tentmakers, either by marriage, as is the case with his brother-in-law, or by blood. The Fattouh brothers are his cousins, and all are the grandsons of the last shaykh of the tentmakers, Mahmoud el-Mikkawi, himself the son of the previous shaykh, called Muhammad. Hany's grandfather was the last person recognized as the shaykh of the craft. After his death in the 1960s, the very notion of the head of the craft fizzled out and was superseded by the idea of the craftsmen as independent shop owners.

Because the shop is small, space is used very economically. In the entrance is a wooden panel which opens to reveal a few shelves bursting with cotton fabric of different colors—these will become the pieces of the appliqué. Having the samples at hand is also useful for dealing with clients who want special orders.

After the 2011 Revolution Hany produced a few figurative pieces capturing the spirit of the events. The first of these was bought by Durham University's Oriental Museum, the second by the Victoria and Albert Museum, and at the time of publication, a third piece is still in Hany's shop. In order to overcome the challenges presented by the recent slump in tourism, Hany and others have been actively trying to promote their work abroad—a prospect made easier by social media like Viber and Facebook.

Owning an independent business

"It was important to set up my own business, to make a name of myself, and thank God, people know me and I have made a name for myself. I have two children, Youssef and Wa'ad, and it is important to set something up for them—so that they have their own entity. My son comes into the shop on his holidays so that he starts getting used to the business; both he and his sister stitch a bit as well.

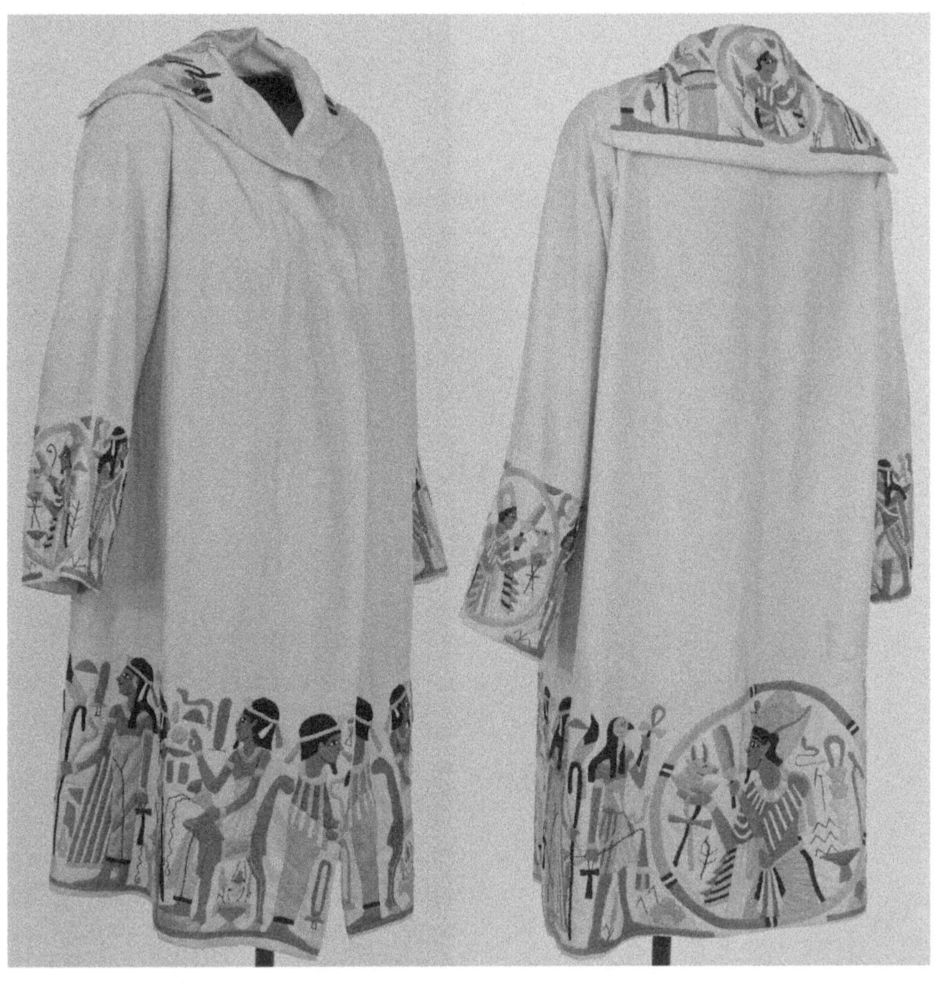

22 Touristic khayamiya coat of the Fashion History Museum, Canada. Photograph by Jonathan Walford.

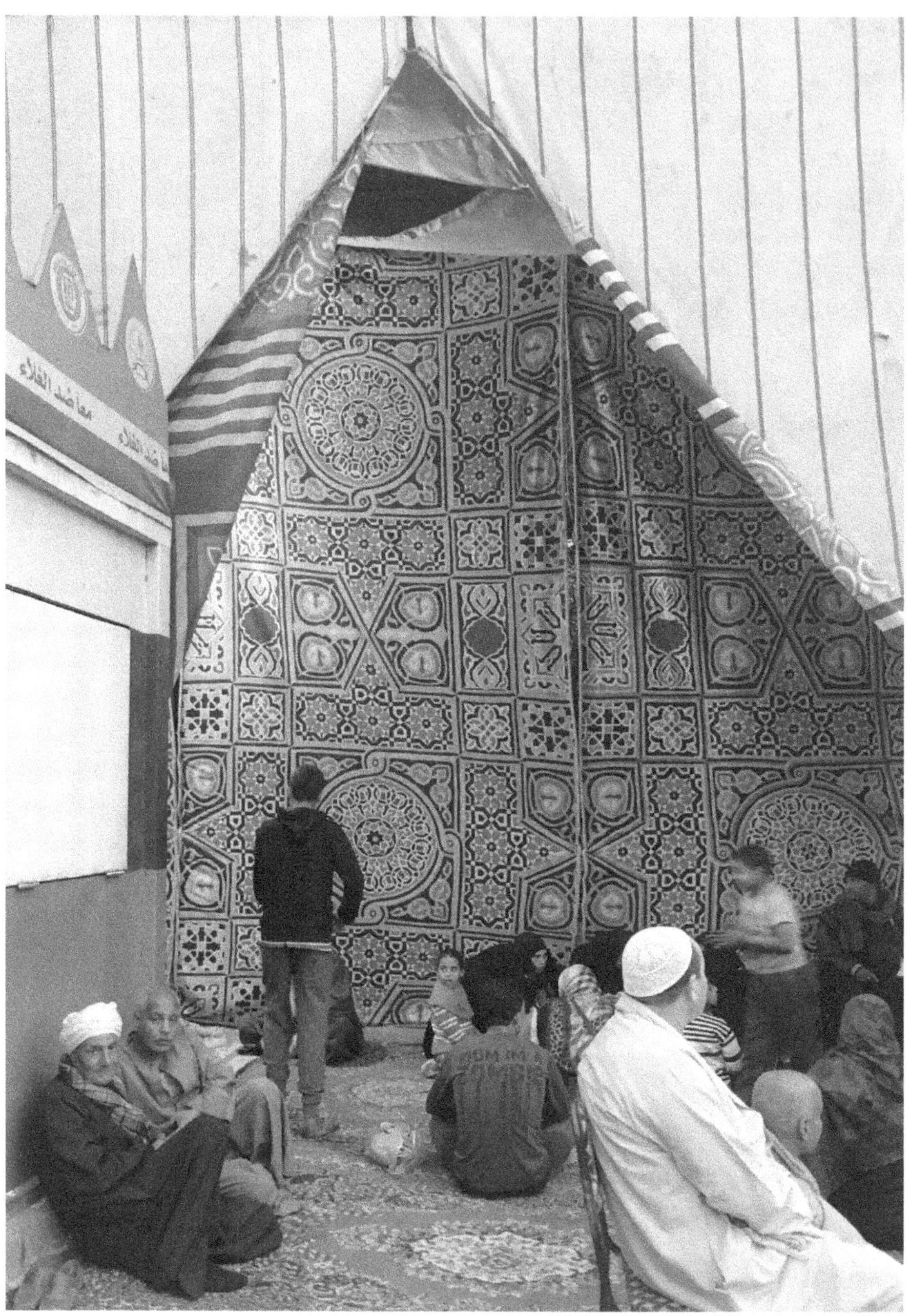

23 The *mawlid* of al-Rifa'i, Cairo, 2017. Handmade *suradiqs* are rare today, but the Sufi orders usually possess their own for important religious occasions. Photograph by Yasmina Abou Youssef.

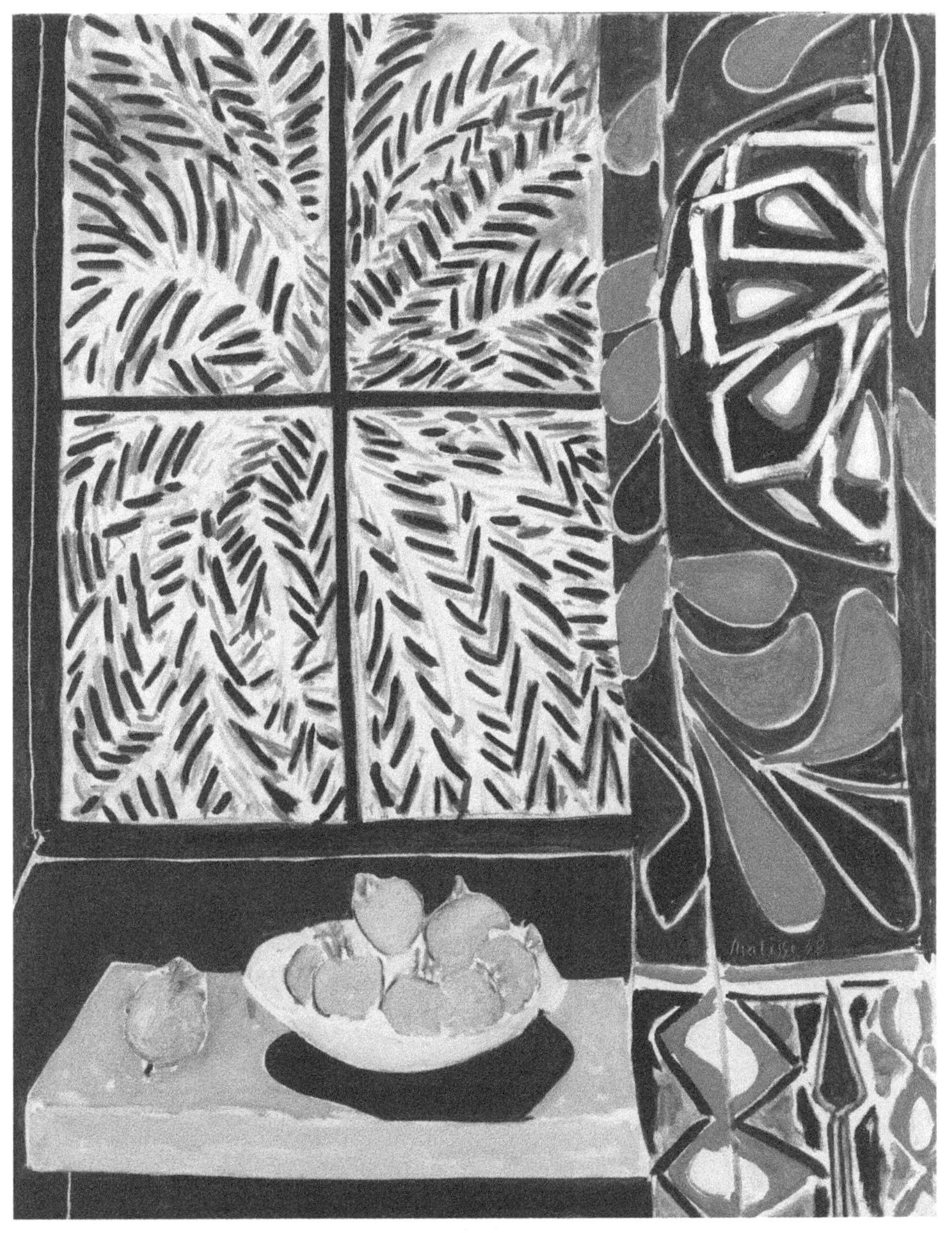

24 Henri Matisse, *Interior with Egyptian Curtain*, 1948. Phillips Collection, Washington DC. Photograph courtesy of Bridgeman Images and the Succession H. Matisse.

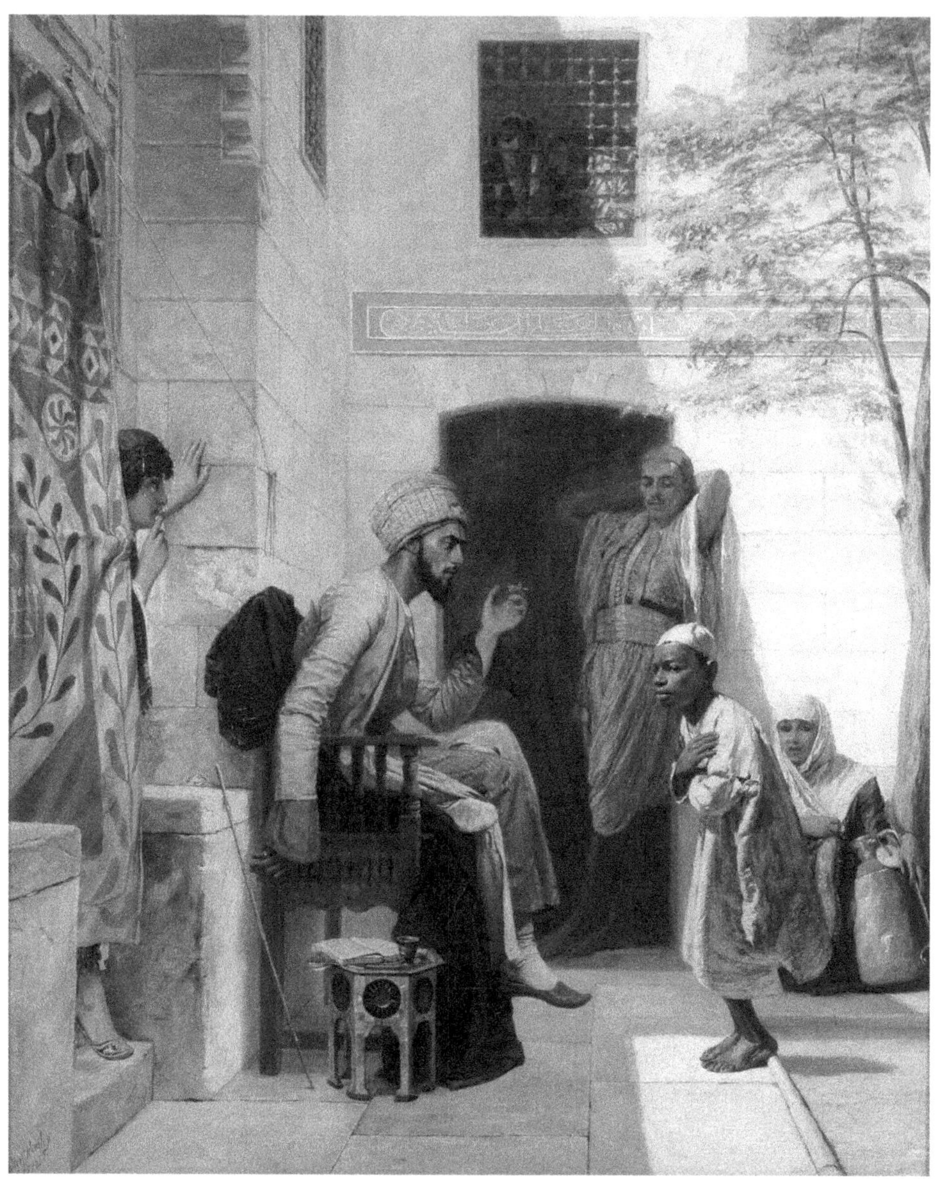

25 Walter Charles Horsley, *Unwilling Evidence,* 1882. Private collection. Photograph courtesy of Bamford's Auctioneers.

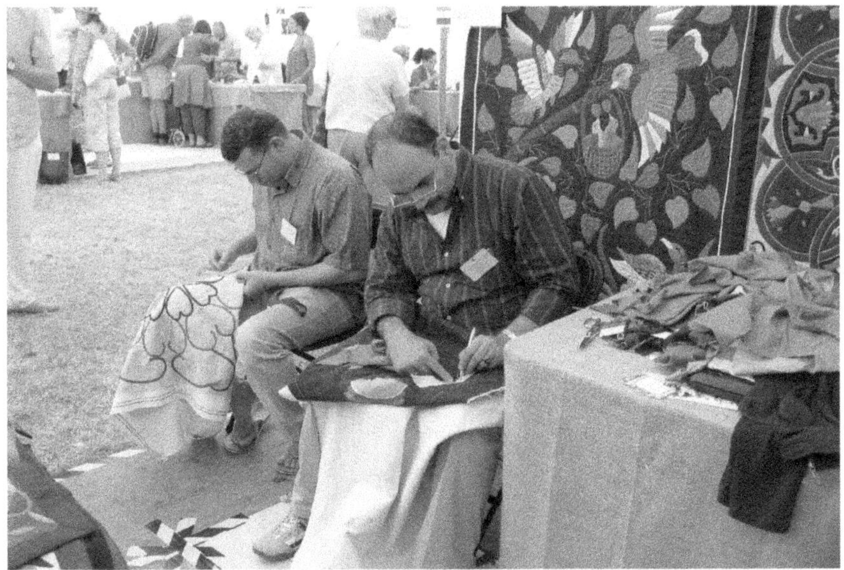

26 Egyptian tentmakers now appear at many international events, especially art, craft, and quilt fairs. Here, Tarek el-Safty and Hossam Hanafy el-Farouk demonstrate their skills in the Netherlands in 2014. Photograph by John Fisher.

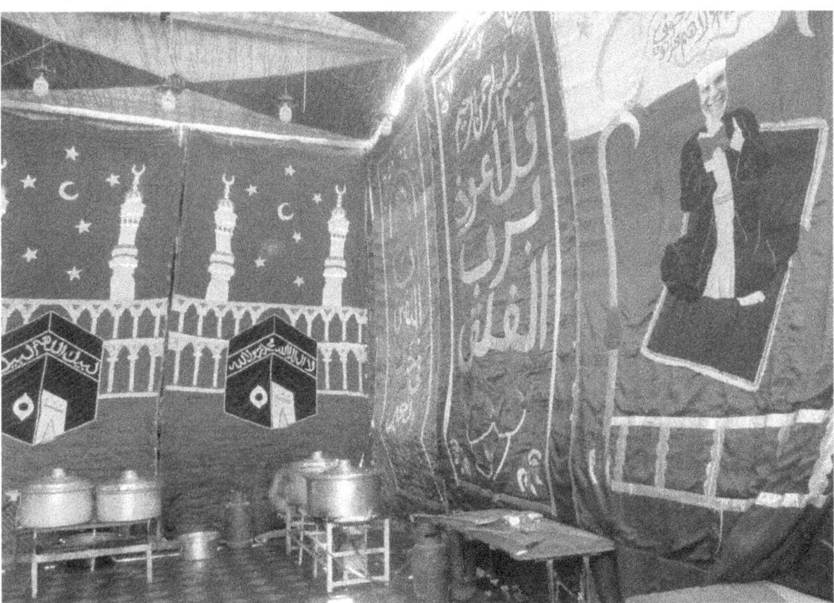

27 This remarkable computer-printed khayamiya panel used in a Ramadan banquet in 2017 depicts the late preacher Shaykh Muhammad Mitwalli al-Sha'rawi, a much-loved household name. Photograph by Seif El Rashidi.

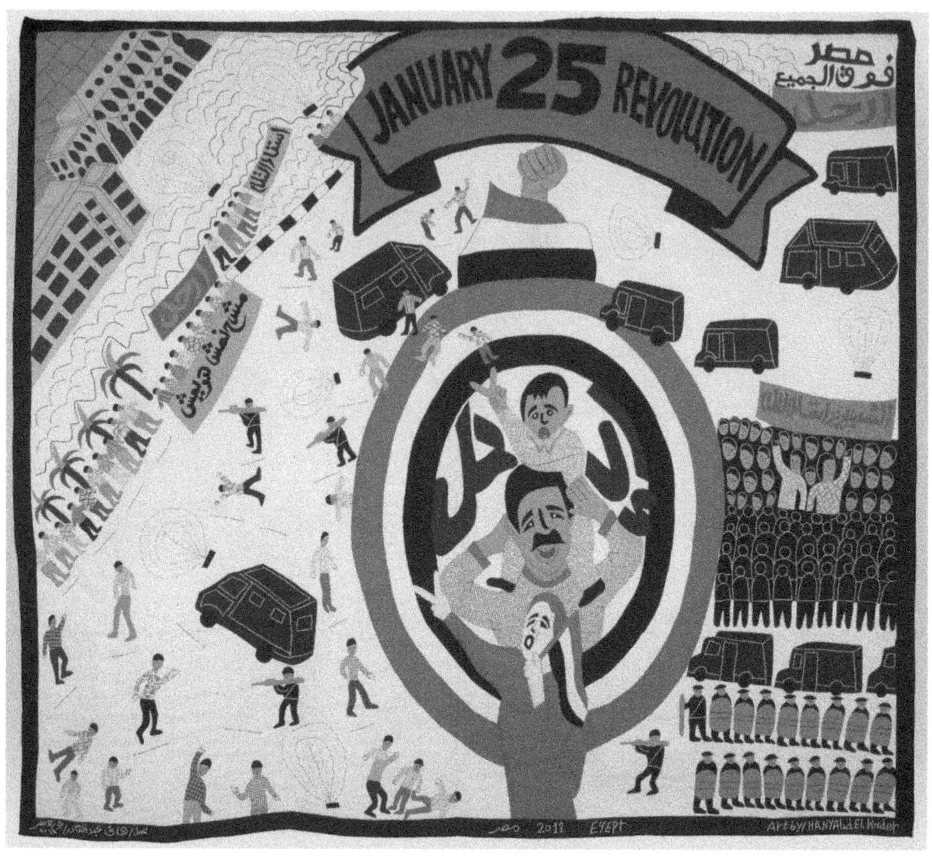

28 Hany Abdel-Kader, *The Second Revolution Khayamiya*, 2012. Collection of the Victoria and Albert Museum, London. Photograph by Timothy Crutchett.

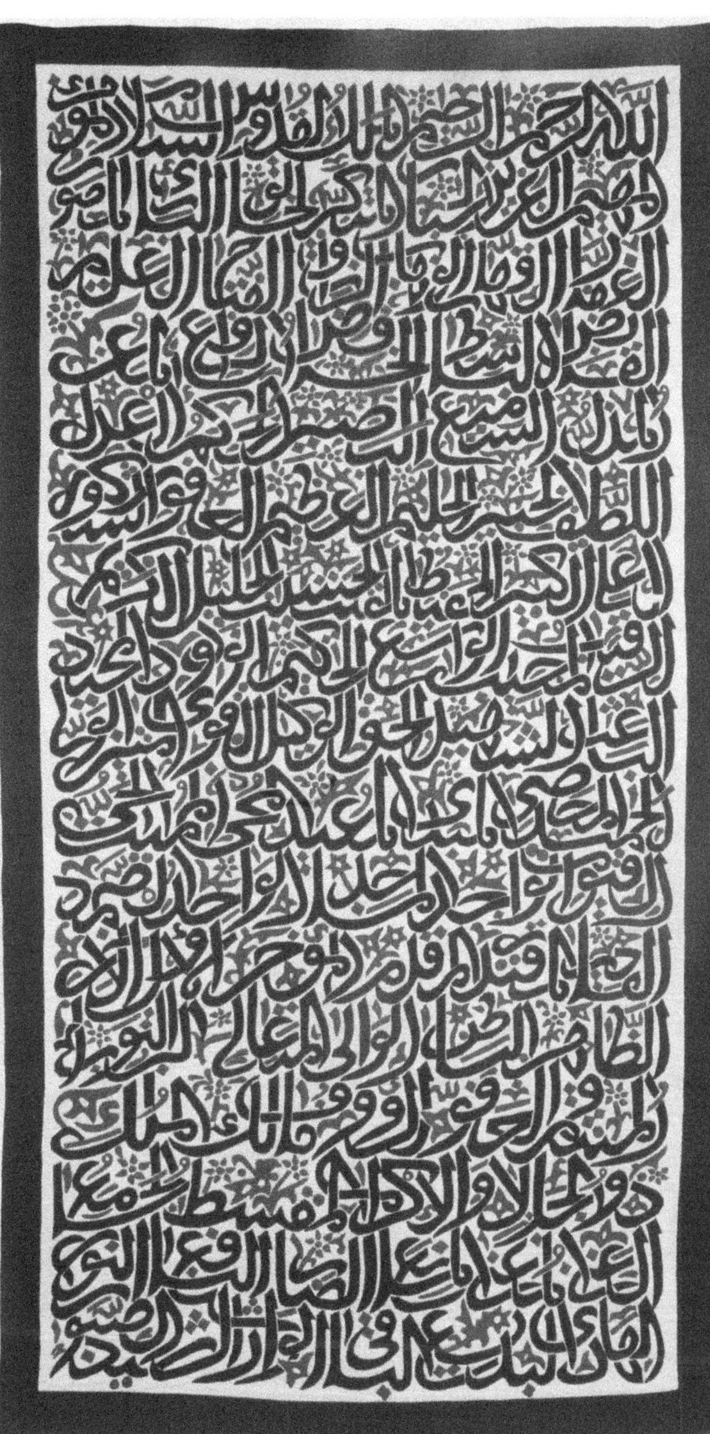

29
Muhammad Dendon, *The Ninety-nine Names*, 2010. Photograph by Timothy Crutchett.

30 A contemporary khayamiya from the collection produced by Ahmad Hamid in the 1980s. It is inspired by an Ottoman tulip design. Photograph by Ahmad Hamid.

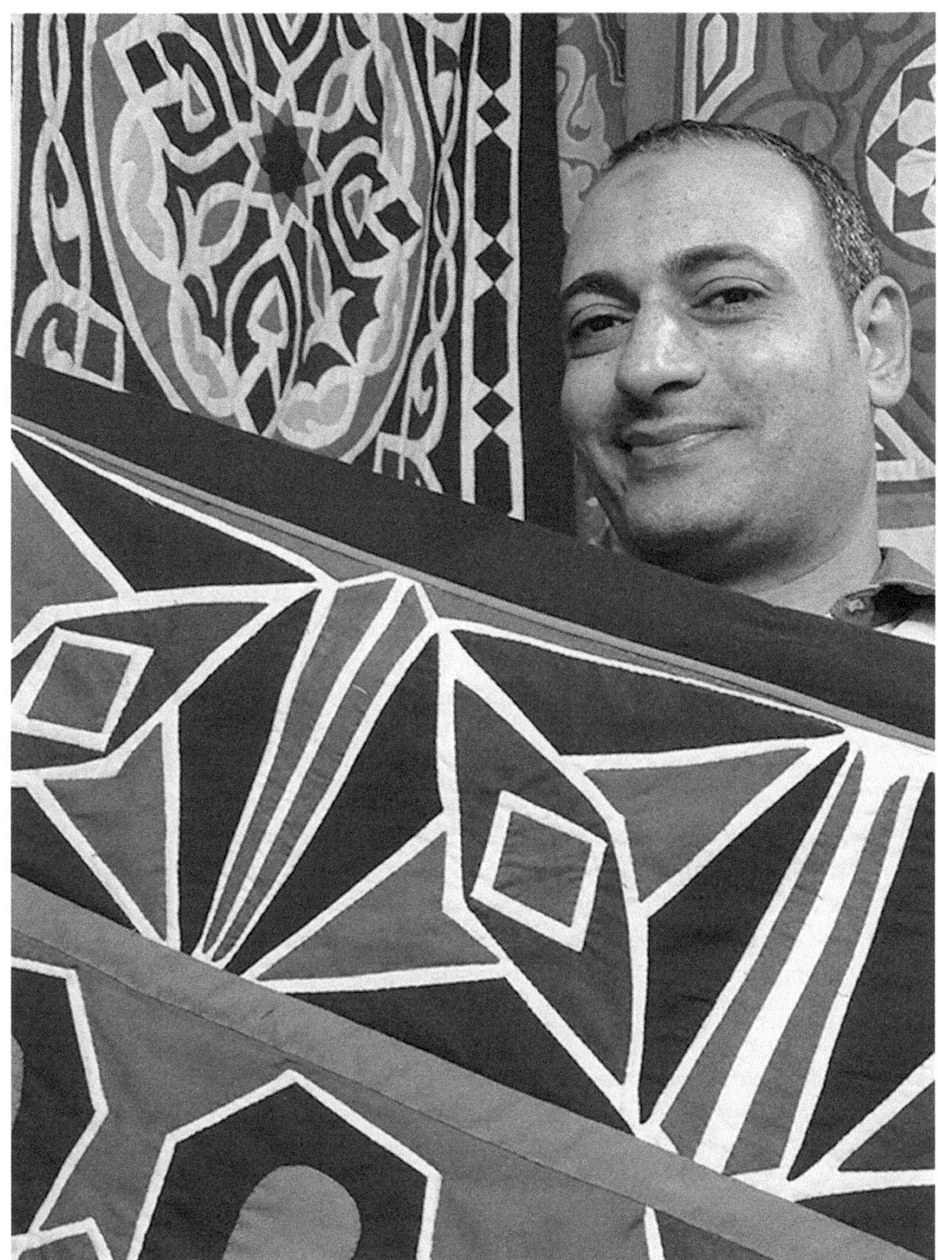

Figure 28 Hany Abdel-Kader, tentmaker. Photograph by Ola Seif.

"I chose this place away from the Street of the Tentmakers because it is much easier—I can get on with my work with no interference, I have peace of mind, it's much more relaxing here. I am also on the way to Bab Zuwayla, so even though I am slightly off the main road, people can find me, people coming and going stop by, and I have placed a sign on the street so that people notice. *Al-hamdullilah*, my shop is the first one many people come across."

His family history

"I have been working for twenty-five years—I inherited this craft from my maternal grandfather, Mahmoud el-Mikkawy, the shaykh of the tent-makers in the 1960s, and my cousins, who taught me the craft. They too worked here on the Street of the Tentmakers. We started working by making the *tark*—the large tent panels, which had only three colors until orange was added thirty or forty years ago. These panels were used in the *suradiq*s for weddings and funerals, and it was all handmade. My grandfather also worked on the *kiswa*, and he employed half of the tentmakers in Cairo. He had around forty people working for him in the *mandara* of a house nearby here in Zuqaq al-Misk. We still have some of the calligraphy pieces he worked on in our houses. Like others, I started off doing basic things—cleaning, ironing, and so on—'I drank the craft,' as we say.

"Around forty years ago, in the 1970s, handmade khayamiya became unaffordable and the khayamiya workers weren't making enough for a living, so they sought other jobs, and shortly after printing workshop owners started to buy designs from some of the khayamiya craftsmen. They silkscreened them and printed them on fabric. Nothing compares to the real thing though, printing is just a secondary technique—it is cheap and the designs are not good, you can't really compare them to the handmade work. Today, tents are still being made, but usually by request—the last time I made one was around seven years ago. It was for Saudi Arabia and was about 70 m x 70 m—it was *gigantic*—and admirable, because anything that is handmade gives me the chance to be creative. It took us two years of work and there were many craftsmen working on it, not just me. I have a tent, a very beautiful handmade one, if anyone wants to buy one, though."

New khayamiya products

I make a wide range of products so that we can appeal to every type of client. For example, I make Ramadan lanterns out of canvas and printed fabric—people like them because they look traditional—they are inexpensive and anyone can afford them. I also make little toy tents in different sizes for children to play with. They are popular, too. It's the little lanterns that are rocking the world—I've almost sold out—and it's three weeks before Ramadan even starts!

"Here are the catalogs of the modern tents. They are very popular in rural areas, especially this new pleated design *(mikashkish)*. The two most popular colors are red and white for weddings, and blue and yellow for funerals. It's all machine-made of course, but they need me because what the factory produces is just a printed panel—what I do is apply the backing canvas and the strings needed to tie the panels to the wooden frame to finish it, basically. With this computer work you can get any design you want—for example, one thing that's quite popular for Muslim clients, both for weddings and funerals, is the panel with the ninety-nine names of God. There's also the virgin, for churches, and there's the back of the Qu'ran design that we used to make by hand. The other thing about this computer work is that you can have any color you want and the fabric is satiny, not cotton like our traditional work."

Does anyone help the tentmakers?

"Recently, a friend of mine told me that there is a syndicate called the Syndicate of Heritage Crafts. I subscribed to it, and now I'm a chairman of it. I hope there will be more support for the craft, because it is on the verge of extinction. Now we work with our own hands, but in ten years we will lose our eyesight, our backs will be weaker, and our fingers will be old. This craft depends on three things: eyesight, back, and steady hands. This craft has a lot of risks in it. When I go to exhibitions in the United Kingdom and such I make a lot of effort. I spend four or five days but the effort is enormous, because everybody there is so eager to see me making tents, they have a hunger for handmade crafts. Last year, I gave an educational class there; I trained a lot of people and they were very happy. They are mainly in their fifties and sixties, and they were professionals. They learned quickly because they make patchworks in their homes. One woman got in touch with me three weeks after I left the United Kingdom and asked me to assess her work. It was a beautiful gesture."

Working in the current climate

"Hopefully, Durham [Cathedral] will like the samples I am making for them, but it's not always easy to get the colors you want—as you know there are shortages for certain things, and I like to use 100 percent cotton, which you can't always get. Well, you can't always get all the colors you need.

"Purple? No, *Wallahi* [I swear], there is no purple—except this one. . . . I know . . . you think it is gray, but it is the closest thing we've got.

"What I really want is to continue going to exhibitions abroad—that's the best thing for me. There you really sell, and when people see me working they appreciate what my work involves. The first time I went to Durham, the women that came to see the exhibition were amazed by my work—they kept on asking questions and looking at the stitches."

Looking at an old piece from the early 1900s

"Hmm. . . . Honestly, honestly, but don't be annoyed, this work isn't very good—look at the stitches, they are wide, and you can see them, and then notice how they haven't changed the color of the thread to match each piece of fabric. . . . Look at this stitching—can you see the difference? The other thing to notice is what they have sewn it on—straight on the canvas. Look around you, at today's work, can you see any of the canvas showing? No—although we used to do it that way. Of course, the old way is easier—why? Because the canvas gives you a good structure to follow—it's like a grid; you don't get that with a normal cotton backing. . . . but I will copy the piece if you want. The fabric is different as well. . . . Can you see it's much thinner *batista*, now we use *topoklin*, which is thicker cotton. . . . I'll see what I can find.

"The colors are great of course . . . that's what happens when you give it a wash or two. . . . *Ya sallam* . . . wonderful."

A lack of awareness

"When I tell someone that I'm a tentmaker, they always ask me, wondering, "What is a tentmaker?!" There is no awareness! Even when I went to an interview at the American embassy in Cairo to obtain a visa to attend an exhibition in New Mexico, they didn't know what a tentmaker was! Even though I had an invitation. I explained to them what it was. I showed them pictures and a book in which I collaborated—it is called *Goha, the Wise Fool*. An American journalist visited me in 2004 and photographed all khayamiya works that depict the story of Goha, and then came back after two weeks and told me that she wants to make a book about Goha, and she needs fifteen handmade panels using khayamiya, which will also be exhibited in the United States, and that a famous author called Denys Johnson-Davies would write the story, and I said okay. It took me a year to make the pieces, and the book was then published in 2005. I loved that year—it is the year the book came out and it is the same year I got married—it was a good year."

Thinking about the future

"Today, there are twenty-nine workshops left, and three or four craftsmen. Today tentmaking is more of a trade than a craft, and that is why it is vanishing. These four do as I do, they design their own work. As for the people who actually execute the work, they are workers, not craftsmen. It's hard to tell how many there are of those, as some of them work from home. I would estimate around two hundred people. Personally I only work with experienced workers, because I have been exposed to the outside world and know what they want. In all honesty, I design what I like—what I like, my clients will like too.

"We are the younger generation of tentmakers. When we inherited the craft from our parents we started to innovate in design, quality, and technique. Our parents were not educated, they didn't have the knowledge we have now, and that knowledge has helped us to create and innovate.

"Youssef, my nine-year-old son, really wants to become a tentmaker. He loves it, but he is still too young, he has to be at least twelve to learn khayamiya. My job is hard and part of me doesn't want him to become a tentmaker—as I said, it strains my eyesight, my health, and lots of other things. If tentmaking got more support maybe I would change my position, but I am a bit of a democratic father, I will leave the choice up to him."

Mohsen el-Khayamy ('The Tentmaker')

Mohsen is one of the most renowned tentmakers who makes work using Arabic calligraphy. Unlike many, his family was not one in the tentmaking trade, but he started off as a young boy of eight.

About his introduction to the craft

"I did not do well at school, so my mother asked our neighbor to take me as an apprentice. He was a stitcher with some of the *farrashin*; you know, those who provide the large tents for events like weddings, condolences, and other outdoor events. I left school in third grade and worked as a *sabi* where Amm Ismail worked. I would fetch the stitchers food and things . . . I started with the minor tasks and then gradually I could do the entire *tark* from beginning to end. I would buy the fabric of the sails, cut it and assemble it on the sewing machine, then I would mark the design and 'dust' it, then I would stich it all by hand. Eventually I made a template for it. I loved this craft . . . I loved making those *tark*s by myself, with my own hands. Over the years I moved from one *firasha* workshop to another, went as far as Alexandria and Ismailiya, then back to Cairo."

Responding to a changing climate

"Years passed, I got married and continued doing this work until after our victory in 1973, when suddenly the printed *tark* appeared. What I did all these years was no longer in demand. The *farrashin* would buy the printed fabric that was cheaper and faster to provide for the events. I asked myself: What could I do? Then I thought of taking those masterpieces from the *tark* and implementing them on smaller, more modern items, such as pillowcases and drapes. I started making those items in a shop in the Street of the Khayamiya; the owner died, God bless his soul. I would sit there stitching and he would hang the products on the walls of the shop. Passersby would watch then buy the piece of their choice. Soon the entire Khayamiya Street followed suit and became like an open market for those handmade masterpieces. By the beginning of the 80s we had already trained a younger generation of workers to do what we do. I went away from the Khayamiya Street to work for a man named Raouf Messiha, who owned a workshop in al-Zaytoun district. He came to Khayamiya to look for skilled craftsmen, *sanay'iya*, to work with him and that is how we met. He is not a tentmaker himself but he stitches as a hobby and is a true artist, a very respectable man, a Christian; Christian or Muslim, we did not make the difference, all our lives we were like brothers, and there is nothing but love between us. I was in charge of the workshop, employing young men to work with me and young women to finish the work, until 2000, when he took the gallery back here in Khayamiya. That is where we started to innovate our designs. We found that many had started basing their new designs on postcards. We too started to bring postcards of pharaonic and Arabic masterpieces, draw from them, and stitch. We used to buy those postcards from Opera Square in Downtown and the used book market along the Azbakeya Gardens fence. Exquisite Arabic patterns were implemented from these postcards, like that one of the Holy Family that I showed you . . . beautiful, isn't it? And this one with *kufi* style calligraphy . . . all those verses from the Holy Qu'ran and names of God, and so on. I developed myself a lot during that period that I worked with Raouf. I learnt a lot from him; I respect him a great deal. He personally met President Sadat and President Mubarak; he had good connections with the Ministry of Tourism and entered many exhibitions. He only stopped working when he had a heart attack and sold the gallery, but we are still in touch till today; he considers me his friend."

Setting up a business

"When Raouf sold the gallery, I bought this little workshop for myself. I did not feel like working for someone else any more. Here I do what we

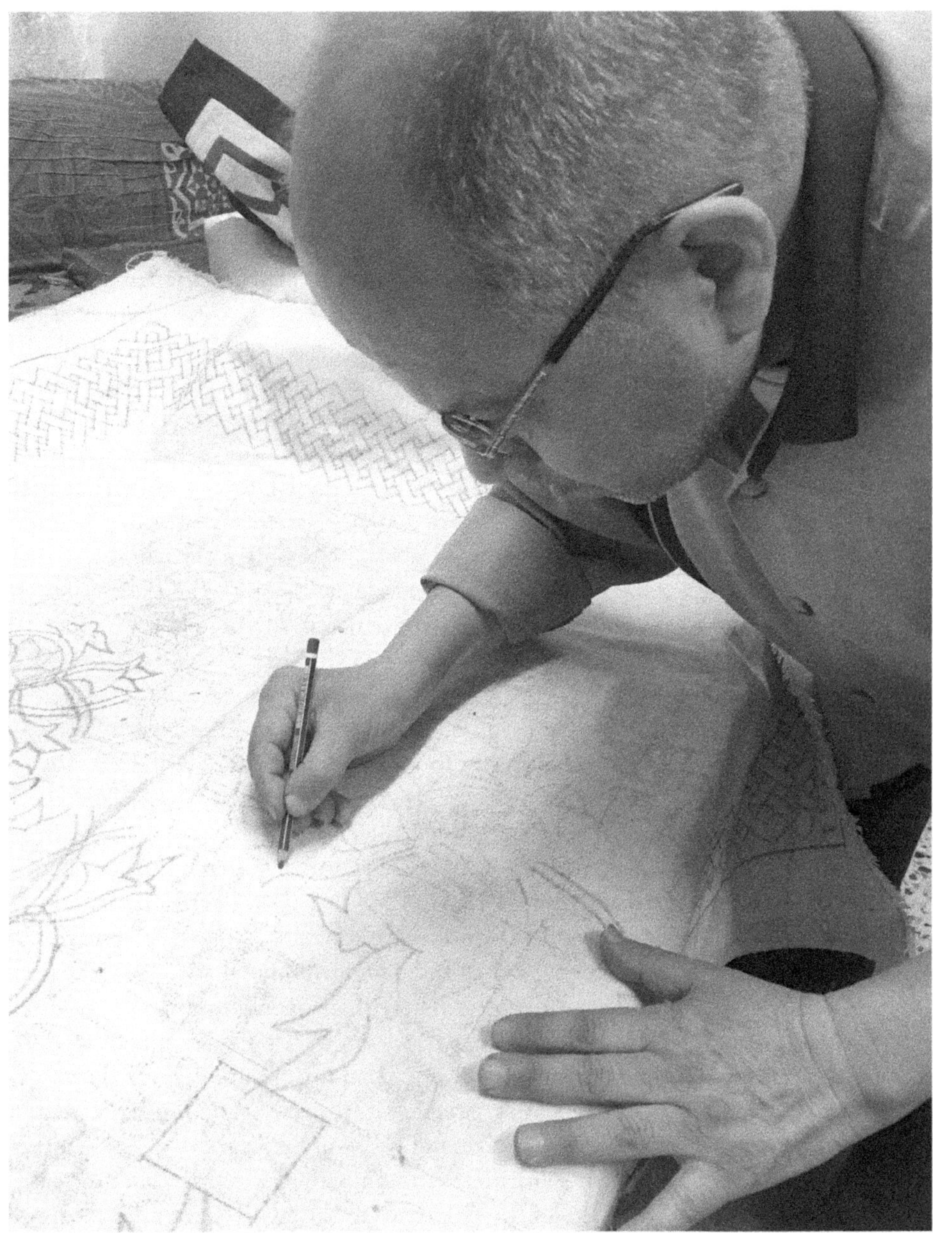

Figure 29 Mohsen el-Khayamy, tentmaker. Photograph by Ola Seif.

used to do at Raouf's. I like doing things myself, the whole thing, until I sell the piece. I did not even want to employ anyone because I am a bit picky about my work. Only my son works with me, Muhammad. He tells me, "No craftsman could work with you," but he puts up with me and he learns from me. I would not want anyone to criticize his work; he bears my name. He is the apprentice of *usta* Mohsen, he should never produce something that is not up to the standards of that name.

"However, even though I refuse to have a full-time craftsman working with me, my son and I do not always carry out the work ourselves. If the work is 'standard' or does not require our caliber of craftsmanship, I would delegate it to a craftsman who works piecemeal, or young women who have started to learn the craft. There are quite a few young women who are being taught the basics of our craft nowadays; some are from Qena or Mansura, and some are from here in al-Darb al-Ahmar as well. There are youth in Mansura who are dedicated to teaching young women khayamiya. However, one cannot hire a young woman the same way one hires a *sanay'i* ; the young women are still learning and would never match up to a craftsman who has years of experience in the field."

The future

"The craft is unfortunately dying out, very few are trying to learn it nowadays and even less are attempting to teach it to others, and that is not to mention that it is becoming an expensive craft to get into; materials are getting more expensive by the day. When I decide to make a new piece there are many factors to take into account; I have to know how much the material would cost and how much I would sell it for afterwards, while taking into account the time I invest in making it as well as the price for my own labor. To be honest, at the end of the day our craft does not pay off very well, but we convince ourselves it's better than staying home, and we do it for the love of the craft and to keep this form of art alive as long as we can. It is for these reasons that I would prefer that my children practice a different vocation; it would be easier for them in the long run. The only people who value our craft and appreciate our work are foreigners. They say it is an intricate, beautiful, true form of art, unlike their Egyptian counterparts, who ask me, "What do you do?" I answer, "I am a *khayamy*." The reply would most commonly be, "What is a *khayamy*?" Here in Egypt our craft hasn't been publicized to the people until very recently, our own countrymen do not even know what khayamiya is. I remember back in the old days, when I was still a young man looking to propose to a young woman . . . her parents would ask me, "And what do you do for a living?" And once again, I would answer, "I am a *khayamy*." Even back then their response would be, "What does that mean?" Most Egyptians don't know our craft.

"You see, our craft is a very fine art one and few truly appreciate it here, which is why our profession is highly dependent on tourism; any minor blow to tourism in Egypt directly impacts our sales. Another point is that what we sell is not a commodity or a necessity to anyone, it is for fun that you buy it when you have money to afford it, so you can unfortunately never count on it to provide you with a stable income.

"I truly believe that the government could play a major role in keeping this craft alive. I do not know why it is that until this day we, the Khayamiya, do not have an official union or support from our government for our craft. If we were to have a union of our own, which would bring all craftsmen in the field together, artisans of our craft would be able to pass down their knowledge to the younger generations of tentmakers who would come to learn, and our industry would grow immensely. As I said, our craft is slowly dying. Every other day we lose people in our business, some younger ones choose to leave the craft behind and find new paths; some work as *ahwagiya* to serve coffee, others became painters, and so on. If our craft is to grow then we need governmental support to lower the prices of the materials we need . . . I mean, how would one invest in innovation when the craft barely covers the expenses of providing for one's home and family, it's either one or the other! Do not get me wrong though; for me, my khayamiya work is as precious as gold, one never gives it up, and this is the beauty of our craft. If I had cash flow like merchants who have shops, I would produce more pieces and keep them till the market improves, but as a craftsman I do not have this option."

Happily recalling the past

"I was the one who made the *kiswa* for the Sayyida Zaynab Mosque [the textile covering of the shrine of the granddaughter of the Prophet]. Hassan el-Tohamy was the person in charge from the Awqaf at the time, and we went to dress her up together. I was even allowed to enter the shrine of Sayyida Zaynab while we were covering it. Her veil was a masterpiece; they even used to hold a festival when they would clad her in our work. This was back in 1979 I think, at the time I was working for Hanafy el-Halawany, and we would make all four sides of her [shrine's] fabric covering as well as one for the dome itself. At that time her [shrine] was covered all in black, in commemoration of the death of President Abd al-Nasser, ten years earlier. We removed the black covering and replaced it with ours."

Recalling the mawlid of al-Husayn and the role of the tentmakers

"At the al-Husayn *mawlid* people would congregate in front of al-Rifa'i Mosque at the foot of the Citadel. They would start walking right after *al-'Asr* [the afternoon prayer], to reach al-Husayn by sunset. It was a big festivity with horsemen and banners to indicate the different congregations of the different sufi *tariqa*s [sects or orders]—al-Refa'iya and al-Shazleya and others. The police also played a major role, as they would stop traffic in al-Qal'a [the Citadel] and Muhammad 'Ali Street and along the route to al-Azhar Street until al-Husayn Mosque. Brass bands in military uniform would play music and march with the congregations. It was always a great *zaffa* [procession] like that of a wedding. Onlookers would gather all along the streets, watching the procession. Around the call for al-maghrib prayers, the procession would reach al-Husayn Mosque, each congregation holding their banners high. Onlookers would comment, "Here is this *tariqa*, there is that *tariqa*." We, the tentmakers, used to make these banners; double-sided with decorative calligraphy indicating the sect of each congregation. You don't see this happening any more [banned by the government since 2006]."

"The *tannura* is another item that we make until now," Mohsen adds. "It is a very special skirt worn by the whirling dervish dancers, who perform in *mawlid*s and wedding parties. It is made of a special fabric, a fabric that looks creased. All colors are used in the modern *tannura*. The performer comes to us and we have to fit it on him so he can swirl it around his waist and his neck and hold it up with his hand, see like this . . . of course, all this is done with machine stitching now."

Tentmaking being a unique tradition

"No one in the world can do the same work we do here . . . they tried to imitate it abroad before and failed. Moreover, machinery can never replace what we do. A machine needs simple and straightforward designs and patterns to be able to stitch, but our craft requires elaborate designs and intricate stitching. These are things that no one else can attempt to do. We have no equivalent in the world, no competition; our khayamiya is unique, and it is only found here."

Ahmad Hamid: Khayamiya from a Designer's Perspective (Reflections on a Forty-piece Collection)

Ahmad Hamid is an architect, engineer, and designer whose work draws its inspiration from design languages, patterns, and spatial relationships

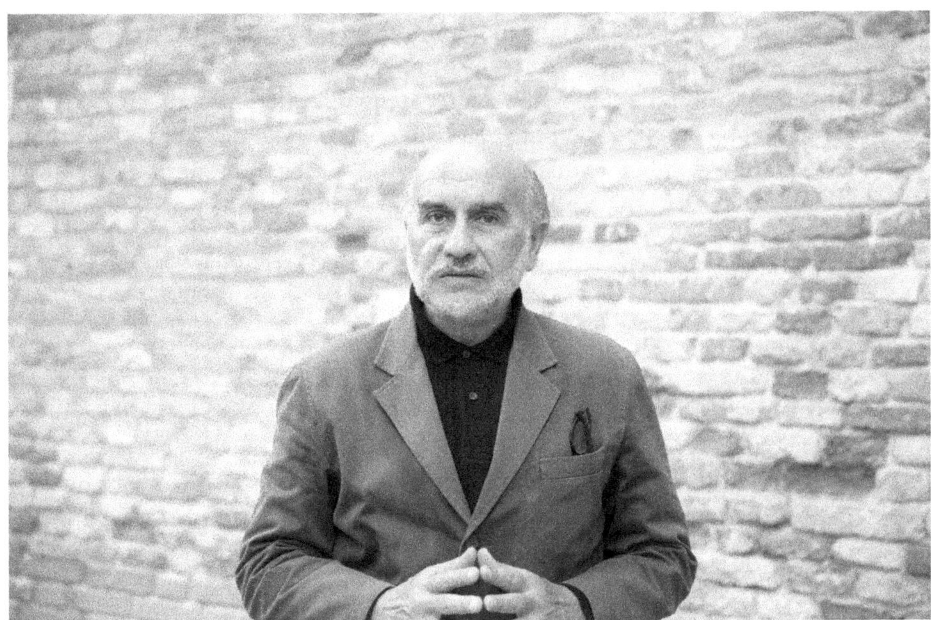

Figure 30 Ahmad Hamid, designer. Photograph by Rachele Maistrello.

from different contexts. Distinctively, in Hamid's professional career as an architect, he oversees the processes of building and making, and in fact much of his design work takes its cues from the manufacturing process. Hamid's work espouses a diverse modernity with a culturally inclusive grammar of forms, surfaces, and space. He produced a collection of khayamiya patchworks in the late 1980s, which received great acclaim both in Egypt and abroad (see plate 30). He reflects below on his work with the tentmakers and on his method used to produce the collection. "Good design evokes a memory and is then remembered as well," he says.

"It was because of Frau Ursula Rindlisbacher, the cultural attaché of Pro-Helvetia, the Swiss government's cultural organization in Egypt, that I first became interested in khayamiya. She always had a nice bedspread or a throw on the sofa from the khayamiya and insisted that the khayamiya craft could be for modern living. It triggered in me the feeling that there was great opportunity and great potential, and made me think about the possibilities of a craft that was completely untapped by designers, and how to use it for modern contemporary living, neither as museum pieces nor as folk art pieces on the wall.

"So I sought to understand a bit more. In Egypt, us architects are educated completely in isolation from the craftsmen and manufacturing process of architecture—one isn't taught to experience that first hand. The first piece I designed in 1983 triggered a whole new sense: that there is a place for the craftsman directly in the spaces of modern living—in a domestic sense, not in a folkloric sense. It is not about bringing folklore into your living room or your bedroom or workspace. I had the insistence that they had something fresh to say today—not like reincarnating or reenacting the past once more, not at all.

"I understood through Ursula that by changing the colors I could move away from those that we associated with a funerary tradition. This is what triggered me to create my first collection in 1985. The master craftsman, Salah el-Ouzy was, as a matter of fact, her discovery.

"I went to meet him and made him understand that this work needed to be engineered and executed very precisely, much more so than for a normal customer—the color palette had to be extremely precise—there was no scope for him to say, "I didn't find mustard so I used lime yellow." He was a bit scared at the beginning, and that is why we created samples, before producing bigger-sized pieces. It was a chance to reinterpret traditional patterns from the world of Islamic art. Suddenly, a whole treasure trove was opened in front of my eyes. Whatever technique we had that had not lasted, or had disappeared, or was impossible to achieve because the secrets of a craft had died out, we could adapt to fabric rather than losing the pattern completely.

"At the beginning we thought that fabric was easy—in fact, fabric is easy in many cases, but not in others. I realized that there was a certain minimum size and scale beyond which the craftsman could not go. Each medium has its parameters, after all. When we got to silk pieces, that was the climax, we were producing our best, producing and selling, and we thought, "Let's try silk." Our first silk piece still hangs in the client's house today—Madame Barakat, a friend of my dear mother and the daughter of Egypt's former prime minister Bahieddine Barakat Pasha. People think it is an original seventeenth- or eighteenth-century textile, but it's a fully contemporary piece made in 1986!

"Later on, many collectors both in Egypt and abroad sought to have one of the fabric pieces I designed. As a matter of fact, the owner of a shop in Zurich called Fox Interiors, which did very high-end interior design sold out of a small but really exquisite store, heard about the collection and I was introduced to him. He asked to see a sample, and the moment I opened a black-and-white chintamani design piece, his exclamation was a big, "Ahhh, how beautiful . . . how modern." He didn't even ask me about the origins of the design or its antecedents, he just said, "We are in business." He immediately bought it and the next day, I was really amazed to find that it had replaced the centerpiece in his shop window, a textile by Pierre Frey. Beside it was a Joseph Hoffman lamp and beside it an exquisite leather Japanese camera bag. It was a big surprise for a designer like myself, warranting a feast.

"We created an ongoing business—he asked for certain patterns and certain colors and we would send them to him in Zurich. He was straight enough to say: "Look, I am buying the piece from you for $1,000, but I need to sell it tomorrow for $2,000, and I am able to." The shortcoming of working with Switzerland, though, was that it wasn't considered important that these pieces were made or designed in Egypt; the people who bought them just liked them for what they were—design pieces.

"Upon reflection, it's not necessarily a bad thing—it shows you that khayamiya can be an international item. We don't always have to know whether a table has been made in Malaysia or Indonesia or China—or in Italy. The global economy today blurs such a demarcation. The point is that it is well styled, well manufactured, well detailed, and that it fits.

"Next came a request from the Egyptian presidential guest palaces, through one of the top connoisseurs of silver around the world, and an expert in personal arms. He came across the collection through the Danish ambassador's wife at the time, who was a great fan of my work. The ambassador came and visited me and started to request some of the pieces for the palaces. All of these stories tell us about how styling and coloring enable khayamiya fabrics to enter realms not tapped upon by their traditional contexts as tents, funerary or temporary structures.

"Coming back to the way they are stitched, I came to understand bit by bit that it was a long process—it takes a craftsman forty days to produce a 2.5 m x 2.5 m piece. It requires discipline and a state of mind that comes close to meditation. With my collection, all of the craftsmen were working under the hegemony of Salah el-Ouzy; they suggested working off the street so that they wouldn't get distracted, or robbed of the patterns, or questioned by others. It was very different from the commercial work sold to tourists, and like me, they too believed in the evil eye and wanted seclusion.

"On one occasion, one lady who had seen an example of my collection, which appeared on the covers of a Saudi engineering magazine, *al-Binaa*, and of *Arts and the Islamic World*, went to Salah and tried to convince him to work for her.

"Salah said, "If you can bring us fame and acclaim and honor, as he does, we are ready to work with you. But you have to know that whatever we ask for in fees, he pays. So we are happy with our work—we have no reason to leave and work with you. What do you have to offer us?" And this is where the conversation ended. It's a story that has meant a lot to me, and is one that I am keen to remember, almost as much as another story. . . . Salah told me that because of the collection he was able to save enough to pay for the trousseau of his eldest daughter. It was the real first realization for me that working with the craftsmen could have some sort of social impact. "You save me from continuously bargaining with the tourist, over whether it is fifteen, twenty, or thirty pounds," he said.

"There was sometimes a problem in acquiring the most basic of equipment—good quality needles, which I sometimes had to buy from Europe, as the ones found in Egypt did not last. Salah was ecstatic—these new needles didn't break as easily—and they were also stainless steel, so did not rust. We also realized that the fabric used for the commercial work was not the best fabric, so we started to buy exquisite deluxe cotton that was very well dyed, sold by the roll. This was important to guarantee that our color palette was consistent and resistant (there were gaps in the production market that we needed to control).

"In 1994 I received a request from Ralph Lauren, who were interested in exploring a line of handmade patchworks. My sister had a piece in New York—a very beautiful red and black chintamani design, and they wanted to know how many we could produce per month, what color palettes were possible, shipping costs, and so on. When I thought about it, I realized that I would never be able to produce the quantities that Ralph Lauren expected—I was, after all, a single designer, hiring freelancers and subject to lapses in the market and in its raw materials. I tried to pique the interest of some of my wealthier friends of the time, as I knew it would require a much larger infrastructure than my previous operation. However, everyone shrugged their shoulders—they were more interested in investing in chicken and fish farms! So I refused the offer. Bluntly said, I think it was a mistake. I should have realized that Ralph Lauren was not the first, nor the last, and that I had found a global upper niche.

"One of the things that struck me most about the craftsmen is that they work with templates. As engineers, we marvel at templates. The tentmakers create patterns according to a certain module, they fix the size of the star so that it isn't too bulky or too small, so that it is appropriate for the viewer's perception. From these templates other perforated templates are created, from which comes a stencil print on the fabric, and then they start stitching—it's like a collage. They have a way of knowing what needs to be stitched before what—a structure. For example, the stems of a tulip should be stitched first, and then the major tulip second, and then the more delicate elements on top—it is all about layers, and you need to think about how these layers come together. This process belongs to our design world of making things.

"I thought about the weight of the fabric as well—to ensure that the piece did not get too heavy to support itself. Of course, I paid for very close stitching to ensure durability. We washed all of the fabric before stitching so that it would lose its extra dye, to prevent future color run and so that the fabric became more supple in the hands of the stitcher. At the end, all of the pieces were ironed using a foot iron, which produces a better result.

"The craftsmen marveled at the design world I opened for them, and at the outcome. I hardly ever invented designs. I looked at patterns that had existed before, changed colors, compiled, and collated. In most cases, I took the patterns as they were. I understood that with textiles the main field has a set of patterns, while the borders have their own language and their own set of patterns, similar to the world of carpets. It was a whole exercise to design these to add value to the centerpiece.

"When I did invent, I had been immersed in the patterns for so long that my designs were a natural continuum to a branch of a tradition that broke away, not by renovating nor innovating, but evolving spontaneously from its roots.

"I introduced a new color palette that was more fresh and more promising, but also more sober. It had a different vibrancy from the striking contrasts of the traditional pieces that come from the star plates, small and large, and the way they borrow space and air and breathe from one another. In my collections I was aware of the vibrancy of the lines and surfaces and patterns. I intentionally did not use the star patterns in order to steer away from what is associated today with a funerary culture. The colors I used are dynamic, but not overly so—it is not op art. Sometimes the volumes of the design itself were in motion.

"I should add that it wasn't easy to find somebody who was willing to work with a designer. Most people don't want to hear another voice saying: "No, this curve is wrong—no, this stitch is wrong—no, this fabric is awful." Most want to do whatever they want, and you as the client have to applaud, pay, take what they give you, and leave. We knew we would have to find somebody willing to work using a different approach—that of a well-engineered operation that was meticulous, specified, and clear—not a happy-go-lucky approach. Fortunately, Salah's craftsmen came to see the merits of this method.

"When I had twenty pieces stored, I had my first exhibition at Extra Gallery. Like Fox Interiors, the gallery owner, Mina Sarofim, an acclaimed art connoisseur, saw a piece not yet fully open, and said: "You have a show—in three months—are you ready?" I said: "I am ready today!"

"It was a joint show with the potter Mohamed Mandour, who produces exquisite modern work inspired by tradition. It worked well, as pottery is 3D while patchwork is 2D—there was no conflict.

"We weren't sure what the demand would be like, and I was happy that I sold half of the pieces. To our surprise, more than 90 percent of the buyers were from Egyptian families, who marveled at what this product was. They saw the pieces as something completely new—even though the designs were traditional, it was the radiating beauty of the pieces that took the eye from any historical or technical context. The questions of where is it from, by who, how is it done, by hand or machine, came later. I lost my favorite piece, a silk *bohjce* with its difficult curves, which I would have loved to keep for myself.

"What struck me about the craft is how from fabric, needle, and thread, all very fragile and frail, one creates a *structure* that is useable. You go from 1D to 2D, to 3D, to 4D, with minimum investment in material and structural elements—it is a beautiful product, so well optimized. In fact, I produced a wonderful tent in Jeddah—not all appliqué, but with huge sections based on designs of Mamluk marblework from a floor in the Museum of Islamic Art. It's not unusual in Islamic art for a pattern to travel from one medium to the next—with limits, of course.

"Upon reflection, I had found that heritage had acquired a negative connotation, almost a handicap, and my role as a designer who fell in love with the aesthetic itself was to bring it out of its box. That's what attracted people. They said, "It's heritage, but it isn't—it's modern." They were surprised—where was the trick? There *is* a trick!

"The end of my patchwork collection came as I reached the saturation point in terms of individual demand. By then I had a young, growing family, and I no longer had the luxury of time to invest in producing high-end textile pieces. People often tell me that I should do another collection. Maybe I should."

Conclusion

The emergence of a cosmopolitan traveling tentmaker, the 'rock star of the quilt world,' has raised esteem for the profession within the Street of the Tentmakers and beyond. But it has also introduced changes in the language of khayamiya as it is influenced more extensively from the design traditions of other cultures, more than it was in the past. Some tentmakers are highly regarded internationally for their craft, and are starting to sell tuition in appliqué as a new product. This shift from making to teaching focuses on a new set of skills—including eligibility for visas, English and other languages, and charisma—and has disrupted working relationships as emboldened tentmakers abandoned their former employers to start their own businesses.

The challenge now facing the tentmakers is to promote their own voices and cherish their own design tradition, while both addressing the aspects of their heritage which resonate with global audiences in particular and trying to stay afloat in a local market at a time when purse strings are tight.

Changes in khayamiya since the mid-nineteenth century are remarkable. Contemporary khayamiya are so far removed from those of even the khedival period that many tentmakers are unaware of the extent of their own visual and material heritage. In an ideal future, demand for the tentmakers' art will be maintained not by foreign interest, but by Egyptians.

The Street of the Tentmakers has moved around Cairo and around the world. It is the heart of khayamiya and the source of the magnificent pavilions that have hosted so many Egyptian celebrations. It is a local marketplace that inspires a global audience of collectors, scholars, artists, and patrons. The Egyptian tentmakers have adapted and reinvented their work, from the Mamluk to the Ottoman and khedival periods, through the souvenirs of tourists and venues for weddings and funerals, to extraordinary works of contemporary art.

In today's market, the tentmakers are finishers of machine-made tents and the makers of fine pieces of handstitched appliqué. Even just thirty-five years ago there was no separation, and they were still the manufacturers of handmade tents, following centuries of an evolving tradition.

The reevaluation of khayamiya should prompt a new interest in their history, for an understanding of this craft's origins is essential to its vitality. This is an art that reaches far beyond the Street of the Tentmakers. As anonymous tentmakers once sewed into their canvas: "Behold, for you have seen a great work. In Egypt, you will find the greatest of all art. Look closely, for this will take a long time to explain."

Notes

Notes to Preface

1 Ramadan, "Tradition vs. modernism in the street of the tentmakers," *Egypt Independent*, Saturday, August 21, 2010.
2 Atasoy, *Otağ-ı Hümayun: The Ottoman Imperial Tent Complex*, 19–41.
3 The earliest depiction of khedival khayamiya is found in photographs of *ulama* posing with a khayamiya backdrop taken by Emile/Henri Béchard during the 1870s–1880s.

Notes to Chapter 1

1 al-Maqrizi, *al-Mawa'iz wa-l-i'tibar bi-dhikr al-khitat wa-l-athar*, vol. 2, 308.
2 al-Maqrizi, *al-Mawa'iz wa-l-i'tibar bi-dhikr al-khitat wa-l-athar*, vol. 2, 308.
3 Sanders, *Ritual, Politics, and the City in Fatimid Cairo*, 22, 25, 26.
4 One cubit was slightly less than 50 centimeters long.
5 al-Maqrizi, *al-Mawa'iz wa-l-i'tibar bi-dhikr al-khitat wa-l-athar*, vol. 2, 308.
6 al-Maqrizi, *Itti'az al-hunafa' bi-akhbar al-a'ima al-Fatimiyyin al-khulafa'*, 160.
7 al-Maqrizi, *Itti'az al-hunafa' bi-akhbar al-a'ima al-Fatimiyyin al-khulafa'*, 160.
8 al-Maqrizi, *al-Mawa'iz wa-l-i'tibar bi-dhikr al-khitat wa-l-athar*, vol. 2, 4, 125.
9 al-Maqrizi, *al-Mawa'iz wa-l-i'tibar bi-dhikr al-khitat wa-l-athar*, vol. 2, 308.
10 al-Maqrizi, *al-Mawa'iz wa-l-i'tibar bi-dhikr al-khitat wa-l-athar*, vol. 2, 308, 413.
11 al-Qalqashandi, *Subh al-'asha*, 503.
12 Bin Tabataba, *al-Fakhri fi-l-adab al-sultaniya wa-l-duwal al-islamiya*, 252; McKinney, *The Case of Rhyme Versus Reason: Ibn Al-Rumi and His Poetics in Context*, 249.
13 al-Maqrizi, *al-Mawa'iz wa-l-i'tibar bi-dhikr al-khitat wa-l-athar*, vol. 2, 309.

14 al-Maqrizi, *al-Mawaʿiz wa-l-iʿtibar bi-dhikr al-khitat wa-l-athar*, vol. 2, 309.
15 al-Maqrizi, *Ittiʿaz al-hunafaʾ bi-akhbar al-aʾima al-Fatimiyyin al-khulafaʾ*, 233.
16 al-Nuwayri, *Nihayat al-arab fi funun al-adab*, 3500.
17 al-Nuwayri, *Nihayat al-arab fi funun al-adab*, 3500. Translation provided by Dr. Hassan Hilmy.
18 al-Maqrizi, *al-Mawaʿiz wa-l-iʿtibar bi-dhikr al-khitat wa-l-athar*, vol. 2, 402.
19 al-Maqrizi, *al-Mawaʿiz wa-l-iʿtibar bi-dhikr al-khitat wa-l-athar*, vol. 2, 309.
20 al-Maqrizi, *al-Mawaʿiz wa-l-iʿtibar bi-dhikr al-khitat wa-l-athar*, vol. 2, 309, 310.
21 al-Maqrizi, *al-Mawaʿiz wa-l-iʿtibar bi-dhikr al-khitat wa-l-athar*, vol. 2, 402.
22 Sanders, *Ritual, Politics, and the City in Fatimid Cairo*, 105 (quoting Ibn al-Tuwayr).
23 Sanders, *Ritual, Politics, and the City in Fatimid Cairo*, 106.
24 al-Maqrizi, *al-Mawaʿiz wa-l-iʿtibar bi-dhikr al-khitat wa-l-athar*, vol. 2, 416; Cornu, "Rideaux et tentures dans le monde arabo-islamique oriental jusqu'à l'époque mamluke," 313 (Islamic Museum Guide Book 1955, 17).
25 Cornu, "Rideaux et tentures," 315.
26 Sanders, *Ritual, Politics, and the City in Fatimid Cairo*, 105.
27 Goitein, *Letters of Medieval Jewish Traders*, 77.
28 Cornu, "Rideaux et tentures," 315.
29 *Book of Curiosities*, fol 34b.
30 *Book of Curiosities*, fol 34b.
31 Levy, *Saladin in Egypt*, 136.
32 *The Travels of Ibn Jubayr*, 88.
33 *The Travels of Ibn Jubayr*, 88.
34 *The Travels of Ibn Jubayr*, Ramadan 579 AH (1183 AD), 148.
35 *The Travels of Ibn Jubayr*, Ramadan 579 AH (1183 AD), 150.
36 Eddé, *Saladin*, 210.
37 Noyles Colvin, ed., *Godeffroy of Boloyne*, 213.

Notes to Chapter 2

1 al-Maqrizi, *al-Suluk li-maʿrifat duwal al-muluk*, 853.
2 al-Qalqashandi, *Subh al-ʿasha*, 533.
3 Ibn Iyas, *Histoire des mamelouks circassiens*, Dhul Hijja 902 AH (1497 AD), 415.
4 Ibn Iyas, *Journal d'un bourgeois du Caire*, vol. 1, Muharram 907 AH (1501 AD), 15.
5 Ibn Iyas, *Journal d'un bourgeois du Caire*, vol. 1, Shawwal 908 AH (1502 AD), 47.
6 Ibn Iyas, *Histoire des mamelouks circassiens*, Rabi I 890 AH (1486 AD), 241.
7 Ibn Iyas, *Histoire des mamelouks circassiens*, Jumada II 890 AH (1494 AD), 339.
8 Ibn Iyas, *Histoire des mamelouks circassiens*, Shawwal 875 AH (1471 AD), 64.
9 Ibn Iyas, *Histoire des mamelouks circassiens*, Shawwal 905 AH (1500 AD), 473.
10 al-Maqrizi, *al-Suluk li-maʿrifat duwal al-muluk*, 109.

11 Folda, *The Art of the Crusaders in the Holy Land: From the Third Crusade to the Fall of Acre, 1096–1187*, 237.

12 Gabrieli, *Arab Historians of the Crusades*, 302.

13 Philips, *Holy Warriors*, 273, 274–75.

14 Philips, *Holy Warriors*, 275.

15 Shoshan, *Popular Culture in Medieval Cairo*, 74.

16 Shoshan, *Popular Culture in Medieval Cairo*, 74; al-Maqrizi, *al-Suluk li-ma'rifat duwal al-muluk*, 938–40; Ibn Taghribirdi, *al-Nujum al-zahira fi muluk Misr wa-l-Qahira*, vol. 8, 165–68.

17 al-Maqrizi, *al-Suluk li-ma'rifat duwal al-muluk*, 150.

18 al-Maqrizi, *al-Suluk li-ma'rifat duwal al-muluk*, 150.

19 al-Maqrizi, *al-Suluk li-ma'rifat duwal al-muluk*, 895.

20 Ibn Iyas, *Journal d'un bourgeois du Caire*, vol. 1, Shaaban 914 AH (1508 AD), 137.

21 Ibn Iyas, *Journal d'un bourgeois du Caire*, vol. 1, Shaaban 912 AH (1506/1507 AD), 99.

22 Ibn Iyas, *Journal d'un bourgeois du Caire*, vol. 1, Muharram 915 AH (1509 AD), 147, 148.

23 Ibn Iyas, *Journal d'un bourgeois du Caire*, vol. 1, Rabi 913 AH (1506–07 AD), 113; Ramadan 914 AH (1508–09 AD), 139.

24 Ibn Iyas, *Journal d'un bourgeois du Caire*, vol. 1, Muharram 918 AH (1512 AD), 237; Dhul Qa'ada 917 AH (1511 AD), 232, 233.

25 Ibn Taghribirdi, *History of Egypt*, 172.

26 al-Maqrizi, *al-Suluk li-ma'rifat duwal al-muluk*, 887.

27 Shoshan, *Popular Culture in Medieval Cairo*, 75.

28 Ibn Iyas, *Journal d'un bourgeois du Caire*, vol. 1, Dhul Hija 912 AH (1507 AD), 107.

29 Ibn Iyas, *Journal d'un bourgeois du Caire*, vol. 1, Muharram 913 AH (1507 AD), 110.

30 We cannot be certain that saffron was the dye used for yellow as it is known to fade easily. Any association with saffron yellow, however, was prestigious.

31 al-Qalqashandi, *Subh al-'asha*, 531, 532.

32 al-Qalqashandi, *Subh al-'asha*, 244.

33 al-Qalqashandi, *Subh al-'asha*, 244.

34 Ibn Iyas, *Histoire des mamelouks circassiens*, Shawwal 879 AH (1475 AD), 117.

35 Ibn Iyas, *Histoire des mamelouks circassiens*, Muharram 904 AH (1498 AD), 440.

36 The word *fusus* could also mean 'bosses' or 'studs'; in other words, not necessarily 'jewels' in the literal sense.

37 Ibn Iyas, *Bada'i' al-zuhur fi waqa'i' al-duhur*, vol. 2, 1498.

38 al-Maqrizi, *al-Mawa'iz wa-l-i'tibar bi-dhikr al-khitat wa-l-athar*, vol. 2, 226; see Rahbet Aqbugha, vol. 3, 90.

39 As well as in a third location by the Mosque of Ibn Tulun.

40 al-Maqrizi, *al-Mawa'iz wa-l-i'tibar bi-dhikr al-khitat wa-l-athar*, vol. 3, 184.

41 al-Maqrizi, *al-Mawa'iz wa-l-i'tibar bi-dhikr al-khitat wa-l-athar*, vol. 3, 184.

42 Ibn Iyas, *Journal d'un bourgeois du Caire*, vol. 2, 235.
43 Ibn Iyas, *Journal d'un bourgeois du Caire*, vol. 1, Jumada I 913 AH (1507 AD), 115.
44 Ibn Iyas, *Journal d'un bourgeois du Caire*, vol. 1, Jumada II 918 AH (1512 AD), 257.
45 Ibn Iyas, *Journal d'un bourgeois du Caire*, vol. 1, Rabi II 919 AH (1513 AD), 292; Rajab 919 AH (1513 AD), 309.
46 Ibn Iyas, *Journal d'un bourgeois du Caire*, vol. 1, Shaaban 919 AH (1513/14 AD), 312.
47 Ibn Iyas, *Journal d'un bourgeois du Caire*, vol. 1, Shaaban 919 AH (1513 AD), 312.
48 Ibn Iyas, *Journal d'un bourgeois du Caire*, vol. 1, Shaaban 919 AH (1513 AD), 313, 314.

Notes to Chapter 3

1 Salmon, *An Account of the Ottoman Conquest of Egypt in the Year A.H. 922 (A.D. 1516)*, 17.
2 Salmon, *An Account of the Ottoman Conquest of Egypt in the Year A.H. 922 (A.D. 1516)*, 4, 6.
3 Salmon, *An Account of the Ottoman Conquest of Egypt in the Year A.H. 922 (A.D. 1516)*, 10.
4 Salmon, *An Account of the Ottoman Conquest of Egypt in the Year A.H. 922 (A.D. 1516)*, 14, 15.
5 Salmon, *An Account of the Ottoman Conquest of Egypt in the Year A.H. 922 (A.D. 1516)*, 35.
6 Salmon, *An Account of the Ottoman Conquest of Egypt in the Year A.H. 922 (A.D. 1516)*, 43.
7 Salmon, *An Account of the Ottoman Conquest of Egypt in the Year A.H. 922 (A.D. 1516)*, 44.
8 Winter, *Egyptian Society Under Ottoman Rule, 1517–1798*, 8.
9 Ibn Iyas, *Bada'i' al-zuhur fi waqa'i' al-duhur*, vol. 2, 1498.
10 Ibn Iyas, *Bada'i' al-zuhur fi waqa'i' al-duhur*, vol. 2, 1474.
11 Translation kindly provided by Professor Robert Dankoff.
12 Dankoff, *An Ottoman Traveller*, 414.
13 Dankoff, *An Ottoman Traveller*, 416.
14 Dankoff, *An Ottoman Traveller*, 417, 421.
15 Dankoff, *An Ottoman Traveller*, 421.
16 Dankoff, *An Ottoman Traveller*, 422.
17 Dankoff, *An Ottoman Traveller*, 422.
18 Dankoff, *An Ottoman Traveller*, 422, 423.
19 Dankoff, *An Ottoman Traveller*, 423.
20 Dankoff, *An Ottoman Traveller*, 424.
21 Dankoff, *An Ottoman Traveller*, 430.

22 Dankoff, *An Ottoman Traveller*, 424.
23 Dankoff, *An Ottoman Traveller*, 425.
24 Dankoff, *An Ottoman Traveller*, 431.
25 Dankoff, *An Ottoman Traveller*, 435.
26 Dankoff, *An Ottoman Traveller*, 440.
27 Dankoff, *An Ottoman Traveller*, 396.
28 Ghazaleh, *Masters of the Trade*, 24, 25.
29 Faroqhi, *Artisans of Empire*, 73.
30 Ghazaleh, *Masters of the Trade*, 35.
31 Ghazaleh, *Masters of the Trade*, 30, 55.
32 Faroqhi, *Artisans of Empire*, 130.
33 Faroqhi, *Artisans of Empire*, 29.
34 Ghazaleh, *Masters of the Trade*, 69, 88.
35 Faroqhi, *Artisans of Empire*, 74.
36 Ghazaleh, *Masters of the Trade*, 66.
37 Faroqhi, *Artisans of Empire*, 130; Ghazaleh notes on page 30 that there were 289 guilds listed by Evliya Çelebi in the seventeenth century, 193 guilds listed by the French Expedition around 1800, and 198 listed by 'Ali Mubarak later in the nineteenth century.
38 Faroqhi, *Artisans of Empire*, 130.
39 Faroqhi, *Artisans of Empire*, 132.
40 Raymond, *Artisans et Commerçants du Caire*, 190, 228.
41 Raymond, *Artisans et Commerçants du Caire*, 210.
42 Raymond, *Artisans et Commerçants du Caire*, 349; al-Jabarti, *'Abd al-Rahṃān al-Jabarti's History of Egypt*, vol. 1, 92 (The Year 1133 AH–Nov 2 1720–Oct 21 1721 AD).
43 al-Jabarti, *'Abd al-Rahṃān al-Jabarti's History of Egypt*, vol. 1, 95 (The Year 1133 AH–Nov 2 1720–Oct 21 1721 AD); vol. 1, 147 (Necrology of Amirs, 1106–42 AH–1694–1730 AD).
44 al-Jabarti, *'Abd al-Rahṃān al-Jabarti's History of Egypt*, vol. 1, 631 (The Year 1187 AH–March 25 1773–March 13 1774 AD).
45 Raymond, *Artisans et Commerçants du Caire*, 213, 230, 231, 236.
46 al-Jabarti, *'Abd al-Rahṃān al-Jabarti's History of Egypt*, vol. 2, 17 (The Year 1191 AH–1777–78 AD), 184 (The Year 1200 AH (1785–86 AD)).
47 Raymond, *Artisans et Commerçants du Caire*, 555–56.
48 Raymond, *Artisans et Commerçants du Caire*, 423.
49 Raymond, *Artisans et Commerçants du Caire*, 349.
50 For an excellent study of the complex of Radwan Bey see Nicholas Warner, "Commerce and Spirituality: The Urbanism of Rīdwān Bey." In *Cities in the Pre-Modern Islamic World: The urban impact of religion, state and society*, eds. A. Bennison

and A. Gascoigne, 196–224. London: Routledge, 2007.

51 Maury, *Palais et Maisons du Caire du XIVe au XVIIIe siècle*, vol. 2, 132.

52 Warner, "Commerce and Spirituality: The Urbanism of Rīdwān Bey," 201, 211.

53 Raymond, *Artisans et Commerçants du Caire*, 263.

54 al-Jabarti, *'Abd al-Rahmān al-Jabarti's History of Egypt*, vol. 2, 221 (Safar 1201 AH–Nov 23–Dec 21 1786 AD).

55 Behrens-Abouseif, *Islamic Architecture in Cairo: An Introduction*, 162.

56 al-Jabarti, *'Abd al-Rahmān al-Jabarti's History of Egypt*, vol. 1, 163 (Necrology of Amirs 1106–42 AH (1694–1730 AD)). (Account of Amir Abd al-Rahman Bey.)

57 "An Ottoman Royal Tent in Wawel Castle," *Hali*, July 10, 2013.

58 Correspondence between Walter Denny and James Piscatori, May 9, 2014.

59 Correspondence between Walter Denny and James Piscatori, May 9, 2014.

60 Faroqhi, *Artisans of Empire*, 80.

61 Prisse d'Avennes, *L'Art Arabe*, 290.

62 Atil, *Levni and the Surname: The Story of an Eighteenth-Century Ottoman Festival*, 42.

63 al-Jabarti, *'Abd al-Rahmān al-Jabarti's History of Egypt*, vol. 2, 223 (Safar 1201 AH–Nov 23–Dec 21 1786 AD), 233 (Ramadan 1201 AH–June 17–July 16 1787 AD).

64 al-Jabarti, *'Abd al-Rahmān al-Jabarti's History of Egypt*, vol. 2, 246 (Necrology of 1201 AH–1786–87 AD).

Notes to Chapter 4

1 al-Jabarti, *'Abd al-Rahmān al-Jabarti's History of Egypt*, vol. 3, 1 (Safar 1213 AH–June 15 1798–June 4 1799 AD).

2 al-Jabarti, *'Abd al-Rahmān al-Jabarti's History of Egypt*, vol. 3, 2 (Safar 1213 AH–June 15–Aug 12 1798 AD).

3 al-Jabarti, *'Abd al-Rahmān al-Jabarti's History of Egypt*, vol. 3, 3, 9 (Safar 1213 AH–July 15–Aug 12 1798 AD).

4 al-Jabarti, *'Abd al-Rahmān al-Jabarti's History of Egypt*, vol. 3, 9 (Safar 1213 AH–July 15–Aug 12 1798 AD).

5 al-Jabarti, *'Abd al-Rahmān al-Jabarti's History of Egypt*, vol. 3, 5 (The Year 1213 AH–June 15–Aug 12 1798 AD), 10 (Safar 1213 AH–July 15–Aug 12 1798 AD).

6 al-Jabarti, *'Abd al-Rahmān al-Jabarti's History of Egypt*, vol. 3, 11 (Safar 1213 AH–July 15–Aug 12 1798 AD).

7 al-Jabarti, *'Abd al-Rahmān al-Jabarti's History of Egypt*, vol. 3, 39 (Jumada I AH–Oct 11–Nov 9 1798 AD).

8 al-Jabarti, *'Abd al-Rahmān al-Jabarti's History of Egypt*, vol. 3, 81 (Shawwal 1213 AH–March 8–April 5 1799 AD), 73 (Ramadan 1213 AH–Feb 6–March 7 1798 AD).

9 al-Jabarti, *'Abd al-Rahmān al-Jabarti's History of Egypt*, vol. 3, 61 (Rajab 1213 AH–Dec 9 1798–Jan 7 1799 AD).

10 al-Jabarti, *'Abd al-Rahmān al-Jabarti's History of Egypt*, vol. 3, 51 (Jumada II 1213 AH–Nov 10–Dec 8 1798 AD).
11 al-Jabarti, *'Abd al-Rahmān al-Jabarti's History of Egypt*, vol. 3, 68 (Shaaban 1213 AH–Jan 8–Feb 5 1799 AD).
12 al-Jabarti, *'Abd al-Rahmān al-Jabarti's History of Egypt*, vol. 3, 71 (Ramadan 1213 AH–Feb 6–March 7 1799 AD).
13 al-Jabarti, *'Abd al-Rahmān al-Jabarti's History of Egypt*, vol. 3, 153 (Shawal 1214 AH–Feb 26–March 26 1800 AD).
14 *Description de l'Egypte*, Etat Moderne II, vol. 6, 796; vol. 7, 515, 722.
15 al-Jabarti, *'Abd al-Rahmān al-Jabarti's History of Egypt*, vol. 3, 316 (Ramadan 1216 AH–Jan 5–Feb 3 1802 AD).
16 al-Jabarti, *'Abd al-Rahmān al-Jabarti's History of Egypt*, vol. 3, 289 (1801–02), (Safar 1216 AH–June 13–July 11 1801 AD), 317 (Ramadan 1216 AH–Jan 5–Feb 3 1802 AD).
17 al-Jabarti, *'Abd al-Rahmān al-Jabarti's History of Egypt*, vol. 3, 293 (Rabi I 1216 AH–July 12–Aug 10 1801 AD), 340 (Rabi I 1217 AH–July 1802 AD).
18 al-Jabarti, *'Abd al-Rahmān al-Jabarti's History of Egypt*, vol. 3, 343 (Rabi II 1217 AH–Aug 1–29, 1802 AD).
19 al-Jabarti, *'Abd al-Rahmān al-Jabarti's History of Egypt*, vol. 3, 355 (Shawal 1217 AH–Jan 25–Feb 22 1803 AD).
20 al-Jabarti, *'Abd al-Rahmān al-Jabarti's History of Egypt*, vol. 3, 330 (Necrology 1801/1802 AD).
21 al-Jabarti, *'Abd al-Rahmān al-Jabarti's History of Egypt*, vol. 3, 459 (Safar 1219 AH–May 12–June 9 1804 AD).
22 al-Jabarti, *'Abd al-Rahmān al-Jabarti's History of Egypt*, vol. 3, 414–15, 459 (Ramadan 1218 AH–Dec 15 1803–Jan 13 1804 AD).
23 al-Jabarti, *'Abd al-Rahmān al-Jabarti's History of Egypt*, vol. 3, 530 (Shaaban 1220 AH–Oct 25–Nov 22 1805 AD).
24 al-Jabarti, *'Abd al-Rahmān al-Jabarti's History of Egypt*, vol. 4, 276, 277 (beginning of 1229 AH–Dec 24 1813–Dec 13 1814 AD).
25 al-Jabarti, *'Abd al-Rahmān al-Jabarti's History of Egypt*, vol. 4, 6 (beginning of the year 1221 AH–March 21 1806–March 10 1807 AD), 23 (Jumada II 1221 AH–Aug 16–Sept 13 1806 AD).
26 al-Jabarti, *'Abd al-Rahmān al-Jabarti's History of Egypt*, vol. 4, 204 (Shaaban 1227 AH–August 10–Sept 7 1812 AD).
27 al-Jabarti, *'Abd al-Rahmān al-Jabarti's History of Egypt*, vol. 4, 210 (Dhul Hijja 1227 AH–Dec 6 1812–Jan 3 1813 AD).
28 al-Jabarti, *'Abd al-Rahmān al-Jabarti's History of Egypt*, vol. 4, 239–40 (Safar 1228 AH–Feb 3–March 1813 AD), 249 (Ramadan 1228 AH–Aug 28–Sept 26 1813 AD).

29 al-Jabarti, *'Abd al-Rahmān al-Jabarti's History of Egypt*, vol. 4, 418 (beginning of 1234 AH–Oct 31 1818–Oct 19 1819 AD).
30 al-Jabarti, *'Abd al-Rahmān al-Jabarti's History of Egypt*, vol. 4, 215 (Dhul Hijja 1227 AH–Dec 6 1812–Jan 3 1813 AD).
31 al-Jabarti, *'Abd al-Rahmān al-Jabarti's History of Egypt*, vol. 4, 218 (Dhul Hijja 1227 AD–Dec 6 1812–Jan 3 1813 AD).
32 al-Jabarti, *'Abd al-Rahmān al-Jabarti's History of Egypt*, vol. 4, 229 (Necrology of 1227 AH–1812–13 AD).
33 al-Jabarti, *'Abd al-Rahmān al-Jabarti's History of Egypt*, vol. 4, 234 (Necrology of 1227 AH–1813 AD).
34 Bowring, *Report on Egypt 1823–1838*, 95.
35 Fahmy, *All the Pasha's Men*, 72.
36 Loti, *Egypt*, 20.

Notes to Chapter 5

1 James Carlile McCoan, *Egypt under Ismail: A Romance of History* (London: Chapman and Hall, 1889), 106.
2 Celik, *Displaying the Orient: Architecture of Islam at Nineteenth-Century World's Fairs*, 149.
3 Georges Douin, *Histoire du Règne du Khédive Ismaïl*, vol. 3, part 2, 461.
4 Celik, *Displaying the Orient*, 147.
5 Butler, *Court Life in Egypt*, 82.
6 Malet, *Egypt, 1879–1883*, 51.
7 Butcher, *Things Seen in Egypt*, 36.
8 Porter and Saif, "The Mahmal Revisited," in *The Hajj: Collected Essays*, 201.
9 See Warner, "Commerce and Spirituality: The Urbanism of Rīdwān Bey."
10 al-Tukhi, *Tawa'if al-hiraf fi Medinat al-Qahira f-il-nisf al-thani min al-qarn al-tasi' 'ashar, 1841–1890*, 52.
11 'Abd al-'Al, *al-Madrasa al-sina'iya al-ilhamiya*, 55–57.
12 'Abd al-'Al, *al-Madrasa al-sina'iya al-ilhamiya*, 172–86.
13 van Gelder, "Beautifying the Ugly and Uglifying the Beautiful: The Paradox in Classical Arabic Literature," 330–31.
14 Blair, *Islamic Inscriptions*, 8.
15 Translation by Seif El Rashidi.
16 Adam Talib in correspondence with Seif El Rashidi, September 20, 2014 and June 2017.
17 Another potential example, yet to be seen within khedival khayamiya, might be, "Have the poets left a single spot for a patch to be sewn?" This is the opening question of the *mu'allaqa* of 'Antara bin Shaddad, essentially asking the reader if anything 'new' can yet be said.

18 These are calligraphic panels in the collection of Professor James Piscatori of Durham University, acquired from a Swiss collection, circa 1900.

19 Late- (post-) khedival *sitara* (panel) from the Newark Museum, collected by John Cotton Dana in 1929.

20 al-Ibshihi, Shihab al-Din Muhammad, *al-Mustatraf fi kul fan mustadhraf* (Dar Al-Kotob Al-'Ilmiyah, 2014), 330.

21 It is more surprising that this panel was discovered in Australia and bears an ink stamp with the address 174 Regent Street in London which, prior to 1933, was the textile shop of the interior designer F.B. Goodyer.

22 For an introduction to the "Mu'allaqat," see Levin, "On the Hanging Odes of Arabia"; for a complete annotated text, see Frank E. Johnson's translation *The seven poems suspended at the Temple at Mecca (al-Sab' al-mu'allaqat)*: https://archive.org/details/alsabalmuallaqat00johnrich

23 The Jackson Hole tent was inherited by Jennie and Hogan Smelker and was originally purchased in Egypt by Paul and Aloha Browne from California and Darien, Connecticut. Aloha (née Perry) was the daughter of the owner of the Standard Dredging Company, a New York-based business, who married Paul Browne in 1929. Renée Howard Smelker (Hogan's mother) acquired it from the Browne family for the Bar BC Ranch in Jackson Hole, Wyoming, in 2015. This tent is now part of the museum of the Jackson Hole Historical Society.

24 Komaroff, ed., *Gifts of the Sultan: The Art of Giving at the Islamic Courts*, 1–32.

25 Translated by Seif El Rashidi.

26 Christies, 'An Egyptian Cotton Appliqué-lined Marriage Tent,' Lot 270/*Sale 6499 - Oriental Rugs and Carpets*, London, 2001. http://www.christies.com/lotfinder/LotDetailsPrintable.aspx?intObjectID=3049384. This source also claims this tent was used "for a wedding by the daughter of the last Khedive of Egypt in 1903," which is impossible, as the last Khedive (Abbas Hilmi II) was born in 1941. Such myths about khayamiya provenance are common, such as the Saunders Tent in Berryville, Texas, which was allegedly sewn by an "Arabian sheik's harem of 200 wives," and won in a shooting contest.

27 A *rubaiya* is an Arabic quatrain—a short poem in two parts, with two halves to each part. The translators of the inscription include France Meyer, Huda Al-Tamimi, Yahya Haidar, and Zahra Taheri at the Centre for Arab and Islamic Studies at the Australian National University in Canberra.

28 Specifically, these are excerpts from "Panegyric to Saif al-Daula on his departure from Antioch" by al-Mutanabbi, in *Poems of al-Mutanabbi*, 54.

29 al-Mutanabbi, in *Poems of al-Mutanabbi*, 54.

30 Discussions with *One Thousand and One Nights* expert, Chirine al-Ansary.

31 'Abd al-'Al, *al-Madrasa al-sina'iya al-ilhamiya*, 283.

Notes to Chapter 6

1 This scene appears adapted from the illustration by Faucher-Gudin after a photograph by Gayet, published in Maspero, *A History of Egypt*.

2 From correspondence collected by Gareth Strong in 2015 between Ethel Aston and her brothers Gordon and Ernest Moffat, both of whom died in World War I as members of the Australian Imperial Forces. According to the Reserve Bank of Australia, earning two shillings a day in 1915 was the equivalent of ten Australian dollars a day in 2015. This also suggests that these small touristic panels were valued in piasters, not Egyptian pounds, though the value of the Egyptian pound was aligned to the British pound during World War I.

3 "The Ladies' Page," *Otago Witness*, Issue 3351, 5 June, 1918.

4 "A blouse with Egyptian decoration," *Weekly Times*, 28 July, 1923, page 55.

5 It is now in the collection of his son, Charles Anthony Ashcroft. This piece is in particularly good condition with close to original colors, a clear provenance, and an unusually fine-legged camel.

6 Australian advertisements for David Jones and Myer (1930/1931), and Liberty of London, in Gillow, *African Textiles*, 93.

7 Sladen, *Oriental Cairo: The City of the "Arabian Nights"*, 24.

8 Sladen, *Oriental Cairo: The City of the "Arabian Nights"*, 24, 72.

9 Sladen, *Oriental Cairo: The City of the "Arabian Nights"*, 102.

10 Sladen, *Queer Things about Egypt*, 144.

11 Sladen, *Oriental Cairo: City of the "Arabian Nights"*, 81–82.

12 Sladen, *Oriental Cairo: City of the "Arabian Nights"*, 81–82.

13 Sladen, *Queer Things about Egypt*, 239.

14 Sladen, *Queer Things about Egypt*, 73, 239.

15 This three-bodied fish motif may have appeared on many ceramics, but at least one is known from the collections of the Egyptian Museum in Berlin.

16 See Bailleul-LeSuer, *Between Heaven and Earth: Birds in Ancient Egypt*.

17 Williamson and Williamson, *It Happened in Egypt*.

18 Teichmann and Vögler (eds.), *Faszination Orient: Max von Oppenheim*, 38–39. For travelers in Palestine, see this photograph: https://www.loc.gov/item/2004674260/

19 The back of this photograph reveals that their enthusiastic waiters had attempted to teach them the Arabic numbers and letters.

20 Roberts Rinehart, *Nomad's Land*, 31.

21 Roberts Rinehart, *Nomad's Land*, 32.

22 Sladen, *Queer Things about Egypt*, 239.

23 As depicted for *Time Magazine* by photographer Robert Landry.

24 Humphries, *Grand Hotels of Egypt*, 70–71.

25 Hillcourt and West, *The Scout Jamboree Book: American Scouts at the 4th World Jamboree*, Chapter 7.

26 Flynn, "Adirondack Attic: Dr. Warner's Egyptian Tent."

27 The Gregg Museum Tent was acquired by Jeff and Betsy Penn in the 1960s and was probably made within the preceding decade. It features a single central pole, two side panels of seven sections each, and a plain white canvas conical roof, approximately 4 m tall and 4.1 m in diameter. The two additional poles for holding the entrance awning aloft are just over 1.8 m high (information provided by Mary Hauser, Registrar and Associate Director of the Gregg Museum of Art & Design).

28 Lile, "Quilt show to include everything from 'Old Abe' to tent covered in Egyptian hieroglyph appliqués," *Marshall–Democrat News*, September 19, 2002.

29 Long, "Saunders Museum turns 50," *Carroll County News*, June 13, 2005. http://www.carrollconews.com/story/1388524.html

30 Ektachrome by Dwight Nichols.

31 Hilmi and Sonbol, eds., *The Last Khedive of Egypt: Memoirs of Abbas Hilmi II*, 72. Additional boxes of Abbas Hilmi's archival papers and correspondence are now held in Durham University Library.

32 Barakat, *Beyond Boundaries*, 48–49. The stepped crenellations, rather than a more typical *'arusa* border, are distinctive but not unique to this tent. They can be seen as references to thirteenth- and fourteenth-century architectural precedents in Cairo, such as the complex of Salar and Sanjar, the al-Maridani Mosque, the shrine of Imam al-Shafi'i, the madrasa of Al-Salih Ayyub, and the complex of Qalaun.

33 The calligraphy of this tent is a *qasida* like that of the IAMM, but referring to warm greetings and the bestowal of love upon a friend and a nation, selflessly and without envy. The door panel bears calligraphy referring to "the lovers within," and might be intended as a layered reference to both function and symbolism. When assembled, it closely resembles the Harvard tent. There are two overlapping roof panels, one with decorations on the inside and then a plain canvas cloth roof. A separate panel serves as a door. The tent pole is two pieces, while the Harvard pole is a single piece.

34 McAdams, ed., *Oriental Institute Annual Report 1982–1983*, 62–64. The Oriental Institute also possesses several touristic panels donated by Clara Klingman in 1980.

35 The tent was gifted by Mrs. William C. Prescott and Mrs. Gordon B. Thayer.

36 Reed, "Love Nest."

37 Translation by Seif El Rashidi. The last line is not from the original poem but appears on the tent.

38 Information provided by Tricia Runzel, curator at the Ellwood House Museum.

39 "It was exceedingly pleasant taking tea under the trees or resting under the beautiful Egyptian tent kindly lent by Mr. E.M. Crookshank, J.P. of East

Grinstead." From "Account of the Bank Holiday events at Forest Row, Kidbrooke Park," *The Sussex Express, Surrey Standard, Wealth of Kent Mail, Dants and Country Advertiser*, August 6, 1898, page 9.

40 "The Primrose League at Saint Hill – Alarming collapse of tent," *Sussex Express, Surrey Standard and Kent Mail*, August 1, 1903, page 105.

41 "Marriage of Isabelle Milne Garlick to John D. King Scott, ceremony held at 'Banool', Yarra Glen," *Bendigo Advertiser*, December 20, 1899, page 2.

42 "Annual Assembly Ball at South Shields," *Shields Daily Gazette*, January 28, 1880, page 8.

43 "Grand Bazaar," *The Lincoln, Rutland, and Stamford Mercury*, July 6, 1894, page 6. If this provenance is true, then it would have been acquired on September 13, 1882, possibly as one of many seized from the field following the defeat of Ahmad 'Urabi's forces, which also enabled the British control of the Suez Canal and the reinstatement of Khedive Tewfik.

44 "Staff Ball to Sir Evelyn and Lady Wood at Colchester – Grand Gathering at the Gymnasium," *The Essex Standard*, Wednesday, January 2, 1889, page 2.

45 "Chelmsford," *The Essex Country Chronicle*, July 12, 1912, page 8.

46 "Grand Fancy Bazaar at Ruthin Castle," *North Wales Chronicle*, August 30, 1879, page 4.

Notes to Chapter 7

1 "Misr turahhib bi-qudum al-rayyis al-jalil," *al-Nil Magazine*, October 30, 1924.

2 Reid, *Whose Pharaohs?*, 277–78.

3 Rizk, "The Making of a King," *al-Ahram Weekly*, 29 September–5 October, 2005: 762, http://weekly.ahram.org.eg/2005/762/chrncls.htm

4 One cache is known from a theatrical props company in London.

5 Lynn Smith, "From the Village to the Stage: Shaping Traditional Dance for the Concert Venue."

Notes to Chapter 9

1 Flam, *Matisse on Art*, 296.

2 Published as plate 98 of J. Cowart and D. Fourcade, *Henri Matisse: The Early Years in Nice, 1916–1930*, 146.

3 Gottlieb, "The Role of the Window in the Art of Matisse," 416. For more information about this particular palm tree view, see Frigeri, "How Matisse was seduced by the palm tree."

4 Perreault, "Matisse Refabricated," in Rathbone and Halford-MacLeod, *Art beyond Isms: Masterworks from El Greco to Picasso in the Phillips Collection*, 102.

5 Oard, *A Window on Matisse: Interior with Egyptian Curtain, 1948.*

6 Darlene Hammond, "'Tifaifai' of eastern Polynesia: Meaning and communication

in a women's reintegrated art form," 38–75; de Chazeaux and Frémy, *Le Tifaifai: Arts et Artisanats de Polynésie Française*, 91–93.

7 Dumas, *Matisse: The Fabric of Dreams*, 212.

8 Johnson, "A Note on Mahdist Flags."

9 Laura Karp Lugo, "Du Synthétisme à l'arrière-garde: le parcours d'Emile Bernard," in Emile Bernard. Au-delà de Pont-Aven, Les catalogues d'exposition de l'INHA, 2012.

Notes to Chapter 10

1 Interview with Hany Abdel-Kader in April 2017.

2 Betty Wass, 1979, cited in Blaire Gagnon, "Egyptian Appliqués: Tourism and Tradition," 87.

3 Information taken from the oral histories collected for the Tentmakers of Cairo project at Durham University, 2014.

4 Sladen, *Queer Things about Egypt*, 144.

5 Roberts Rinehart, *Nomad's Land*, 126.

6 Blaire Gagnon and Betty Wass, cited in Gagnon, "Egyptian Appliqués: Tourism and Tradition," 87.

7 Betty Wass, 1979 field notes, cited in Gagnon, "Egyptian Appliqués: Tourism and Tradition," 87.

8 Correspondence with Gillian Vogelsang-Eastwood, Textile Research Centre in Leiden, January 14, 2015.

9 Simpson reports this from observations made in 1928, cited in Gagnon, "Egyptian Appliqués: Tourism and Tradition," 86.

10 Interviewed by Betty Wass in 1979, cited by Gagnon, "Egyptian Appliqués: Tourism and Tradition," 79.

11 Feeney, "Tentmakers of Cairo."

12 Interview with Dina Shehayeb in 2014, commissioned by Durham University.

13 Correspondence with Peter Alford Andrews, 2016 and 2017.

14 *Stitch like an Egyptian* exhibition at the 2007 Australasian Quilt Convention in Melbourne, at which Ahmed Naguib and Ayman Ahmed represented the tentmakers of Cairo.

15 Interview with John Fisher, London, May 2017.

16 Jenny Bowker, 2013.

17 Marcus, "Music," in D.W. Reynolds, ed., *The Cambridge Companion to Modern Arab Culture*, 148.

18 Saeed Mokhtar cited in Ramadan, "Tradition vs. modernism in the street of the tentmakers."

19 Bowker, "The Tentmakers of Cairo: Kim Beamish in coversation with Sam Bowker," *Ibraaz*, June 8, 2016, https://www.ibraaz.org/interviews/194

20 Bowker, "The Tentmakers of Cairo: Kim Beamish in coversation with Sam Bowker."

21 Robert Bowker demonstrated problematic engagements with the tourist economy and Egyptian government intervention as a marginalized professional community in his book *Egypt and the Politics of Change in the Arab Middle East* (Edward Elgar Publishing, 2010), 131–63.

22 Interview with Seif El Rashidi, 2016.

23 Victoria and Albert Museum website, http://www.vam.ac.uk/info/jameel-prize-4

24 An example of Chant Avedissian's textiles inspired by khayamiya can be seen in the British Museum.

25 See Drew, *New Tent Architecture*.

26 Translation provided by France Meyer, Lecturer in Arabic at the Center for Arab and Islamic Studies at the Australian National University.

27 Interview with Dina Shehayeb for the Tentmakers of Cairo project at Durham University.

Bibliography

ʻAbd al-ʻAl, M. *al-Madrasa al-sinaʻiya al-ilhamiya*. Cairo: Longman, 2000.

Abdul-Yazid, A. "Khayamiya: The textile of life and death." *Al-Arabi Magazine* 7, no. 536 (2003).

Aly Shawky, A. "Streets of Cairo: Tent-making and endangered crafts around Khayamiya." *Egypt Independent*, August 13, 2011, http://www.egyptindependent.com/streets-cairo-tent-making-and-endangered-crafts-around-khayamiya/

Ammoun, D. "Tentmaking." In *Crafts of Egypt*, 51–57. Cairo: American University in Cairo Press, 1991.

Andrews, P.A. *Felt Tents and Pavilions. The Nomadic Tradition and its Interpenetration with Princely Tentage*. London: Melisande, 1999.

Atasoy, N. *Otağ-ı Hümayun: The Ottoman Imperial Tent Complex*. Istanbul: Aygaz, 2000.

Atil, E. *Levni and the Surname: The Story of an Eighteenth-Century Ottoman Festival*. Istanbul: Kocbank, 1999.

Baedecker, K. *Egypt and the Sudan: Handbook for Travellers*. Leipzig: Karl Baedecker, 1908 (1st ed.) and 1929 (2nd ed.).

Bailleul-LeSuer, R. *Between Heaven and Earth: Birds in Ancient Egypt*. Chicago: University of Chicago Oriental Institute Publications, 2012.

Barakat, H. *Beyond Boundaries: Tents of the Islamic World*. Kuala Lumpur: Islamic Arts Museum Malaysia, 2003.

Beamish, K. *The Tentmakers of Cairo*, film, 94 min., produced by Non D'Script, 2015, http://www.tentmakersofcairo.com/

Behrens-Abouseif, D. *Cairo of the Mamluks: A History of the Architecture and its Culture*. London: I.B.Tauris, 2007.
———. *Islamic Architecture in Cairo: An Introduction*. Leiden: Brill, 1989.
Belzoni, G.B. *Travels in Egypt and Nubia*. Vercelli: White Star, 2007.
Bin Tabataba, M. *al-Fakhri fi-l-adab al-sultaniya wa-l-duwal al-islamiya*. Qom: Dar al-Sadar, 1993.
Blair, S. *Islamic Inscriptions*. Edinburgh: Edinburgh University Press, 1998.
Blair, S., and J. Bloom. *Cosmophilia: Islamic Art from the David Collection, Copenhagen*. Boston: McMullen Museum of Art, 2006.
Book of Curiosities. Online, www.bodley.ox.ac.uk/bookofcuriosities
Bowker, J. "Looking at the Australasian Quilt Convention through Egyptian eyes." *Vic Quilter—The Victorian Quilters Journal*, July (2007): 28–29.
———. *Stitch Like an Egyptian: The Tentmakers of Cairo Exhibit*. Catalogue for the American Quilter's Society, 2012.
———. "Teaching, travelling and traditions." *Machine Quilting Unlimited* 15, no. 3 (2010): 56–60.
———. "The Tentmakers of Chareh El Khiamiah—the film." *Down Under Quilts* 158 (2013): 54–59.
Bowker, S. "Matisse and the Khayamiya: An Egyptian Curtain Unveiled." *The Burlington Magazine* 157, December no. 1353 (2015): 843–45.
———. "Pavilions of Splendour." *Hali* 179 (2014): 71–77.
———. "The Symmetry of Khayamiya and Quilting: International Relations of the Egyptian Tentmakers." *Craft + Design Enquiry* Issue 6 (2014), http://press-files.anu.edu.au/downloads/press/p288791/html/ch03.xhtml?referer=1177&page=5
———. "The Urban Fabric of Cairo: Khayamiya and the Suradeq." *International Journal of Islamic Architecture* 3, no. 2 (2014): 475–501.
Bowring, J. *Report on Egypt, 1823–1838: Under the Reign of Mohamed Ali*. London: Triade, 1998.
Browning, B.K., A. Reynolds, and J. Bowker. *The Ancient Art of Appliqué: Patterns from the Tentmakers of Cairo*. Burlington: American Quilter's Society and Collector Books, 2013.
Butcher, E.L. *Things Seen in Egypt*. London: Seeley Service and Co. Ltd., 1910.
Butler, A.J. *Court Life in Egypt*. London: Chapman and Hall, 1888.
Celik, Z. *Displaying the Orient: Architecture of Islam at Nineteenth-Century World's Fairs*. Los Angeles: University of California Press, 1992.
de Chazeaux, M., and M.-N. Frémy. *Le Tifaifai: Arts et artisanats de Polynésie française*. Tahiti: Au Vent Des Iles, 2014.

Cornu, G. "Rideaux et tentures dans le monde arabo-islamique oriental jusqu'à l'époque mamluke." In *Mélanges de l'Ecole Française de Rome - Moyen Age*, 307–22. Paris: Persée, 1999.
Cowart, J., and D. Fourcade. *Henri Matisse: The Early Years in Nice, 1916–1930*. Washington, DC: National Gallery, 1986.
Dankoff, R., and S. Kim, eds. *An Ottoman Traveller: Selections from the Book of Travels of Evliya Çelebi*. London: Eland, 2010.
Description de l'Egypte. Online, http://descegy.bibalex.org/
Douin, G. *Histoire du Règne du Khédive Ismaïl*. 3 vols. Cairo: Société Royale de Géographie d'Egypte, 1934.
Drew, P. *New Tent Architecture*. London: Thames & Hudson, 2008.
Dumas, A. *Matisse, His Art and His Textiles: The Fabric of Dreams*. London: Royal Academy of Arts, 2005.
Eddé, A.-M. *Saladin*. Cambridge, MA: Harvard University Press, 2011, 210.
Fahmy, K. *All the Pasha's Men: Mehmed Ali, His Army and the Making of Modern Egypt*. Cairo: American University in Cairo Press, 2002.
Faroqhi, S. *Artisans of Empire*. London: I.B.Tauris, 2009.
Feeney, J. "Tentmakers of Cairo." *Saudi Aramco World* 37, no. 6, November/December (1986), http://archive.aramcoworld.com/issue/198606/tentmakers.of.cairo.htm
Flam, J. *Matisse on Art*. Los Angeles: University of California Press, 1995.
Flynn, A. "Adirondack Attic: Dr. Warner's Egyptian Tent." Radio interview, 12 min., *NCPR North Country Public Radio*, June 18, 2014, http://www.northcountrypublicradio.org/news/story/25176/20140618/adirondack-attic-dr-warner-s-egyptian-tent
Folda, J. *The Art of the Crusaders in the Holy Land: From the Third Crusade to the Fall of Acre, 1096–1187*. Cambridge: Cambridge University Press, 1995.
Frigeri, F. "How Matisse was seduced by the palm tree." *Tate Blog*, August 22, 2014, http://www.tate.org.uk/context-comment/blogs/how-matisse-was-seduced-palm-tree
Gabrieli, F. *Arab Historians of the Crusades*. Los Angeles: University of California Press, 1984.
Gagnon, B.O. "Egyptian Appliqué." *Uncoverings* 24 (2003): 131–62.
———. "Egyptian Appliqués: Tourism and Tradition." Master's thesis, University of Rhode Island, 2002.
Ghazaleh, P. *Masters of the Trade: Crafts and Craftspeople in Cairo, 1750–1850*. Cairo: American University in Cairo Press, 1999.
Gillow, J. *African Textiles*. London: Chronicle Books, 2003.

———. *Textiles of the Islamic World*. London: Thames and Hudson, 2010.
Goitein, S.D. *Letters of Medieval Jewish Traders*. Princeton: Princeton University Press, 2015.
Gostelow, M. *Embroidery: Traditional Designs, Techniques and Patterns*. London: Marshall Cavendish, 1982.
Gottlieb, C. "The Role of the Window in the Art of Matisse." *The Journal of Aesthetics and Art Criticism* 22, no. 4, Summer (1964): 393–423.
Gruber, C., ed. *Islamic Architecture on the Move: Motion and Modernity*. Chicago: University of Chicago Press, 2016.
Hammond, J.D. "'Tifaifai' of eastern Polynesia: Meaning and communication in a women's reintegrated art form." PhD thesis, University of Illinois at Urbana-Champaign, 1981.
Hanna, N. *Artisan Entrepreneurs in Cairo and Early Modern Capitalism*. Cairo: American University in Cairo Press, 2011.
———. "Language, Literature and Society in 17th and 18th Century Cairo." *Majalla Misr al-Haditha* (2012): 7–25.
———. "Literacy among artisans and tradesmen in Ottoman Cairo." In *The Ottoman World*, edited by C. Woodhead, 319–32. London: Routledge, 2011.
———. *Ottoman Egypt and the Emergence of the Modern World*. Cairo: American University in Cairo Press, 2014.
Hillcourt, W., and J.E. West. *The Scout Jamboree Book: American Scouts at the 4th World Jamboree*. New York: G.P. Putnam's Sons, 1933.
Hilmi, A., and A. Sonbol, eds. *The Last Khedive of Egypt: Memoirs of Abbas Hilmi II*. Cairo: American University in Cairo Press, 2006.
Humphries, A. *Grand Hotels of Egypt*. Cairo: American University in Cairo Press, 2011.
Hussein, Al-Sayyed. "The Egyptian Art of Tent-making." *Ahram Online*, July 24, 2012, http://english.ahram.org.eg/NewsContent/32/99/48580/Folk/Special-Files/The-Egyptian-art-of-tentmaking.aspx
Ibn Iyas, Muhamad Bin Ahmad. *Bada'i' al-zuhur fi waqa'i' al-duhur*. 2 vols. Cairo: Madbouly, 2005.
———. *Histoire des mamelouks circassiens*. Vol. 2. Translated by Gaston Wiet, 872–906. Cairo: Imprimerie de l'Institut Français d'archéologie orientale, 1945.
———. *Journal d'un bourgeois du Caire*. Vols. 1 and 2. Translated by Gaston Wiet. Rennes: Armand Collin, 1955.
Ibn Jubayr. *The Travels of Ibn Jubayr*. Translated by R.J. Broadhurst. London: Darf Publishers, 2003.
Ibn Taghribirdi, Y. *History of Egypt, 1382–1469*. Berkeley: University of California Press, 1954–1963.

———. *al-Nujum al-zahira fi muluk Misr wa-l-Qahira*. 16 vols. Cairo, 1938.

al-Jabarti, A. *'Abd al-Raḥmān al-Jabartī's History of Egypt: 'Ajā'ib al-Āthār fi'l-Tarā jim wa'l-Akhbār*. Vols. 1–4. Edited by Thomas Philipp and Moshe Perlmann. Stuttgart: Franz Steiner, 1994.

Johnson, D. "A Note on Mahdist Flags." In *The Sudan Special 1884–98*, special issue, *Savage and Soldier magazine* (1998), http://www.savageandsoldier.com/sudan/MahdistFlags.html

Komaroff, L., ed. *Gifts of the Sultan: The Art of Giving at the Islamic Courts*. Los Angeles: Los Angeles County Museum of Art, 2011.

Lane, E.W. *An Account of the Manners and Customs of the Modern Egyptians*. Cairo: American University in Cairo Press, 2012.

Levin, G. "On the Hanging Odes of Arabia." *Parnassus: Poetry in Review* 30, nos. 1 & 2 (2008), http://parnassusreview.com/archives/408

Levy, Y. *Saladin in Egypt*. Leiden: Brill, 1999.

Loti, P. *Egypt*. Translated by T. Werner. London: T. Werner Laurie Ltd., 1909.

Lynn Smith, K. "From the Village to the Stage: Shaping Traditional Dance for the Concert Venue." *Habibi: Journal of Middle Eastern Dance* 17 no. 3, Spring (1999), http://thebestofhabibi.com/vol-17-no-3-spring-1999/village-to-the-stage/

Malet, E. *Egypt, 1879–1883*. London: John Murray, 1909.

al-Maqrizi, T. *Itti'az al-hunafa' bi-akhbar al-a'ima al-Fatimiyyin al-khulafa'*. Online, http://www.alwaraq.net/Core/SearchServlet/searchabsone?docid=144&searchtext=2KfZhNmB2KfYt9mF2YrZitmG&option=1&offset=1&WordForm=1&AllOffset=1

———. *al-Mawa'iz wa-l-i'tibar bi-dhikr al-khitat wa-l-athar*. 4 vols. Beirut: Dar Al-Kotob Al-'Ilmiyah, 1998.

———. *al-Suluk li-ma'rifat duwal al-muluk*. Online, http://www.alwaraq.net/Core/SearchServlet/searchabsone?docid=22&searchtext=2K7ZitmF2Kk=&option=1&offset=1&WordForm=1&AllOffset=1

Marcus, S. "Music." In *The Cambridge Companion to Modern Arab Culture*, edited by D.W. Reynolds, 135–63. Cambridge: Cambridge University Press, 2015.

Maspero, G. *A History of Egypt*. Vol 2. London: Grolier Society, 1903.

Maury, B. *Palais et maisons du Caire du XIVe au XVIIIe siècle*. Vol. 2. Cairo: Imprimerie de l'Institut Français d'archéologie orientale, 1975–1983.

McAdams, R., ed. "Curator's Report." *Oriental Institute Annual Report 1982–1983*, 62–64. Chicago: University of Chicago, 1983.

McKinney, R.C. *The Case of Rhyme Versus Reason: Ibn Al-Rumi and His Poetics in Context*. Leiden: Brill, 2004.

Meisami, J.S., and P. Starkey, eds., with Smoor, P. "Baha' al-Din Zuhayr

581–656 / 1186–1258." *Encyclopedia of Arabic Literature*. Vol 1, 127. London: Routledge, 1999.

al-Mutanabbi. *Poems of al-Mutanabbi*. Translated by A.J. Arberry. 2nd edition. Cambridge: Cambridge University Press, 2009.

Noyles Colvin, M., ed. *Godeffroy of Boloyne; or, The Siege and Conqueste of Jerusalem*. New York: Kraus Reprint Co., 1987.

al-Nuwayri, S. *Nihayat al-arab fi funun al-adab*. Online, http://www.alwaraq.net/Core/SearchServlet/searchone?docid=101&searchtext=2K7ZitmF2Kkg2KfZhNmB2LHYrA==&option=1&offset=3&WordForm=1&exactpage=3500&totalpages=4&AllOffset=1

Oard, B.A. *A Window on Matisse: Interior with Egyptian Curtain, 1948*. Online, https://sites.google.com/site/beautyandterror/Home/window-on-matisse

O'Kane, B. "From Tents to Pavilions: Royal Mobility and Persian Palace Design." *Ars Orientalis* 23 (1993): 249–68, https://archnet.org/system/publications/contents/4668/original/DPC1274.pdf?1384786368

Perreault, J. "Matisse Refabricated." Arts Journal website, July 25, 2005, http://www.artsjournal.com/artopia/2005/07/matisse_refabricated.html

Philips, J. *Holy Warriors: A Modern History of the Crusades*. London: Random House, 2010.

Phillips, R.B., and C.B. Steiner, eds. "Art, Authenticity and the Baggage of Cultural Encounter." In *Unpacking Culture: Art and Commodity in Colonial and Postcolonial Worlds*, 3–19. Los Angeles: University of California Press, 1999.

Porter, V., and L. Saif, eds. "The Mahmal Revisited." In *The Hajj: Collected Essays*, 195–205. London: British Museum Press, 2013.

Prisse d'Avennes, E. *L'Art Arabe*. Paris: l'Aventurine, 2002.

al-Qalqashandi, A. *Subh al-'asha*. Online, http://www.alwaraq.net/Core/SearchServlet/searchone?docid=77&searchtext=2KfZhNiu2YrYp9mF&option=1&offset=4&WordForm=1&exactpage=503&totalpages=16&AllOffset=1

Rathbone, E.E., and J. Halford-MacLeod. *Art beyond Isms: Masterworks from El Greco to Picasso in the Phillips Collection*. London: Third Millennium, 2002.

Raymond, A. *Artisans et Commerçants du Caire*. Damascus: Presses de l'Ifpo, 1973.

Reed, C. "Love Nest." *Harvard Magazine*, July–August, 2009, https://harvardmagazine.com/2009/07/love-nest

Reid, D.M. *Whose Pharaohs? Archaeology, Museums, and Egyptian National Identity from Napoleon to World War I*. Los Angeles: University of California Press, 2002.

Roberts Rhinehart, M. *Nomad's Land*. New York: George H. Doran, 1926.

Sachs, S. "Cairo Journal; A Tentmaker's Wish: Make the Bazaar Splendid!" *New York Times*, August 18, 2000.

Salmon, W.H. *An Account of the Ottoman Conquest of Egypt in the Year A.H.*

922 (A.D. 1516): translated from the Third Volume of the Arabic Chronicle of Muhammed Ibn Ahmed Ibn Iys, an Eye-Witness of the Scenes He Describes. London: Royal Asiatic Society, 1921.

Sanders, P. *Creating Medieval Cairo: Empire, Religion, and Architectural Preservation in Nineteenth-Century Egypt.* Cairo: American University in Cairo Press, 2007.

———. *Ritual, Politics, and the City in Fatimid Cairo.* New York: SUNY Press, 1994.

Schleicher, S. *Adaptive Toldo Systems.* Master's thesis, Massachusetts Institute of Technology, 2009, https://dspace.mit.edu/handle/1721.1/46802

Shoshan, B. *Popular Culture in Medieval Cairo.* Cambridge: Cambridge University Press, 1993.

Simpson, O.B. "Embroidery in Egypt." *The Embroideress* 29 (1928): 693–95.

Sladen, D. *Oriental Cairo: The City of the "Arabian Nights."* London: Hurst & Blackett, 1911.

———. *Queer Things about Egypt.* Philadelphia: J.B. Lippincott Company, 1911.

Stone, C. "Movable Palaces." *Saudi Aramco World*, April 2010.

Stuart, H.W. *The Funeral Tent of an Egyptian Queen.* London: John Murray, 1882.

Teichmann, G., and G. Vögler, eds. *Faszination Orient: Max von Oppenheim, Forscher, Sammlet, Diplomat.* Ostfildern: DuMont Reiseverlag, 2003.

al-Tukhi, N. *Tawa'if al-hiraf fi madinat al-Qahira fi al-nisf al-thani min al-qarn al-tasi' 'ashar, 1841–1890.* Cairo: The Egyptian General Book Authority, 2009.

van Gelder, G.J. "Beautifying the Ugly and Uglifying the Beautiful: The Paradox in Classical Arabic Literature." *Journal of Semitic Studies* 48, Autumn (2003): 330–31.

Walker, Bethany. "Rethinking Mamluk Textiles." *Mamluk Studies Review* 4 (2000): 167–217, http://mamluk.uchicago.edu/MSR_IV_2000-Walker.pdf

Warner, N. "Commerce and Spirituality: The Urbanism of Rīdwān Bey." In *Cities in the Pre-Modern Islamic World: The Urban Impact of Religion, State and Society*, edited by A.K. Bennison and A.L. Gascoigne, 196–224. London: Routledge, 2007.

———. *The Monuments of Historic Cairo: A Map and Descriptive Catalogue.* Cairo: American University in Cairo Press, 2005.

Wass, B. "The Tentmakers of Cairo." In *Islamic Art from Michigan Collections*, edited by C.G. Fisher and A. Washburn, 17–26. Dexter: Michigan State University, 1982.

Williamson, C.N., and A.M. Williamson. *It Happened in Egypt.* New York: Garden City, 1914, http://www.gutenberg.org/cache/epub/9799/pg9799.txt

Winter, M. *Egyptian Society Under Ottoman Rule, 1517–1798.* Abingdon: Routledge, 1992.

Index

Page numbers in italics refer to figures.
p refers to an image in the plate sections.

Abdel-Kader, Hany 181, 183–85, 206–11
American Quilter's Society *see* quilting
ancient Egypt 91, 108–109, 117–19, 127, 165, 168, 194
appliqué: creating appliqué 165, 168–69; Mamluk period 30–33 (*see also* Hajj textiles); Ottoman appliqué in Europe *p8*, 62–63
apprenticeship 161, 164; *see also* guild system
architecture and khayamiya: Mamluk marblework *p6*, 31, 36–37; in the nineteenth century 76–79; Ottoman architecture 58–61 (*see also sabil-kuttab*); khedival doorways 83–85
'arusa 111, 170
Ashcroft Panel 113, *p20*
Ashmolean Museum 32, 62
Australia 107, 113, 129, 234n2; Syme Panel *p17*, 102, 233n21
Ayoub, Raouf 171, 191–94

Barakat, Heba 126
Barakat, Zayni 40
Bedouin 50–52, 68, 173
birds 2, 29, 39, 117–18, 119, 175
border 169–70
Bowker, Jenny 175, 176–77
British Museum 114, 119, 126, 238n24

celebrations: Fatimid ceremonies 10–11; inauguration of Suez Canal 81–82; khedival celebrations 88, *89*; Mamluk times 24–28; military conquests 16–17, 22–24, 43–45, 73–74; modern period 143–45
celebrities 133–35, 139, 141
color 2, 13, 16–17, 23, 75–76, 81–82, 116, 123, 167
competition among the tentmakers 171–72
contemporary khayamiya: Avedissian, Chant 181–82; collaborations 180–81, 183; design of 161–63; design of *suradiq* panels 163–64;

Hamid, Ahmad *p*30, 181–82, 216–22; Koraichi, Rachid 181, *182*; *Revolution Khayamiya p28*, 183–185
cotton 2, 16, 29, 30, 54, 61, 74, 85, 167, 168–69

dancers 71, 120, 129, 141, *142*, 143, 150, 158, 159, 160, 216
al-Darb al-Ahmar 74–75, 83, 214
Description de l'Egypte 68–69, *70*
Doddington Hall Tent 121, 126, 128–29
Doris Duke Collection *p*14, 98–99
dyes 168, 169; in the Fatimid era 13; in the nineteenth century 75–76, 167; in the Ottoman era 56; Tanis 14–15; *see also* tentmaking technique

Egyptian nationhood 131–33, 135–37; Egyptian coat of arms 138–39; *see* Mokhtar, Mahmoud
exhibitions *p*26, 113, 174–75, 176–77

Fabbi, Fabbio 158–59
fabric 1–2, 168–69, 177–78; *Bahnasi* fabric 14; *dabiqi* linen 11; *see also* dyes
farrashin: el-Hendy family 147–48, 151–52; Wahdan, Lotfy 148, 152–53
Fattouh, Atef 196–201
figuration 11, 14, 39, 82, 99, 114, 118
Fuad, King 131, 133–34
funeral tents 144–45
fustat tent: Fatimid era 2–3, 7; khedival era 102–103; Mamluk era 29; *mustatib* tent 3; al-Qatul 6; tent of al-Yazuri 3–4

Gagnon, Blair 122, 173
garments 12, 20, 25–26
Gomaa, Ahmed 201–205
guild system 52–54, 185, 229n37

Hajj textiles 34–35; Ka'ba 15–16; *see also mahmal*
Harvard Tent 126–28
Horsley, Walter Charles *p*25, 159
humor 116–17

Ilhamiya School of Arts 93–94, 106
imitation khayamiya *p*27, 144, 177–78; computer-printed panels 178
inherited tents 27, 34–35, 55–56
international audiences 108–109, 112–13, 175, 179–80
Islamic Arts Museum Malaysia (IAMM) 175–76; IAMM tent *p*21, 103, 125–26

Jackson Hole tent 103, 233n23

khayamiya and the church 33, 96, 142, 145, 170, 178, 196
el-Khayamy, Mohsen 211–16
khedival khayamiya: calligraphy 97–98, 110; epigrams 94–106
*khirka*s 29–30
kiswa 33–34, 35, 73, 77, 198, 208, 215

el-Leithy, Moustafa 187–96
el-Leithy, Yasser 171, 186, 187–96
Liberty's of London 109, 114
'Look Again' quatrain 99–100
lotus (flowers) 137–38

*mahmal p*5, 33–34, 35, 90
Mamluk tents 22–30; of King Louis IX 23; of Sultan al-Ghuri 27; of Sultan Qaytbay 37
Matisse, Henri *p*24, 155–58, 159
*mawlids p*10, *p23*, *89*, 145, 216; of Sayyid al-Badawi 48–52; *see also* Sufi
modern khayamiya: in art 158–60; in cinema 142–43
Mokhtar, Mahmoud 133, 137
mosques 85–87; Aslam al-Silahdar Mosque *p*6, 37; of Muhammad 'Ali 76; in the Ottoman period 58–59
Morton Tent 126
Mubarak, Hosni 184, 212

Muhammad 'Ali 72–73; Ottoman baroque style 76–78; state production of tents 74–76
musicians *101*, 160

al-Nasser, Gamal Abd 135–37
Newark Museum 126
New Zealand 112, 113

orientalism 158–59
Ottoman conquest of Egypt 45–47
Ottoman tents 51, 62–64, *70*, 145, 158, 175

palanquin 30, 38–39
poetry 50, 71, 94–101, 103–106, 127, 200
Prisse d'Avennes, Emile 63
Prophet's banner 66
provenance 125–26, 177

quality 38, 52, 55–56, 133, 186, 204, 205
quilting 173–75, 176–77; international quilt shows *see* exhibitions; *tifaifai*

Ramadan tents 29, 143–44
Revolution of 2011 181, 183–84
Rhode Island Panel *p*19, 105

sabil-kuttab: nineteenth century *p*7, 77, *78*; Ottoman period 60–61
Sadat, Anwar 139
el-Safty, Tarek 186
Salah al-Din 15–17
Saunders Museum Tent 125
scissors 164, 189, 196
Shepheard's Hotel *122*, 123
shisha cafés *see suradiq*; modern era
Sladen, Douglas 114–17, 123
the Street of the Tentmakers: in Mamluk times 38; in Ottoman times 57–58, 90
Sufi: *mawlids* 87, 91, 216; poetry 104; al-Rifa'i 85
suradiq: design of *suradiq* panels 163–64; Fatimid 'House of Watermelons' tent 6–7; IAMM Tent 103, 125–26, 235n33, *p*21; khedival era *92*; modern era *132*, *136*, *138*, 134–35, 137, 139–45, 183; nineteenth century 68–69; 'tent of deliverance' 7–9; *see also* tentmaking technique
sutur 11, 39–41

tark x, 148, 163, 168, 195–96, 208
tent of Muhammad Bey Abu al-Dahab 55
tentmaking technique 165–66; design around 1900 91–94
Thackeray, Lance 117
tifaifai 173; *see also* Matisse, Henri
touristic khayamiya *p*20, 108–12; camp tents 124–25; international retail 113–14, *p*22; provenance 125–26; *sha'bi* (folkoric) motifs 120
tughra 78–79

Wahhabis 73–74
war: First World War 107–108; Second World War 113
weddings 72–73, *138*, *140*, 142, 150–51
women tentmakers 172

Zaghlul, Sa'd 131–33

www.ingramcontent.com/pod-product-compliance
Ingram Content Group UK Ltd.
Pitfield, Milton Keynes, MK11 3LW, UK
UKHW032122080525
458352UK00005B/20